T4-ADP-707

CAPITAL BUDGETING

CAPITAL BUDGETING
Theory, Quantitative Methods, and Applications

Anthony F. Herbst
University of Texas at Arlington

HARPER & ROW, PUBLISHERS, New York
Cambridge, Philadelphia, San Francisco,
London, Mexico City, São Paulo, Sydney

Sponsoring Editor: John Greenman
Project Editor: Pamela Landau
Production Manager: Jeanie Berke
Compositor: York Graphic Services, Inc.
Printer/Binder: The Murray Printing Company
Art Studio: Vantage Art

CAPITAL BUDGETING
Theory, Quantitative Methods, and Applications
Copyright © 1982 by Harper & Row, Publishers, Inc.

All rights reserved. Printed in the United States of America. No part of this book may be used or reproduced in any manner whatsoever without written permission, except in the case of brief quotations embodied in critical articles and reviews. For information address Harper & Row, Publishers, Inc., 10 East 53d Street, New York, NY 10022.

Library of Congress Cataloging in Publication Data

Herbst, Anthony F., 1941–
    Capital budgeting.

    Includes index.
    1. Capital budget.   I. Title.
HG4028.C4H45   658.1'54   81-13382
ISBN 0-06-042795-7   AACR2

Contents

Preface xi

A Note on Course Uses xiii

I. THE BASIC FRAMEWORK 1

1. Introduction 3

Magnitude of Capital Investment 4   General Perspective on Capital Investment 4   Capital Budgeting 7   Cash Flows 8   Cost of Capital 9   Risk and Uncertainty 9   Questions 11

2. Objective of Capital Budgeting 12

A Normative Model for Capital Budgeting 13   Basic Valuation Model 14   Cash Flows and the Public Sector 16   Questions 16   Problems 17

3. Estimating Project Characteristics 18

Project Types 18   Project Characteristics 19   Initial Cost 20   Useful Life 23   Cash Flows 26   Taxes and Depreciation 29   Questions 36   Problems 36

4. Cost of Capital 38

Introduction 38   Cost of Capital Components 39   Overall Cost of Capital 42   Optimal Capital Structure 44   Interaction of Financing and Investment 46   Questions 47   Problems 47

II. TRADITIONAL METHODS OF PROJECT EVALUATION 51

5. Traditional Methods that Ignore Time Value of Money 53

Payback and Naive Rate of Return 53   Accounting Method: Alias Average Return on Average Investment 58   Comprehensive Example 59   Questions 61   Problems 62

6. Traditional Methods that Recognize Time Value of Money: Internal Rate of Return 64

Definition of the IRR 64   A Caution and a Rule for IRR 67   Payback and IRR Relationship 68   Mathematical Logic for Finding IRR 69   A Digression on Nominal and Effective Rates 72   Questions 74   Problems 75

7. Traditional Methods that Recognize Time Value of Money: The Net Present Value 78

Unequal Project Size 82   Unequal Project Lives 83   Summary and Conclusion 85   Questions 86   Problems 86

8. Reinvestment Rate Assumptions of NPV and IRR and Conflicting Rankings 88

Reinvestment Rate Assumptions for NPV and IRR 88   Conflicting Rankings and Fisher's Intersection 92   Relationship of IRR and NPV 96   Summary and Conclusion 97   Questions 97   Problems 98

III. SPECIAL TOPICS AND METHODS 101

9. The MAPI (Terborgh) Method 103

The Concept of Duality 103 The MAPI Framework 105 Application of the MAPI Method 109 Conclusion 113 Questions 113 Problems 114

10. The Problem of Mixed Cash Flows: I 116

Internal Rate of Return Deficiencies 116 Descartes' Rule 117 The Teichroew, Robichek, and Montalbano (TRM) Analysis 118 The TRM Algorithm 120 The Unique, Real Rate of Return: Caveat Emptor! 126 A New Theorem 128 Questions 130 Problems 130

11. The Problem of Mixed Cash Flows: II 133

The Wiar Method 133 Sinking Fund Methods 136 The Multiple Investment Sinking Fund Method 143 Questions 146 Problems 147

Appendix to Chapter 11: The Problem of Mixed Cash Flows—III: A Two-Stage Method of Analysis 148

Introduction 148 Relationship to Other Methods 149 The Two-Stage Method 149 Formal Definition and Relationship to NPV 154 Conclusion 156 A Brief Digression on Uncertainty 156 Questions 157 Problems 157

12. Leasing 160

Alleged Advantages to Leasing 161 Analysis of Leases 161 Summary and Conclusion 169 Questions 170 Problems 170 Appendix 171

13. Leveraged Leases 174

Methods of Leveraged Lease Analysis 175 Application of the Methods 176 Analysis of a Typical Leveraged Lease (Childs and Gridley) 179 Conclusion 184

14. Alternative Investment Measures 187

Additional Rate of Return Measures 187 Time-Related Measures in Investment Analysis 192 Summary and Conclusion 197 Questions 197 Problems 198

15. Project Abandonment Analysis 201

The Robichek-Van Horne Analysis 201 An Alternative Method: A Parable 204 A Dynamic Programming Approach 210 Summary and Conclusion 211 Questions 212 Problems 212

16. Multiple Project Capital Budgeting 214

Budget and Other Constraints 214 General Linear Programming Approach 215 Zero-One Integer Programming 218 Goal Programming 224 Summary and Conclusion 227 Questions 228 Problems 228

IV. CAPITAL BUDGETING UNDER RISK—WITHOUT DIVERSIFICATION 235

17. Utility and Risk Aversion 237

The Concept of Utility 238 Calculating Personal Utility 240 Measures of Risk 246 Risk of Ruin 250 Summary 251 Questions 252 Problems 252

18. Single Project Analysis Under Risk 255

Payback Method 256 Certainty Equivalents: Method I 256 Certainty Equivalents: Method II 258 Risk-Adjusted Discount Rate 259 Computer Simulation 261 Lewellen-Long Criticism 265 Questions 268 Problems 269

19. Multiple Project Selection Under Risk: Portfolio Approaches 271

Introduction 271 Multiple Project Selection 275 Relating to Investor Utility 280 Epilogue 281 Questions 281 Problems 282

20. Multiple Project Selection Under Risk: Computer Simulation and Other Approaches 285

Decision Trees 285 Other Risk Considerations 288 Conclusion 298 Questions 298 Problems 298

V. CAPITAL BUDGETING UNDER RISK—WITH DIVERSIFICATION   301

21. The Capital Asset Pricing Model   303

Assumptions of the CAPM   304   The Efficient Set of Portfolios   304   The Security Market Line and Beta   307   The CAPM and Valuation   310   The CAPM and Cost of Capital   310   The CAPM and Capital Budgeting   311   Comparison with Portfolio Approaches   312   Some Criticisms of the CAPM   313   Conclusion   314   Questions   314   Problems   315

VI. CURRENT AND FUTURE CHALLENGES IN CAPITAL BUDGETING   319

22. Capital Investment in the 1980s   321

Introduction   321   Entering the 1980s   321   Inflation   324   Productivity   330   Government Regulations   332   Contingency Planning   341   Conclusion   343

VIII. APPENDIX: FINANCIAL MATHEMATICS TABLES AND FORMULAS   345

Index   391

Preface

The aim of this book is to tie together the theory, quantitative methods, and applications of capital budgeting. Consequently, its coverage omits few, if any, topics important to capital investment. My intention was to effect a harmonious blend of the old, such as the MAPI method of capital investment appraisal, with the new, such as the Capital Asset Pricing Model (CAPM). I have tried to provide a balanced treatment of the different approaches to capital project evaluation and have explored both the strengths and weaknesses of various project selection methods.

A work on this subject necessarily uses mathematics, but the level of mathematical sophistication required here is generally not above basic algebra. Although I have favored clarity and readability over mathematical pyrotechnics, the book's level of mathematical rigor should be sufficiently high to satisfy most users.

The book's treatment of risk is deliberately deferred to later chapters. The decision to do this, rather than treating risk earlier, was based on my belief that readers new to the subject are less overwhelmed by the added complexities of risk considerations—and better able to comprehend them—after they have become thoroughly familiar with capital budgeting in an environment assumed to be risk-free.

In Chapter 21 I try to present a balanced treatment of the CAPM, including some of the important criticisms of its use in capital budgeting. I know that some readers prefer an earlier introduction of the CAPM, as well as its subsequent use as a unifying theme. (See the last paragraph of A Note on Course Uses for the chapter sequence which meets that need.) I chose not to employ that structure for three reasons.

First, although the CAPM may be adaptable to capital budgeting decisions involving major projects (e.g., the acquisition of a new company division), serious questions exist concerning its applicability to more typical projects for which estimation of expected returns alone is difficult, to say nothing of also estimating the project's beta. Second, company managers increasingly appear to be placing primary emphasis on the survival of the firm rather than on diversification in their capital investment decisions, thereby diluting the implications of the CAPM. In other words, top management does indeed care about unsystematic (or company) risk, which portfolio diversification may, in some cases, undermine. To the management of a company, such risk may not always be reduced easily, and, if intensified by diversification, may imperil the company.

Third, the CAPM is concerned with risk. For the reasons stated earlier, I felt that the book would better serve its audience if it examined capital investment under assumed uncertainty first, without the added complexities that a simultaneous treatment of risk would entail.

I want to thank those reviewers and others who helped to improve the book through their constructive criticism and suggestions, especially Don Panton, University of New Mexico; James B. Henry, University of South Carolina; G. David Quirin, University of Toronto; J. Daniel Williams, University of Akron; Ron Rizzuto, University of Denver; Wayne Perg, Bowling Green State University; and Phil Horvath, Bradley University. For any remaining errors or omissions in the final text, I alone bear responsibility. I would appreciate hearing from users of the book who are willing to pass on their suggestions for improvement to me at the Department of Finance and Real Estate, UTA Box 19449, The University of Texas at Arlington, Arlington, TX 76019.

Finally, I want to thank my wife Betty, and our children, Mya and Geoff. Betty typed the entire manuscript at least three times and took care of the details relating to correspondence and permissions. Only those who have themselves gone through the writing of a book can appreciate the sacrifices the author's family members are called upon to make.

A.F.H.

A Note on Course Uses

Choices had to be made in the sequencing of this book's chapters. The final arrangement represents the author's own preferences, but others may well choose a different sequence of chapter topics, depending upon their course objectives, their time constraints, and their students' backgrounds. Some instructors, for example, may prefer to omit the chapter on leveraged leasing, whereas others may give it detailed consideration.

Instructors of courses in which students have had an introductory-level finance course may wish to move fairly quickly through the early chapters, using them to review material previously studied and to emphasize certain points.

The special topics and methods covered in Chapters 9 through 16 are independent of one another, so each of these chapters may be dealt with individually in whatever sequence the instructor prefers, or omitted altogether. However, there is certainly no reason not to cover all of them if time permits.

There are as many alternative sequences for teaching capital budgeting as there are ways to teach the subject. If one's students have sufficient background, it is possible to cover Chapters 1 through 8 quickly and use the time gained to assign several cases. I often compress the time allocated to these chapters and include cases with Chapters 4 and 9, and following Chapter 22. With MBA classes I always include cases, even though some students may have to work harder to keep up. The specific cases employed are described in the Instructor's Manual that accompanies the text. They have been selected to provide in-depth applications of concepts and methods contained in the chapters.

In a 16-week semester course carrying three credits and meeting twice a week, I suggest the following sequence: First week, Chapters 1, 2, and beginning of 3; second week, finish Chapters 3 and 4; third week, Chapter 5 and beginning of 6; fourth week, finish Chapters 6 and 7; fifth week, Chapter 8, plus first examination; sixth week, Chapter 9; seventh week, Chapter 10; eighth week, Chapter 11; ninth week, Chapters 12 or 13 and 14; tenth week, Chapter 15, plus second examination; eleventh week, Chapter 16 and first part of 17; twelfth week, finish Chapter 17, cover 18; thirteenth week, Chapter 19; fourteenth week, Chapter 20; fifteenth week, Chapter 21; sixteenth week, Chapter 22 and course review.

In an 11-week, quarter-system course of 4 credits meeting twice a week, I propose this sequence and approximate time on each subject: First week, Chapters 1, 2, and first part of 3; second week, second part of Chapter 3 and first part of Chapter 4; third week, second part of Chapter 4 and Chapter 5; fourth week, Chapters 6 and 7; fifth week, Chapters 8 and 9, plus midterm examination; sixth week, Chapter 10; seventh week, Chapter 11 and Chapter 12 or 13; eighth week, Chapters 14 and 15; ninth week, Chapters 16 and 17; tenth week, Chapters 18 and 19; eleventh week, Chapters 20 and 21.

Another alternative sequence based on 1 1/2-hour lecture periods is suggested by Don Panton, University of New Mexico: Chapters 1 and 2 combined into one lecture; Chapters 3 and 4 each split into two lectures; Chapter 5, one lecture; Chapter 6 split into two lectures; Chapters 7 and 8, one lecture each. Chapters 10 and 11 combined into two lectures; Chapters 17, 18, and 19, one lecture each; Chapter 21, two lectures. Then Chapters 12 and 13 combined into one lecture, and finally Chapter 16 in one lecture. He would omit Chapters 9, 15, 19, 22, and 14 in undergraduate classes.

For those who wish to cover the Capital Asset Pricing Model earlier in the course, another sequence would be to assign chapters in this order: 1, 2, 3, 4, 5, 6, 7, 8, then 17, 18, 19, and 21 (which contains the CAPM). Then a selection from Chapters 9, 10, 11, 12, 13, 14, 15, 16, 20, and 22 might be made, according to class needs and instructor's interests, in whatever sequence seems appropriate.

Part I
THE BASIC FRAMEWORK

Chapter 1
Introduction

Once we consciously think about the nature of capital investment decisions, we realize that such decisions have been made for millenia, since humans first awakened to the idea that capital[1] accumulation could improve life. The earliest investment decisions involved what today would be considered very primitive. But to the early nomadic hunter-forager the first capital investment decisions were quite significant. To the extent that time and energy had to be diverted from the immediate quest for food and for security from enemies, to the production of tools for the hunt and to defense installations, food storage facilities, and so on, capital investments were made. Such primitive capital creation required time and effort. And the benefits that could have been expected to result were uncertain; it took foresight to build capital.

As society evolved, the benefits of capital accumulation gradually became more indirect and complex, involving specialization and cooperation not previously envisioned, and the associated commitment of resources more permanent. Additionally, social norms and institutions had to be developed to facilitate the evolution. For example, the changeover from nomadic to agrarian life required a great in-

---

[1] The word *capital* is used in several senses. It may refer to physical plant and equipment (economic capital) or the ownership claims on the tangible capital (financial capital). In this book, unless otherwise indicated in a specific instance, the word shall refer to physical or economic capital.

crease in capital: in the form of land clearing, construction of granaries, mills, irrigation, canals, tools, and fortifications. The fortifications were a necessary adjunct to deter those who would, by force, seize the benefits achieved. The changeover required a commitment that, at least in the short run, tended to be irreversible. And it became more and more irreversible, for the change caused social and economic institutions to be developed to support it and coordinate the various requisite activities.[2]

MAGNITUDE OF CAPITAL INVESTMENT

In the United States in 1979, business capital expenditure on new plant and equipment amounted to $177 billion out of a gross national product (GNP) of $2369 billion. This meant that 7.5 percent of measured national economic activity was used for business capital investment. If government expenditure on capital goods (plant and equipment) was reported separately from total government expenditure on goods and services, the total of business and government capital expenditure would likely exceed 10 percent of GNP. Inclusion of expenditures on owner-occupied dwellings would raise the total still higher.[3] Figure 1.1 displays the trend in business investment since 1972, in contrast to government spending over the same period. Figure 1.2 illustrates business spending on plant and equipment alongside corporate profits and taxes. It is readily apparent that capital investment is an important component of economic activity, both absolutely and relatively.

GENERAL PERSPECTIVE ON CAPITAL INVESTMENT

Because resources are scarce (as economists have long maintained) and because capital investment figures prominently in the economy, decisions on capital budgets ought to be made on as sound and rational a basis as possible. The general irreversibility of capital investments, and their legacy for future costs as well as benefits, make such decisions of great importance both from the standpoint of the individual firm and at the level of national policy.

Economic theory recognizes that for any given level of technology, the factors of production (land, labor, and capital) *together* in combination are required to produce goods and services. Production of any good or service, then, is a function of combined factors, with the function corresponding to the state of known technology.

At the national policy level the dual goals of high employment (low unemployment) and increasing standard of living are normally accorded primary importance. These goals require that for given levels of technology the stock of capital increases

---

[2] C. Northcote Parkinson writes of such differences between agricultural and nomadic societies in his book *East and West* (New York: New American Library, 1963).
[3] "Gross private domestic investment" as a percentage of GNP in the United States was slightly above 16 percent for 1979.

Figure 1.1 Selected components of GNP. (*Source:* Board of Governors of the Federal Reserve System, Federal Reserve Chart Book.)

Figure 1.2 Corporate profits (left) and plant and equipment spending (right). (*Source:* Board of Governors of the Federal Reserve System, Federal Reserve Book.)

apace with growth in the labor supply or, if technological growth is toward the more capital-intensive side, to exceed it. As long as the goals are the same, this will hold for every type of government because political philosophy cannot change the feasible mix of land, labor, and capital for a given technology.

Few in business and industry would dispute the view that the press and media generally tend to emphasize labor's employment problems while generally ignoring the problems of underemployment of capital, reduced or negative capital accumulation, and return on investment. Such imbalanced editorial policy, however, is understandable to the extent it exists because much of the public identifies their interests with labor rather than with capital. However, it reinforces popular notions that, although not clearly incorrect, are at least suspect and thus tend to contribute further to problems faced by labor and capital alike. The notion that the interests of labor and capital are mutually exclusive may be useful to left-wing rhetoricians, but it fails to address the problems of underemployment and sagging productivity in societies in which labor and capital are undichotomized. In the industrial nations of North America, Europe, and Asia, for example, it is common for workers to own shares in their own employer or other corporations either directly or through their pension fund. Worker representation on corporate boards has been accepted in some European nations for many years and the practice seems to be growing. Thus the interests of labor and capital are not easily separable, if at all, because so many are neither entirely worker nor entirely capitalist.

The proper mix of factors of production is necessary to minimize unemployment of labor without resorting to government "make work" projects. But it depends on wages that reflect productivity and value product. Adoption of government policies that ignore capital in order to aim at direct treatment of labor unemployment, or low minimum wages, is bound to failure in a broader sense. Still, we see such policies being publicly advocated, whereas capital investment necessary to create a real expansion in jobs is ignored. Return on capital investment in the United States is today generally less than can be earned on the same funds if put into government bonds, after taking capital consumption into account. This has the effect of dampening enthusiasm for capital investment and consequently moving funds to nonproductive uses. Since capital must complement labor, fewer productive jobs are created, which leads to higher labor unemployment, more public policies to treat the symptoms, and still more disincentive to capital investment. In fact, recent studies at the University of Chicago indicate that in the United States, capital is being consumed at a faster rate than it is being created; industry is paying liquidating dividends. This has serious implications for the economic policies of government.

Concern that capital will replace labor may be legitimate in the short run, if myopic. If the relative costs of labor and capital should favor a capital-intensive production mix of factors, this should present no problem provided the distribution of benefits is equitable. In other words, replacement of some labor by capital may increase the quality of life for labor provided that the benefits are shared by labor. The laying-off of some workers while others are put on extended overtime or continue to work a normal 40-hour week does not further equitable distribution. But a reduction in the standard work week to fewer than 40 hours may. If it were not for capital accumulation and improved technology yielding increased productivity, workers would not have a 40-hour standard week but one of 60 hours or so, as was once the standard not so many decades ago.[4]

Most of the developing nations are capital poor, but have abundant labor that is not highly skilled or educated. For them it makes sense to adopt labor-intensive methods of production, gradually shifting to capital-intensive technologies as their capital stock is increased and the quality of labor increases. In the developed, relatively capital rich nations it is not sensible to adopt labor-intensive methods of production, for this wastes productive capacity. It is very ironical that although developing nations strive to accumulate capital, developed nations often follow policies that discourage capital growth and may cause the capital stock to shrink relatively if not absolutely. One may well wonder if it would not be more honest and efficient simply to donate capital to the developing nations to raise their capital intensity while lowering that of the donor nation.

Capital investment decisions have repercussions that may extend far beyond the immediate time frame, because they involve long-term commitments that are not readily undone. The decision *not* to invest is a capital investment decision also. And future repercussions may be compounded by the often very long planning periods for capital goods and the fact that it takes capital and labor together to produce more capital goods. The "production process" to create "human capital"—skilled labor—is a lengthy one, and the more sophisticated the capital goods to be produced generally the higher the quality of human capital required.

CAPITAL BUDGETING

In the private sector, capital investment and the analysis surrounding it are generally referred to as *capital budgeting*. Capital budgeting focuses on alternative measures of project acceptability. Tangible factors are emphasized, although, to the extent that their effects can be weighed, intangibles must be considered. Capital investment in the private sector has perhaps tended to pay less attention to intangibles than its public sector counterpart, *cost-benefit analysis*. This may well be due to the inherently more qualitative nature of social and political goals and constraints.

In private enterprise, profitability provides the principal criterion for the acceptability of particular prospective investment projects through its effect on the market value of the enterprise. Capital budgeting centers on an objective function that the management seeks to maximize, subject to various constraints. Often the primary constraint is imposed by the funds available for investment. When this constraint is binding, it is referred to as *capital rationing*. In the public sector, a reasonable alternative is provided by minimizing a cost function, constrained by specifying minimum levels of services to be provided. The aggregate effect of private and public support for capital investment is to raise a nation's standard of

---

[4] Determination of what is equitable and what is not is a matter that must be decided outside the scope of this book.

living, both in tangible benefits and in terms of intangible benefits such as greater security and less social stress. To the extent that the benefits accrue to a few rather than to the many, it is the social and political institutions that are responsible.[5]

Emphasis throughout this book is on private sector capital budgeting. Yet, some of the methods covered are applicable without modification to public sector investment, and others are applicable with modification.

The following sections set forth some principles that will be used throughout the remainder of the book.

CASH FLOWS

Emphasis will be on *net, after-tax cash flows*. *Pretax, net cash flow* is defined as total cash inflow associated with the capital investment less its net cash outflow. After removing the portion that will be paid out for income taxes, at the enterprise's marginal rate, we are left with net, after-tax cash flow for the time period over which we have measured or estimated the flows. Cash flows will be estimated for *each* division of a capital investment's life, although some may well be zero. Normally the divisions will be annual, but they can be quarterly, semiannual, or for some other time period if desired. The major focus in this book will be on what is to be done with the cash flow estimates once they are obtained, rather than on how to make cash flow estimates, although Chapter 3 does address the subject.

Cash flow estimates in practice will normally be as much, or more, the result of experienced judgment by persons in such diverse functional areas as production engineering, marketing, and accounting than the result of objective measurement. We can estimate future results a priori, but measure them only after they occur. The management charged with responsibility for capital budgeting must insure that adequately accurate estimates are obtained and, where possible, objective forecasts used. It may be necessary to stress to those participating in the process through which estimates are obtained that it is cash flows that are sought, not accrued profits or cost savings. It is cash that may be used to pay dividends, employee wages, and vendor bills and it is cash that may be invested in new plant and equipment.

It is vitally important that all relevant cash flows attributable to a capital project be included. An early survey reported by Soldofsky [5] suggested that many firms, even some fairly large ones, failed to include all associated cash flows in their analysis. Today we may expect that fewer firms would be making the errors he found. However, such omissions as do occur can seriously bias the measures of project acceptability and destroy the usefulness of whatever technique is employed.

COST OF CAPITAL

The organization's cost of capital, expressed as a decimal or percentage, is used in two basic ways in capital budgeting: as a minimum profitability rate that prospec-

---

[5] For a lucid presentation of a rationale for aggressive national policy encouraging capital formation, see E. A. G. Robinson [4].

tive project returns are required to exceed and as a discount rate applied to cash flows.

The literature dealing with cost of capital is voluminous; yet the concept and the measurement of cost of capital are still unsettled. For our purposes cost of capital will be assumed to be independently derived, along the lines suggested in Chapters 4 and 21, except where it is explicitly stated otherwise. The reader is referred to the suggested readings at the end of those chapters for works dealing in depth with this topic. The importance of cost of capital should not be minimized: An adequate estimate is *crucial* to proper application of capital-budgeting techniques, because all but the crudest techniques incorporate it in one way or another.

In the author's experience the importance of obtaining good estimates of the firm's cost of capital is often overlooked. The result is that capital budgeting may, in practice, become somewhat a burlesque: sophisticated techniques yielding accept/reject decisions based on crude and incorrect data. One of the largest firms in the United States in the 1970s was using 8 percent as its overall, marginal cost of capital. At the time, by generally accepted measure, the firm had a cost of capital above 10 percent. In capital investment methods that employ discounted cash flows, and these methods are all conceptually better, this was a serious error. Paradoxically, the same firm went to considerable effort to obtain finely detailed project cash flow data from its marketing, engineering, production, and accounting staffs at the same time. As a result, projects were undoubtedly undertaken that, had an adequate cost of capital been used, would have been rejected. The stock market performance of this firm during the 1970s, vis-à-vis comparable firms in its industry, tends to support this view.

RISK AND UNCERTAINTY

For better or worse we live in a world of probabilities, with little more than the proverbial death and taxes certain. In general, capital-budgeting projects are no exception, although some specific classes of capital investment, such as in leasing, may approach certainty sufficiently to be treated as if they were risk free.

Risk

Risk is usually defined to prevail in situations in which, although exact outcomes cannot be known in advance, the probability distributions governing the outcomes are either known or may be satisfactorily estimated. In a risky environment, probabilities may be associated with the various results that may occur. Life insurance companies, for example, can predict within close tolerance how many policyholders in any age grouping will survive to age 65, even though they cannot predict accurately which individuals within the group will reach that age. Those poker players who are successful in the sense of being net winners over the long run understand risk. Winning card combinations have associated probabilities, and successful players must take these into account, at least intuitively, to win on balance. In gambling games probabilities can generally be determined with precision, whether the players know the odds explicitly or through a sense gained by experience in playing.

In games of chance the thrill of risk-bearing itself may be more important than the prospect of gain. And in capital investment the taking on of risk for the sake of doing so may hold appeal to some individuals in management. However, if management is to serve the interests of the organization's owners and creditors, it must manage risk, not be managed by it. Managers may undertake risky investments (later we show that this can be actually beneficial to the enterprise), but they must strive to commit funds to investments that in the aggregate promise a greater probability of gain than loss. This is not to say that individual projects offering a small probability of great gain in return for a great probability of small loss must never be undertaken. For example, often such probabilities can be altered by managerial action. Such projects, however, will constitute a relatively small proportion of the firm's total capital budget. Managers could do worse than be guided by the Machiavellianlike principle that a single loss on a clearly high risk project may do more harm to their reputation than a string of gains on other projects. When portfolio effects are taken into account, this is an unhappy state of affairs, but one those making capital investment decisions must be aware of.

Later we treat in detail the topic of portfolio risk—risk of the total of the enterprise's investments. Although it is both informative and a necessary beginning to examine individual investment projects by themselves, it is important to recognize such interrelationships of investments as may exist and to analyze the effect on the total enterprise that acceptance of any particular project would likely cause.

Uncertainty

The generally accepted distinction in the literature between risk and uncertainty is that in the case of uncertainty we know the possible outcomes are random variables, *but* we do not know the probability distribution that governs the outcomes, or its parameters, and cannot estimate them a priori. Because capital-budgeting decisions are one of a kind, there is insufficient prior experience with similar situations for indicating the probabilities associated with the possible outcomes. Because they are unique, such capital investments are not amenable to Bayesian revision; they will not be repeated. In the more extreme cases even the entire range of outcomes that could reasonably be expected to occur may be unknown.

In the following chapters we shall first consider project analysis in a certainty environment for all project parameters. This has the advantage of allowing us to concentrate on basic principles and gain a firm understanding of them before complicating matters. Later the assumption of certainty is relaxed in order to deal with risk in individual projects and risk relationships between capital investment projects and the enterprise. Uncertainty considerations will be mentioned where appropriate as a complicating factor requiring attention and planning for unforeseen contingencies.

QUESTIONS

1. Why does a commitment made to a capital investment imply irreversible consequences, at least in the short run?
2. Can you describe a product that is produced solely with labor or capital alone?
3. What are the likely long-term consequences of government policies that discourage capital investment with (a) population and labor force constant and (b) with population and labor force increasing?
4. Discuss the question of whether increasing capital intensity in production will necessarily be detrimental to the environment and quality of life.
5. Explain briefly the following terms:
   Cash Flow
   Cost of Capital
   Risk
   Uncertainty
6. Explain how the following creatures other than humans employ capital in their lives:
   Ants
   Bees
   Beavers
   How is capital beneficial to these creatures? How does their social organization differ from other creatures that do not use capital?

Bibliography

1. Board of Governors of the Federal Reserve System, *Federal Reserve Bulletin*, Vol. 66, No. 6 (June 1980).
2. ———, *Federal Reserve Chart Book*, May 1980.
3. Parkinson, C. Northcote, *East and West* (New York: New American Library, 1963).
4. Robinson, E. A. G., *The Structure of Competitive Industry* (Chicago: University of Chicago Press, 1958).
5. Soldofsky, Robert M., "Capital Budgeting Practices in Small Manufacturing Companies," in *Studies in the Factor Markets for Small Business Firms*, eds. Dudley G. Luckett and Karl A. Fox (Ames: Iowa State University Press, 1964), pp. 46-94.

Chapter 2
Objective of Capital Budgeting

Unless one restricts attention to the very general social goal of accumulating capital in order to increase national welfare, it is difficult to define only *one* objective for capital budgeting to achieve. The classical economics assumption of profit-maximizing entrepreneurs may not be considered appropriate for government or nonprofit, private institutions. Furthermore, that assumption is not operationally feasible, and doubts have been expressed as to whether it represents the true motivation of managers in either private enterprise or in government.

Alternatives to the classical assumption of profit maximizing behavior have been proposed. Among these, the more prominent include the concepts of "satisficing" and organizational decision-making. Satisficing owes much of its development to Herbert Simon, who observed that "Administrative theory is peculiarly the theory of intended and bounded rationality—of the behavior of human beings who *satisfice* because they have not the wits to *maximize*."[1] This view is supported by the observation that managers make decisions without the complete information classical economic theory assumes they possess. Managers may intuitively take into account the classical concepts of rationality, including marginal analysis and game theory. However, there is no evidence to support the notion that managers attempt to

[1] Herbert A. Simon, *Administrative Behavior*, 2nd ed. (New York: Macmillan, 1957), p. xxiv.

perform the complex calculations demanded by classical economic theory in other than rare individual instances. Even if they wished to do so, managers usually do not have the detailed and exhaustive data that classical theory would require.

Other, behaviorally oriented theories of management decision-making have been developed, including those of Cyert and March,[2] which expand and supplement the satisficing concept, and Galbraith,[3] who views managements of large, widely held corporations as serving their own interests above those of the owners, and in some cases above those of the nation. Because of the diversity of human behavior and the evolution of attitudes and institutions, it is likely that additional behavioral theories will be developed that attempt to elaborate or offer alternatives to those proposed to date.

The behavioral theories, although realistically portraying management in human rather than mechanistic terms by incorporating a wider spectrum of behavioral assumptions than profit maximization, have contributed to better understanding of organizations. Like the classical model of profit maximization, however, they are not operational. Although profit maximization provides a normative model of management behavior, the behavioral models are descriptive: They describe what management *does* rather than what management *should* do or, more specifically, they fail to specify what objective criteria that management should use in reaching decisions that best serve those who employ them. Also, although profit maximization provides a nomothetic model, the behavioral models to date are ideographic, or nonuniversal.

Our intent is to develop capital budgeting as much as possible within a normative framework. Therefore, we shall leave the behavioral models at this point and proceed to define a normative model that can be operationalized. The model that is adopted can be applied to both private and public enterprise.

A NORMATIVE MODEL FOR CAPITAL BUDGETING

A serious deficiency of the classical economics principle of profit maximization, which prevents its adoption as operating policy, is that it does not indicate whether long-run or short-run profits are to be maximized. A firm's management, for example, might maximize short-run profits by formulating a policy that would simultaneously alienate customers, employees, and creditors over a period of a few months. It might attempt charging the highest prices the market will bear while lowering quality, paying minimum wages, letting the firm's financial structure, plant, and equipment deteriorate, and so on. Such behavior would surely injure the firm's chances to survive beyond the short run. Once owners of a firm have decided to liquidate it, they might adopt such an irresponsible mode of operation, but they could not thus operate and expect the firm to survive for long.

---

[2] Richard M. Cyert and James G. March, *A Behavioral Theory of the Firm* (Englewood Cliffs, N.J.: Prentice-Hall, 1963).
[3] John K. Galbraith, *The New Industrial State* (Boston: Houghton Mifflin, 1967).

A less extreme manifestation of short-run profit syndrome is not uncommon. It has taken root in firms that neglect proper maintenance of plant and equipment and steadfastly refuse to abandon worn or technologically obsolete equipment until a new replacement can "pay for itself" in one or two years. This thinking blossoms into the specious yet appealing notion that plant and equipment, although seriously worn and obsolete, should not be abandoned because they have been "paid for" years ago. In other words, such assets are considered "free" resources to the firm because they were fully depreciated in the past. In truth, the firm pays increasingly more in high scrap rates, in higher than necessary labor content, and in machine repair and tooling costs as time goes on. The assets were paid for when acquired, *not* when depreciated. Depreciation merely enabled the firm to recover the cost of the investments through tax remission over the years of their useful or economic lives.

The opposite of this obsession with short-run profits is preoccupation with the prospect of profits in the long-run future. This, in the extreme, is a much less common pathological condition than short-run profit obsession. Probably this is, at least in part, due to the fact that firms that seriously neglect short-run profits cannot survive for long. A firm may be able to neglect long-run profits and yet survive as an economic cripple; a firm that neglects short-run profits is likely to be an early fatality.

A tendency toward overly great emphasis on long-term profits may be observed in firms that, although showing poor current performance, spend lavishly on public relations, landscaping and lawn care around factory and office facilities, excessive employee benefits, research and development, and so on. The key word here is "lavishly." All firms are expected to spend reasonable amounts on such indirectly beneficial things that make the world more pleasant and that may not be strictly defensible in terms of expected tangible benefits. It is ultimately for the owners and creditors of the enterprise to determine what is reasonable, although in reality management may to a considerable extent be protected by the shield of ignorance surrounding the enterprise's operations. It is uncommonly difficult for ordinary stockholders to obtain the detailed information necessary to challenge successfully the mishandling and largess by management.

It would appear that management is caught between the horns of a dilemma. Short- and long-run profit maximizations seem to be contradictory. Is there any way to resolve the conflict, the ambiguity? Yes, there is, if we recognize that money, our economic *numeraire*, has time-value.

BASIC VALUATION MODEL

The model of managerial behavior we adopt is that of modern financial management, which is not part of classical economics although it might be considered a direct descendant:

$$\text{Maximize Wealth, or Value, } V = \sum_{t=0}^{\infty} \frac{R_t}{(1+k)^t} \qquad (2.1)$$

subject to governmental, economic, and managerial constraints.

The terms of this basic valuation model are:

t is Time Index
R_t is Net Cash Flow in Period t
k is The Enterprise Cost of Capital

This model resolves the ambiguity over whether it is long- or short-run profits that should be maximized. It is the *total discounted value* of all cash flows that is to be maximized. The theoretical *value of the enterprise is defined in terms of its profitability over time*. One may, of course, adopt the continuous analog of this discrete-time model, although traditionally this has not been common or especially useful.

The nature of this model is such that its maximization may be powerfully facilitated by an effective financial management that can raise adequate funds at minimum cost. This becomes clear if one considers that denominator terms containing k are raised to progressively higher powers. And it underscores the need for good estimates of the enterprise cost of capital.

Contemporary literature recognizes that there is interaction between the cost of capital k and the risk characteristics of the cash flow stream R_t over time. In other words, if the firm undergoes changes that alter the variability of its overall cash flows over time, this will have an effect on its cost of capital. The theory behind this notion has not yet become operational, and, although we shall deal with it in Chapter 21, for now it will suffice to adopt the principle that the cost of capital will not be increased if the enterprise invests its funds in capital projects of similar risk to the existing assets of the firm. If projects are accepted that are *less* risky than the existing asset base of the firm, a tendency will be for the cost of capital to decrease. This principle will be useful for a certain time; however, it ignores portfolio effects that imply that certain investments that are *more* risky than the existing asset base may actually serve to reduce the enterprise's risk and thus its cost of capital. Portfolio effects are considered in detail later.

Operational Adaptation

We adopt the simple convention of accepting prospective investments that add to the value of the enterprise. In an environment in which there is no *capital rationing*—that is, where funds are sufficient to accept all projects contributing to the value of the enterprise—we accept all profitable projects. In the more common situation in which funds are scarce compared to the investment cost of the array of acceptable investments, we should try to accept those projects that contribute the maximum amount to the value of the firm. Nothing in this contradicts the behavioral theories of management. Other motivations may deter achievement of *maximum* value increase. But even satisficing management, or management merely interested in remaining in control, should still try to attempt to increase the value of the enterprise, even if not to the fullest possible extent. Management that habitually does otherwise does so at its peril because the owners may replace the existing management.

The Cash Flows

For individual projects that consist of only one of many items of capital equipment it is difficult, if not impossible, to associate net cash flows or even accounting revenues directly. In these cases it may sometimes be possible to treat a package of such individual items of plant and equipment as a single, large capital-budgeting proposal. This is likely to be the most useful when the package alone will support a new product line, or when replacing an entire production facility is contemplated.

Alternatively, the cash flows associated with the individual capital equipment components may result from cost reduction. Cost reduction may be considered a positive cash flow because it represents the elimination of an opportunity cost. Such costs are defined as those attributable to inaction or the result of adopting some alternative to the best available action.

CASH FLOWS AND THE PUBLIC SECTOR

Because the equivalent of positive cash flows may be obtained from a reduction in costs, the basic valuation model can be useful in public sector cost benefit analysis. Cost reduction frees resources that would otherwise be wasted, so that they may satisfy other public demands. Also, maximization of the value of public enterprise may be considered beneficial, because such institutions are owned by all citizens of the community, state, or nation. Maximization of their value therefore serves to maximize the public wealth of society. Value in such cases is drawn from the tangible and intangible benefits provided to the citizens and not in the funds accumulated by the institution, which should be minimal. In other words, the money accumulated by public enterprise should be distributed as it is accumulated in the form of social dividends, paid through reduction in required external funding by taxes or government borrowing, or by increase in desired services provided. Unfortunately, the performance of some government institutions may lead one to believe that this, in fact, is not done, perhaps because the bureaucrats managing them are not answerable to the citizens nor held accountable by elected officials.

QUESTIONS

1. Explain why neither the theory of classical economics nor the behavioral theories of the firm provide operational guidelines for capital investment analysis.
2. Contrast the classical economics assumption of profit maximizing entrepreneurship with the notion of satisficing management.
3. Can we properly consider fully depreciated capital goods "free" resources? Is depreciation a cost, so that when an asset is fully depreciated this cost component vanishes?
4. Why do we consider the value of a firm to be the *discounted* value of all cash flows from now into the future? Why not just add up the undiscounted cash flows?
5. It is reasonable to expect the firm's cost of capital to be inversely related to the riskiness (variability) of its net cash flows. Explain.
6. Explain why reduction in a cash cost may be treated the same as an increase in a cash inflow or benefit. Can you think of a situation in which it is easier to measure cost

reduction through capital investment than increase in cash revenue from the investment?
7. Comment on the statement that maximization of the value of public institutions serves to maximize the wealth of the beneficiary (owner) community's public wealth.

PROBLEMS

2.1 Two firms each have 12 percent annual cost of capital. From the sixth year onward, it is expected that both will have net, after-tax cash flows of $2 million each year. In years zero through five their net, after-tax cash flows, in millions of dollars, are:

			Year			
Company	0	1	2	3	4	5
A	2	4	6	8	10	12
B	4	2	6	10	8	12

(a) Which firm has the higher discounted cash value? Why?
(b) If a third firm, C, has the same characteristics but uniform net, after-tax cash flows of $7 million in years zero through five, how does its value compare?
(c) If the cost of capital for all three firms could be zero, which would have the greatest value?

Bibliography

1. Brigham, Eugene F., and James L. Pappas, *Managerial Economics* (Hinsdale, Ill.: Dryden, 1972).
2. Cyert, Richard M., and James G. March, *A Behavioral Theory of the Firm* (Englewood Cliffs, N.J.: Prentice-Hall, 1963).
3. Galbraith, John K., *The New Industrial State* (Boston: Houghton Mifflin, 1967).
4. Johnson, Robert W., *Capital Budgeting* (Belmont, Cal.: Wadsworth, 1970).
5. McGuire, Joseph W., *Theories of Business Behavior* (Englewood Cliffs, N.J.: Prentice-Hall, 1964).
6. Simon, Herbert A., *Administrative Behavior*, 2nd ed. (New York: Macmillan, 1957).
7. Weston, J., and Fred and Eugene F. Brigham, *Managerial Finance*, 6th ed. (Hinsdale, Ill.: Dryden, 1978).

Chapter 3
Estimating Project Characteristics

In order to apply any systematic method of capital-budgeting evaluation and project selection it is necessary to first obtain estimates of relevant project characteristics or parameters. The methodologically superior methods of evaluation also require an estimate of the firm's cost of capital, which is the subject of the next chapter. This present chapter focuses on those characteristics of a particular project or aggregation of projects that become manifest in cash flows attributable to the project.

PROJECT TYPES

Let us define those capital investment projects as *major* projects, that in themselves generate net cash inflows, and as *component* projects those that do not in themselves directly generate net cash flows. Examples will serve to clarify the distinction. Investment in plant and equipment to produce a new product line that will generate sales revenues as well as production, marketing, and other costs would be classified as a major project. Investment in a new toolroom lathe would be classified as a component project. It will be used to service other capital equipment in the plant or produce prototype parts. The lathe then will not produce directly attributable cash inflows, but will necessitate directly attributable cash outflows for operator wages and fringe benefits, electric power, and so on. A new spline rolling machine that will replace several milling machines in a plant producing transmissions would also be considered a component project. The spline rolling machine in such a production facility would not produce a product that is sold without other machining and assembly operations being performed on it. Thus, product revenue cannot be directly associated with this machine except through rather tenuous cost accounting procedures that may not properly reflect its revenue contributions.

Major projects have *both* cash inflows *and* cash outflows directly associated with themselves. Component projects ordinarily do not. Therefore, although attention to value maximization may be appropriate for major projects, cost minimization will generally be more suitable an approach to component projects. For instance, a cost reduction brought about by replacing an older (component project) machine by a newer and more efficient machine contributes to net cash inflow as much as an increase in revenue with costs held constant. In this case the net cash flow is attributable to eliminating opportunity cost that is associated with less than the most efficient production equipment for the particular operation.

To further clarify the distinction between project types, assume that for a given cost of capital and risk level we want to maximize net cash flows by holding costs constant while increasing cash revenues. For major projects this may be appropriate. On the other hand, for component projects we may more easily achieve the same result by minimizing costs for a given level of cash revenue. An analogy may be made with the terminology of mathematical programming, with the major project considered the *dual* problem of cost minimization. Generally, we may expect an equivalence between maximizing some objective function subject to cost constraints and that of minimizing cost subject to some performance constraints.[1]

Most capital-budgeting techniques have been oriented to selecting projects that will contribute toward maximization of some measure of project returns. However, the MAPI method proposed by George Terborgh departs from these by selecting projects that contribute to minimization of costs. The MAPI method is treated in detail in a subsequent chapter.

PROJECT CHARACTERISTICS

The quantitative parameters of an investment that are relevant to the decision to accept or reject the project are:

Initial Cost
Project Useful Life
Net Cash Flows in Each Time Period
Salvage Value at End of Each Time Period

These parameters, together with the enterprise's cost of capital, provide information on which a rational decision may be based according to objective criteria. In addition to the above quantitative parameters, sometimes qualitative considerations

---

[1] A. O. Converse, *Optimization* (New York: Holt, Rinehart and Winston, 1970), p. 5.

will also affect the investment decision. For example, one production facility may use a collection of custom-designed machinery, whereas another employs more or less standard production machines. If the specialized machinery cannot practicably be converted to producing other machined products, and if the probability that the particular products, for which this specialized machinery is acquired, will be abandoned prematurely is high, then the decision to adopt standard production machinery may be superior even though it may promise somewhat lower benefits if things go well for the product line.

Qualitative considerations may be crucial, especially in the area of contingency planning. In answering the "what if" question of what alternative use may be made of capital investment projects if things do not go as well as expected, management may prefer the array of projects that offers flexibility over the somewhat more efficient, but highly specialized, alternative. For example, a firm that produced automobile fabric convertible tops and decided in 1970 to acquire new automated equipment to stitch the seams, predicated on a 15-year useful machine life, would have found in 1976 that original equipment market sales were vanishing. In 1976, Cadillac, the last of the United States automakers to produce fabric-covered convertibles, announced it was phasing out such models. Unless the replacement market would continue to provide sufficient sales into the mid-1980s, the firm would need to find alternative products suitable for production on the specialized equipment. Perhaps fabric camper-trailer tops or similar items could be produced as profitably on the specialized machinery. If not, the firm would find that its decision in 1970 was, with benefit of hindsight, the wrong decision.

No general rules or procedures have been developed for contingency planning in capital budgeting. Each case has its own unique attributes that prevent uniform application of rigorous principles. It is in such aspects of decision-making that there is no reasonable alternative to the judgment of management. For instance, how should a firm that produces barrel tubes for shotguns incorporate in its decisions the possibility that a Congress will be elected that is disposed to outlaw private firearms ownership or restrict ownership drastically? Given that such a Congress is elected, what is the contingent probability that it will find time to act? Will a later change in congressional composition reverse such legislation? If so, would consumer demand return to its former level? Such a firm must incorporate factors such as these into its capital-budgeting decisions in order to ensure flexibility in using its physical capital in case the environment in which it operates suddenly changes. And is there any firm not subject to environmental changes?

INITIAL COST

Capital-budgeting projects will generally require some initial cash outlay for acquiring the project. Such cost may arise from construction outlays, purchase cost or initial lease payment, legal fees, transportation, and installation, and possibly from tax liability on a project that is being replaced by the new one or from penalty costs associated with breaking a lease on the replaced project. Cash costs attributable to the decision to accept a capital project should be included in the initial project cost. Costs that would be incurred regardless of whether or not the project were accepted—"sunk costs"—should not be allocated to the project cost. With some projects, especially large ones involving design and construction over several years, initial costs should be considered as the negative net cash flows incurred in each period prior to the one in which net cash flow becomes positive.

Sunk Cost

Unrecoverable costs associated with previous decisions should not be allocated to a new project under consideration. For instance, assume that a firm purchased a $400,000 machine 5 years ago, which had at the time an estimated useful life of 20 years, and that $228,571 has still to be claimed as depreciation against taxes on income at a 48 percent rate, which yields a tax reduction of $118,857 spread over the next 15 years. Assume now that a technologically improved machine is available to replace it. Should the unrecovered tax reduction be added to the other costs of the new machine? The answer is "no," in this case. However, the unrecovered tax reductions may be included as costs in the years in which they would have been realized. Now, what if the $400,000 machine suddenly breaks down and cannot be repaired? In this event the unrecovered tax reductions from depreciation should not be charged to a replacement machine, either in the initial cost or in the cash flows over the remaining depreciable life of the broken machine. For tax purposes the broken machine's remaining value will be charged to the firm's operations as a loss which will have no effect on the replacement decision. Similarly, equipment that is discarded because of a change in the firm's operations should not have any of its cost charged to new equipment that is subsequently acquired.

The problem of what costs to include and what costs to exclude from a particular capital investment project will be resolved by focusing on cash flows and ignoring accounting costs. Does acceptance of the candidate project increase or decrease cash flow in years zero through the end of its anticipated economic life? If acceptance of the project precipitates changes in cash flows, then these must be taken into account in evaluating the project. Noncash items, and items such as sunk costs, must *not* be included in project evaluation, even though specific dollar figures are associated with them.

What if costly preliminary engineering studies have been completed and research and development costs incurred? Should these be included in the cost of the project for capital-budgeting evaluation? No, they should not, for they represent sunk costs—water over the dam—and subsequent acceptance or rejection of the project will not affect them. The handling of such sunk costs in the accounting framework may be a different matter; for tax or control reasons they may be associated with the project. Since in this book our concern is capital budgeting and not accounting, such matters will be ignored. They are irrelevant to the decision of whether or not to accept a project, except to the extent that they affect *cash flows*.

Components of Initial Cost

In addition to the obvious component of initial cost, namely, the basic price of the capital project in question, some less obvious costs must be included. Among them are:

    Transportation and Insurance Charges
    Installation Costs, including special machine foundations, movement of other equipment to get the new project to its location in the plant, installation of service facilities such as electric, hydraulic and pneumatic lines, and so on.
    License or Royalty Cost
    Required Additional Working Capital Investment
    Operator Training Costs

Transportation and insurance costs may be included in the vendor's price. In many instances, however, delivery will be F.O.B. the vendor's plant. In these cases failure to include the proper transportation and insurance costs will understate the project's initial cost, perhaps seriously so when heavy equipment is difficult and expensive to ship.

Installation costs may include the full expense of project installation. With industrial machinery that will be placed in an existing plant, it may be necessary to move intervening equipment to allow room for the new equipment. In some instances the plant structure itself may have to be temporarily or permanently modified or the disassembled equipment moved in pieces to its site in the plant. Worker safety may require installation of sound-dampening materials, special ventilation equipment, dust collectors, fire extinguisher systems, and so on. Heavy machines usually require a concrete "anchor" to be poured prior to installation, with the foundation sometimes being several feet thick and as large or larger than the machine attached to it. Machinery often requires foundations to be built so that vibrations created are not communicated through the plant floor. Adequate vibration dampening can increase installation cost considerably, but it is required in environments in which precision may be affected by this type of unwanted disturbance.

License or royalty cost for use of patented equipment or processes may require an initial payment as well as the customary periodic payments as production gets underway. These should be included in the project cost.

Required additional working capital investment is an item that is easy to overlook. Usually, this will not be a significant factor with component projects, but will be important for most major projects as defined earlier in this chapter. Additional net working capital required to support accounts receivable, inventory, or other current asset increases (net of current liability increases) are included in project cost. Recovery of such net working capital requirements at project termination may be incorporated in salvage value or the last period's cash flow, which are equivalent means of handling this factor.

Operator training costs, if not included by the vendor in the basic equipment cost, must be added to the project cost by the purchaser. Such training is to be expected with capital equipment employing a new technology or capital equipment whose operation by nature is complex. For instance, it is generally required when large-scale computer systems are acquired, that operators and support personnel be trained properly in correct use of the equipment. This is true even though the new machine replaced an older model of the same vendor, or a smaller machine of the same series with a different operating system or fewer options than the new one.

In addition to these initial cost items, others may be found in particular cases. The rule to follow in determining whether a cost item should be included in the initial cost of a capital investment project is to answer the two following questions. If the answer to both is in the affirmative, the cost should be included in the initial cost of the project.

1. Is the cost incurred only if the capital project is undertaken, that is, accepted?
2. Is the cost represented by a cash outflow?

If the answer to both is "yes," then only the cash outflow associated with the cost should be included in the initial cost of the project. Noncash costs should be excluded. For this purpose we assume net working capital increases to be cash flows, although "internal" to the firm. Increased working capital requirements must be funded, and the money committed will generally not be released until the end of the project's useful life.

USEFUL LIFE

The investment merit of a project will depend on its useful economic life. Useful economic life of capital equipment may end long before it becomes physically deteriorated to the point of inoperability. Economic life, and decline in the value of capital equipment over the economic life, may mean that project abandonment prior to the end of the originally anticipated *project* life will be of greater benefit to the firm than holding the project to the end. This topic is taken up in detail later.

Terborgh defined the cumulative effects on decline in capital serviceability over the period the equipment is held as *operating inferiority*.[2] This is a meaningful concept, and it will be adopted here. Operating inferiority is determined by two components: physical deterioration and technological obsolescence. Physical deterioration is what is normally considered to be the determinant of project life. However, technological obsolescence will be far more important in determining the economic life of some projects.

Consider an accounting firm that purchased a large number of mechanical calculating machines in 1970, assuming an economic life of ten years. If the machines were to be kept in service over the full ten years, they could be expected to undergo steady physical deterioration. As time went on, more frequent and more serious breakdowns would be expected, and expenditures for repairs would increase accordingly.

[2] George Terborgh, *Dynamic Equipment Policy* (Washington: Machinery and Allied Products Institute, 1949), pp. 61–62.

Some rotary, mechanical calculators cost $1000 or more in 1970. At about the same point in time, due to advances in technology, a variety of electronic calculators came on the market. Not only was the cost substantially less, as little as one-fourth the cost of their mechanical predecessors for some of them, but they were superior in several respects. The electronic models were substantially faster, immensely quieter, less subject to mechanical problems because of the dearth of moving parts, and provided number displays that were larger (sometimes), illuminated, and generally easy to read. Thus it was that the mechanical calculator fell victim to technological obsolescence. They simply were inferior in most respects to their modern descendants, even if still quite serviceable.

In firms whose employees devote a large portion of their working time to calculation, by 1975 few mechanical calculators were in use. Why? Because replacement with the best technology allowed less wasted time waiting for results, a quieter atmosphere more conducive to productive work, and reduced repair costs. If an employee spent half of each day working with a calculator, and the new calculator was 25 percent faster, the same employee could do the equivalent of one hour additional work in the same four hours. Such efficiency gains are easily translated into money terms. An office employing four such people, by equipping each with the new technology, could avoid hiring the fifth person when the workload expanded by as much as 25 percent.

Physical Deterioration

For many types of capital, experience with similar facilities in the past may provide useful guidelines. For instance, we would expect that the physical life of a punch press purchased today would, on the average, be similar to that of a new punch press of 20 years ago.

With capital that employs new technology, or a new application of existing technology, managers and engineers experienced with production equipment may provide useful estimates. However, capital goods produced by a firm not likely to stay in the business and maintain a supply of replacement parts may negate an otherwise good estimate of useful life. Unavailability of a crucial part from a supplier will mean either producing the part in the toolroom, contracting to have it custom made, modifying the machine to take a similar standard part, or abandoning the machine. This last alternative obviously ends the useful life.

Physical deterioration of major projects, as defined earlier, may well be concerned with that of plant and equipment components. It is not meaningful to speak of *the* physical deterioration of a major project unless this is taken to be synonymous with deterioration of the buildings housing the operation, or unless the major project is indeed one major item of capital equipment that dominates all others. If our major project is a division of the firm composed of one or more buildings, each housing 100 or more items of capital equipment, what meaning can we attach to physical deterioration of the project? The answer is none; at least this is true if component projects are added and replaced as time goes on. On the other hand, if our division is based on operation of one dominating item of capital, such as a toll bridge or a carwash, it may well be meaningful to refer to physical deterioration of the major project.

Technological Obsolescence

Although we may often be able to obtain workable estimates of physical life for capital equipment and corresponding physical deterioration over time, it is a very different matter for technological obsolescence. Technological innovations that contribute to the obsolescence of existing capital tend to occur randomly and unevenly over time. Sometimes technological changes are implemented rapidly during relatively short intervals of time: The technological advances in computer equipment since the 1950s have been profound, and in the 1980s may not only continue but may continue at a rapid pace for some time yet. Theoretical developments, such as holographic, laser-directed computer memories, once the engineering obstacles have been overcome, and artificial intelligence software promise yet further waves of innovation in the industry.

Terborgh's approach to incorporating technological obsolescence into the operating inferiority of capital equipment is difficult to improve upon. His recommendation, basically, is to assume, in the absence of information to the contrary, that technological obsolescence of existing capital will accumulate at a constant rate as time goes on.[3] In the absence of information to the contrary, such extrapolation from the past into the future is reasonable. However, should information be available that implies more rapid or less rapid technological change, this information should be employed, even if only qualitatively.

Should the firm delay an investment when technological changes are expected in the near future? The answer to this question may be found in evaluating the merit of investing today with replacement when the technologically improved capital becomes available, and evaluating the merit of the alternative—that of postponing investment until the improved capital is available. Comparison of the merits of the alternatives will serve to determine the better course of action. Methods for performing such analysis, once the net cash flows are determined, are covered in later chapters.

The subject of technological obsolescence in capital budgeting is not limited to the firm's physical capital; it may apply also to the human capital of the enterprise, and certainly does apply to the product lines on which the cash flows of investment projects are predicted. For example, the replacement of vacuum tubes with transistors and integrated circuits, and later with miniaturized circuits made possible by large-scale integration, caused televisions incorporating vacuum tubes to be obsolete. A firm that based its capital investment decisions on continued demand for sets with vacuum tubes found that later it had still serviceable equipment for a product no longer in demand. Similar examples are to be found in mechanical versus elec-

[3] Ibid., p. 65.

tronic calculators, automatic versus manual automobile transmissions, and piston versus jet propulsion aircraft engines, to name just a few of the more obvious.

CASH FLOWS

In capital budgeting we must base our analysis on the net cash flows of the project under consideration, not on accounting profits. Only cash can be reinvested. Only cash can be used to pay dividends and interest and to repay debt. Only cash can be used to pay suppliers, workers and management, and tax authorities.

Over the long run, both total firm cash flow and total accounting profits provide measures of management performance. However, in the short run the two will generally not be highly correlated. The firm, for example, may have had a very profitable year as measured by "generally accepted accounting principles" and yet have no cash to meet its obligations since the "profits" are not yet realized but are tied up in accounts receivable that may or may not be eventually collected.

Determination of net cash flows involves consideration of two basic factors: (1) those that contribute to cash inflows or cash receipts and (2) those that contribute to cash outflows or cash costs. Major projects, as defined earlier, will have both these factors affecting them throughout their economic lives. Component projects, after the initial outlay, will be directly involved with cash outflows, but only *indirectly* with cash inflows.

Estimation of cash inflows for major projects generally requires the joint efforts of specialists in marketing research, marketing management, and design engineering, and perhaps staff economists and others as well. If the firm does not have the required expertise itself, it may hire the services of appropriate consultants.

For cash outflow estimation, joint contributions of design, production, and industrial engineering, production management, and cost accounting are required for major projects. Additionally, staff economists and labor relations personnel may contribute information relevant to probable cost increases as time goes on.

Financial management will be responsible to top management for analyzing the effects on the firm's financial strength if the project is undertaken and for obtaining the funds necessary to finance the undertaking. Finance personnel will undoubtedly be involved in recommending which major projects should be accepted and which rejected based on their analysis of the project, its interactions with the existing assets of the firm, and consequently its profitability in cash terms. Accounting staff will be concerned with the project's effect on reported profits and tax liabilities and all the attendant details.

Cash inflows for a major project will be determined by (1) price at which each unit of output is sold; (2) the number of units of output sold; and (3) the collection of accounts receivable on credit sales. Estimation of these items is not easy, especially for a product dissimilar to product lines with which the firm may already have had experience. Proper estimation, as mentioned earlier, involves persons from different functional areas within the firm, and possibly external to it.

For component projects we will be concerned with cash outflows. If a given task must be performed by capital equipment, then we shall seek to obtain capital that will do so at lowest cost. Thus, on initial selection of mutually exclusive candidate projects, we will select the project that minimizes cost or, alternatively and equivalently, the project for which the saving in cash opportunity cost is maximized. Of course, we must assume that all component projects admitted to candidate status are capable of performing the tasks that must be done within the environment of a major project. Projects that cannot should not be treated as candidates.

Cash Inflows (Cash Receipts)

Assume that we are examining a *combination of several* machines that will produce a single product our new firm plans to sell. The principals of our firm are experienced in sales and engineering of such a product; both worked for years for a larger company that produced similar products. Some preliminary orders have already been obtained from firms that will purchase the product we will produce. It is estimated that at a price of $17.38 per unit, our firm can reasonably expect sales of 100,000 units per year.

If we assume that sales and cash receipts on sales will be uniform throughout each year, and that unit price and sales volume will be constant from year to year, the task of cash inflow estimation is trivial. If we have no uncollectable accounts receivable, our cash inflows each year will be unit price times number of units, that is, $1,738,000.

Life is usually not so simple as this, however. Sales probably will not be uniform throughout the year, but there will be seasonal variations. Sales from year to year will seldom be even nearly constant. Possibly sales will grow from year to year along a trend of several years' duration, or decline for several years. Such variations are very difficult to predict in advance, and are aggravated by unforeseen developments in competition, the national economy, and other factors.

In the final analysis, estimation of cash inflows will depend on managerial judgment, conditioned by the economic environment and knowledge of the firm's competition and trends in product design and improvement. Also, in many industries revenues may be influenced by advertising expenditures, so that firms may, in fact, individually and collectively, influence the level of demand for their products. Seldom will a firm be in the position of having a mathematical model that provides reliable demand and revenue forecasts, especially for periods beyond one year. There are too many qualitative, vague, and intangible factors at work that cannot be quantified given the current state of the art in mathematical modeling. Proper incorporation of these factors requires human judgment, and perhaps not a little luck.

It will often be useful to prepare several forecasts, including a "worst case" forecast in which it is assumed that whatever can go wrong for the firm's sales will go wrong. Of course, unanticipated factors and events may make actual events still worse, but we would assume that for a proper "worst case" forecast, actual experience would be no worse, say, 95 times out of 100. In other words, a good "worst case" forecast should have a *small* probability associated with it that actual events will turn out worse. "Best case" and "most likely" forecasts may similarly be made.

The population projections of the United States Bureau of the Census, in fact, have been prepared on the basis of high, low, and most likely. Because we can never expect an exact forecast, it is extremely useful to be able to bracket the actual outcome, so that we may say that the probability is p percent that the actual outcome will fall between the best case and worst case estimates, where p is a number close to 1.0. For this approach to be useful, the best case and worst case forecasts cannot be so far apart as to make them meaningless.

Let us now go back to our example. If $17.38 per unit and 100,000 units are taken to be our most likely forecast for the coming year, we may determine that $14.67 and 40,000 units is the worst that is likely and $23.00 and 200,000 the best that is likely to happen. If we can attach a (albeit subjective) probability of .05 or 5 percent that the actual revenue will fall short of the worst case, we have useful information. The chances of sales revenues being less than the worst case are then only five in 100.

Cash Outflows

To some extent estimates of cash outflows may be made with more confidence than those for cash inflows. For example, the initial investment outlay is made at the beginning of the project's life, and may often be estimated precisely. In fact, the supplier may provide a firm price for the cost of the investment. However, other cost components may prove to be almost as difficult to forecast as factors affecting cash receipts.

What specific items do we consider as cash outflows? Anything requiring cash to be paid out of the firm or to be made unavailable for other uses. Suppose that the machines we are considering for purchase are to be treated as one project. Assume that the project costs $3 million for purchase and installation. For simplicity, assume also that we plan to run production on a constant level, so that labor, electricity, and materials will be constant for at least two years. In addition, cash will be tied up in raw materials and finished goods inventory and in accounts receivable. Setting aside the notion of worst and best case forecasts for now, let us deal with the most likely production and cost forecast, and the most likely annual cash revenue forecast. We obtain the following:

Year 0	*Cash Outflow*	*Cash Inflow*
Initial Investment	$3,000,000	
Wages	100,000	
Fringe Benefits	50,000	
F.I.C.A., etc.	20,000	
Raw Materials Inventory	200,000	
Finished Goods Inventory	500,000	
Accounts Receivable Investment	400,000	
Electric and Other Direct Variable Costs	10,000	
	$4,280,000	
Cash Receipts on Sales, Net of Discounts, and Bad Debt Losses		$1,738,000
Net Cash Flow		($2,542,000)

Note that no overhead or sunk cost items have been included in the cash flows. In the second year of operations, if no new investment in inventories or accounts receivable is required, and the same amounts of labor, electricity, and so on, at the same rates are employed, we obtain:

Year 1	Cash Outflow	Cash Inflow
Wages	$100,000	
Fringe Benefits	50,000	
F.I.C.A., etc.	20,000	
Electric and Other Direct Variable Costs	10,000	
	$180,000	
Cash Receipts on Sales, Net of Discounts, and Bad Debt Losses		$1,738,000
Net Cash Flow		$1,558,000

Wages and fringe benefits include those of direct labor plus the portion of indirect labor that services the machinery: machine set-up, materials handling, and so on.

Ordinarily, in expositions of the various capital-budgeting techniques, we assume for simplicity of explanation that cash flows occur only at the end of a period (usually a year) and not over that period. Period zero in such treatment includes only the installed cost of the capital equipment. Subsequent periods include net cash flows arising from cash receipts minus cash disbursements, the latter including whatever additional investment that may be required in capital equipment, inventories, and so on.

Interest expenses are specifically excluded from cash costs because methods of project evaluation that employ discounting already incorporate the interest costs implicitly—they are imbedded in the discount rate and not in the cash flows.

TAXES AND DEPRECIATION

Since firms generally pay income taxes on earnings and depreciation is deductible as an expense, there is an effect on cash flow. Cash that does not have to be paid as tax to the government serves to increase net cash flow because it is a reduction in cash outflow.

The rationale behind allowing depreciation to be tax deductible is that it represents recovery of investment rather than profit. And since the benefits of capital investment occur over the economic life of the project, it is deemed appropriate to spread recognition of the investment outlays, as expenses, over the same period. Various accounting conventions and tax authority rulings on how the depreciation charges may be calculated, and what depreciation lifetimes may be used for various asset types, have complicated a basically simple concept. Profitable disposal of capital equipment may subject the firm to additional taxes on residual salvage value. Such details are covered in texts in accounting and in financial management. Here we are concerned only with basic concepts and the effect of depreciation on cash flow, not on the details of tax rules. Tax laws change from time to time, not only for various theoretical reasons, but as part of the economic "fine-tuning" of the federal government to encourage or discourage new investment, as the situation of the national economy may indicate.

Several methods of calculating depreciation for each year of a capital investment's life have been devised. Because cash may be invested, it is generally better to charge as much depreciation as possible in the early years of a project's life, thus deferring taxes to later years and simultaneously retaining more cash in the early years. This is especially true during times of rapid inflation. Unless the firm has tax losses larger than it can use to offset taxable income, it will charge the maximum allowable depreciation in the early years of a capital investments' life. Given that money has time value, to do otherwise would not be in the best interests of the owners of the enterprise. The more rapid the rate of price inflation, the more incumbent it is to charge the maximum depreciation in the early years for tax purposes. However, for management control purposes the firm may use the depreciation schedule that is considered to match most closely the actual economic deterioration in the capital project from year to year. Yet, with high rates of price inflation in capital goods, the depreciation charged against the original cost if unadjusted may be of little usefulness. Such adjustment, however, is beyond the scope of this book.

ADR Depreciation

In the United States there are currently two basic depreciation frameworks: (1) the general guidelines (GG) and (2) class life asset depreciation range system (ADR). The general guidelines may be used for any depreciable asset. The ADR system was authorized in the Revenue Act of 1971.

A firm may select the ADR system in preference to the general guidelines for any depreciable assets acquired after the year 1970. There are provisions dealing with assets acquired prior to 1970, but since we are concerned here with the decision to acquire or not acquire *new* assets, we shall not go into these. The firm elects annually to use the ADR system or not to use it for those depreciable assets acquired during the fiscal year.

Under the ADR system, assets correspond to various classes. For example, one class is 00.241—light general purpose trucks. The range for this class is three years at the lower limit, four years "guideline," and five years upper limit. The firm may choose the lower limit, three years, to achieve the most rapid depreciation.

It will be useful to review the basic methods of depreciation used in the United States before going into the differences between the GG and ADR systems.

Straight-Line Depreciation

The notion behind the straight-line depreciation is that the investment's residual value declines by a *constant dollar amount* from year to year uniformly over the useful life. Therefore, the initial investment is divided by the number of years of useful life, and the result used as the annual depreciation charge. This is the least useful method for deferring taxes to the later years of the project's life.

Double-Declining-Balance Depreciation

With declining-balance depreciation it is assumed that the residual value of the investment at the end of any year is a *fixed percentage* of the residual value at the end of the previous year. Alternatively, we take as declining-balance depreciation a constant *percentage* of the residual value at the end of the previous period. In United States practice, the method used is that of *double*-declining balance (DDB), in which the percentage value of decline is multiplied by a factor of two. This results in accelerating the depreciation charges and deferring larger amounts of taxes to later years. Salvage value is excluded from the calculations in this method.

Sum-of-the-Years' Digits Depreciation

The method of sum-of-the-years' digits (SYD) depreciation is implemented by writing the years in the asset's lifetime in reverse order, and then dividing each by the sum of the years in the useful life. Depreciation for each year is then determined by multiplying the original asset cost by the factor corresponding to each year. A project lasting five years will therefore have 5/15 (or 1/3) of the original value charged to depreciation in the first year and 1/15 charged in the fifth and last year. This method, like that of double-declining balance, provides for accelerated asset depreciation.

Comparison of the Basic Depreciation Methods

Assume we have an asset that cost the form C and has a depreciable lifetime[4] of N years. Then the annual depreciation charges with the three methods for $0 < t \leq N$ are:

Straight Line $\quad C/N$

Double-Declining Balance $\quad C(1 - 2P)^{t-1}2P \quad$ where $P = 1/N$

Sum-of-Years' Digits $\quad C(N - t + 1)/[N(N + 1)/2] \quad$ since

$$\sum_{t=1}^{N} t = \frac{N(N + 1)}{2}$$

Example 3–1

For illustration, let us take a project with $C = \$100,000$, $N = 10$, and calculate depreciation at the end of each year with each method. We assume zero salvage value.

---

[4] The depreciable lifetime of an asset will often be different from the useful economic life. This happens because tax authority rulings concerning the lifetime that may be used for depreciation may not properly reflect the useful economic life of such asset in any particular firm.

Table 3-1. COMPARISON OF DEPRECIATION METHODS UNDER GENERAL GUIDELINES, WITH ZERO SALVAGE

Year	Straight Line	Double-Declining Balance	Sum-of-Years' Digits
1	$ 10,000	$ 20,000	$ 18,182
2	10,000	16,000	16,364
3	10,000	12,800	14,545
4	10,000	10,240	12,727
5	10,000	8,192	10,909
6	10,000	6,554	9,090
7	10,000	5,243	7,273
8	10,000	4,194	5,455
9	10,000	3,355	3,636
10	10,000	13,422 [a]	1,819
	$100,000	$100,000	$100,000

[a] $2684 plus remaining $10,738 undepreciated balance.

The *total* depreciation charged with each method is equal to the cost of the project. Total depreciation cannot, of course, exceed the investment acquisition cost. Note that with double-declining-balance depreciation, the final year's depreciation charge is the sum of the double-declining-balance amount plus the undepreciated balance.

In practice, firms will usually switch from one method of depreciation to another when it is advantageous to do so, and when the tax authorities will allow the change. For instance, under GG a firm may switch from double-declining-balance depreciation to straight-line depreciation. Of course, the straight-line depreciation charge will not be based on the original cost and lifetime, but on the *undepreciated balance* and remaining depreciable life at the time of the switch.

In this example the firm could, under the GG, switch to straight-line depreciation in year six. In this year straight-line depreciation of the remaining balance yields the same dollar depreciation as the double-declining-balance method. However, in years seven, eight, and nine the amount charged to depreciation is larger with straight line.

In no case may the firm depreciate more than 100 percent of an asset. This means that if an asset costs $C, and is expected to have a salvage value of $S, no more than $(C − S) may be depreciated. Let us now consider an example in which salvage value must be taken into account. *Note that DDB depreciation ignores salvage*, although no more than $(C − S) may be charged.

Example 3-2

Let us take a project with $C = \$130,000$, $N = 10$, and $S = \$10,000$. We shall assume the firm will switch to straight-line from DDB depreciation, as allowed by the GG, as soon as this is advantageous.

Table 3-2. COMPARISON OF DEPRECIATION METHODS UNDER GENERAL GUIDELINES, WITH SALVAGE

Year	Straight Line	Double-Declining Balance	Sum-of-Years' Digits
1	$ 12,000	$ 26,000	$ 21,818
2	12,000	20,800	19,636
3	12,000	16,640	17,455
4	12,000	13,312	15,273
5	12,000	10,650	13,091
6	12,000	8,520	10,909
7	12,000	6,816	8,727
8	12,000	5,754[a]	6,545
9	12,000	5,754	4,634
10	12,000	5,754	2,181
	$120,000	$120,000	$120,000

[a]Straight-line depreciation in years 8, 9, and 10 on the remaining balance. No more than 100 percent of the asset may be depreciated. Salvage is expected to be $10,000 and $102,738 has been charged by the end of year seven. The straight-line amount is obtained by dividing $(120,000−102,738) by 3. This yields $5,754, which is larger than the DDB charge of $5,453 would be, so the switch is advantageous.

Example 3-3

With ADR system, salvage is treated the same way as with DDB under the GG; that is, it is ignored. As always, however, no more than 100 percent of the asset value may be depreciated. The following example shows the results of using ADR with the same asset just considered. *In practice, because ADR allows a choice of depreciable asset life, we should not expect that the asset life will remain ten years.* If a shorter life is allowed, the firm will take it to maximize accelerated write-off.

General Guidelines allows the firm to switch from DDB to straight line only; *ADR allows the firm to switch to SYD from DDB.* This allows for the greatest amount of depreciation in the early years. Switching from DDB to SYD will always be advantageous in the second year of the project's life. Applying this to Example 3-2 yields the following results: Actual depreciation in the second year will be the same; SYD will yield greater depreciation in the subsequent years.

Canadian Depreciation

Depreciation is generally called "capital consumption allowance" in Canada, or "capital cost allowance." Because the *Income Tax Act* was changed in 1949, only the declining-balance method has been generally allowed. This is not a double-declining balance as discussed earlier, but a declining balance based on assigned, fixed rates. The rate is applied to the undepreciated book balance of the asset, and the firm need not charge depreciation in years when it has losses.

All assets acquired within a tax year qualify for a full year's depreciation. There

34 THE BASIC FRAMEWORK

Table 3-3. COMPARISON OF DEPRECIATION METHODS UNDER ADR SYSTEM, WITH SALVAGE

Year	Straight Line	Double-Declining Balance	Sum-of-Years' Digits
1	$ 13,000	$ 26,000	$ 23,636
2	13,000	20,800	21,273
3	13,000	16,640	18,909
4	13,000	13,312	16,545
5	13,000	10,650	14,182
6	13,000	8,520	11,818
7	13,000	6,816	9,455
8	13,000	5,423	4,182
9	13,000	4,362	0
10	3,000	3,487	0
	$120,000	$120,000	$120,000

Table 3-4. COMPARISON OF OPTIMUM DEPRECIATION TO DDB AND SYD, WITH SALVAGE

Year	Optimum Depreciation	Method Used	Double-Declining Balance	Sum-of-Years' Digits
1	$ 26,000	DDB	$ 26,000	$ 23,636
2	20,800	SYD	20,800	21,273
3	18,489	SYD	16,640	18,909
4	16,178	SYD	13,312	16,545
5	13,867	SYD	10,650	14,182
6	11,556	SYD	8,520	11,818
7	9,245	SYD	6,814	9,455
8	3,865	SYD	5,423	4,182
9	0	SYD	4,362	0
10	0	SYD	3,487	0
	$120,000		$120,000	$120,000

are 25 asset classes, each assigned a fixed capital cost allowance rate. All assets of a class are pooled together. Total capital consumption is calculated by multiplying the book balance of each pool by its corresponding capital cost allowance rate and adding the products together.

Capital gains and losses result only when a given asset pool, not an individual asset, is sold. Capital cost allowances due to a specific asset can remain in effect indefinitely if the given asset expires without salvage value, if there are other assets in the same asset pool, and if the firm generates income from which the capital cost allowance can be deducted.

Summary on Depreciation

1. Under the general guidelines, the only switch that can be made is from DDB to straight-line depreciation.
2. Under the general guidelines, only the DDB method ignores salvage value.
3. With ADR system the depreciable life is chosen from an IRS guideline range for the type of asset to be depreciated.

4. In the ADR system, salvage value is ignored (as it is with DDB under the general guidelines) in calculating depreciation with SYD and straight line as well as DDB.
5. Under the ADR system, it is permitted to switch from DDB to SYD when this becomes advantageous to the firm. The switch will be made in the second year in order to maximize the early write-off of an asset.
6. Although salvage is ignored under ADR (and DDB with the general guidelines), the maximum that may be depreciated is the difference between the asset cost and its salvage value.

It can be shown that under the ADR system, maximization of the tax deferral in the project's early years will always be achieved by using double-declining-balance depreciation in the first year, and sum-of-the-years' digits depreciation in the second and subsequent years.

Because depreciation rules change from time to time, it is wise to consult the current tax code.

Investment Tax Credit

From time to time the federal government has provided special tax credit on new asset purchases in order to encourage aggregate investment in the economy. In recent years the credit has been increased from 7 percent to 10 percent (more in certain special cases) on new investment. The effect on cash flow is much the same as that of depreciation: It facilitates cash recovery during the first year of the asset's life. Because the rules governing application of the investment tax credit contain some complications, and may change from year to year, the current tax code should be checked when estimating the cash flows for an investment project that may qualify for the investment tax credit. At the time of this writing the investment tax credit is affected by the useful life of the asset. If the asset life is less than three years, no credit may be claimed. The credit applies to one-third the asset cost if the asset has an economic life of three years but less than five; and two-thirds if the asset cost is five years but less than seven. The credit applies to assets described as "qualified investment" under Section 38 of the Tax Code. It is equal to the amount allowed on new assets under Section 38 plus as much as $100,000 of the cost of newly acquired used assets qualified under Section 38. In no case may the investment tax credit exceed the firm's total tax liability for the year.

Unused portions of the investment tax credit are treated in the manner of capital losses: They may be carried back three years and forward five. The firm is restricted in applying the tax credit. If its tax liability is above $25,000, the credit claimed for the year may not exceed $25,000 plus 50 percent of the tax liability exceeding $25,000. If an asset is abandoned prior to the end of its estimated life, a portion of the tax credit claimed may have to be added to the firm's tax bill in the year. The amount will equal the difference between the credit actually claimed and the amount that would have been used had the actual asset life been used originally to calculate the credit.

Inflation

Over a span of time when price levels are fairly constant, depreciation rules and practices may be reasonably equitable in allowing the cost of the project to be recovered. A capital investment costing, for example, $150,000 will provide recovery of $150,000, which may be used to purchase a successor project at the end of its useful life. However, if capital equipment prices were to increase at 12 percent per annum, at the end of only ten years it would cost $465,870 just to replace the worn machine with an identical new one. Existing depreciation rules do not take this into account, and therefore capital recovery is inadequate to provide for replacement investment when required. This is one of the many matters that will be treated in some detail later, because of its significant effect on investment.

QUESTIONS

1. Classify each of the following as a *major* or *minor project* and justify your choice:
   (a) A new factory to produce a new product.
   (b) A grinding machine that will be part of the new factory.
   (c) A grinding machine that may be added to the new factory in a year or two.
   (d) An automatic carwash system that a hotel will construct adjacent to its building.
   (e) Addition to a customer parking lot at a retail store.
2. Explain why cost minimization will normally provide a more appropriate approach than net revenue maximization for component projects. Why may cost minimization not be the best approach for major projects?
3. Why will firms usually prefer accelerated depreciation for tax purposes?
4. What is the difference between cash flow and accounting earnings? Can you give an example in which the two are different?
5. A firm has spent $5000 for a feasibility study on a capital project. If the project is undertaken, should this cost be included in the cost of the project? Explain.
6. Discuss the concept of contingency planning in capital budgeting. Why is it difficult to formulate general principles for contingency planning?

PROBLEMS

3.1 Prove that, as allowed under ADR system rules, a switch from double-declining balance in year one to sum-of-the-years' digits in the second and subsequent years will yield the maximum depreciation of the methods described in this chapter.

3.2 A firm has purchased new equipment that will result in accounts receivable and inventory increases of $15,000. It is estimated that 40 percent of this amount will be provided by accounts payable trade credit. What will be the increase in net working capital? Should this be treated as a cost of the project?

3.3 XXX corporation has purchased a clam digger for $60,000, and must pay $2000 to have it delivered. The useful life of the machine is five years and salvage is estimated to be $5000. Calculate the effects on cash flow of straight line, sum-of-years' digits, and double-declining balance under the general guidelines, and the ADR under the method of Problem 3.1. What effect would there be if salvage were $15,000? Zero? Assume the applicable income tax rate is 48 percent, and under ADR the digger may be depreciated over four years instead of five.

3.4 Assuming alternative costs of capital of 10 percent, 15 percent, and 20 percent per annum, compare the effects of straight line, sum-of-the-years' digits, double-declining balance, and the ADR method of Problem 3.1. (*Hint:* Assume cash tax deferrals can be invested at a minimum return equal to the firm's cost of capital. Ignore salvage and let cost be $100,000, lifetime five years.)

3.5 A machine costing $100,000 has an anticipated useful life of five years. Over this period the replacement cost is expected to increase by 10 percent each year. Will the taxes deferred by depreciation, invested at 10 percent return compounded annually, accumulate to an amount sufficient to buy a replacement machine at the end of this one's useful life? Use the ADR method of Problem 3.1. What if the inflation rate in replacement cost was 15 percent per year? The useful life was ten years? Assume a 48 percent tax rate.

Bibliography

1. Converse, A. O., *Optimization* (New York: Holt, Rinehart and Winston, 1970).
2. DeGarmo, E. Paul, and John R. Canada, *Engineering Economy*, 5th ed. (New York: Macmillan, 1973).
3. Gehrlein, William V., and Thomas K. Tiemann, "Optimal Depreciation Policies for Regulated Firms," *The Engineering Economist*, Vol. 25, No. 2 (Winter 1980), pp. 79–90.
4. Hirschmann, W. B., and J. R. Brauweiler, "Investment Analysis: Coping with Change," *Harvard Business Review* (May–June 1965).
5. Johnson, Robert W., *Capital Budgeting* (Belmont, Cal.: Wadsworth, 1970).
6. Osteryoung, Jerome S., *Capital Budgeting: Long-Term Asset Selection*, 2nd ed. (Columbus, Ohio: Grid, 1979).
7. Scheuble, Philip A., Jr., "How to Figure Equipment Replacement," *Harvard Business Review* (September–October 1955).
8. Soldofsky, Robert M., "Capital Budgeting Practices in Small Manufacturing Companies," in Dudley G. Luckett and Karl A. Fox, eds. *Studies in the Factor Markets for Small Business Firms* (Ames: Iowa State University Press, 1964).
9. Terborgh, George, *Dynamic Equipment Policy* (Washington: Machinery and Allied Products Institute, 1949).

Chapter 4
Cost of Capital

The cost of capital is a complex and still unsettled subject. It is discussed in finance texts in detail far beyond what we can devote to it in this text. In this chapter, intended primarily as a review, some of the more important considerations from the theory on cost of capital will be discussed, and some operational principles illustrated. Cost of capital is treated further in Chapter 21, within the context of the capital asset pricing model.

INTRODUCTION

Stated succinctly, the traditional view has been that the firm's cost of capital is the combined cost of the debt and equity funds required for acquisition of fixed, or permanent, assets used by the firm. Under this definition, even such things as permanent, nonseasonal working capital requirements are acquired with capital funds. Short-term financing with trade credit and bank lines of credit is generally excluded from cost of capital considerations. "Short term" is understood to include periods of one year or less, in which such balance sheet items as accounts payable and line-of-credit financing would be expected to be turned over at least once, or eliminated. Alternatively, the firm's cost of capital is the rate of return it must earn on an investment so that the value of the firm is neither reduced nor increased.

In terms of the firm's balance sheet, cost of capital relates to the long-term liabilities and capital section, to the firm's capital structure.

Although the specific account titles to be found for the various components of capital structure may differ, depending on the nature of the firm's business, the preferences of its accountants, and tradition within the industry, certain communalities exist. There will usually be long-term debts in the form of bond issues outstanding or long-term loans from banks or insurance companies. There will always be equity: For corporations this means common stock, retained earnings, and perhaps "surplus"; for proprietorships and partnerships it may be just an "equity" account. Because, for a variety of reasons, the corporate form of organization is dominant, and because the principles for dealing with corporate organization may be straightforwardly applied to proprietorships and partnerships, we will concentrate on corporate organization.

Each component item in the firm's capital structure has its own specific cost associated with it.

COST OF CAPITAL COMPONENTS

Debt

An important characteristic of debt is that interest payments are tax deductible,[1] whereas dividend payments are not. Thus the after-tax cost of debt is $(1 - \tau)$ times the pretax cost, where τ is the firm's marginal tax rate.

If a firm borrows $1 million for 20 years at annual interest of 9 percent, its before-tax cost is $90,000 annually, and if the firm's marginal income tax rate is 48 percent, the after-tax cost is $46,800, or 4.68 percent. The cost of debt is defined as the rate of return that must be earned on investments financed solely with debt,[2] in order that returns available to the owners be kept unchanged. In our example, investment of the $1 million would need to generate 9 percent return pretax, or 4.68 percent after tax, to leave the common stockholders' earnings unaffected.

For purposes of calculating the component cost of an item of debt, it is not important whether the particular debt component is a long-term loan from a bank or insurance company, or whether it is a mortgage bond or debenture, or whether sold publicly or privately placed. There is one important exception, however—that of convertible debentures. Such bonds are convertible at the option of the purchaser into shares of common stock in the firm. Because of this feature, they are hybrid securities, not strictly classifiable as either debt or equity. It is beyond the scope of this book to treat such issues, and the reader is referred to the bibliography at the end of the chapter as a starting point in the analysis.

[1] Although interest payments are tax deductible, principal repayments are *not*. This is a point often overlooked, although not a conceptually difficult one to understand.
[2] Note that this view ignores risk and the interactions between cost of capital components. In practice, the firm should evaluate potential investments in terms of its overall cost of capital whether or not the actual financing will be carried out by debt, equity, or some combination.

Preferred Stock

Preferred stock fills an intermediate position between debt and common stock. Ordinary preferred stock has little to distinguish it from debt, except that preferred dividends, in contrast to interest payments on debt, are not tax deductible. And the firm is under no legally binding agreement to pay preferred dividends. However, such dividends must be paid before any dividends to common shareholders may be paid, and unpaid preferred dividends are usually cumulative. If they are not paid in any period, they are carried forward (without interest) until paid.

The cost of preferred stock may be defined similarly to that of debt. It is the rate of return that investments financed solely with preferred stock must yield in order that returns available to the owners (common stockholders) are kept unchanged. Since preferred issues generally have no stated maturity, they may be treated as perpetuities,[3] as may securities issues with exceptionally long maturities.[4] Therefore, the component cost of a preferred stock that pays a dividend D_p and can be sold for a net price to the firm of P_p is given by:

$$k_p = \frac{D_p}{P_p} \tag{4.1}$$

There are many variations of preferred stock, including callable issues, participating, voting, and convertible stocks. Convertible preferreds, like convertible bonds, present problems of classification that are beyond the scope of this book. Principles established for treating convertible bonds are also applicable to convertible preferreds.

Common Stock and Retained Earnings

We will consider equity to exclude preferred stock and to include only common stock and retained earnings. In other words, we take equity to mean only the financial interest of the residual owners of the firm's assets: Those that have a claim (proportionate to the shares held) of assets remaining after claims of creditors and preferred shareholders are satisfied in the event of liquidation.

The cost of equity has two basic components: (1) the cost of retained earnings and (2) the cost of new shares issued. In general terms, the cost of equity can be defined as the minimum rate of return that an entirely equity-financed investment must yield to keep unchanged the returns available to the common stockholders, and thus the value of existing common shares.

There are two different but theoretically equivalent approaches to measuring the firm's cost of equity capital. The first is a model premised on the notion that the

---

[3] A perpetuity is a security that has a perpetual life, such as the British consols issued to finance the Napoleonic Wars and, more recently, a bond issue of the Canadian Pacific Railroad.
[4] The noncallable 4 percent bonds issued by the West Shore Railroad in 1886 and not redeemable before the year 2361 (475 year maturity) could be considered perpetuities. Unfortunately for the bond owners, many firms do not have perpetual life, and thus there is risk that the firm will fail and the bonds will be rendered worthless.

value of a share of common stock is the present value of all expected cash dividends it will yield out to an infinite time horizon. We shall refer to this as the *dividend capitalization model*.[5] It is derived under the assumption that the cash dividend is expected to grow at a constant rate g from period to period. The model is:

$$k_{re} = \frac{D}{P} + g \qquad (4.2)$$

where D is the expected annual dividend for the forthcoming year, P is the current price per share, and g is the annual growth rate in earnings per share.[6]

Unfortunately, estimation of the cost of equity capital is not as simple and objective as Eq. (4.2) suggests. Dividends may be quite constant for some firms, but price per share is subject to substantial volatility, even from day to day. This may require that one obtain an average, or normalized price. For corporations whose shares are not actively traded there may be no recent market price quotation. Growth is affected not only by the individual firm's performance, but also by the condition of the economy. Therefore, estimation of the firm's cost of equity capital is not simply employing a formula, but also a substantial amount of human judgment. More complex formulations than Eq. (4.2) have been devised, but still no means for bypassing the need for exercising judgment have been seriously proposed. The more complex formulas suffer from the same problems as Eq. (4.2).

The second approach to estimating the firm's cost of equity capital is with what has come to be known as the capital asset pricing model, or CAPM. Although the dividend capitalization model could be characterized as inductive, the CAPM might be better characterized as deductive. The CAPM yields the following equation:

$$k_e = R_F + \beta(R_M - R_F) \qquad (4.3)$$

where R_F is the rate of return on a risk-free security, usually meaning a short-term United States government security[7] such as treasury bills, and R_M is the rate of return on the market portfolio—an efficient portfolio in the sense that a higher return cannot be obtained without also accepting higher risk. The beta coefficient relates the return on the firm's stock to the return on the market portfolio. It is obtained by fitting a least-squares regression of the historical returns on the firm's stock to the historical returns on the market portfolio; it is the slope coefficient of the regression. Beta measures the risk of a company's shares that cannot be diversi-

---

[5] For detailed development of this and related models, see James C. T. Mao, *Quantitative Analysis of Financial Decisions* (New York: Macmillan, 1969), chap. 10.

[6] The cost of new shares is found similarly, except that the share price must be adjusted for flotation costs. Thus, if we denote flotation costs, as a proportion of the share price, by f, the cost of new equity is given by:

$$k_e = \frac{D}{P(1-f)} + g$$

[7] Even U.S. government bonds are not entirely risk free because of risk of change in their value caused by change in the market rate of interest. With short-term securities, however, such risk is slight, at least for magnitudes of market changes usually seen.

fied away, and provides an index that indicates the responsiveness of returns on a particular firm's shares to returns on the market portfolio.[8]

The CAPM thus provides us with a means for estimating the firm's cost of capital with market data and the β coefficient, which relates the firm to the market. The dividend capitalization model, in contrast, requires only the current market price of our firm's common shares. Because of this, the CAPM data requirements are greater. Furthermore, the question of stability of the betas over time has not been resolved.

Example

If we assume that we have obtained the beta for our firm, which is 1.80, and the risk-free interest rate is 6 percent and the return on market portfolio is 9 percent, we obtain as our estimate:

$$k_e = 6\% + 1.80(9\% - 6\%) = 11.4\%$$

The CAPM deals with risk *explicitly* through the firm's β coefficient. The dividend capitalization model, on the other hand, implicitly assumes risk is fully reflected in the market price of the firm's shares.

OVERALL COST OF CAPITAL

The overall cost of capital is obtained by calculating an average of the individual components, weighted according to the proportion of each in the total. Suppose a firm has the following capital structure:

Debt (Debentures Maturing 1998)	$30,000,000
Preferred Stock	20,000,000
Common Stock	15,000,000
Retained Earnings	35,000,000
Total	$100,000,000

Assume further that the after-tax costs of the components have been estimated as shown in Table 4-1. Calculation of the weighted average cost of capital is performed as shown.

Note that this average cost of capital is based on historical, balance sheet proportions, and on debt and preferred stock costs that were determined at time of issue of these securities.[9] In capital investment project analysis, we are not concerned with average cost of capital. We are interested in the *marginal* cost, for that is the cost of funds that will be raised to undertake prospective capital investments. We cannot raise money at average historical cost, but at today's marginal rate.

---

[8] In the development of β, capital appreciation is taken into account explicitly in addition to dividends.
[9] Once a bond or preferred stock issue is sold the firm is committed to paying a fixed, periodic return per security. Even though capital market conditions may subsequently dictate higher or lower yields for similar securities of comparable risk if they are to be sold now, the interest and dividend payments on such securities sold in the past do not change.

Table 4-1. CALCULATION OF WEIGHTED AVERAGE COST OF CAPITAL

	(1) $ Amount (Millions)	(2) Proportion of Total	(3) % Cost	(4) (2)×(3)
Debt	30	.30	4.16	1.25%
Preferred	20	.20	9.00	1.80
Common	15	.15	15.00	2.25
Retained Earnings	35	.35	14.00	4.90
	Weighted average cost of capital			10.20%

Table 4-2. CALCULATION OF MARGINAL COST OF CAPITAL

	(1) $ Amount (Millions)	(2) Proportion of Total	(3) % Cost	(4) (2)×(3)
Debt	3	.30	4.68	1.40%
Preferred	2	.20	12.00	2.40
Common	1.5	.15	17.00	2.25
Retained Earnings	3.5	.35	15.00	5.95
	Marginal cost of capital			11.60%

Now, what if the firm must raise an additional $10 million? If the capital structure is judged to be optimal (more about optimal structure later), funds should be raised in proportion to the existing capital structure. If its profits are adequate, the firm may utilize retained earnings rather than float new common shares, providing that dividend policy will not be seriously affected. Assume that the $10 million will be raised in amounts and at costs illustrated in Table 4.2.

This 11.60 percent *marginal cost of capital* suggests that market conditions have changed, and that investors require higher yields than formerly. The result of raising additional funds at a marginal cost higher than the average historical cost will be to raise the new average cost figure somewhat. The new average cost is given by:

$$10.33\% = (100 \times 10.20\% + 10 \times 11.60\%) \div 110$$

One may be tempted to ask why the entire $10 million should not be raised with debt, thus at the lowest attainable marginal cost. This question arises naturally, but ignores the interrelated nature of financing decisions. Investors and creditors have notions about the proper mix of debt and equity for firms. Therefore, although today the firm might raise the entire $10 million with debt, at a later date it could find it has no reserve borrowing capacity, and also cannot borrow on favorable terms or at acceptable cost. In such a situation the firm may find that to raise funds it must float a new issue of common stock at a time when required yields are higher than normal, in a depressed stock market. This, however, would be a disservice to the current stockholders. The cost of any one capital component alone cannot be considered the true cost of capital for yet another reason. The cost of capital associated with any particular component is for that component to be a part of the whole firm, within the context of the firm. Bond purchasers are not merely buying bonds, they are buying bonds of a firm with a balanced financial structure. Because the overall results of the firm are what matters to the suppliers of funds, and because funds are not segregated by their origin, it would be inappropriate to use the cost of a component as a substitute for the overall cost.

Analysts have observed that stock and bond prices often move in opposite directions. Therefore, the financial manager has some flexibility in establishing the appropriate financing mix over the short run. Indeed, it is expected that financial management will use its best judgment in such matters. Sometimes it is better to raise funds with bonds, at other times with common stock. However, future price and yield trends must be anticipated; investors and creditors will not willingly tolerate marked deviation in capital structure from established norms over long periods. And the indenture agreements of prior bond issues or loans may well restrict the firm's latitude in using more leverage.

OPTIMAL CAPITAL STRUCTURE

In the early 1960s considerable controversy erupted over the theory proposed by Modigliani and Miller that the firm's cost of capital is invariant with respect to its capital structure, depending only on the risk class to which the firm belonged. The original M and M theory did not take taxes into account, particularly the tax deductibility of interest payments on debt.[10] Subsequent modification of the M and M theory to include tax effects weakened their original conclusions. Since business income taxes are a reality in most nations, and interest payments for businesses a tax deductible expense, most authorities today agree that there is an optimal capital structure or range of optimal structures for any particular firm. The theory of M and M is elegantly developed and well worth reading. But it will not be discussed here because we cannot take up the required space. Instead, we shall examine the implications of optimal capital structure.

Existence of an optimal capital structure for any given firm suggests that financial management should try to obtain the optimal. Examination of the basic valuation model introduced in Chapter 2 reveals why this is desirable. Attainment of the lowest overall cost of capital will do proportionately more to increase the value of the firm than will an increase in the net cash flows, because of the compounding of terms containing k, the cost of capital.

We must recognize, however, that the world does not remain stationary. The quest for optimal capital structure requires that one follow a moving target, adjusting and readjusting sights as capital market conditions and investor and creditor attitudes change. Optimal capital structure, in practice, is not a once and for all time achievement. Rather, it involves periodic review and adjustment. Within a

---

[10] Modigliani and Miller also assumed perfect capital markets, with investors able to borrow and lend at the same interest rate and zero transactions costs. This created arbitrage opportunities not found in the real world.

Figure 4.1 Cost of capital schedule for a firm.

range of leverage, the firm may at times choose to finance more heavily with debt than with equity. Such a process, however, cannot continue indefinitely or the firm's leverage will become excessive, and with this the risk of insolvency, so that the cost of debt increases and onerous indenture conditions are imposed, not to mention the financial leverage effects on variability in common stockholder returns.

At other times the firm may finance more heavily with equity, or employ preferred shares. An analogy may be drawn to a driver who must use accelerator and brakes to adjust to a speed that is optimal for road conditions—a speed that is safe and yet gets the driver to one's destination in minimum time or with minimum fuel consumption. The driver may use the brakes several times in sequence before using the accelerator, or the accelerator for some time without braking. (Unlike debt and equity, however, we may surmise that brake and accelerator will never be used simultaneously.)

The following example assumes constant capital market conditions and investor attitudes for purposes of illustration. Figure 4.1 illustrates the cost of capital schedule for a hypothetical firm. For simplicity, it is assumed that debt and equity may be raised in arbitrarily small increments, although this abstracts from real world considerations that militate against small issues of either debt or equity.

Note that the cost of equity capital, k_e, rises continuously as leverage increases. This reflects the increasing risk to the common shareholders as financial leverage increases: Shareholders require a greater return as variability in earnings allocated to them increases. The cost of debt, in contrast, begins at 4.68 percent [9 percent pretax $\times$ (1 − 48 percent marginal tax rate)] and does not rise until leverage goes beyond 20 percent. Beyond this amount creditors become increasingly sensitive to the risk of firm insolvency as earnings become less and less a multiple of the interest that must be paid.

Lowest overall cost of capital is reached at 40 percent leverage, even though at this leverage the component costs of equity and debt are not at their lowest levels.

Beyond 40 percent leverage the overall cost of capital rises for additional leverage at a faster rate than it declined prior to the optimum, thereby reflecting the rapidly rising debt and equity schedules.

If one could find an industry in which the firms were similar except for leverage, a schedule like that in Figure 4.1 could be produced. Each set of observations for a given leverage would correspond to one firm, or the average of several if multiple observations at the same leverage were obtained. However, it is difficult to find an industry in which the firms are really similar, because most firms today are in varying degree diversified in their operations, and are normally classified on the basis of their major activity. Furthermore, size disparity between firms would present problems to the extent that there may be differences in access to capital markets, industry dominance, product brand differentiation, and so on.

INTERACTION OF FINANCING AND INVESTMENT

The foregoing discussion of the firm's cost of capital assumed that cost of capital was independent of the firm's capital investment decisions. In practice this view may be unrealistic.

If the firm consistently follows the practice of investing in capital projects that yield a return equal to or greater than its existing cost of capital, and do not affect the riskiness of overall returns to the firm on its investments, *then* we may assume independence of cost of capital and investment. However, if the firm adopts a policy of adopting investments that alter its overall profitability or variability in earnings, we must recognize that there are likely to be resultant changes in the cost of capital components and thus the firm's overall cost of capital.

Changes in the firm's cost of capital through pursuit of investment policy that alters the characteristics of risk (that is, variability in return and probability of insolvency) are not necessarily adverse. The firm may reduce its cost of capital by reducing risk.[11] On the other hand, the firm may increase its cost of capital if it consistently adopts investments that, although offering high expected returns, at the same time contain commensurately high risk. This will not necessarily be so, but discussion of this point is deferred to Chapter 21, after portfolio effects have been considered. Depending upon the correlation between project returns on new investments and the existing capital assets of the firm, risk may actually be reduced *overall* by adopting a very risky new investment.

A simple example with an intuitive interpretation will serve to illustrate this point. Assume that the firm undertakes a very risky capital investment project, but has returns that are expected to be highly negatively correlated with the firm's existing assets. Acceptance of the project will reduce the overall riskiness of the firm. If, in a particular year, the existing assets provide high cash returns, the new investment will provide low returns. However, if the cash returns on existing assets were low, then the new investment would provide high returns. The overall result will be to smooth out variability in earnings and thus reduce risk.

[11] Some portfolio-approach advocates would argue that, since investors can diversify their portfolios to reduce risk, it is unnecessary, and perhaps even detrimental to stockholder interests, for the firm to diversify its investments.

QUESTIONS

1. What is the difference between the average and the marginal costs of capital? Which is more appropriate in capital budgeting? Why?
2. It has been said that since dividends do not have to be paid, the cost of retained earnings is zero. Comment critically on this statement.
3. Why should we not simply divide the cost of retained earnings [formula (4.2)] by $(1 - f)$ to estimate the cost of new common stock equity?
4. If the actual growth term in formula (4.2) should happen to be negative, and to dominate the D/P term, does this mean cost of equity capital can be negative? Comment. (*Hint:* The growth term may be viewed as long-run *expected* growth.)
5. An investment project is to be financed entirely through the sale of 9 percent mortgage bonds. The firm's marginal income tax rate is 48 percent. The firm's current overall cost of capital is 14 percent. Why can we not properly evaluate the project by using the 4.32 percent after-tax cost of the mortgage bond issue?
6. Explain the major differences between common stock, preferred stock, mortgage bonds, and debentures. (*Suggestion:* Summarize the characteristics in a table.)

PROBLEMS

4.1 The earnings of the XXXX corporation over the period 1970 through 1976 (in millions of dollars) were as follows:

1970	1971	1972	1973	1974	1975	1976
10	24	11	17	28	14	42

(a) Calculate the percentage rate of growth from 1970 to 1976 using only the earnings for those two years. Calculate the growth rate from 1971 to 1975 by using data for only those two years.
(b) Using the average earnings for 1970–1971 and for 1975–1976, calculate the growth rate between these two periods.
(c) By using the relationship $P_0(1 + g)^n = P_n$ for discrete growth each year, and $P_0 \exp(gn) = P_n$ for continuous growth, calculate the discrete and the continuous growth rates using least squares. Note that by taking logarithms of these equations, we obtain $\log P_n = \log P_0 + n \log(1 + g)$ and $\ln P_n = \ln P_0 + gn$. Why are these methods superior to those used in parts (a) and (b)?

4.2 From the 1981 annual report for Easterline Corporation we derive the following information:

Year	1977	1978	1979	1980	1981
Net Income Per Share	$.17	.32	.42	.58	.80
Cash Dividends Per Share	$.30	.30	.30	.30	.31

It is probable that 1982 dividends will be $.32 per share or more. The price per share of common stock during the fourth quarter of 1981 ranged between $6 and $7. Now it is $9. Estimate the cost of retained earnings for this company.

4.3 The ZZZZ Company has the following liability and equity structure:

9% Debentures	$10,000,000
8% Mortgage Bonds	7,000,000
$4 Preferred Stock (100,000 shares)	5,000,000
Common Stock (1,9000,000 shares)	22,000,000
Retained Earnings	55,000,000

where the common stock and preferred stock are listed at current market value. The growth rate in earnings per share of common has been 15 percent per year. The dividend expected by the shareholders to be paid next year is $.96 per share. The firm's marginal tax rate is 48 percent. Calculate (a) the firm's average cost of capital (b) the firm's marginal cost of capital if it floats a new 8 1/2 percent bond issue of $15 million to replace the existing debentures, 600,000 new shares of common stock at a price to the public of $12.50 per share (assume flotation costs of 1 1/2 percent), and increases retained earnings by $10 million, and (c) the firm's average cost of capital after the new financing. The dividend payout ratio is 50 percent of earnings.

4.4 The 1975 annual report of Simmonds Precision Products, Inc., which is traded on the New York Stock Exchange, contains the following information, which is quoted verbatim:

Long-term debt (excluding current installments) consisted of the following:

	1975	1974
Notes payable to bank (interest at 1% above prime rate, $8\frac{1}{4}$% at December 31, 1975)	$4,250,000	$3,500,000
$6\frac{1}{4}$% promissory note to insurance company payable in 1977	500,000	850,000
Bank obligations of foreign subsidiaries at 7% to $9\frac{1}{2}$% payable in installments through 1981 (secured by property, plant and equipment carried at a net book value of $1,378,000)	786,000	980,000
Other, principally mortgage loans	49,000	100,000
	$5,585,000	$5,430,000

The notes payable to banks are under an unsecured bank credit agreement that provides for maximum borrowings of $5 million to 1978 with the unused portion subject to a 1/2 percent per annum commitment fee. The amount available and permitted to be outstanding will be reduced to $4 million in 1978, $3 million in 1979, with the latter amount expiring or maturing in 1980. Under the agreement the amount of unrestricted retained earnings available for the payment of dividends on common stock in 1976 is $748,000.

(a) Calculate the firm's average cost of debt capital for 1974 and 1975. Assume a prime rate of 10 1/2 percent for December 31, 1974.
(b) What effect would a change to 10 1/4 percent or to 6 1/4 percent in the prime rate have on the 1975 average cost of debt capital?
(c) Discuss the effect of a 20 percent upward revaluation or a 20 percent devaluation of the U.S. dollar on the 1975 average cost of debt capital under

the assumption that the company is responsible for the bank obligations of its foreign subsidiaries.

Bibliography

1. Beranek, William, "Some New Capital Budgeting Theorems," *Journal of Financial and Quantitative Analysis*, Vol. XIII, No. 5 (December 1978), pp. 809–829.
2. Bierman, Harold, Jr., and Jerome E. Hass, *An Introduction to Managerial Finance* (New York: Norton, 1973).
3. Boudreaux, Kenneth J., et al., "The Weighted Average Cost of Capital: A Discussion," *Financial Management*, Vol. 8, No. 2 (Summer 1979), pp. 7–23.
4. Brick, John R., and Howard E. Thompson, "The Economic Life of an Investment and the Appropriate Discount Rate," *Journal of Financial and Quantitative Analysis*, Vol. XIII, No. 5 (December 1978), pp. 831–846.
5. Brigham, Eugene F., "An Analysis of Convertible Debentures: Theory and Some Empirical Evidence," *The Journal of Finance*, Vol. XXI (March 1966), pp. 35–54.
6. Dobrovolsky, Sergei P., *The Economics of Corporation Finance* (New York: McGraw-Hill, 1971).
7. Donaldson, Gordon, *Corporate Debt Capacity* (Homewood, Ill.: Irwin, 1961).
8. Durand, David, "The Cost of Debt and Equity Funds for Business," reprinted in E. Solomon, *Management of Corporate Capital* (Chicago: University of Chicago Press, 1959).
9. ———, "The Cost of Capital in an Imperfect Market: A Reply to Modigliani and Miller," *American Economic Review* (June 1959).
10. Gahlon, James M., and Roger D. Stover, "Debt Capacity and the Capital Budgeting Decision: A Caveat," *Financial Management*, Vol. 8, No. 4 (Winter 1979), pp. 55–59.
11. Haley, Charles W., and Lawrence D. Schall, *The Theory of Financial Decisions*, 2nd ed. (New York: McGraw-Hill, 1979).
12. ———, "Problems with Concept of the Cost of Capital," *Journal of Financial and Quantitative Analysis* (December 1978), pp. 847–870.
13. Henderson, Glenn V., "In Defense of the Weighted Average Cost of Capital," *Financial Management*, Vol. 8, No. 3 (Autumn 1979), pp. 57–61.
14. Johnson, Robert W., *Financial Management*, 4th ed. (Boston: Allyn & Bacon, 1971).
15. Lewellen, Wilbur G., *The Cost of Capital* (Belmont, Cal.: Wadsworth, 1969).
16. Miles, James A., and John R. Ezzell, "The Weighted Average Cost of Capital, Perfect Capital Markets, and Project Life: A Clarification," *Journal of Financial and Quantitative Analysis*, Vol. XV, No. 3 (September 1980), pp. 719–730.
17. Miller, M. H., and F. Modigliani, "Dividend Policy, Growth and the Valuation of Shares," *Journal of Business*, Vol. XXIV (October 1961), pp. 411–433.
18. ———, "Some Estimates of the Cost of Capital to the Electric Utility Industry: 1954-57," *American Economic Review*, Vol. LVI (June 1966).
19. Modigliani, F., and M. H. Miller, "Corporate Income Taxes and the Cost of Capital: A Correction," *American Economic Review*, Vol. LIII (June 1963).
20. ———, "The Cost of Capital, Corporation Finance and the Theory of Investment," *American Economic Review* (June 1958), pp. 361–397.
21. Mumey, Glen A., *Theory of Financial Structure* (New York: Holt, Rinehart and Winston, 1969).

22. Myers, Stewart C., "Interactions of Corporate Financing and Investment Decisions—Implications for Capital Budgeting," *The Journal of Finance*, Vol. XXIX, No. 1 (March 1974), pp. 1-25.
23. Solomon, Ezra, *The Theory of Financial Management* (New York: Columbia University Press, 1963).
24. Weston, J. Fred, and Eugene F. Brigham, *Managerial Finance*, 6th ed. (Hinsdale, Ill.: Dryden, 1978).

Part II
TRADITIONAL METHODS OF PROJECT EVALUATION

Chapter 5
Traditional Methods That Ignore Time-Value of Money

PAYBACK AND NAIVE RATE OF RETURN

Payback

The payback period criterion has been demonstrated to be the single most popular measure of project merit used in practice by Mao [8], Soldofsky [13], Christy [2], Istvan [5], and Amling [1]. Possibly, the payback criterion is the oldest of capital budgeting measures as well.

The payback method is extremely simple to employ and intuitively appealing. To apply the method to a project costing amount C with uniform cash flows of amount R each period, one need only take the ratio of C to R:

$$\text{Payback} \equiv \frac{C}{R} \tag{5.1}$$

when R is uniform each period. In cases in which cash flows are not expected to be uniform, the method is somewhat more complicated.

$$\text{Payback} \equiv P + \frac{C - \sum_{t=1}^{P} R_t}{R_{t+1}} \tag{5.2}$$

54 TRADITIONAL METHODS OF PROJECT EVALUATION

Figure 5.1 Project A.

where

$$C - \sum_{t=1}^{P} R_t > 0 \quad \text{and} \quad C - \sum_{t=1}^{P+1} R_t \leq 0$$

Two illustrations will serve to make the procedure clear. We consider first a project designated as project A. This investment requires an outlay today (at $t = 0$) of $5000, and will yield uniform net cash flows of $2500 each year over its economic, or useful life, of ten years.

Applying formula (5.1), since the cash flows are uniform, we obtain a payback for project A of:

$$P(\text{A}) = \frac{C}{R} = \frac{5000}{2500} = 2.0 \text{ years}$$

The parenthetical A with P serves to distinguish this from the payback on other projects.

Next let us consider project B, which, although requiring the same initial outlay in year $t = 0$ of $5000, has a nonuniform net cash flow sequence. Cash flows for B in years $t = 1$ through $t = 4$ are $500, $1000, $2000, and $4000, respectively. In years $t = 5$ through $t = 10$, the cash flows are uniformly $8000. Since project B has nonuniform cash flows, formula (5.1) is not applicable. We must instead use (5.2). To do this we proceed as follows, taking the absolute value of C, and successively subtracting the net cash flows:

$$
\begin{array}{rl}
C = & \$5000 \\
-R(1) = & 500 \\
\hline
 & 4500 \quad P = 1 \\
-R(2) = & 1000 \\
\hline
 & 3500 \quad P = 2 \\
-R(3) = & 2000 \\
\hline
 & 1500 \quad P = 3 \\
\end{array}
$$

Figure 5.2 Project B.

The remaining $1500 is less than the cash flow in year four. It represents the unrecovered portion of the initial outlay. The question now is how far into year four we must go to recover this remaining amount. Implicit *in the payback method is the assumption that cash flows are uniform over a particular period* even if nonuniform from period to period. Therefore, we must go into year four:

$$\frac{\$1500}{R(4)} = \frac{1500}{\$4000} = \frac{3}{8} \quad \text{or} \quad .375$$

Combining results, we obtain the payback period for project B of:

$$P(B) = P + .375 = 3.375$$

This procedure for calculating payback is in the form of an *algorithm*. An algorithm is a systematic, multiple step procedure for obtaining a solution to a problem. Other, more complicated algorithms will be introduced in later chapters. Many may be converted into computer programs in order to reduce human effort and with it the chance of calculation errors.

The Naive Rate of Return

When a manager who relies on the payback criterion speaks of rate of return, this normally refers to something other than time-adjusted return on investment. For example, a project that promises a two-year payback will be said to offer a 50 percent per year rate of return. This we refer to as *naive* rate of return (NROR), since it ignores the effects of cash flows beyond the payback period as well as the effects of compounding from period to period.

$$\text{NROR} \equiv 1/\text{Payback (in years)} \tag{5.3}$$

The criticisms of payback are thus equally applicable to naive rate of return.

Strong Points of Payback

1. It is easily understood.
2. It favors projects that offer large immediate cash flows.
3. It offers a means of coping with risk due to increasing unreliability of forecasted cash flows as the time horizon increases.
4. It provides a powerful tool for capital rationing when the organization has a critical need to do so.
5. Because it is so simple to understand, it provides a means for decentralizing capital budgeting decisions by having nonspecialists screen proposals at lower levels in the organization.

Weak Points of Payback

1. It ignores all cash flows beyond payback period.
2. It ignores the time value of funds.
3. It does not distinguish between projects of different size in terms of investment required.
4. It can be made shorter by postponing replacement of worn and deteriorating capital until a later period.
5. It emphasizes short-run profitability to the exclusion of long-run profitability.

To illustrate, let us consider along with projects A and B another project, C. This project also requires an investment of $5000, and yields net cash flows of $5000, $1000, and $500 in years one, two, and three, respectively. It offers no cash returns beyond year three. Payback for project C is easily seen to be 1.0 year.

If we rank the three projects now in terms of payback, we obtain:

Project	Payback	Ranking
C	1.0	1
A	2.0	2
B	3.375	3

If we assume that A, B, and C are mutually exclusive, the reliance on payback alone implies that project C will be selected as the best project because it has the shortest payback of the three. In the absence of project C, A would be selected as preferable to B. But which project would management prefer to have at the end of four years? Clearly, project B is preferable at that point, if there is any reliability in the estimates of project characteristics, and if we can assume reasonable certainty of these estimates.

Let us next consider the effects of a large negative salvage value for project C in year four. Has the payback measure for this project been changed? No, it has not, because cash flows beyond payback are ignored.

Terborgh [12, p. 207] has provided perhaps the most clever and effective statement of the way payback favors delaying replacement of an already deteriorated capital project until it has deteriorated still further. Payback treats relief from losses

Figure 5.3 Project C.

caused by undue delay in replacements as return on the new investment. Consider Terborgh's analogy:

> A corporation has a president 70 years of age who in the judgment of the directors can be retired and replaced at a net annual advantage to the company of $10,000. Someone points out, however, that if he is kept to age 75, and if he suffers in the interval the increasing decrepitude normally to be expected, the gain from replacing him at that time will be $50,000 a year, while it should be substantially higher still, say $100,000 at the age of 80. It is urged, therefore, that his retirement should be deferred. The genius advancing this proposal is recognized at once as a candidate for the booby hatch, yet it is not different in principle from the rate-of-return requirement.
>
> No one can deny that the advantage of $100,000 a year (if such it is) from retiring the president at 80 is a real advantage, given the situation then prevailing. The question is whether this situation should be deliberately created for the sake of reaping this gain. Similarly, the question is whether a machine should be retained beyond its proper service life in order to get a larger benefit from its replacement. The answer in both cases is obvious. The executive who knowingly and wilfully follows this practice should sleep on a spike bed to enjoy the relief of getting up in the morning.

Considering the strong and weak points of payback all together, is there any merit on balance in using this method? Absolutely not, *unless* payback is not the sole criterion employed. As a single criterion, payback may be worse than useless because its implicit assumptions disregard important information about events beyond payback. As a tie-breaker to supplement other methods, payback has considerable merit if we assume that, *other things being equal,* rapid cash flow in the early years of an investment is preferable to the later years. This view is reinforced if one considers that the further from the present we attempt to estimate anything, the less reliable our estimates become. In other words, once we introduce risk into our considerations, we will *ceteris paribus* prefer early return of our investment to later recovery of it.

Unrecovered Investment

A concept related to payback, but taking the time value of money into account, is *unrecovered investment*.[1] Again taking C to be the cost or investment committed (at $t = 0$) to a capital project, and taking rate k as the firm's per period opportunity cost of the funds tied up in the project, unrecovered investment is defined by

$$U(k, t) = C(1 + k)^t - \sum_{i=1}^{t} R_i(1 + k)^{t-1} \tag{5.4}$$

Note that if we set $k = 0$ for values of $U \geq 0$, and $k = \infty$ for $U < 0$, we find that $U = 0$ defines payback as in the previous section.

If for all periods we take k as the firm's cost of capital, then it follows that the value of t for which $U = 0$ provides us with a time-adjusted payback period. The value of t for which this is true will not necessarily be an integer. The t value thus obtained suggests how long it will take for the firm to recover its investment in the project plus the cost of the funds committed to the project. If k is in fact a precise measure of the enterprise's opportunity cost, then the t for which $U(k, t) = 0$ corresponds to the time at which the firm will be no worse off than if it had never undertaken the project. Since we assume cash flows occur at the end of each period, this relationship will be approximate but nevertheless useful.

The subject of unrecovered investment is treated further in Chapter 14. The concept of time-adjusted payback is used in the method of analysis discussed in the appendix to Chapter 11.

ACCOUNTING METHOD: ALIAS AVERAGE RETURN ON AVERAGE INVESTMENT

The accounting method[2] involves calculation of an average net cash return on the average investment committed to a project. It is not as popular a method of capital-budgeting project analysis as payback, but it is nonetheless frequently encountered today, as reported by Amling [1] and others. It is easy to apply: It requires only that one:

1. Calculate average *accounting profit*[3] by $\frac{1}{N}\sum_{t=1}^{N} A_t$.
2. Calculate average investment by $(C + S)/2$.
3. Divide average return by average investment, and express as a percentage.

Thus the average return on average investment (ARAI) is defined as:

---

[1] David Durand, "Time as a Dimension of Investment," *Proceedings of the Eastern Finance Association* (April 1973), pp. 187–192.
[2] National Association of Accountants, *Financial Analysis to Guide Capital Expenditure Decisions*, Research Report 43, 1967.
[3] Note that this is at odds with our stated use only of net, after-tax cash flows in capital investment project analysis.

$$\text{ARAI} \equiv \frac{\sum_{t=1}^{N} \dfrac{A_t}{N}}{(C+S)/2} \neq \frac{\sum_{t=1}^{N} \dfrac{R_t}{N}}{(C+S)/2} \tag{5.5}$$

Note that if A were uniform, with straight-line depreciation and $S = 0$, ARAI would be similar to the naive rate of return (NROR). This is because the A_t terms include depreciation, whereas the R_t terms include the cash flow dollars shielded from taxes by depreciation.

Strong Points of Accounting Method

1. It is easily understood.
2. It does not ignore any periods in the project life.
3. It is, in a sense, more conservative than payback and naive rate of return.
4. It explicitly recognizes salvage value.
5. Because it is easy to understand, it (like payback) may provide a means for decentralizing the process of preliminary screening of proposals.

Weak Points of Accounting Method

1. Like payback, it ignores the time value of funds.
2. It assumes that capital recovery is linear over time.
3. It does not distinguish between projects of different sizes in terms of the investment required.
4. It conveys the impression of greater precision than payback since it requires more calculation effort, while suffering from faults as serious as that method.
5. It does not favor early returns over later returns.
6. The method violates the criterion that we consider only net cash flows. We can only pay out dividends in cash and reinvest cash; not book profits.

COMPREHENSIVE EXAMPLE

Consider the following two projects. They have net, after-tax cash flows and depreciation charges as shown. It is assumed that the class life asset depreciation range system is used, with a switch from double-declining balance to sum-of-the-years' digits method in year two. Project D has zero salvage, E has salvage of $20,000. The depreciable lifetime for D is five years, for E it is eight years. Note that project D's economic life is a year longer than the depreciation life used.

	Project D	*Project E*
Initial Outlay	$100,000	$100,000
Cash Flow/ Depreciation for Year:		
1	$25,000/$40,000	$40,000/$25,000
2	35,000/ 24,000	30,000/ 18,750

60 TRADITIONAL METHODS OF PROJECT EVALUATION

3	40,000/ 18,000	20,000/ 16,071
4	40,000/ 12,000	20,000/ 13,393
5	40,000/ 6,000	20,000/ 6,786
6	40,000/ 0	20,000/ 0
7	0	20,000/ 0
8	0	20,000/ 0

Payback periods are calculated as follows:

Project D

$100,000
− 25,000
─────────
  75,000 $P = 1$
− 35,000
─────────
  40,000 $P = 2$
− 40,000
─────────
       0   $P = 3$

The payback for project D is exactly three years.

Project E

$100,000
− 40,000
─────────
  60,000 $P = 1$
− 30,000
─────────
  30,000 $P = 2$
− 20,000
─────────
  10,000 $P = 3$

and $10,000/20,000 = 1/2$

So the payback for project E is $3\frac{1}{2}$ years.

We calculate ARAI on the basis of accounting profits, not cash flows. If we assume that the timing of accounting profits and cash flows is approximately the same, the accounting profit in any year t, A_t, will be equal to the net, after-tax cash flow, R_t, less the depreciation charged in that year: $A_t = R_t - D_t$.

Then ARAI for the investment projects is:

Project D

$\frac{1}{6}$ ($25,000 − $40,000 +
     35,000 − 24,000 +
     40,000 − 18,000 +
     40,000 − 12,000 +
     40,000 −   6,000 +

$$\frac{40{,}000 - 0)}{\frac{1}{2}(\$100{,}000 + 0)}$$

$= \$20{,}000/\$50{,}000$

$= 40\%$

Project E

$$\frac{\frac{1}{8}\;(\$40{,}000 - \$25{,}000 + 30{,}000 - 18{,}750 + 20{,}000 - 16{,}071 + 20{,}000 - 13{,}393 + 20{,}000 - 6{,}786 + 20{,}000 - 0 + 20{,}000 - 0 + 20{,}000 - 0\;)}{\frac{1}{2}\;(\$100{,}000 + \$20{,}000)}$$

$= \$13{,}750/\$60{,}000$

$= 22.92\%$

If we assume the firm has a 10 percent annual cost of capital, the unrecovered investment at the end of year three for each project is:

Project D
$\$100{,}000\,(1.10)^3 - \$25{,}000\,(1.10)^2$
$\phantom{\$100{,}000\,(1.10)^3} - 35{,}000\,(1.10)^1$
$\phantom{\$100{,}000\,(1.10)^3} - 40{,}000\,(1.10)^0$
$= \$133{,}100 - \$111{,}585$
$= \$\;21{,}515$

Project E
$\$100{,}000\,(1.10)^3 - \$40{,}000\,(1.10)^2$
$\phantom{\$100{,}000\,(1.10)^3} - 30{,}000\,(1.10)^1$
$\phantom{\$100{,}000\,(1.10)^3} - 20{,}000\,(1.10)^0$
$= \$133{,}100 - \$101{,}400$
$= \$\;31{,}700$

QUESTIONS

1. What reasons would seem to account for the popular use of the payback, NROR, and ARAI measures, given their deficiencies?
2. Discuss the merits of using payback as a screening criterion at the lower operating levels of an organization, or for low-cost projects. Would this apply to major projects involving significant amounts of the organization's capital?
3. It often happens that the NROR and ARAI measures give conflicting results in ranking two or more investment projects. Carefully enumerate the conditions under which such conflict is likely to result.

62 TRADITIONAL METHODS OF PROJECT EVALUATION

4. Discuss the statement that use of the payback criterion causes bad situations to become worse before action is taken. Compare this to the view that, if too low a payback criterion is adopted, unwarranted, unprofitable investments will be made.
5. In times of capital funds crisis, firms may adopt stringent payback criteria, one year, for instance. Analyze the appropriateness of this policy in such circumstances in comparison to normal times.
6. Why may payback (or NROR) be useful in tie-breaking between projects that more refined measures may rank almost equal? Check one or more of the references to studies in the chapter bibliography. Is reference made to payback as a tie-breaker?
7. Explain why payback may be worse when used for replacement decisions than for de novo capital investments in light of Terborgh's analogy.

PROBLEMS

5.1 Describe the conditions (if any) under which the ARAI method can favor an investment project with low salvage value over the same project with high salvage value.

5.2 Calculate payback, NROR, and ARAI for the following projects. Under these criteria which project is most attractive? Assume salvage is zero for each.

Net Cash Flows in Period

Project	$t=0$	$t=1$	$t=2$	$t=3$	$t=4$	$t=5$	$t=6$	$t=7$
A	−50	7	3	20	18	4	15	40
B	−50	40	15	2	3	7	4	7
C	−50	20	20	20	20	20	20	25

5.3 Provide a specific example, if possible, of a project for which the NROR and ARAI are equal. Specify fully the required conditions the investment must meet.

5.4 Develop a flow chart and computer program to implement the payback method. Demonstrate that the program functions properly.

Bibliography

1. Amling, Frederick, *Some Determinants of Capital Expenditure Decisions in the Largest Industrial, Public Utility, Transportation, and Merchandising Corporations in the United States* (Oxford, Ohio: School of Business Administration, Miami University, 1963).
2. Christy, G. A., *Capital Budgeting: Current Practices and Their Efficiency* (Corvallis, Ore.: Bureau of Business Research, University of Oregon, 1966).
3. Durand, David, "Time as a Dimension of Investment," *Proceedings of the Eastern Finance Association* (April 1973).
4. Hoskins, Colin G., and Glen A. Mumey, "Payback: A Maligned Method of Asset Ranking?," *The Engineering Economist*, Vol. 25, No. 1 (Fall 1979), pp. 53–65.
5. Istvan, Donald E., *Capital Expenditure Decisions—How They Are Made in Large Corporations* (Bloomington, Indiana: University Business Report No. 33, 1961).
6. Klammer, T., "Empirical Evidence of the Adoption of Sophisticated Capital Budgeting Techniques," *Journal of Business* (July 1972), pp. 387–394.
7. Lewellen, Wilber G., Howard P. Lanser, and John H. McConnell, "Payback Substitutes

for Discounted Cash Flow," *Financial Management*, Vol. 2, No. 1 (Summer 1973), pp. 17–23.
8. Mao, James C. T., *Quantitative Analysis of Financial Decisions* (New York: Macmillan, 1969).
9. ———, "Survey of Capital Budgeting: Theory and Practice, *The Journal of Finance* (May 1970), pp. 349–359.
10. National Association of Accountants, *Financial Analysis to Guide Capital Expenditure Decisions*, Research Report 43, 1967.
11. Oblak, David J., and Roy J. Helm, Jr., "Survey and Analysis of Capital Budgeting Methods Used by Multinationals," *Financial Management*, Vol. 9, No. 4 (Winter 1980), pp. 37–41.
12. Petty, J. William, David F. Scott, and Monroe M. Bird, "The Capital Expenditure Decision—Making Process of Large Corporations," *The Engineering Economist* (Spring 1975), pp. 159–172.
13. Soldofsky, Robert M., "Capital Budgeting Practices in Small Manufacturing Companies," *Studies in the Factor Markets for Small Business Firms* (Ames: Iowa State University Press, 1964), pp. 46–94.
14. Terborgh, George, *Dynamic Equipment Policy* (Washington: Machinery and Allied Products Institute, 1949).
15. Weingartner, H. Martin, "Some New Views on the Payback Period and Capital Budgeting Decisions," *Management Science*, Vol. 15, No. 12 (August 1969), pp. B594–B607.

Chapter 6
Traditional Methods That Recognize Time-Value of Money

INTERNAL RATE OF RETURN

DEFINITION OF THE IRR

The internal rate of return (IRR) is defined as the rate of interest compounded from period to period, which exactly equates all net cash flows to the required outlay. Alternatively, the IRR is the rate for which the net present value (NPV) of the cash flows is equal to zero. Thus IRR is the rate of discount r, which satisfies the relationship:

$$C = \frac{R_1}{(1+r)^1} + \frac{R_2}{(1+r)^2} + \frac{R_3}{(1+r)^3} + \cdots + \frac{R_N}{(1+r)^N} \tag{6.1}$$

If we rename C to R_0, this can be restated as:

$$0 = \frac{R_0}{(1+r)^0} + \frac{R_1}{(1+r)^1} + \frac{R_2}{(1+r)^2} + \cdots + \frac{R_N}{(1+r)^N} \tag{6.2}$$

or in the more compact equivalent forms:

$$0 = \sum_{t=0}^{N} \frac{R_t}{(1+r)^t} = \sum_{t=0}^{N} R_t(1+r)^{-t} \tag{6.3}$$

Equations (6.1), (6.2), and (6.3) define a polynomial equation with real coefficients $R_0, R_1, \ldots, R_n$. The IRR is thus the root of a polynomial. Unfortunately, under some circumstances there may be two or more real roots, or an economically misleading root, and this creates some significant problems. The general case of multiple roots will be dealt with later. For now we consider only investment projects that have only one sign change in the coefficients, which we are assured by Descartes' rule of signs can have but one real, positive root. Cost C, or as we will normally call it from now on, R_0, we assume to be negative, and $R_1, R_2, R_3, \ldots, R_N$ to be positive. In later chapters this assumption may be relaxed.

In general, finding the IRR can be a troublesome task when the cash flows after R_0 are nonuniform. We shall therefore deal first with a project with uniform cash flows. To illustrate the calculation of IRR when cash flows are uniform, let us consider project A from Chapter 5 again, and use Eq. (6.1):

$$\$5000 = \frac{\$2500}{1+r} + \frac{\$2500}{(1+r)^2} + \cdots + \frac{\$2500}{(1+r)^{10}} \tag{6.4}$$

which, since the R_t are uniform, can be rewritten:

$$\$5000 = \$2500 \sum_{t=1}^{10} \frac{1}{(1+r)^t} = \$2500 \sum_{t=1}^{10} (1+r)^{-t} \tag{6.5}$$

so that we have:

$$2.0 = \frac{\$5000}{\$2500} = \sum_{t=1}^{10}(1+r)^{-t} = \frac{1-(1+r)^{-10}}{r} \equiv a_{\overline{10}|r} \tag{6.6}$$

Since the last term on the right here is the summation representing the present value of an annuity of one for ten periods at r percent,[1] we look in appendix Table A-4.[2] Moving across the row that corresponds to the ten periods, we find the factor 2.003 under 49 percent. Since this is very close to 2.0, we might conclude that the IRR for project A is essentially 49 percent (the actual rate is 49.1 percent to the nearest one-tenth percent).

Now let us see what must be done when cash flows are not uniform for all periods beyond $t = 0$. Finding the IRR for project B is not so easy, because the cash

---

[1] The term is derived from the formula for the summation of a geometric progression, which is:

$$\text{Sum} = \alpha \frac{\rho^N - 1}{\rho - 1}$$

where ρ is the common ratio (in the case above, $\rho = (1+r)^{-1}$), α the first term in the progression, and N the number of periods. For an ordinary annuity this becomes:

$$(1+r)^{-1}\frac{(1+r)^{-N} - 1}{(1+r)^{-1} - 1} = (1+r)^{-1}\frac{(1+r)^{-N} - 1}{-r(1+r)^{-1}}$$

$$= \frac{1 - (1+r)^{-N}}{r} \equiv a_{\overline{N}|r}$$

[2] Modern hand-held calculators provide a better approach: Calculate the factor for a trial r, and revise the estimate until the result is satisfactorily close. If a table is readily available, it provides a good first guess, of course. Many reasonably priced calculators are available with circuitry preprogrammed to provide very precise solutions for r.

66 TRADITIONAL METHODS OF PROJECT EVALUATION

flows are not uniform. To find r we use the appendix tables for single-amount present worth and for annuity present worth.

First, let us estimate that r is 60 percent. We then proceed as follows:

Year	Present Worth Factor	×	Cash Flow	=	Present Value
1	.62500		$ 500		$ 312.50
2	.39063		1000		390.63
3	.24414		2000		488.28
4	.15259		4000		610.36
5					
6					
7	.2391		8000		1912.80
8	(1.6515 − 1.4124)				
9					
10					

Project present value at 60% = $3714.57

Since the cash flows in years five through eight are a uniform $8000, we need multiply this amount only once by the present worth of annuity factor for ten years at 60 percent *less* the present worth of annuity factor for four years at 60 percent. Notice that the latter is equal to the sum of the single-amount present worth factors for years one through four. The project present value at 60 percent is $3714.57, which is less than the $5000 investment outlay. Therefore we know that 60 percent is too high a discount rate, and that IRR is less than this. Let us next try 50 percent.

Year	Present Worth Factor	×	Cash Flow	+	Present Value
1	.66667		$ 500		$ 333.33
2	.44444		1000		444.44
3	.29360		2000		592.60
4	.19753		4000		790.12
5					
6					
7	.3604		8000		2883.20
8	(1.9653 − 1.6049)				
9					
10					

Project present value at 50% = $5043.69

This is just slightly above the $5000 investment cost. We have bracketed the IRR, and now know that it is very close to 50 percent. We can now refine our result by interpolation.

$$\begin{bmatrix} 60\% \\ r \\ 50\% \end{bmatrix} \quad \begin{bmatrix} 3714.57 \\ 5000 \\ 5043.69 \end{bmatrix}$$

$$\frac{-10}{50 - r} = \frac{1329.12}{43.69}$$

$$r = 50 + \frac{436.90}{1329.12} = 50.329\% \text{ or } 50.3\%$$

This interpolation assumes a linear relationship, whereas we have an exponential one, so our result is only approximate. However, for capital-budgeting applications it will normally be precise enough. We should generally give interpolated answers to only one decimal or the nearest percent or tenth of a percent in order not to convey the impression of greater precision than we in fact have. The actual rate, correct to the nearest tenth of a percent, *is* 50.3 percent in this case. In general, the smaller the range over which we bracket the rate, the more precise our interpolated result will be.

By this point it should be clear that calculation of IRR is a tedious task when cash flows are not uniform. In fact, to ease the computational burden, computer programs have been developed to calculate IRR and today some of the better handheld calculators are programmed to solve for IRR.[3] Programs to calculate IRR are not difficult to write; the Newton-Raphson or interval bisection methods, in conjunction with Horner's method of polynomial evaluation, both yield good results efficiently.

A CAUTION AND A RULE FOR IRR

Assume we have a project costing $4000 that will last only two years and provides cash flows of $1000 and $5000 in years one and two. To find the IRR for this project we may use the quadratic formula $(-b \pm \sqrt{b^2 - 4ac})/2a$, since (dropping the $ signs):

$$4000 = \frac{1000}{1+r} + \frac{5000}{(1+r)^2} \qquad (6.7)$$

is equivalent to:

$$-4 + \frac{1}{1+r} + \frac{5}{(1+r)^2} = 0 \qquad (6.8)$$

Multiplying by $(1 + r)^2$, we get:

$$-4(1+r)^2 + (1+r) + 5 = 0 \qquad (6.9)$$

Letting $x = 1 + r$, we obtain the quadratic equation:

$$-4x^2 + x + 5 = 0 \qquad (6.10)$$

which has roots given by:

$$\frac{-1 \pm \sqrt{1 + 80}}{-8}$$

of $x = -1.0$ and $+1.25$. Converting to r, we have IRR of -200 percent *and* $+25$ percent! Which do we take as *the* IRR for this project? The rule to follow in such cases is:

> In the case of one positive or zero root and one negative root, choose the negative root only if the project cost is strictly greater than the undiscounted sum of the cash flows in periods 1 through N.

---

[3] Texas Instruments "MBA" calculator, and TI-59 programmable (Securities Analysis Module, and Real Estate Module) and Hewlett-Packard HP-38E just to mention some of the more prominent ones.

In this case 4000 < 1000 + 5000, so we choose +25 percent for IRR. A *negative IRR makes no economic sense in cases in which the total cash return is greater than or equal to the project cost.* Conversely, in cases in which the cost exceeds the undiscounted cash flows, a positive IRR makes no economic sense. A *negative IRR < −100 percent makes no economic sense* because it is not possible to lose more than all of what is lost on a bad investment when all cash flows attributable to the project are included.

PAYBACK AND IRR RELATIONSHIP

In Chapter 5 the naive rate of return (NROR) was defined as the reciprocal of payback. Is there any relationship between NROR and IRR? Yes. Provided that certain conditions are met, the NROR may approximate the IRR.

Assuming uniform cash flows, $R = R_1 = R_2 = \ldots = R_N$. Then payback = C/R, NROR = $1/\text{payback} = R/C$, and IRR is the r such that:

$$C = \sum_{t=1}^{N} \frac{R}{(1+r)^t} = R \sum_{t=1}^{N} (1+r)^{-t} \tag{6.11}$$

$$\frac{C}{R} = \sum_{t=1}^{N} (1+r)^{-t} \tag{6.12}$$

so that:

$$\frac{R}{C} = \frac{1}{\sum_{t=1}^{N} (1+r)^{-t}} = \frac{r(1+r)^N}{(1+r)^N - 1} = \frac{r}{1 - (1+r)^{-N}} \tag{6.13}$$

which is defined as the *capital recovery factor* for N periods at rate r per period. Now, letting N increase without limit, we obtain:

$$\frac{R}{C} = \lim_{N \to \infty} \frac{r}{1 - (1+r)^{-N}} = r \tag{6.14}$$

which is the same result as the NROR provides.

Therefore, under certain conditions, the NROR may provide a useful approximation to IRR. What are the conditions? The first condition is that the project life should be at least twice the payback period. The second is that the cash flows be at least approximately uniform:

1. $N \geq 2C/R$ and
2. uniform R.

Today, some hand-held calculators make the task of finding the IRR of a uniform cash flow series almost trivial. For projects with nonuniform cash flows, however, it may be useful to employ a computer if one is readily accessible, especially if many cash flow periods are involved, or if it is desired to deal with the problem of mixed cash flows according to methods described in Chapter 10 and those following.

Figure 6.1 IRR polynomial.

MATHEMATICAL LOGIC FOR FINDING IRR

For projects that we know will have only one real, positive root, by Descartes' rule of signs,[4] several methods can be easily programmed for computer solution. The most straightforward are interval bisection and Newton-Raphson. A capital investment with one real positive IRR yields a net present value polynomial function that looks like Figure 6.1, that is, concave from above.

Note that the IRR is the discount rate for which the discounted value of the project, including the cost $C(R_0)$, is zero. In other words, the IRR is the discount rate for which the project NPV is zero. Thus, to find the IRR we must find the rate for which the polynomial intersects the horizontal axis.

Interval Bisection

With the interval bisection method, we select a high value and a low value that we think will bracket the IRR. If we are wrong, we will try higher values the next time. Assume we first select 0 as our low value and h as our high value. This is shown in Figure 6.2. We evaluate the NPV polynomial at rate 0 and at rate h. Since the NPV is positive for rate 0 and negative for rate h, we know the function has a root (crosses the horizontal axis) between these rates.

Next we improve our results by bisecting the interval between 0 and h and testing to determine in which subinterval the function crosses. We also test for the possibility that the midpoint of our earlier range, m, may actually be the IRR, even though unlikely. If we determine that the IRR lies in the interval between m and h, we bisect this range again, and repeat the process. We determine at the outset to stop when the difference between the low and high interval values is less than or equal to an arbitrarily small value. This error tolerance cannot be too small, however, because all digital computers have intrinsic round-off errors in computation

---

[4] Descartes' rule states that the number of unique real roots to a polynomial with real coefficients cannot exceed the number of changes in the sign of the coefficients and that complex roots must be in conjugate pairs. That is, if $x + ci$ is a root, $x - ci$ is also a root.

70 TRADITIONAL METHODS OF PROJECT EVALUATION

Figure 6.2 Interval bisection.

and different capability for precision calculation.[5] In general, however, a tolerance of .0001 or .01 percent should cause no problems. If it does, a change to double-precision calculation may remedy the difficulty. If it does not, a computer specialist may have to be called in or a different computer used. The manual method of IRR solution is similar to this, except that the final IRR estimate is made by interpolation rather than continued iteration, once it is known that the IRR value has been bracketed.

Newton-Raphson Method

This method is somewhat more sophisticated than the interval bisection approach, and in some cases marginally more efficient.[6] Any increase in efficiency it yields will likely result in very small savings in computer time, however.

The approach with this method is to modify the original "guess" at the IRR by using the intersection of the tangent line to the NPV curve with the rate axis as the improved "guess." The process is repeated until the NPV is sufficiently close to zero. This might be expressed as an error less than or equal to some small percentage of the project cost, for example, or alternatively an NPV less than some small money amount.

The Newton-Raphson method requires that the numerical value of the derivative with respect to rate of the NPV be obtained at the current rate estimate. If we refer to r_n as the current IRR estimate and r_{n+1} as the revised estimate, $f(\ )$ as the NPV function, and $f'(\ )$ its derivative, then:

$$r_{n+1} = r_n - \frac{f(r_n)}{f'(r_n)}$$

---

[5] This is potentially a very serious problem, especially as the number of cash flows becomes large. Logically correct programs may yield totally incorrect results for which the program user is unprepared after testing the program with small problems having few cash flows and getting correct results.

[6] Marginal is used here in the sense that one or two seconds of computer time is not usually significant unless a program is run very frequently.

Figure 6.3 Newton-Raphson method.

The value of r_{n+1} is our revised estimate of the IRR. Graphically, the Newton-Raphson approach may be visualized as shown in Figure 6.3.

For the NPV function at rate i, the polynomial is:

$$\text{NPV} = f(i) = R_0(1 + i)^{-0} + R_1(1 + i)^{-1} + \cdots + R_n(1 + i)^{-n}$$

and the derivative:

$$f'(i) = -R_1(1 + i)^{-2} - 2R_2(1 + i)^{-3} - \cdots - nR_n(1 + i)^{-(n-1)}$$

Computer evaluation of $f'(i)$ involves modification of $f(i)$ by dropping the first term containing R_0, negating all the subsequent cash flow terms, multiplying each by the corresponding exponent, and then decrementing each of the exponent powers by one.

Other Methods

In the case of capital-budgeting projects having more than one real root, or if it were desired to find complex roots in addition to real roots, other, more sophisticated, techniques must be employed. However, as we shall see in a later chapter, if a project has multiple real IRRs, the IRR is not a proper measure of the project's rate of return. Nevertheless, it may sometimes be interesting to examine the NPV function and its roots even though other evaluations of the project must be used.

To obtain other roots to the NPV polynomial one may employ any of several easily obtained, standard computer programs. FORTRAN program (really a subroutine) DPOLRT in IBM Corporation's Scientific Subroutine Package (SSP) is one such program.[7] The SSP also contains some additional programs that use alternative methods, such as PRQD.

The Dartmouth University Amos Tuck School BASIC language time-sharing

---

[7] It is possible that double roots (or roots of greater multiplicity) may be missed in computer solution. Application of Sturm's theorem prior to computer solution will help by determining the number of real roots that exist.

program PVROR finds the real roots of NPV polynomials by the method described in the article by Lawrence Fisher, "An Algorithm for Finding Exact Rates of Return," published in the *Journal of Business* in 1966. It has the additional feature of allowing the NPV function to be plotted on the time-sharing terminal if desired. Shan S. Kuo's book, *Numerical Methods and Computers,* contains a thoroughly explained and documented FORTRAN program of less than 100 statements that the interested reader of this book may find useful. Since the program requires initial guesses for two parameters, it could be beneficial to convert the program to time-sharing use in FORTRAN, BASIC, or APL.

Strong Points of IRR

1. It is conceptually superior to payback and accounting methods.
2. It does not ignore any periods in the project life nor any cash flows.
3. It takes into account the time value of funds.
4. It is consistent with the basic valuation model expressed in Chapter 2.
5. It yields a percentage that management can examine and make judgment about when k is not known with confidence.
6. It favors early cash flows over later ones.

Weak Points of IRR

1. It requires an estimate of the organization's cost of capital, or at least a range of values in which this is likely to be found.
2. It is much more difficult to apply without a computer than payback or accounting methods, and when cash flows are nonuniform, much more difficult to apply than the net present value method.
3. It does not distinguish between projects of different size and/or different economic lives. However, adjustment for this may be made along lines similar to such adjustments for net present value.
4. It often yields multiple, and thus ambiguous, results when there is more than one sign change in the cash flows.
5. Some have criticized the method on the basis that it implicitly assumes that cash flows may be reinvested at a return equal to the IRR.

A DIGRESSION ON NOMINAL AND EFFECTIVE RATES

Investment-Financing Relationship

The mathematics of the internal rate of return are identical to those required for finding the effective interest rate on a loan or the yield to maturity or call on a bond. To the lender, a loan or a bond purchase is an investment. Symmetry of the loan or bond relationship requires that the effective cost rate to the borrower (bond issuer) be the same as the rate of return to the lender (bond purchaser) on a pretax basis. Mathematically, the only difference in a loan or bond from the perspectives of borrower and lender is that the signs of the cash flows will be reversed.

Consider a bond that has a face value of $1000, a nominal interest yield or coupon rate of 7 percent, and a 20-year maturity. It sells when first issued for $935. Interest will be calculated semiannually and we assume the bond will not be called prior to its maturity date. To the purchaser of the bond who buys at issue, it is an investment with cash flows in periods zero through 40 (semiannual payments over 20 years) and the IRR equation is, dropping the $ signs:

$$-935 + 35(1 + r_s) + 35(1 + r_s)^2 + \cdots \\ + 35(1 + r_s)^{40} + 1000(1 + r_s)^{40} = 0 \qquad (6.15)$$

To the issuer of the bond, the equation to calculate the effective cost is:

$$+935 - 35(1 + r_s) - 35(1 + r_s)^2 - \cdots \\ - 35(1 + r_s)^{40} - 1000(1 + r_s)^{40} = 0 \qquad (6.16)$$

The solution to the real, positive root of Eq. (6.15) is the same as that to Eq. (6.16).

Nominal Rate and Effective Rate

Note that the rate in Eqs. (6.15) and (6.16) is denoted by r_s. This is to flag it as a semiannual rate. The corresponding nominal annual yield or cost rate is two times r_s. The effective annual rate is that rate that would be equivalent if interest payments were made annually at the end of each year instead of at the end of each semiannual period.

For the bond in question the (pretax) rates are:

Semiannual Effective Yield $r_s = 3.81964\%$
Nominal Annual Yield $r_n = 2r_s = 7.63928\%$
Effective Annual Yield $r = (1 + r_s)^2 - 1 = 7.78518\%$

It is usual United States financial practice to report yields in terms of nominal annual rates rather than effective annual rates. If the investor has the opportunity to reinvest interest payments as they are received at the effective per-period rate, however, the period-to-period compounding implicit in this should be recognized. The effective annual yield recognizes such compounding; the nominal annual rate does not.

Clarification of Nominal and Effective Rates

Let us examine here a problem that may help to clarify the relationship between and meaning of the various rates. In the case of a bond, the *coupon rate* is the rate applied to the face or par value of the bond to determine the dollar interest to be paid. The coupon rate is a nominal annual rate. The rate advertised by thrift institutions, which is compounded so many times per year, is also a nominal annual rate.

74 TRADITIONAL METHODS OF PROJECT EVALUATION

For example, $5\frac{3}{4}$ percent compounded quarterly is a nominal annual rate. If we divide it by the number of compounding periods, we obtain the effective rate per quarter, which is 1.4375 percent per quarter. Money left on deposit will thus earn 1.4375 percent every three months. If $1000 is deposited at the beginning of a year under these terms, it will grow to $1058.75 at year end. This is thus an effective increase of 5.875 percent, not $5\frac{3}{4}$ percent.

In general, nominal annual (coupon) rate, per period effective rate, and effective annual rate are related as follows:

I. Nominal annual rate (r_N) ÷ number of compounding periods in a year (M)
    = effective per period rate (r_p).
II. The quantity one plus the effective per period rate raised to the power corresponding to the number of compounding periods in a year
    = one plus the effective annual rate.

$$\frac{r_N}{M} = r_p$$
$$(1 + r_p)^M - 1 = r$$

Or, comprehensively in one equation:

$$r = \left(1 + \frac{r_N}{M}\right)^M - 1$$

Unless it is perfectly clear from the context in which the term is used, r_N should never be called the "annual rate," but should be called the "nominal annual rate" or "annual rate compounded M times per year." To do otherwise is imprecise, confusing, and misleading.[8]

IRR With Quarterly Cash Flows

Consider an investment project costing $5000 that will last an estimated five years and provides net, after-tax cash flows at the end of each *quarter* of $300 in all, but in the final quarter which, with salvage, amounts to $1000.

The quarterly, per-period IRR is $r_p = 2.701$ percent. The nominal annual IRR, r_N is 10.804 percent *compounded quarterly*. The effective annual IRR rate, $r = 11.249$ percent. If we were to ignore the fact that the cash flows occur quarterly and instead treat the flows for each year as if they fell on the last day of the year, we would get an IRR of $r = 9.880$ percent. Note that this is significantly less than if the cash flows were treated as falling at the end of every three months, because the cash flows, on average, are pushed into the future some one-and-one-half quarters or some four-and-one-half months (see Figure 6.4).

---

[8] See, for example, Anthony F. Herbst, "Truth in Lending, Regulation Z: Comments on Closed-End Contract Interest Rate Disclosure Requirements," *Journal of Bank Research*, Vol. 3, No. 2 (December 1972).

TRADITIONAL METHODS THAT RECOGNIZE TIME-VALUE OF MONEY 75

Figure 6.4 Quarterly versus annual cash flows for IRR calculation.

QUESTIONS

1. What is the difference between taking the reciprocal of payback as the rate of return on a project and finding the IRR?
2. What is the difference between using a present value formulation to find the IRR and using a future value formulation?
3. How would you explain the concept of IRR to operating management that is familiar only with payback and the NROR?
4. Why can we use the IRR formulation to find the effective interest we will pay on a loan, just as we use it to determine the yield on an investment?
5. Why is the IRR method conceptually superior to payback and to the NROR?
6. How does the IRR method attach more significance to early cash flows than to later ones?
7. Explain how the interval bisection and Newton-Raphson methods can be used to find IRR.
8. How is the method of interpolation related to the interval bisection method for finding IRR?

PROBLEMS

6.1 Show that if the project cash flows are uniform, and the project life is at least twice the payback period, that the NROR provides a useful first approximation to the IRR.

6.2 Calculate the IRRs of these projects, using tables and interpolating:

Project	Cost	R_1	R_2	R_3	R_4	R_5	R_6	R_7	R_8	R_9	R_{10}	R_{11}
I	1000	100	200	200	200	300	300	300	100	100	50	50
II	1000	150	150	200	200	200	250	250				
III	1000	175	175	175	175	175						

6.3 Calculate the IRRs of the following projects:

Project	Cost	R_1	R_2	R_3	R_4
I	1000	500	700	900	1100
II	1000	900	600	300	100

6.4 Calculate the IRR of this project:

R_0	R_1	R_2
−10	50	−50

This project has *mixed* cash flows. Would you accept it for a cost of capital $k = 15$ percent? Do you notice anything strange about the IRR for this project?

6.5 Show that this project has two solutions for IRR. Note that it has *mixed* cash flows:

R_0	R_1	R_2
−400	1100	−700

At what value of discount rate does this project's NPV reach its maximum value?

Bibliography

1. Ayres, Frank, Jr., *Mathematics of Finance* (New York: Schaum, 1963).
2. Bernhard, Richard H., "A Simpler Internal Rate of Return Uniqueness Condition which Dominates that of deFaro and Soares," *The Engineering Economist*, Vol. 24, No. 2 (Winter 1979), pp. 71–74.
3. Cissell, Robert, and Helen Cissell, *Mathematics of Finance*, 4th ed. (Boston: Houghton Mifflin, 1973).
4. DeFaro, Clovis, "A Sufficient Condition for a Unique Nonnegative Internal Rate of Return: Further Comments," *Journal of Financial and Quantitative Analysis*, Vol. XIII, No. 4 (September 1978), pp. 577–584.
5. ———, and Luiz Soares, "A Flexible Sufficient Condition for a Unique Nonnegative Internal Rate of Return," *The Engineering Economist*, Vol. 23, No. 2 (Winter 1978), pp. 117–127.

6. Dorn, William, S., and Daniel D. McCracken, *Numerical Methods with FORTRAN IV Case Studies* (New York: Wiley, 1972).
7. Fisher, Lawrence, "An Algorithm for Finding Exact Rates of Return," *The Journal of Business*, Vol. XXIX, No. 1, part II (January 1966), pp. 111–118.
8. Hadley, George F., *Elementary Business Mathematics* (Homewood, Ill.: Irwin, 1971).
9. Herbst, Anthony F., "Truth in Lending, Regulation Z: Comments on Closed-End Contract Interest Rate Disclosure Requirements" *Journal of Bank Research*, Vol. 3, No. 2 (December 1972).
10. International Business Machines Corporation, *Systems/360 Scientific Subroutine Package (360A-CM-03X) Version III Programmer's Manual*.
11. Johnson, Robert W. *Capital Budgeting* (Belmont, Cal.: Wadsworth, 1970).
12. Kuo, Shan S., *Numerical Methods and Computers* (Reading, Mass.: Addison-Wesley, 1965).
13. Mao, James C. T., *Quantitative Analysis of Financial Decisions* (New York: Macmillan, 1969).

Chapter 7
Traditional Methods That Recognize Time-Value of Money: The Net Present Value

The internal rate of return considered in the last chapter involved finding the unique real root to a polynomial equation with real coefficients. At best this is a tedious calculation when performed manually, particularly for projects with unequal cash flows for many periods. The net present value (NPV), which is considered here, involves the much simpler task of evaluating that polynomial equation with real coefficients for a given discount rate, which usually will *not* be a root to the polynomial. The NPV is defined in the equation:

$$\text{NPV} \equiv C + \sum_{t=1}^{N} \frac{R_t}{(1+k)^t} \quad \text{or} \quad \sum_{t=0}^{N} \frac{R_t}{(1+k)^t} \tag{7.1}$$

if we let $C = R_0$, or in the more compact form:

$$\text{NPV} \equiv \sum_{t=0}^{N} R_t(1+k)^{-t} \tag{7.2}$$

    This equation appears to be identical to the basic valuation model in Chapter 2. There is a subtle difference, however, that the notation does not reflect. In the basic valuation model the R_t are the total or aggregated net, after-tax cash flows in each period. In Eq. (7.1), on the other hand, the R_t are the net, after-tax cash flows of the project under analysis. Although the same symbol is used in each, the meaning is somewhat different.

The NPV of a particular project provides a measure that is compatible with the valuation model of the firm. This much is perhaps obvious because of the mathematical form of the equations. Since we take as given the management goal of maximization of the enterprise's value, we recognize that acceptance of individual projects with a positive NPV will contribute to the increase in that value. In the absence of capital rationing, in other words, if there is no shortage of money to accept all projects with positive NPVs, the enterprise should do so.

In reference to the calculation of NPV, the conventional approach has been to calculate first the *gross* present value, which is the present value of all the net, after-tax cash *inflows*, and then subtract the initial outlay that is assumed to be at present value since it is incurred at $t = 0$. For projects requiring net outlays beyond the initial period, the outlays are brought to present value in the same manner as the cash receipts.

In the calculation of NPV we take the discount rate, k, as *given*. The rate used is generally[1] the organization's cost of capital; more particularly, it is the *marginal* cost of capital. If an investment yields a discounted return greater than its discounted cost, it will have NPV > 0. Conversely, if the discounted cost exceeds the discounted returns, it will have NPV < 0. Therefore the rule for project adoption under the NPV criterion is:

If NPV ≤ 0, reject
> 0, accept

The discounting process employed simply allows cash flows to be compared after they have been adjusted for the time value of money. The time reference we use is immaterial: We could just as easily have used net *future* value by adjusting the cash flows to their compounded (rather than discounted) value at $t = N$ rather than at $t = 0$. However, it is a traditional convention that NPV rather than net future value be used.

The NPV method may be further clarified by means of an example. Let us assume that k, the discount rate, is 15 percent per annum and find the NPV for project A, considered in the previous chapter. This project requires an initial outlay of $5000 and returns $2500 each year over a ten-year useful life, net after taxes. Table 7.1 illustrates the NPV calculations. Notice that because the cash flows for this project are a uniform $2500, we could have summed the present worth factors and then multiplied the sum once by $2500 to get the NPV. However, this summation has already been done: The results are listed in the table in the appendix for annuity present worth factors.[2]

---

[1] In the case of risky projects, which we are not considering in this section of the text, a "risk-adjusted discount rate" or "hurdle rate" is sometimes used as an alternative to other methods for dealing with risk.
[2] Alternatively, if we have a modern calculator, we can find the present worth of annuity factor for N periods and rate k from the relationship

$$a_{\overline{N}|k} = \frac{1 - (1 + k)^{-N}}{k}$$

Table 7-1. THE NPV CALCULATIONS FOR PROJECT A

Year	Present Worth Factor	×	Cash Flow	=	Present Value
1	.86957		$2,500		$2,173.92
2	.75614		2,500		1,890.35
3	.65752		2,500		1,643.80
4	.57175		2,500		1,429.38
5	.49718		2,500		1,242.95
6	.43233		2,500		1,080.82
7	.37594		2,500		939.85
8	.32690		2,500		817.25
9	.28426		2,500		710.65
10	.24718		2,500		617.95
	5.01877				$12,546.92

Table 7-2. THE NPV CALCULATIONS FOR PROJECT B

Year	Present Worth Factor	×	Cash Flow	=	Present Value
1	.86957		$ 500		$ 434.78
2	.75614		1,000		756.14
3	.65752		2,000		1,315.04
4	.57175		4,000		2,287.00
	−2.85498				$4,792.96
5	.49718		8,000		$3,977.44
6	.43233		8,000		3,458.64
7	.37594		8,000		3,007.52
8	.32690		8,000		2,615.20
9	.28426		8,000		2,274.08
10	.24718		8,000		1,977.44
	5.01877				
	2.16379	×	8,000	=	17,310.32
				Gross PV	$22,103.28
				Less C at $t = 0$	−5,000.00
				NPV	$17,103.28

Now, to obtain *net* present value, we need remove only the $5000 project cost that, since it occurs at $t = 0$, is already at present value. (That is, the present value factor for $t = 0$ is 1.00000.)

Therefore the NPV for project A is:

$7546.92 = $12,546.92 − $5000

at $k = 15$ percent. Since NPV > 0, the project is acceptable for investment.

Next, let us find the NPV for project B (also considered in a previous chapter). The calculations are shown in Table 7.2.

Note that since cash flow in years five through ten is a uniform $8000, the present value of these flows can be obtained by multiplying by the present worth of

Figure 7.1 NPV functions for projects A and B.

annuity factor for ten years *less* the present worth of annuity factor for four years: $8000(5.01877 - 2.85498)$.

If we were considering A and B as mutually exclusive projects, B would clearly be preferred since its NPV of $17,103.28 is more than $2\frac{1}{2}$ times larger, *and* the required $5000 investment is the same for both projects.

The internal rate of return (IRR), which the previous chapter covered, is a special case of NPV. The IRR is that discount rate for which the NPV is equal to zero. In other words, the IRR is that rate of discount for which the present value of net cash inflows equals the present value of net cash outflows.

Figure 7.1 illustrates the NPV functions for projects A and B for various discount rates. Negative rates are for purposes of illustration only, not because of any economically meaningful interpretation of such rates as cost of capital. Note that the IRR of each project is at that rate of discount where the NPV of that project intersects the horizontal axis, and that NPV = 0 at these points. It can be shown that for all investments with $R_0 = C < 0$, and $R_t \geq 0$ for all $0 < t \leq N$, that the NPV function is concave from above. For projects having *some* $R_t \geq 0$ for $0 < t \leq N$ this will not necessarily be true.

Let us consider an investment project that has some negative cash flows after $t = 0$. We will call this project AA. The cash flows over a four-year economic life are:

R_0	R_1	R_2	R_3	R_4
-1000	1200	600	300	-1000

This project has two "IRRs": -8.14 percent and $+42.27$ percent. Quotation marks are placed on the IRR because, as we shall see in Chapter 10, neither rate is internal to the project and neither measures the return on investment for this project. Figure 7.2 contains the graph of the NPV function for this project. Note that

82 TRADITIONAL METHODS OF PROJECT EVALUATION

Figure 7.2 NPV curve for project AA.

NPV is positive until the discount rate reaches 42.27 percent, but that the NPV is concave from *below* up to this point.

We shall consider such projects in later chapters in more detail. For now it will be useful to make a mental note that they are neither purely investments nor purely financing projects (loans to the enterprise) but a mixture of these. Because many projects are of this nature, it is important that we have means for their proper analysis, although we shall defer this until later.

UNEQUAL PROJECT SIZE

A difficulty that arises with NPV is that marginally valuable projects may show a higher NPV than more desirable projects simply because they are larger. For example, consider projects D and E.

	Project D	Project E
Cost = R_0	$100,000	$10,000
Cash Flows, R_1 through R_{10}	30,000	10,000
R_{11}	0	0

Again using $k = 15$ percent, we see that the NPV for project D is $50,570, whereas that for project E is only $40,190. Therefore, D would seem preferable to E. However, D costs *ten times* as much as E. The extra NPV is only 11.5 percent of the additional $90,000 required investment—an amount less than the 15 percent cost of capital.

This problem is a serious one, especially when capital is limited and consequently there is capital rationing within the organization. Fortunately, this problem is easily corrected.

The Profitability Index

The problem of unequal project size with the NPV is easily corrected by using what is called the *profitability index* (PI). The PI may be defined in two ways; these are identical except for a constant of 1.0. The more common way is by the ratio of *gross* present value to project cost. Under this definition an acceptable project, one with NPV > 0, will have a PI > 1.0.

This author's preference is to define PI as the ratio of *net* present value to project cost:

$$PI \equiv \frac{NPV}{C} \quad \text{or} \quad \frac{NPV}{R_0} \tag{7.3}$$

Thus, if NPV > 0, PI > 0. On the other hand, if NPV ≤ 0, PI ≤ 0. It is immaterial which definition is used, provided that it is used consistently. They are identical except that definition (7.3) yields a PI that is 1.0 less than that obtained under the alternative definition.

Let us look again at projects D and E in terms of their PI.

PI	D	E
	.5057	4.019

The results obtained favor project E, because the return on the investment is much better proportionately than that on project D.

UNEQUAL PROJECT LIVES

Another problem exists with the NPV and the derivative PI. This is due to the effect of unequal project lives. For example, let us assume that a given operation is expected to be required for an indefinite time, and that two mutually exclusive projects, F and G, both have acceptable NPVs and IRRs. However, project F will last for ten years and project G will last for only five, after which it will have to be replaced. Can we determine which should be accepted on the basis of PI as defined earlier? No. We must take into account the effect of the difference in project lives. As an aid in defining how this should be done, let us consider specific projects F and G.

Net Cash Flows

Year	Project F	Project G
0	$100,000	$100,000
1	30,000	40,000
2	·	40,000
3	·	40,000
4	·	40,000
5	·	40,000
6	·	0
7	·	·
8	·	·
9	·	·
10	30,000	0

Letting $k = 15$ percent, we obtain for the projects:

	F	G
NPV	$50,563	$34,086
PI	.506	.341

Since project G will have to be replaced at the end of year five, we need to take this into account systematically. (We assume it can be replaced for $100,000 at that time, ignoring the effects of inflation.) One way is to assume that if it is adopted, project G will be replaced by an identical project at the end of year five and then treat the cash flows over the entire ten-year period explicitly. In other words, we calculate NPV and PI for project G that now has cash flows:

	Net Cash Flows		
Time	First Project G	Replacement	Combined
0	$-100,000		$-100,000
1	40,000		40,000
2	40,000		40,000
3	40,000		40,000
4	40,000		40,000
5	40,000	$-100,000	-60,000
6		40,000	40,000
7		40,000	40,000
8		40,000	40,000
9		40,000	40,000
10		40,000	40,000

The values obtained now for project G are:

NPV = $51,033
PI = .510

so that, contrary to the unadjusted results previously obtained, project G is preferable. The method illustrated for adjusting for unequal lives can be tedious to apply, since it requires us to calculate NPV over the least common denominator number of years of the project lives. In this example project F lasted exactly twice as long as project G, so this presented no problem. However, what if we had one project lasting 11 years and another lasting 13 years (both prime numbers)? In this case we would have to evaluate 143 cash flows for each project!

Level Annuities

A much easier equivalent method is to calculate the time-adjusted annual average (level annuity) for each project. This is done by multiplying the unadjusted NPV by the capital recovery factor (also called annuity with present value of 1.0) for the number of years of useful life in the project. The capital recovery factor (CRF) is the reciprocal of the present value of annuity factor.[3]

[3] The CRF is defined by the equation $k/[1 - (1 + k)^{-N}]$ for rate k and N periods. The CRF enables us to spread out any given present value over a specified number of years as well as providing a means for finding a time-value-adjusted average present value.

For projects F and G, the time-adjusted annual averages are:

Project F $50,563 × .19925 (10-year CRF) = $10,075
Project G $34,086 × .29832 (5-year CRF) = $10,169

It is apparent that project G offers a higher NPV on an annual basis than does F. Now, to convert these results to adjusted NPVs for the projects over the longest-lived project, in this case ten years, we need only multiply by the present value of annuity factor corresponding to this number of years. Thus, we obtain adjusted NPVs of:[4]

Project F $10,075 × 5.0188 = $50,564
Project G $10,169 × 5.0188 = $51,036

And the corresponding profitability indexes are .506 and .510.

SUMMARY AND CONCLUSION

Now that we have seen how two difficulties with NPV may be surmounted with the profitability index and uniform annual equivalents, what can we say in summary about NPV?

Strong Points of NPV

1. It is conceptually superior to payback and accounting methods.
2. It does not ignore any periods in the project life nor any cash flows.
3. It takes into account the time value of funds.
4. It is consistent with the basic valuation model expressed in Chapter 2.
5. It is easier to apply than internal rate of return since it involves evaluating a polynomial rather than finding a root.
6. It favors early cash flows over later ones.

Weak Points of NPV

1. It, like IRR, requires that we have an estimate of the organization's cost of capital, k. Also, the given k is embedded in the NPV, whereas with IRR the internal rate can be judged by management. Management will determine whether it is reasonable that the IRR is greater or less than k when k is not known with confidence.
2. It is more difficult to apply than payback or accounting method, and thus less suitable for use by lower levels in the organization without proper training in its application. That may not be feasible.
3. Unless modified by conversion to uniform annual equivalents and converted to profitability index, NPV will give distorted comparison between projects of unequal size and/or unequal economic lives.

[4] Minor rounding errors make the calculated result different by a small amount.

QUESTIONS

1. Explain the difference in method between finding IRR and calculating NPV.
2. Why does the method of uniform annual equivalents yield the same results as evaluating projects over the least common denominator of their useful lives?
3. Compare the NPV Eq. (7.1) to the basic valuation model in Chapter 2, Eq. (2.1). How will adoption of projects with NPV > 0 serve to increase the firm's value?
4. What is the basic difference between finding NPV and net future value? What is the relationship between them?
5. If the firm makes an error in estimating its cost of capital why will this result in magnified errors in calculated NPV?
6. How would you explain the concept of NPV to operating management that is familiar only with payback? To management familiar with payback and IRR? What arguments would you advance to get them to adopt NPV or PI as their capital-budgeting criterion?
7. Calculate, using the method of uniform annual equivalents, the NPVs and PIs of these projects, taking into account the different project lives. How many cash flow periods would you have to evaluate if you used the method of least common denominator? Let $k = 10$ percent, 12 percent, and 15 percent.

Project	Cost	R_1	R_2	R_3	R_4	R_5	R_6	R_7	R_8	R_9	R_{10}	R_{11}
I	1000	100	200	200	200	300	300	300	100	100	50	50
II	1000	150	150	200	200	200	250	500				
III	1000	250	250	250	250	250						

8. Show that a uniform (level) annuity of 355.76 ($k = .10$) is equivalent to cash flows at the end of years one through five of 600, 500, 300, 150, and 100. In what sense is the level annuity equivalent? In a world where cash flows become increasingly uncertain the further in the future they occur, is the level annuity fully equivalent? Explain.

PROBLEMS

7.1 Show that the profitability indexes defined as gross present value/cost and net present value/cost differ by a constant of 1.0.

7.2 Prove that the net present value and net future value are identical except for a factor of proportionality. What is the factor?

7.3 Prove that the method of uniform annual equivalents yields the NPV identical to that obtained by evaluating projects over the least common denominator number of periods.

7.4 Calculate the NPVs for the following projects for $k = 5$ percent, 10 percent, 15 percent, and 20 percent. Plot the results. Explain what you observe.

Project	Cost	R_1	R_2	R_3	R_4
I	1000	500	700	900	1100
II	1000	900	600	300	100

7.5 Show by use of the present value of annuity tables or calculated factors, what effect errors of 1 percent, 2 percent, 3 percent, and 5 percent in k will have on NPV for projects having uniform cash flows. (*Hint:* Work with gross present value, since R_0 will not be affected.)

7.6 Project Delta has $R_0 = -\$10,000$ and cash flows of $2000 at the end of each *quarter* of its economic life of five years. Project Gamma has $R_0 = -\$20,000$ and cash flows of $15,000 at the end of each *year* of its seven-year life. Neither project is expected to have any salvage value. The discount rate that the firm uses is 12 percent per annum. The projects are mutually exclusive.
(a) Which project is preferred?
(b) If project Delta's cash flows were assumed to occur at year end rather than end of quarter, how would your answer to part (a) be affected?
(c) If a project has uniform cash flows at the end of each quarter, and the annual discount rate is k, can you find a factor that will adjust for the effect of treating the cash flows as occurring at year end? Draw a time diagram to illustrate.

Bibliography

1. Beranek, William, "The AB Procedure and Capital Budgeting," *Journal of Financial and Quantitative Analysis*, Vol. XV, No. 2 (June 1980), pp. 391–406.
2. Bierman, Harold Jr., and Seymour Smidt, *The Capital Budgeting Decision*, 3rd ed. (New York: Macmillan, 1971).
3. Haskins, C. G., "Benefit-Cost Ratios versus Net Present Value: Revisited," *Journal of Finance and Accounting*, Vol. 1, No. 2 (Summer 1974), pp. 249–265.
4. Johnson, Robert W., *Capital Budgeting* (Belmont, Cal.: Wadsworth, 1970).
5. Osteryoung, Jerome, *Capital Budgeting* (Columbus, Ohio: Grid, 1974).
6. Smith, Gerald W., *Engineering Economy* (Ames: Iowa State University Press, 1968).

Chapter 8
Reinvestment Rate Assumptions for NPV and IRR and Conflicting Rankings

This chapter discusses some controversial conceptual problems that have figured prominently in the literature of capital budgeting. Discussion is not limited to examination of the work of other authors, but includes this author's views, which in themselves may be somewhat controversial to other writers in the field of capital investments. The author hopes that this chapter will move readers who are already familiar with the standard lore of capital budgeting to think critically of some things that may have been taken for granted, and judge for themselves.

REINVESTMENT RATE ASSUMPTIONS FOR NPV AND IRR

Comparison of Eqs. (6.3) with (7.1) and (7.2) shows that the internal rate of return (IRR) is nothing more nor less than a special case of net present value (NPV). The IRR is defined as the rate for which NPV is zero. With this in mind, let us examine a general equation combining (6.3) and (7.1):

$$X = \frac{R_0}{(1+d)^0} + \frac{R_1}{(1+d)^1} + \cdots + \frac{R_N}{(1+d)^N} \tag{8.1}$$

or

$$X = \sum_{t=0}^{N} \frac{R_t}{(1+d)^t} = \sum_{t=0}^{N} R_t(1+d)^{-t} \tag{8.2}$$

If the discount rate d is such that $X = 0$, we say that d is the IRR. If $X \neq 0$, we say that X is the NPV for cost of capital $k = d$. Therefore, by employing Eqs. (8.1) and (8.2) we can deal simultaneously with both IRR and NPV.

So far, all mathematical formulations for IRR and NPV have been in terms of present value. We can convert to *future value* by multiplying both sides of the equation by $(1 + d)^N$, where d is either the IRR or cost of capital k, as the case may be. If we do this with Eqs. (8.1) and (8.2), we obtain:

$$X(1 + d)^N = R_0(1 + d)^N + R_1(1 + d)^{N-1} + \cdots + R_N \qquad (8.3)$$

$$X(1 + d)^N = \sum_{t=0}^{N} \frac{R_t}{(1 + d)^{t-N}} = \sum_{t=0}^{N} R_t(1 + d)^{N-t} \qquad (8.4)$$

Note that if d is the IRR, then $X = 0$ and $X(1 + d)^N$ is zero. Therefore, IRR could be as easily obtained from a future value formulation as from the conventional present value formulation. Also, if X were not zero, that is, if X were an NPV for $k = d$, the effect of multiplying by $(1 + d)^N$ simply moves the reference point from $t = 0$ to $t = N$.

In other words, looking at Eq. (8.3), we obtain the same results except for a constant of $(1 + d)^N$ times the NPV by assuming the cash flows are *reinvested* at earning rate d, rather than being discounted at that rate. The R_0, which for most projects will be the cost or initial outlay, is "invested" for N periods at rate d compounded each period. For the initial outlay this may be interpreted as the *opportunity* cost of committing funds to this project instead of to another purpose in which rate d could be earned. Or in the case where $d = k$, the opportunity cost may arise from the decision to undertake the project requiring funds to be raised, whereas without the project no new funds would need to be raised. The mathematical symmetry between these formulations has been a cause for concern among finance theorists. Let us consider the source of their concern.

The implication of future value formulation is that the project return, whether measured by IRR or by NPV, will depend on the rate at which cash flows can be reinvested. For a firm in a growth situation in which profitable investment opportunities abound, the IRR assumption that cash flows may be reinvested at a rate of earning equal to the IRR may thus not be unreasonable. For other firms, and government institutions, analysts think it more realistic to assume that the cash flows can be reinvested at a rate equal to the cost of capital k. Here we have the usual formulation of the reinvestment rate assumption.

Let us now consider the IRR and reinvestment rate in another light. Consider a loan of $100,000 that is made by a bank to an individual business proprietor for a period of five years. The loan is to be repaid in equal installments of $38,438.[1] From the bank's viewpoint this is an investment, with cash flows:

$t = 0$	$t = 1$	$t = 2$	$t = 3$	$t = 4$	$t = 5$
−$100,000	$33,438	$33,438	$33,438	$33,438	$33,438

and yield (that is, IRR) of 20 percent.

[1] To the nearest whole dollar.

From the borrower's point of view, the cash flows are identical except that the signs are reversed. The cash flows of the borrower are the cash flows of the lender multiplied by minus one. Therefore, the borrower has cash flows:

$t=0$	$t=1$	$t=2$	$t=3$	$t=4$	$t=5$
+$100,000	−$33,438	−$33,438	−$33,438	−$33,438	−$33,438

and his effective *cost* is 20 percent on the loan. The *borrower* must earn at least 20 percent per period on the loan just to be able to repay it. The pretax return to the lender on the investment (loan) cannot be less than the cost to the borrower. Even if the bank does not reinvest the cash flows as the loan is repaid, its implicit return will still be 20 percent. The return is measured as a time-adjusted percentage of the principal amount outstanding, and is independent of what disposition is made of the cash flows as they are received. This is not to say that the uses to which the cash flows are put will have no effect on the organization, for they will. However, although the yield on the funds originally invested may be increased by such uses, it cannot be reduced by lack of such investment opportunities. This is a strong position to take, and requires explanation.

The payments made by the borrower, once given over to the lender, can earn nothing for the borrower. The borrower must, in the absence of other sources of funds, be able to earn 20 percent per period on the remaining loan principal. If the borrower is unable to earn anything on the remaining loan principal, he or she must still make the required periodical payments. The payments, even if made from other sources of funds, will be the same as those required if the loan were to generate funds at 20 percent per period. If funds must be diverted from other projects to repay the loan, the *opportunity* cost to the borrower may be *more* than 20 percent, if the funds could have earned more than this percentage in other uses. The cost internal to the loan itself, however, is 20 percent.

Table 8.1 provides a breakdown of the loan payments into the principal and interest components implicit in the IRR method of rate calculation. Note that the *interest is computed* at 20 percent per year on the *beginning-of-period principal balance*. The excess of payment over this amount is used to reduce the principal.

The following loan (to the borrower) will have identical cost of 20 percent, but the principal is not amortized but paid in full at the end of the loan:

$t=0$	$t=1$	$t=2$	$t=3$	$t=4$	$t=5$
+$100,000	−$20,000	−$20,000	−$20,000	−$20,000	−$120,000

The borrower may place the loan principal in a (hypothetical) bank account that pays him or her exactly 20 percent annually on the deposit. At the end of each year the borrower withdraws the interest and pays it to the lender. At the end of the loan the borrower withdraws the principal plus interest and repays the loan. Since he or she pays the interest to the lender as soon as it is earned, the person does not earn interest on interest. The bank pays the borrower exactly 20 percent annually on the deposit, which he or she immediately turns over to the lender. The loan costs exactly equal the 20 percent annual interest the bank pays the borrower for the deposit, so

Table 8-1. COMPONENT BREAKDOWN OF CASH FLOWS (AMOUNTS ROUNDED TO NEAREST $)

t	Beginning Principal	Interest on Principal	Principal Repayment
1	100,000	20,000	13,438[a]
2	86,562	17,312	16,126
3	70,437	14,087	19,351
4	51,086	10,217	23,221
5	27,865	5,573	27,865

[a]Assumes that end-of-year payment of $33,438 is composed of interest of 20% on the beginning balance *plus* a repayment of principal (that is, $20,000 + $13,438).

there is no net gain to him or her. (We have ignored transactions costs to simplify discussion.)

For the lender the loan also yields exactly 20 percent. However, there is an important difference: The lender may reinvest the interest payments if desired and thus *increase* the gain. Such increase, significantly, does not depend on the loan itself, but on reinvestment opportunities available for the loan interest when it is received. The 20 percent return is thus a *minimum* return on the loan, and this minimum is independent of reinvestment opportunities. The reinvestment rate could be zero and still the lender would earn 20 percent on the loan.

The only difference between these two loans is the handling of principal repayment: In the first, the principal is amortized over the life of the loan. In the second loan, the entire principal repayment is made at the loan maturity date. The first loan does provide better reinvestment opportunities to the lender since larger payments are received in all but the last year, and the lender may be able to reinvest them and so raise the return on the loan. Once again, however, 20 percent is the minimum return to be expected, even if the reinvestment opportunity rate were to be zero. *The lender earns exactly 20 percent on the principal amount still in the hands of the borrower.* If the lender can earn 20 percent or more on the recovered principal, so much the better for the lender. If he or she cannot, the lender nevertheless continues to earn 20 percent on the still unrecovered principal.

Let us assume a zero reinvestment rate. With the first loan, let us consider that the $100,000 principal is returned in equal annual installments of $20,000 over the five-year loan maturity. This means that $13,438 over and above the principal repayment is earned on the *remaining* principal. The percentage return on the remaining principal in each year is then as shown in Table 8.2. The geometric mean return is 29.4 percent, the arithmetic mean return 30 percent, and the median return 22.4 percent. This treatment differs from the IRR formulation in assuming a fixed allocation of periodical payments to principal amortization[2] rather than a gradually increasing amortization payment. Therefore, the principal is more quickly reduced, consequently yielding a higher return on that which remains.

[2]Straight-line amortization of the principal.

Table 8-2. PER PERIOD RETURN ON REMAINING PRINCIPAL (CONSTANT AMORTIZATION OF $20,000 PER PERIOD)

t	Principal Remaining	% Return
1	$100,000	13.438
2	80,000	16.798
3	60,000	22.397
4	40,000	33.595
5	20,000	67.190

These results do not require any reinvestment rate other than zero. They show that the percentage return on an investment does not depend on the available reinvestment rate. The actual gain to the investor (or lender) may, of course, be higher than this minimum amount if the available reinvestment rate is greater than zero, but that is a condition *external* to the investment. The IRR is concerned with the internal characteristics only, and therefore provides a measure of the minimum return on the investment.

In summary, the conceptual difficulty with the reinvestment rate assumption arises from focusing on the superficial aspects of the mathematics of the IRR while neglecting the economic interpretation of the initial investment and the subsequent cash flows. Mathematics is a tool in financial mathematics, and economics the master. The reinvestment rate problem arises from confusion of this hierarchy—from trying to make the economics conform to the mathematics. The IRR might be called more properly *return on invested capital* to make clear its economic assumptions. However, this term has another specific meaning that is covered later; and is thus reserved for that.

Treatment of the reinvestment rate with the NPV, along lines similar to that of the IRR, is left as an exercise at the end of the chapter.

CONFLICTING RANKINGS AND FISHER'S INTERSECTION

The rules for project acceptance once again are:

	IRR	NPV
Accept if	$r > k$	NPV > 0
Reject if	$r \leq k$	NPV ≤ 0

Now it would seem that if we are comparing two acceptable, yet mutually exclusive, projects, that we should get the same preference ranking by NPV as we do by IRR. However, this will not always be the case. Conflicting rankings may arise because one or both projects have nonuniform cash flows. Irving Fisher recognized this reason for conflicting rankings many years ago, although Alchian [1] was responsible for its widespread recognition. Mao [6] contains a clear treatment of the conflicting ranking problem à la Fisher.

Figure 8.1 Fisher's rate, r_f, and conflicting IRR-NPV project rankings.

To begin, let us consider two projects each costing $7000 at $t = 0$, and each having an economic life of five years, in order that we do not need to correct for unequal project size or life. The projects have the following cash flows (dropping the $ signs):

	Project H	Project I
Cost, R_0	7,000	7,000
CASH FLOW		
$t = 1$	6,000	250
$t = 2$	3,000	500
$t = 3$	1,500	750
$t = 4$	750	4,000
$t = 5$	375	10,000

The internal rates of return are $IRR_H = 35.120$ percent, $IRR_I = 19.745$ percent. As shown in Figure 8.1, the IRR values are fixed. However, the NPV values change, since they depend on the value of d that is used. For $d = 0$ (that is, zero discount) they are for projects H and I $4625 and $8500, respectively.

Notice that the two NPV curves intersect at a discount rate of approximately 11 percent (11.408 percent), which we denote as r_f. For smaller discount rates, project I has an NPV greater than that of project H. However, $IRR_H > IRR_I$ always. Therefore, for discount rates less than r_f, there will always be a conflict between the NPV ranking and the IRR ranking, but, for discount rates greater than r_f, both IRR and NPV will yield the same ranking.

Let us examine these projects further by treating them each as loans and inspecting their repayment schedules. We assume that each net cash flow is composed of two components: an interest payment and a principal repayment. First, we will use as discount rate the Fisher's rate of 11.408 percent.

The project NPVs at $t = 0$ can be found by discounting the amounts in column 4. For project H we have $996.26(1.11408)^{-2} + 1500(1.11408)^{-3} + 750(1.11408)^{-4} + .375(1.11408)^{-5}$, equaling $2592.80. For project I we have $4449.93(1.11408)^{-5}$ or $2592.80. As we should have expected, at Fisher's rate the NPVs of projects H and I are equal, for that is how Fisher's rate is defined.

94 TRADITIONAL METHODS OF PROJECT EVALUATION

Table 8-3. COMPONENT TREATMENT OF PROJECTS H AND I AT FISHER'S RATE OF 11.408% (AMOUNTS IN $)

PROJECT H

t	(1) Beginning Principal	(2) Interest on Principal	(3) Principal Repayment	(4) Excess over (2)+(3)	(5) Total Net Cash Flow
1	7000.00	798.56	5201.44	0	6000.00
2	1798.56	205.18	1798.56	996.26	3000.00
3	0	0	0	1500.00	1500.00
4	0	0	0	750.00	750.00
5	0	0	0	375.00	375.00

PROJECT I

t	(1) Beginning Principal	(2) Interest on Principal	(3) Principal Repayment	(4) Excess over (2)+(3)	(5) Total Net Cash Flow
1	7000.00	798.56	−548.56	0	250.00
2	7548.56	861.14	−361.14	0	500.00
3	7909.70	902.34	−152.34	0	750.00
4	8062.04	919.72	3080.28	0	4,000.00
5	4981.75	568.32	4981.75	4449.93	10,000.00

Notice an important difference between the two projects with respect to column 1, the beginning-of-period principal remaining. The net cash flows for project H were sufficiently high at the end of periods one and two to pay off the entire principal after paying the required interest. In fact, at the end of period two the net cash flow was $996.26 *in excess* of what was required to pay off the interest and remaining principal. This is the meaning of NPV, and why some authors choose to call it *excess present value*. The NPV is the amount, at discount, by which the net cash flows of an investment project exceed what is required for payment of interest on remaining principal and principal repayment. Note that although project H paid off the entire principal by the end of period two, project I did not pay off its principal until the end of period five.

We know that projects H and I are not loans, but are capital investment projects. The principal repayments represent recovery of the initial investment, whereas the interest payments represent the opportunity cost of funds committed to the projects and as yet unrecovered. Which project is preferable? Both have the same NPV of $2592.80 at Fisher's rate. Does this mean that we should feel indifferent about the two projects?

Although projects H and I have identical NPVs at Fisher's rate of 11.408 percent, project H is clearly preferable. The reason is that project H provides for faster recovery of the funds invested in it than does project I. In fact, project I is incapable of paying the interest on beginning-of-period principal in any of periods one through three. Therefore, instead of giving us back our original investment with

Table 8-4. COMPONENT TREATMENT OF PROJECTS H AND I AT 5%, A RATE LESS THAN FISHER'S RATE (AMOUNT IN $)

PROJECT H

t	(1) Beginning Principal	(2) Interest on Principal	(3) Principal Repayment	(4) Excess over (2)+(3)	(5) Total Net Cash Flow
1	7000.00	350.00	5650.00	0	6000.00
2	1350.00	67.50	1350.00	1582.50	3000.00
3	0	0	0	1500.00	1500.00
4	0	0	0	750.00	750.00
5	0	0	0	375.00	375.00

PROJECT I

1	7000.00	350.00	−100.00	0	250.00
2	7100.00	355.00	145.00	0	500.00
3	6955.00	347.75	402.25	0	750.00
4	6552.75	327.64	3672.36	0	4,000.00
5	2880.39	144.02	2880.39	6975.59	10,000.00

interest from the start, project I requires that we wait until the end of period four before any reduction in principal plus accumulated interest can be made. On the principle that a bird in the hand is worth two in the bush, or rather that a dollar today is better than a dollar plus interest tomorrow (if there is any doubt about getting the dollar tomorrow), we prefer project H to project I. The fact that the NPVs of the two projects are identical should not cause us to be indifferent between projects such as H and I, for the NPV is only one criterion by which project merit may be gauged. If the NPVs are equal, we will, of course, prefer the project that offers the more rapid capital recovery. Invested funds recovered early are subject to less uncertainty of receipt than funds to be recovered later, and funds recovered early can be reinvested for a longer period to enhance the earnings of the firm.

We have seen that, at Fisher's rate, project H is preferable to project I even though the NPVs are identical. This preference is consistent with what we would have obtained by choosing between the projects on the basis of their IRRs. Now let us examine these same projects for a rate of discount substantially less than r_f, Fisher's rate. For illustration we will use a discount rate of 5 percent. Table 8.4 contains the results of our calculations.

We may again determine the NPVs by bringing the column 4 amounts to $t = 0$ at a discount rate of 5 percent per period. For project H we obtain an NPV of $3641.98 and for project I an NPV of $5465.56. Since NPV of I > NPV of H, which we would expect for a discount rate less than Fisher's rate, the NPV criterion favors project I. The profitability indexes (PIs) would not suggest a different relationship, because both projects require the same initial investment outlay.

At a cost of capital of 5 percent we find that the NPV (or PI) criterion favors project I. The IRR criterion, however, favors project H. Which criterion should we use? For a cost of capital (discount rate) greater than or equal to Fisher's rate we would have no problem, for both the IRR and the NPV would favor project H. But we have under consideration a rate of 5 percent and a conflict in ranking that must be resolved.

To help us decide which project is preferable, let us again examine columns 1 and 4 of Table 8.4. Notice that project H (column 1) allows us to recover our entire investment plus interest (opportunity cost on the funds committed) and yields an excess of $1582.50 at the end of the second year (column 4). Project I, in contrast, cannot even compensate for our opportunity cost in year one. It does not yield recovery of our investment until the end of the fifth year. In fact, *the entire NPV of project I depends on the large cash flow in period five.* If unanticipated events in year three, four, or five caused all cash flows to be zero, project H would still have a positive NPV of $1582.50(1.05)^{-2} = 1435.37, but project I would have a negative NPV of $-$6308.39$. Not only does project H have a higher IRR (35.120 percent) than project I (IRR = 19.751 percent), but also it does not depend on the accuracy of our cash flow estimates beyond year two to be acceptable.

Hopefully the foregoing analysis illustrates the danger of relying on any single measure of investment merit. This applies to the NPV and the PI as it does to other measures. Some have emphasized the NPV-PI criterion to an extent tantamount to recommending it as a universal prescription for capital-budgeting analysis. We have just seen that the NPV alone does not provide sufficient information to choose between two projects that have the same required investment and useful lives. A formal treatment of risk in capital budgeting is deferred until the latter chapters. However, we must realize that risk is our constant companion whether we deal with it formally or ignore it.

On the premise that point estimates are subject to error, and that the expected error becomes greater the further from the present the event we estimate, *ceteris paribus* we prefer an investment that promises early recovery of funds committed, and early receipt of funds above this amount. In the applied world of capital investments, no single measure has adequately captured the multiple-faceted character of capital-budgeting projects. For this reason industrial firms often examine several measures of a capital investment in their decision-making processes.

RELATIONSHIP OF IRR AND NPV

Mao [6, p. 196] has explicitly shown the relationship of IRR to NPV in an interesting way. Let us again examine Eqs. (6.3) and (7.2).

$$0 = \sum_{t=0}^{N} R_t(1 + r)^{-t} \qquad (6.3)$$

$$\text{NPV} = \sum_{t=0}^{N} R_t(1 + k)^{-t} \qquad (7.2)$$

If we subtract (6.3) from (7.2), we obtain

$$\text{NPV} = \sum_{t=0}^{N} R_t[(1 + k)^{-t} - (1 + r)^{-t}] \tag{8.5}$$

Now, taking any term beyond $t = 0$, we assume that k and r are both positive and R_t nonnegative. For NPV to be positive it is necessary only for the relation $r > k$ to be true. Conversely, for NPV to be negative, it is necessary that the relation $r < k$ be true. This shows the equivalence of the NPV and IRR criteria for projects that have $R_t \geq 0$ for $t > 0$, *in terms of the accept/reject decision*.

SUMMARY AND CONCLUSION

In this chapter we have examined (1) the reinvestment assumptions implicit in the discounted cash flow methods, IRR and NPV, (2) the reasons for conflicting rankings between IRR and NPV, and (3) Mao's treatment of the IRR-NPV relationship.

The reinvestment rate assumptions were seen to arise from the mathematical relationship between present value and future value formulations of the discounted cash flow methods. It was shown that the return on investment, that is, the remaining unrecovered initial investment, is not dependent on reinvestment opportunities. To do this the net cash flows were separated into two components: a payment of "interest" (return) on remaining "principal" (investment), and a repayment of "principal" (recovery of investment).

A treatment similar to that used to deal with the reinvestment assumptions was employed to analyze, in conjunction with Fisher's rate (r_f), the reason for contradictory rankings between IRR and NPV. It was seen that for rates less than r_f that the NPV alone is inadequate to judge which of two projects is better, since the NPV does not distinguish between the timing of cash receipts to recover the investment and those that provide a net return.

Mao's mathematical connection of IRR and NPV in a single equation serves to illustrate the conditions under which the NPV is positive or negative, and to focus more clearly on the IRR-NPV relationship.

QUESTIONS

1. What is the relationship between NPV and IRR?
2. What is meant by the reinvestment rate assumption with the discounted cash flow methods of IRR and NPV?
3. Contrast the view that the IRR depends on the reinvestment opportunities available to the firm with the view that the IRR is internal to the investment. How does this relate to the NPV?
4. How is it that the IRR and NPV may give conflicting rankings of two projects? Explain in terms of Fisher's rate.
5. In what sense is the IRR "internal" to the project and the NPV external to it?
6. Explain why, *ceteris paribus*, a project that returns the required investment quickly is preferable to one that may take several years to do this? What, if anything, does this have to do with reinvestment opportunities?

PROBLEMS

8.1 The NPV method does not require that the initial investment be amortized over the entire project life, but the IRR method does. Show why this is so; show how the IRR method does not allow for full recovery of the investment until the end of the project life.

8.2 Show that, if the entire investment is recovered only at the end of the project's useful life, and the cash flows at the end of years one through N are a uniform \$R, then the IRR is simply R/P, where P is the required investment at $t = 0$. (The total cash flow at end of year N is $R + P$.)

8.3 Prove that, if each of two projects has uniform cash flows and equal lives, the NPV curves may still cross.

8.4 Show, for a project costing \$P and returning \$R at the end of each period (R not necessarily uniform), where $R \geq 0$ and the sum of the cash flows exceeds the project cost, that the NPV curve will be concave from above.

8.5 If two projects require the same investment and have the same useful life, show that the profitability index (PI) will preserve the same ranking that the NPV gives.

8.6 Can the implications of Eq. (8.5) be obtained by adding, rather than subtracting, Eqs. (6.3) and (7.2)? Why, or why not?

Bibliography

1. Alchian, Armen A., "The Rate of Interest, Fisher's Rate of Return over Cost, and Keynes' Internal Rate of Return," *The American Economic Review*, Vol. 45 (December 1955), pp. 938–943.
2. Carlson, C. Robert, Michael L. Lawrence, and Donald H. Wort, "Clarification of the Reinvestment Assumption: The Discounted Flow Techniques." Presented at the Annual Financial Management Association Meetings, October 1972.
3. Doenges, R. Conrad, "The Reinvestment Problem in a Practical Perspective," *Financial Management* (Spring 1972), pp. 124–129.
4. Dudley, Carlton L., Jr., "A Note on Reinvestment Assumptions in Choosing Between Net Present Value, and Internal Rate of Return," *The Journal of Finance* (September 1972), pp. 907–916.
5. Jeynes, Paul H., "The Significance of Reinvestment Rate," *The Engineering Economist*, Vol. 11 (Fall 1965), pp. 1–9.
6. Mao, James C. T., *Quantitative Analysis of Financial Decisions* (New York: Macmillan, 1969).
7. Myer, Richard L., "A Note on Capital Budgeting Techniques and the Reinvestment Rate," *The Journal of Finance*, Vol. XXIV (December 1975), pp. 1251–1254.
8. Robinson, Romney, "The Rate of Interest, Fisher's Rate of Return over Costs, and Keynes' Internal Rate of Return: Comment," *The American Economic Review*, Vol. 46 (December 1956), pp. 972–973.

9. Solomon, Ezra, "The Arithmetic of Capital Budgeting Decisions," *Journal of Business*, Vol. 29 (April 1956), pp. 124–129.
10. Weston, J. Fred, and Nai-fu Chen, "A Note on Capital Budgeting and the Three Rs," *Financial Management*, Vol. 9, No. 1 (Spring 1980), pp. 12–13.

Part III
SPECIAL TOPICS AND METHODS

Chapter 9
The MAPI (Terborgh) Method

George Terborgh, Research Director of the Machinery and Allied Products Institute (MAPI), authored *Dynamic Equipment Policy,* published in 1949. This work still provides perhaps the most useful and theoretically sound practical means for analyzing component projects, despite its early publication date. In 1958 a simplified and streamlined version of the methodology proposed in 1949 was published in *Business Investment Policy,* many points of which are contained in *An Introduction to Business Investment Analysis,* based on an address delivered in 1958 by George Terborgh.

In order to appreciate how the MAPI method relates to the other methods that employ discounted cash flow, it will be useful if first the concept of *duality* is understood. Those familiar with mathematical programming may skip the following section without loss of continuity.

THE CONCEPT OF DUALITY

One of the important contributions of mathematical programming is that of duality. Simply stated, duality means that for every maximization problem there corresponds a minimization problem yielding identical solution values. If the problem at hand, called the *primal* problem, is one of maximization, the *dual* problem will always be a minimization problem. The converse is also true: If the primal is a minimization formulation, the dual will be a maximization formulation. Furthermore, the dual of the dual will be the primal.

Let us examine the general linear programming problem:

Maximize $\quad p_1q_1 + p_2q_2 + \cdots + p_nq_n$ (9.1)
Subject to $\quad a_{11}q_1 + a_{12}q_2 + \cdots + a_{1n}q_n \leq b_1$
$\qquad\qquad a_{21}q_1 + a_{22}q_2 + \cdots + a_{2n}q_n \leq b_2$
$\qquad\qquad \vdots \qquad\qquad\qquad\qquad\qquad \vdots$
$\qquad\qquad a_{m1}q_1 + a_{m2}q_2 + \cdots + a_{mn}q_n \leq b_m$
and for all $i \quad q_i \geq 0$

which in the shorthand notation of matrix algebra becomes:

Maximize (9.2)
Subject to $\quad A \cdot q \leq b$
$\qquad\qquad q_i \geq 0 \quad$ for all i

This particular linear programming problem may be considered that of maximizing total firm profit (price times quantity for each product) subject to constraints on the output of each product associated with limitations on machine time, labor, and so on, and the relative requirements of each product for these limited resources.

If the above maximization problem has a feasible solution, the dual formulation will also have a feasible solution, and the dual will yield the same amounts of each product to be produced.

The corresponding dual problem is:

Minimize $\quad b_1u_1 + b_2u_2 + \cdots + b_mu_m$ (9.3)
Subject to $\quad a_{11}u_1 = a_{21}u_2 + \cdots + a_{m1}u_m \geq P_1$
$\qquad\qquad a_{12}u_1 + a_{22}u_2 + \cdots + a_{m2}u_m \geq P_2$
$\qquad\qquad \vdots \qquad\qquad\qquad\qquad\qquad \vdots$
$\qquad\qquad a_{1n}u_1 + a_{m2}u_2 + \cdots + a_{mn}u_m \geq P_n$
and for all $i \quad u_i \geq 0$

which in matrix algebra notation corresponding to the primal becomes:

Minimize $\quad b'u$ (9.4)
Subject to $\quad A'u \geq p'$
$\qquad\qquad u_i \geq 0 \quad$ for all i

where b' is the transpose of the vector of constraint constants in the primal problem, and so on. The u variables are called *shadow prices* and represent the opportunity costs of unutilized resources. Thus, if we minimize the opportunity costs of nonoptimal employment of our machine, labor, and other resources, we achieve a lowest cost solution.

The important point of all this is that the primal and the dual formulations *both* lead to the *same* allocation of available resources. Therefore, it is not important which of the two formulations we solve. For reasons of ease of formulation, calculation, or computer efficiency, we may choose to work with *either* the primal or the dual formulation.

Now, getting back to the MAPI method of capital-budgeting project evaluation, we may say that the method is analogous to a dual approach to the goal of maximization of the value of the firm expressed in Eq. (2.1). It will be useful to again state Eq. (2.1) here as:

$$\text{Maximize } V = \sum_{t=0}^{\infty} \frac{R_t}{(1+k)^t} \qquad (9.5)$$

If we recognize that the net cash flows R_t are composed of gross cash profits P_t as well as cash costs C_t, then

$$R_t = P_t - C_t \qquad (9.6)$$

And for component projects we may assume that the P_t are fixed: We cannot directly associate cash inflows with the project. Even for major projects we may have to take the cash inflows as given, since to some extent they are beyond our control, at least as far as finance and production are concerned. Marketing staff may influence gross revenues through advertising, salesmanship, and marketing logistics, but still they will be subject to the state of the general economy, the activities of our competition, and "acts of God."

If we take the P_t as given, or fixed, and is thus independent of the capital equipment used in production, then we may reformulate our objective as:

$$\text{Minimize cost} = \sum_{t=0}^{\infty} \frac{C_t}{(1+k)^t} \qquad (9.7)$$

which may be operationalized by accepting the lowest cost projects for performing any given task, subject to their capability of performing the task to our requirements.

This is the basic idea behind the MAPI method, which we will now examine.

THE MAPI FRAMEWORK

The methodology of the MAPI method involves calculating the time-adjusted annual average cost of the project or projects under consideration. However, several concepts vital to intelligent application of the method must first be understood.

Challenger and Defender

In Terborgh's colorful terminology, the capital equipment currently in use is referred to as the *defender*, and the alternative that may be considered for replacement as the *challenger*. The MAPI method as originally developed emphasized capital equipment replacement, but is applicable to nonreplacement decisions as well since, in such cases, the status quo may be considered the defender. Various potential challengers may be compared against one another in a winnowing process, with the project promising the lowest time-adjusted annual average cost selected as *the* challenger.

If the challenger is superior to the defender as well as to presently available rivals, it may still be inferior to future alternatives. The current challenger is the best replacement for the defender only when there is no future challenger worth delaying for. This requires that a series of capital equipment not currently in existence be appraised, and this presents some difficulties:

> Now obviously it is impossible as a rule for mere mortals to foresee the form and character or machines not yet in existence. In some cases, no doubt, closely impending developments may be more or less dimly discerned and so may be weighted, after a fashion, in the replacement analysis, but in no case can the future be penetrated more than a fraction of the distance that is theoretically necessary for an exact, or even a close solution of the problem. What then is the answer? *Since the machines of the future cannot be foreseen, their character must be assumed.*[1]

The exact nature of the necessary assumptions is dependent on some additional terminology, which will be introduced at this point.

Capital Cost

The mechanics of the MAPI method require that we obtain the time-adjusted annual average cost of the project under consideration. The two components that determine what the average cost will be: one capital cost and operating inferiority. Capital cost must not be confused with the firm's cost of capital, because they are different things despite the similarity in labels.

Capital cost in the MAPI framework is the uniform annual dollar amount, including the opportunity cost of funds tied up in the project, that must be recovered if the project is retained for one year, or for two years, or for three years, and so on. To clarify this concept, assume we are examining a project that costs $10,000, and our firm has a 15 percent annual cost of capital. Our opportunity cost for funds committed to the project is at least 15 percent annually since, if funds were not committed to it, our cost of funds would be lower by this amount. That is, our firm would require $10,000 less, for which it is incurring an annual 15 percent cost.

Now, if we accept this project, and then at the end of one year abandon it, what is the capital cost? It is $10,000 *plus* the opportunity cost at 15 percent, or $11,500. What if the project is abandoned at the end of the second year? In this case the total capital cost is $10,000(1.15)^2 or $13,225. However, since the project will be kept for two years, the *annual* capital cost will be much less, not even one-half of the $13,225. The reason for this is that funds recovered in the first year do not incur opportunity cost during the second year. At a 15 percent annual cost of capital, the time-adjusted annual average capital cost in each of the two years will be $6151. If the

---

[1] George Terborgh, *Dynamic Equipment Policy* (Washington: Machinery and Allied Products Institute, 1949), pp. 57, 58.

project were retained for three years, the time-adjusted annual average cost will be $4380. These amounts are obtained by multiplying the initial investment by the *capital recovery factor* corresponding to the annual percentage cost of capital and the number of years the project is retained. The capital recovery factor is the reciprocal of the annuity (uniform series) present worth factor.

The longer a project is retained and kept in service, the lower the amount of investment that must be recovered in each individual year of the project's life. A project that is retained only one or two years must therefore yield a larger cash flow each year to allow recovery of the initial investment, plus opportunity cost of the committed funds, than the same project if kept for many years.

In the present value and internal rate of return methods for capital budgeting, the initial investment is considered only at time period zero. In the MAPI method, the initial investment is spread over the years of the projects's life. With the NPV method, since the discount rate is assumed to be known, that is, it is the firm's cost of capital, it is possible that the initial investment could be treated in the same way as in MAPI; nevertheless, in practice it is not treated thus.

Operating Inferiority

Operating inferiority is defined as the deficiency of the defender, the incumbent, existing project or the status quo, relative to the best available alternative for performing the same functions. Operating inferiority is considered to be composed of two components: physical deterioration and technological obsolescence. In the MAPI method we measure operating inferiority using the best capital equipment as a benchmark:

> In the firmament of mechanical alternatives there is but one fixed star: the best machine for the job. This is base point and the standard for evaluating all others. What an operator can afford to pay for any rival or competitor of this machine must therefore be derived by a top-down measurement. *But the process is not reversible.* He cannot properly compute what he can afford to pay for the best by measurement upward from its inferiors.[2]

PHYSICAL DETERIORATION

Physical deterioration of capital can be determined by comparing the equipment in service with the *same* equipment when new and undegraded by past operation. Physical deterioration, then, will be the sum of the excess of the operating cost of the old machine over its new replica's cost plus the amount that the value of the service provided by the old machine is inferior to machines of the latest technology. We normally would expect rapid physical deterioration to be rapid in the first few years of a project's life, then to accumulate more slowly, perhaps reaching a steady-state equilibrium, with repair costs at a relatively constant level per period, keeping the quality of service approximately constant. The comparison of the equipment in

[2] Ibid., p. 35.

service with its new replica should be in terms of operating costs, including maintenance and repair, additional direct labor required, extra indirect labor required (such as for quality control inspection), and the cost of higher scrap output.

TECHNOLOGICAL OBSOLESCENCE

Although physical deterioration may be considered an internal, age-related aspect of capital degradation, technological obsolescence is external to it and not necessarily related to age. Obsolescence consists of the sum of the excess operating cost of the same capital that is new over that of the *best* alternative now available plus the deficiency in the value of service relative to the best alternative. Physical deterioration is degradation of the firm's existing capital relative to new, *identical* capital. Technological obsolescence is the inferiority of the existing capital relative to the latest generation of capital for doing the job.

Two Basic Assumptions

Unfortunately, although the concept of operating inferiority is not difficult to grasp, implementation poses some problems. Although we may be able to estimate the cost of operating inferiority for this year, and perhaps the next as well, the task becomes increasingly difficult and tenuous as we attempt to carry the process into the future. Physical deterioration may not occur uniformly: It may be substantial in the early years, tapering off later, or it may be just the opposite. Technological developments tend to occur randomly over time. Although some may be anticipated in advance in rapidly developing fields, such as computer technology, prediction of when they will be brought to market is still a somewhat uncertain enterprise.

In addition to the problems inherent in estimating operating inferiority, there is yet another obstacle. This is related to the characteristics of future challengers.

> It is true that the challenger has eliminated all *presently available* rivals. But it has not eliminated *future* rivals. The latter, though at present mere potentialities, are important figures in the contest. For the current challenger can make good its claim to succeed the defender only *when there is no future challenger worth waiting for*. It must engage, as it were, in a two-front war, attacking on one side the aged machine it hopes to dislodge and on the other an array of rivals still unborn who also hope to dislodge the same aged machine, but later.[3]

The MAPI analysis emphasizes the importance of future capital equipment:

> For since the choice between living machines can be made only by reference to the machines of tomorrow, the latter remain, whether we like it or not, an indispensable element in the calculation. It may be said . . . that the appraisal of the ghosts involved is the heart of the . . . analysis. No replacement theory, no formula, no rule of thumb that fails to take cognizance of these ghosts and to assess their role in the play can lay claim to rational justification.[4]

---

[3] Ibid., p. 55.
[4] Ibid., p. 57.

In order to deal with these problems Terborgh proposed two "standard" assumptions on the basis that "The best the analyst can do is to start with a set of standard assumptions and shade the results of their application as his judgment dictates."[5] In other words, if we have information we will use it; if not, we will employ reasonable standard assumptions.

ADVERSE MINIMUM

The key to the MAPI method is the "adverse minimum" for the capital project. This is defined as the lowest combined time-adjusted average of capital cost and operating inferiority that can be obtained by keeping the project in service the number of years necessary to reach this minimum, and no longer.

FIRST STANDARD ASSUMPTION

Future challengers will have the same adverse minimum as the present one.[6]

SECOND STANDARD ASSUMPTION

The present challenger will accumulate operating inferiority at a constant rate over its service life.[7]

The first standard assumption is justified on the basis that there is no alternative that is more reasonable. In the absence of information to the contrary, what compulsion is there for us to assume that future challengers will have either higher or lower adverse minima? If we have information that leads us to believe that future challengers will have different adverse minima, then we may modify the standard assumption. Furthermore, this standard assumption facilitates developing a simpler replacement formula than would be otherwise possible.

The second standard assumption again is justified on the basis of methodological necessity, since the analyst typically does not have data on a sufficient sample size of similar equipment to make a more reasonable assumption. In the absence of information to the contrary, the best we can do is predict the future by extrapolation from the present and past experiences on the basis that there are elements of continuity and recurrence that will be repeated into the future. If we were to reject entirely this continuity and recurrence over time, we would be utterly incapable of dealing with the future in all but those situations in which change is at least dimly visible on the horizon.

APPLICATION OF THE MAPI METHOD

To apply the MAPI method to a potential challenger, we require an estimate of the firm's cost of capital, the cost of the project, and an estimate of the project's first-year accumulation of operating inferiority. From this information we derive the

[5] Ibid., p. 60.
[6] Ibid., p. 64.
[7] Ibid., p. 65.

110 SPECIAL TOPICS AND METHODS

adverse minima of potential challengers, thereby selecting the project with the lowest adverse minimum as *the* challenger. The adverse minimum of the defender, if there is existing capital equipment that may be replaced by the challenger, is determined similarly. In many cases the defender will be found to have already passed the point in time at which its adverse minimum occurs. In such cases Terborgh has recommended that the next-year total of capital cost and operating inferiority be used as the defender's adverse minimum.

Let us assume the firm's cost of capital is 15 percent per annum, and that we have an existing machine (defender) that will have a combined capital cost and operating inferiority of $70,000. There is only one potential challenger. It costs $100,000 and is estimated to accumulate operating inferiority during the first year of service amounting to $7000. Application of the second standard assumption means we assume operating inferiority will be accumulated at $7000 each year the challenger would be in service. We ignore salvage value for now to simplify the exposition. Table 9.1 illustrates the technique of finding the challenger's adverse minimum.

Since the adverse minimum of the challenger of $41,105 per year if held six years is substantially lower than the next-year operating inferiority of the defender, we would replace the defender this year. In fact, even if the challenger were to be replaced itself at the end of the second year of its service by a still better but yet unbuilt new challenger, the decision would still be correct. If kept in service two years, the challenger costs $64,760, whereas the defender will cost $70,000 next year and, if it continues to accumulate operating inferiority, still more the following year. The figures in column 8 of Table 9.1 are average annual costs, adjusted for the time-value of money. The lowest of these, as stated earlier, is the adverse minimum.

The time-adjusted annual average costs are composed of a capital cost component that declines over time, and an operating inferiority component that increases over time. For the project analyzed in Table 9.1, capital cost declines rapidly in the early years of the project's life, whereas operating inferiority rises rapidly. Therefore, this challenger will obtain its adverse minimum in only six years. Some projects may not reach their adverse minimum for many years. For instance, management may have a policy of abandoning equipment at the end of, say, 15 years regardless of its condition. In such an environment the adverse minimum may not be reached. However, if the time-adjusted annual average cost declines constantly, we may then take the last year of service's value as our adverse minimum. Of course, as we go into the future further and further, the reliability of the two standard assumptions employed in the beginning begins to wane. Thus, other things being equal, we would prefer a challenger that reached its adverse minimum within just a few years to one that took 15 or 20 years to reach it.

Figure 9.1 illustrates graphically how the adverse minimum is determined as the minimum point on the total cost function, which is the vertical sum of the individual costs of the component functions for capital cost and for operating inferiority. Readers who are familiar with the derivation of the basic economic order quantity model will note some similarity of the graphs.

Table 9-1. DERIVATION OF THE ADVERSE MINIMUM OF A CHALLENGER COSTING $100,000 WITH INFERIORITY GRADIENT OF $7000 A YEAR. ASSUMES NO CAPITAL ADDITIONS AND NO SALVAGE VALUE. COST OF CAPITAL IS 15%.

Year of Service	(1) Operating Infr[a] for Year Indicated	(2) Present Worth Factor for Year Indicated	(3) Present Worth of Operating Infr[a] (1) × (2)	(4) Present Worth of Operating Infr Accm[b] (3) Accm	(5) Capital Recovery Factor for Year Indicated	(6) Operating Infr[a] (4) × (5)	(7) Capital Cost (5) × $100,000	(8) Both Combined (6) + (7)
1	$ 0	.86957	$ 0	$ 0	1.15000	$ 0	$115,000	$115,000
2	7,000	.75614	5,293	5,293	.61512	3,256	61,512	64,760
3	14,000	.65752	9,205	14,498	.43798	6,350	43,798	50,148
4	21,000	.57175	12,007	26,505	.35027	9,284	35,027	44,311
5	28,000	.49718	13,921	40,426	.29832	12,060	29,832	41,892
6	35,000	.43233	15,132	55,558	.26424	14,681	26,424	41,105[c]
7	42,000	.37594	15,789	71,346	.24036	17,149	24,036	41,185
8	49,000	.32690	16,018	87,364	.22285	19,469	22,285	41,754
9	56,000	.28426	15,919	103,283	.20957	21,645	20,957	42,602
10	63,000	.24718	15,572	118,855	.19925	23,682	19,925	43,607
11	70,000	.21494	15,046	133,901	.19107	25,584	19,107	44,691
12	77,000	.18691	14,392	148,293	.18448	27,357	18,448	45,805

[a] Infr = inferiority
[b] Accm = accumulated
[c] Adverse minimum

Figure 9.1 Graphic representation of columns 7, 8, and 9 of Table 9-1. Time-adjusted annual averages for period ending with year indicated.

The Problem of Capacity Disparities

The existence of alternatives that provide for different production capacities requires some modification to the MAPI method. Assume that the defender, having a next-year operating inferiority of $50,000, is capable of producing 10,000 units of output annually. Assume further that potential challengers A and B have respective adverse minima of $500,000 and $1 million and annual production capabilities of 150,000 and 400,000 units.

At first glance it would appear that the defender should not be replaced, for it has the lowest adverse minimum (next-year operating inferiority). However, if we express the adverse minima in terms of the units of annual production, we find that alternative B promises the lowest cost *per unit* (see Table 9.2).

Now we see that the ordering of the per unit costs is the opposite of the ordering of the adverse minima for the three alternatives. Which should be selected? The answer depends on the firm's annual production requirements. For instance, if the firm requires that 35,000 units be produced each year, then the cost per unit will be $14.28 with alternative A and $28.57 with alternative B. The defender alone cannot produce more than 10,000 units annually. However, if exact duplicates of the defender may be acquired (with the same adverse minimum as the defender), then we would need to add three machines. This would raise capacity to 40,000 units in total—5000 more than required. The cost per unit will be $5.71, which is much less than the per unit costs of machines A and B.

Table 9-2. COMPARISON OF ALTERNATIVES

Machine	Adverse Minimum	Annual Production Capability	Cost per Unit
Defender	$ 50,000	10,000	$5.00
Alternative A	500,000	150,000	3.33
Alternative B	1,000,000	400,000	2.50

Therefore, adverse minima in themselves are meaningless unless the alternative machines have the same annual productive capacity. If they do not, it is necessary to make adjustments. Cost should be expressed in terms of cost *per unit*, since to do otherwise may lead to improper selection of the challenger and on to a wrong replacement decision. And the cost per unit must be based on the firm's requirements, not on the rated machine capacities that may be lesser or greater than the production required by the firm.

CONCLUSION

The MAPI method of capital equipment analysis provides an alternative means of investment evaluation that is based on minimization of costs. It is thus, in a sense, a dual formulation of methods based on maximization of some measure of investment return such as the discounted cash flow (DCF) measures.

Because the MAPI method is based on cost minimization, it is suitable for analysis of projects where the DCF measures are much more difficult, if not impossible, to apply. Such projects are those this author has defined as component projects—they do not have cash revenues directly attributable to them alone. For these projects the cash inflows may be assumed invariant with respect to the production equipment employed, whereas cash costs will vary directly with respect to the choice of equipment. The MAPI method, unlike the DCF methods, requires no estimates of cash inflows. Instead it requires cost estimates that often may be provided more easily, and provided by those personnel whose experience in production promises they may be the best obtainable estimates. Conversely, revenue estimates for component projects are likely to be based on tenuous premises if not pure guesses.

Proper application of the MAPI method requires that the adverse minima of alternative projects be adjusted to reflect production capacity differences or the firm's production requirements. Otherwise the per unit cost of one alternative may be greater than that of another even though it may have a lower adverse minimum.

QUESTIONS

1. The MAPI method is not really a dual formulation of the model of maximization of discounted cash flows because it is concerned with minimization of actual cash costs, not shadow prices or opportunity costs. Comment on this statement.
2. Why must the MAPI adverse minima be adjusted to reflect volume or capacity differences between capital investment projects?

114 SPECIAL TOPICS AND METHODS

3. If projects in fact do not generally follow the two basic MAPI assumptions, why are the assumptions nevertheless useful? How may the MAPI method be adjusted for projects that deviate from one or both of the standard assumptions?
4. Review the critical article by Joel Dean and Winfield Smith, "Has MAPI a Place in a Comprehensive System of Capital Controls?," *Journal of Business* (October 1955); and the reply of George Terborgh, "Some Comments on the Dean-Smith Article on the MAPI Formula," *Journal of Business* (April 1956). What is your evaluation of the articles? Both are reprinted in Ezra Solomon, ed., *The Management of Corporate Capital* (New York: Free Press, 1959).
5. Why is the MAPI method especially useful for evaluating component projects? Is it as indispensable in the initial accept/reject decision for major project analysis? Explain.
6. Explain why capital cost declines as a capital investment is held for additional time periods, whereas operating inferiority increases.
7. Contrast the concept of *capital cost* with that of cost of capital presented in Chapter 4. Can you devise a terminology that is less confusing and as meaningful?
8. For what reasons would you attribute the widespread neglect of the MAPI method in texts dealing with financial management and particularly capital budgeting?
9. Is the MAPI method appropriate to public sector capital investment analysis (referred to as "cost/benefit analysis")?

PROBLEMS

9.1 The ABZ Company owns five gear cutting machines that are used for cutting splines on power-take-off shafts, and similar parts that it supplies to a large-order customer. The machines have a combined estimated next-year operating inferiority of $15,000. One of the firm's engineers proposes replacing these machines with a single spline-rolling machine which promises to quadruple the current capacity of 100,000 splines per year. The new machine would cost $75,000 and accumulate a first-year operating inferiority of $3 thousand. The firm's cost of capital has been determined to be 12 percent per annum. The firm's management estimates that it will need to cut or roll 350,000 splines next year if it accepts a contract that has been offered by a new customer. Should the replacement be made? How would you answer if additional new gear cutting machines were available for $15,000 each? What if the firm's cost of capital were 5 percent per year? 18 percent?
9.2 Calculate the capital cost for each of years one through five of a machine that costs $100,000. Assume a 10 percent annual cost of capital.
9.3 Calculate the level annuities equivalent to the following costs in years one through five at a 10 percent annual cost of capital: $500, $1500, $300, $3000, $200. Carefully interpret the results you obtain. Explain the difference between these calculations and those used to calculate capital cost in Problem 9.2.
9.4 Your company is considering expansion into manufacture of a new line of products, for which combined sales are estimated to be 500,000 units annually. It is determined that the machining cost per unit cannot exceed $1.76. Two alternatives are being considered. Alternative A is a package of five machines, each capable of producing 100,000 units annually. Labor cost per unit is determined

to be 16 cents with this process and each machine costs $100,000. Alternative B is a single machine costing $550,000 and is capable of producing 700,000 units annually. Per unit labor cost with this machine is determined to be 9 cents. The company has a 12 percent annual cost of capital. Ignore other costs and salvage values. The physical lives are expected to exceed 15 years, and alternative A will have a first-year operating inferiority of $30,000, whereas B's is $31,000. Should the expansion be undertaken? If so, which alternative should be selected? What if sales may be expected to grow to 600,000 units after two years? Fall to 300,000 units?

9.5 Perform a sensitivity analysis of the changes in adverse minimum for different costs of capital ranging from 5 percent to 25 percent. For this purpose, use a capital project with $100,000 cost, 25-year maximum life, and first-year operating inferiority of $10,000. How would your results change if the first-year operating inferiority were $20,000? $40,000?

Bibliography

1. Dean, Joel, and Winfield Smith, "Has MAPI a Place in a Comprehensive System of Capital Controls?," *Journal of Business* (October 1955).
2. Terborgh, George, *Dynamic Equipment Policy* (Washington: Machinery and Allied Products Institute, 1949).
3. ————, *MAPI Replacement Manual* (Washington: Machinery and Allied Products Institute, 1950).
4. ————, "Some Comments on the Dean-Smith Article on the MAPI Formula," *Journal of Business* (April 1956).
5. ————, *Business Investment Analysis* (Washington: Machinery and Allied Products Institute, 1958).
6. ————, *Studies in the Analysis of Business Investment Projects* (Washington: Machinery and Allied Products Institute), consisting of a set of six volumes dated 1960 to 1961.
7. ————, *Studies in Business Investment Strategy* (Washington: Machinery and Allied Products Institute), consisting of a set beginning in 1963.
8. ————, *Business Investment Management* (Washington: Machinery and Allied Products Institute, 1967).

Chapter 10
The Problem of Mixed Cash Flows: I

When the internal rate of return (IRR) was discussed in Chapter 6, a restriction was placed on the cash flows that assured there would be only one real IRR in the range −100 percent to ∞—that there be only one change in the arithmetic sign in the flows. In this chapter the restriction is removed, the consequences examined, and a method analyzed that is claimed to provide a unique measure of return on investment.

INTERNAL RATE OF RETURN DEFICIENCIES

Under certain circumstances the IRR may not be unique, and thus we would seem to have to decide which, if any, of the IRR is a correct measure of return on investment. As we shall see, when there are two or more IRRs, none of them is a correct measure of return on investment.

The difficulties with IRR arise because of mixed cash flows. We define mixed cash flows as existing whenever a project has more than one change in arithmetic sign. There must, of course, be one change in sign for us to find any IRR. However, when there is more than one change in sign, the IRR, even if unique, may not measure the return on investment.

Figure 10.1 Net present value.

Example 10.1

Let us consider the following capital-budgeting project, for which we have mixed cash flows of:

$t = 0$	$t = 1$	$t = 3$
−$100	+$320	−$240

This project has two IRRs: 20 percent and 100 percent. The net present value (NPV) is positive for any cost of capital greater than 20 percent but less than 100 percent. Figure 10.1 illustrates the NPV function for this project. The NPV reaches a maximum of $6.25 for a cost of capital of 60 percent. The profitability index (PI) of .0625 (or 1.0625 by the common, alternative definition of PI) is not likely to cause much enthusiasm, but let us retain this example for further analysis.

DESCARTES' RULE

Descartes' rule of signs states that the number of unique, positive, real roots to a polynomial equation with real coefficients (such as the equation for IRR) must be less than or equal to the number of sign changes between the coefficients. If less than the number of sign changes, the number of positive,[1] real roots must be less by any even number, since complex roots come in conjugate pairs, and an nth degree polynomial will have n roots, not necessarily distinct.

---

[1] We are interested in positive, real roots since in solving any given polynomial, we will find the values of $x = 1 + r$, where r is the IRR value in decimal form. Therefore, after solving for the roots of the IRR polynomial, we must make the transformation $r_j = x_j - 1$ for each root, $j = 1, \ldots, n$. Since we work with all net cash flows attributable to the particular project, we therefore cannot lose more than 100 percent or our investment. Thus limiting the r_j to ≥ -1.00 restricts the x_j to ≥ 0.

Example 10.2

The following cash flows yield a third-degree IRR polynomial equation:

$t = 0$	$t = 1$	$t = 2$	$t = 3$
−$1000	+$3800	−$4730	+$1936

The IRR equation is (dropping $):

$$-1000 + 3800(1 + r)^{-1} - 4730(1 + r)^{-2} + 1936(1 + r)^{-3} = 0 \qquad (10.1)$$

or, alternatively, by multiplying by $(1 + r)^3$ to put into future value form, then dividing by 1000 and letting $x = 1 + r$:

$$1x^3 - 3.8x^2 + 4.73x - 1.936 = 0 \qquad (10.2)$$

This equation has three real roots, one with a multiplicity of two (double root). The roots are 10 percent, 10 percent, and 60 percent, which we can verify by generating the equation by multiplication and by comparing with Eq. (10.2). If $r = 10$ percent $= .10$, then $x = 1.1$ and $x - 1.1$ is a zero (root) to the equation. Similarly, $x - 1.6$ is a zero to the equation. Multiplying, we obtain:

$$\begin{array}{r} x - 1.1 \\ \underline{x - 1.1} \\ x^2 - 2.2x + 1.21 \\ \underline{x - 1.6} \\ x^3 - 2.2x^2 + 1.21x \\ \underline{-1.6x^2 + 3.52x - 1.936} \\ x^3 - 3.8x^2 + 4.73x - 1.936 \end{array} \qquad (10.3)$$

which is identical to Eq. (10.2).

We shall leave the matter of multiple roots now, because, as we shall see, when a project has mixed cash flows, even a unique, real IRR is no assurance that the IRR is a correct measure of investment return.

THE TEICHROEW, ROBICHEK, AND MONTALBANO (TRM) ANALYSIS

Teichroew [10], and later Teichroew, Robichek, and Montalbano (TRM) [11, 12] explained that the existence of multiple IRR provided a meaningful interpretation, and proposed an algorithm for determining a unique measure of return on invested capital (RIC). James C. T. Mao [8] was the first to offer a lucid summary of the main points of the TRM work, and his work is still a valuable reference on the topic.

The analysis of TRM realized that projects with mixed cash flows may be neither clearly investments nor clearly financing projects. If, for example, the firm makes a loan, the cash flow sequence will be − + + ··· + + if the loan is amortized with periodic payments. This is identical to a capital investment with the same net cash flows. From the viewpoint of the borrower (or the capital asset, if we can attribute a viewpoint), the cash flow sequence will be the negative of our firm's: + − − ⋯ − −. Depending on whether we view the cash flow sequence through the firm's eyes or those of the borrower, we have what is unambiguously either an investment or a financing project. Since there is only one change in sign between the cash flows, we know the IRR will be unique.

Now, what if we have instead a cash flow sequence of − + + − +, or + − − + − +? Can we say a priori that we have an investment or a financing project based only on examining the signs of the cash flows? The answer is no, we cannot. The TRM analysis recognizes that some projects with mixed cash flows have attributes of *both* investment and financing projects. The returns on such projects are not, as the IRR method assumes, independent of the firm's cost of capital. To understand the TRM analysis, we need to define some terms.

DEFINITIONS

Let

$$a_0, a_1, \ldots, a_n$$

denote the project cash flows.

Let

$$s_t(r) = \sum_{i=0}^{t} a_i(1+r)^i, \quad 0 \leq t < n,$$

and

$$s_t(r) = (1+r)s_{t-1}(r)$$

denote the *project balance* equations, and

$$s_n(r) = \sum_{i=0}^{n} a_i(1+r)^i$$

denote the *future value* of the project.

The minimum rate is $r_{\min}$ for which all the project balance equations are less than or equal to zero: $s_t(r_{\min}) \leq 0$ for $0 < t < n$.

The project balance at the end of period t, at rate r, is interpreted as the future value of (1) the amount the firm has invested in the project or (2) the firm has received from the project from period zero to the end of period t. By using TRM's classifications, *at rate r*, the following occur:

1. If $s_t(r) \leq 0$ for $0 \leq t < n$, we have a *pure investment project*.
2. If $s_t(r) \geq 0$ for $0 \leq t < n$, we have a *pure financing project*.
3. If $s_t(r) \leq 0$ for *some* t, $s_t(r) > 0$ for *some* t, and $0 \leq t < n$, we have a *mixed project*.

A *simple project* is one in which the sign of a_0 is different from the sign of a_i for all $i > 0$. In a mixed project, the firm has money invested in the project during some periods, and "owes" the project money during some other periods.

120 SPECIAL TOPICS AND METHODS

It can be shown that all simple investments are pure investments. However, the converse is not true: Not all pure investments are simple investments.

Let us follow TRM's notation in using PFR to denote the *project financing rate*, the rate applied for periods in which the project can be viewed as providing funds to the firm; that is, as a net financing source, with positive project balance. We use k, the firm's cost of capital for PFR, and PIR to denote the *project investment rate*, $r°$ (TRM use r for this), the rate that the project yields when the project balance is negative. We also refer to the PIR as the RIC, the *return on invested capital*.

To determine the PIR, or RIC, we proceed as follows, first negating all cash flows if $a_0 > 0$:

$$\begin{aligned}
s_0(r, k) &= a_0 \\
s_1(r, k) &= (1 + r)a_0 + a_1 \quad &&\text{if } s_0 < 0 \\
&= (1 + k)a_0 + a_1 \quad &&\text{if } s_0 \geq 0 \\
s_2(r, k) &= (1 + r)a_1 + a_2 \quad &&\text{if } s_1 < 0 \\
&\vdots \quad = (1 + k)a_1 + a_2 \quad &&\text{if } s_0 \geq 0 \\
s_n(r, k) &= (1 + r)a_{n-1} + a_n \quad &&\text{if } s_{n-1} < 0 \\
&= (1 + k)a_{n-1} + a_n \quad &&\text{if } s_{n-1} \geq 0
\end{aligned}$$

In order to find whether, for any $j (0 < j \leq n)$, $s_j(r, k) < 0$ or ≥ 0, we substitute r_{min} for r in evaluating it. Since we will use an estimate of the firm's cost of capital for k, the only unknown in $s_n(r, k)$ is r. We solve this equation for r, and since the solution is a particular value, the RIC, we refer to it as $r°$.

Note that because r_{min} is defined as the smallest real root for which all the project balance equations, $s_t(r_{min})$, are ≤ 0, with $0 \leq t < n$, it is a_n which determines whether the project is pure or mixed. If $s_n(r_{min}) \geq 0$, a greater discount rate r, one for which $s_n(r_{min}) = 0$, will retain the condition that $s_t(r) \leq 0$ for $0 \leq t < n$. In this case, the r for which $s_n(r) = 0$ will be the $r°$ of the project. It will also be the IRR of the project. *From this it follows that the IRR is found by assuming that the project financing rate equals the project investment rate*, so that k does not enter the equation for IRR. In general, this will not be a correct assumption. However, it does not affect our results when $s_n(r, k) = s_n(r)$, a condition we have for all pure investments. *In other words, for pure investments only*, $r° = IRR$, *and k does not affect $r°$: the IRR is "internal" to the project.*

THE TRM ALGORITHM

The foregoing leads to an algorithm for determining the RIC on an investment, either simple or with mixed cash flows. The steps of the algorithm are:

    I. If $a_0 > 0$, negate all cash flows before beginning. Find r_{min}, the minimum real rate for which all the project balance equations, $s_t(r_{min})$ are ≤ 0, for $0 \leq t < n$.

    II. Evaluate $s_n(r_{min})$.

        (1) If $s_n(r_{min}) \geq 0$, then $s_t(r, k) = s_t(r)$ and $r°$ equals the unique IRR as traditionally found.

(2) If $s_n(r_{min}) < 0$, then we proceed to step III.

III. Let k be the firm's cost of capital.

$$\begin{aligned}
s_0 &= a_0 \\
s_1 &= (1 + r)a_0 + a_1 \quad \text{if } s_0 < 0 \\
&= (1 + k)a_0 + a_1 \quad \text{if } s_0 \geq 0 \\
s_2 &= (1 + r)a_1 + a_2 \quad \text{if } s_1 < 0 \\
&= (1 + k)a_1 + a_2 \quad \text{if } s_1 \geq 0 \\
&\vdots \\
s_n &= (1 + r)a_{n-1} + a_n \quad \text{if } s_{n-1} < 0 \\
&(1 + k)a_{n-1} + a_n \quad \text{if } s_{n-1} \geq 0
\end{aligned}$$

In every $s_t(r, k)$, use r_{min} for r to determine whether the project balance is less than zero or greater than or equal to zero.

IV. Solve $s_n(r, k)$ for unique r; call this $r°$, the return on invested capital.

Note that the return on invested capital $r°$ may be the IRR, but in general will not be.

Example 10.3

Let us now take up the project discussed earlier, which had cash flows:

$t = 0$	$t = 1$	$t = 2$
−$100	+$320	−$240

and apply the TRM algorithm.

I. Find r_{min}:

$$-100(1 + r) + 320 = 0$$
$$r = 3.2 - 1 = 2.2 \text{ or } 220\%$$
$$r_{min} = r \quad \text{(In this example there is only one project balance equation.)}$$

II. Evaluate

$$\begin{aligned}
s_n(r_{min}) &= -100(1 + r)^2 + 320(1 + r) - 240 \\
&= -240
\end{aligned}$$
$$-240 < 0$$

So we have a mixed investment.

III. Let k be the firm's cost of capital:

$$\begin{aligned}
s_0 &= a_0 = -100 < 0 \\
s_1 &= s_0(1 + r) + a_1 \quad \text{since } s_0 < 0 \\
&= 0 \quad \text{when evaluated for } r = r_{min} \\
s_2 &= s_1(1 + k) + a_2 \quad \text{since } s_1 \geq 0 \\
&= -100(1 + r)(1 + k) + 320(1 + k) - 240
\end{aligned}$$

IV. Solve for $r° = r$:

$$1 + r = \frac{320(1 + k) - 240}{100(1 + k)} \tag{10.4}$$

122 SPECIAL TOPICS AND METHODS

Figure 10.2 r^* function of k.

$$r^\circ = r = 2.2 - \frac{2.4}{1+k} \tag{10.5}$$

Under the IRR assumption of $r = k$, we find that

$$r = 2.2 - \frac{2.4}{1+r}$$
$$r^2 - 1.2r + .2 = 0$$

and, using the quadratic formula,

$$r = \frac{1.2 \pm \sqrt{1.44 - .8}}{2} = \frac{1.2 \pm .8}{2}$$
$$= 1.0, .20$$
$$= 100\%, 20\%$$

What if $r \neq k$? Figure 10.2 shows the function for r° in terms of k. The figure shows clearly that for only two values of k will $r^\circ = k$ for this project. Under the rule that we accept a project if $r^\circ > k$ and reject if $r^\circ \leq k$, this project is acceptable for the same values of k that we found with the NPV criterion.

Example 10.4

For a second application of the TRM algorithm let us take the project considered earlier that had cash flows:

$t = 0$	$t - 1$	$t = 2$	$t = 3$
$-\$1000$	$+\$3800$	$-\$4730$	$+\$1936$

I. Find $r_{\min}$:
(1) $-1000(1 + r) + 3800 = 0$

$r_1 = 3.8 - 1 + 2.8$ or 280%
(2) $-1000(1 + r)^2 + 3800(1 + r) - 4730 = 0$

$$r_2 = \frac{-3.8 \pm \sqrt{(3.8)^2 - (4)(4.73)}}{-2}$$
$$= \text{complex roots}$$

Therefore, $r_{min} = 2.8 = r_1$.

II. Evaluate $s_n(r_{min})$:

$$s_n(r_{min}) = -1000(3.8)^3 + 3800(3.8)^2 - 4730(3.8) + 1936$$
$$= -16{,}038 < 0$$

Hence this is a *mixed project*.

III. Let k be the firm's cost of capital:

$$s_0 = a_0 = -1000 < 0$$
$$s_1 = s_0(1 + r) + a_1 = 0$$
$$\quad = -1000(1 + r) + 3800 = 0 \text{ at } r = r_{min}$$
$$s_2 = s_1(1 + k) + a_2$$
$$\quad = -1000(1 + r)(1 + k) + 3800(1 + k) - 4730$$
$$\quad < 0 \quad \text{at } r = r_{min}$$
$$s_3 = -1000(1 + r)^2(1 + k) + 3800(1 + r)(1 + k) - 4730(1 + r) + 1936$$

IV. Solve for $r° = r$:

This yields a fairly complicated expression for r in terms of k, although for a specific value of k, the solution can be easily accomplished with the quadratic formula. The expression for k in terms of r is:

$$k = \frac{1.936 - 4.73(1 + r)}{(1 + r)^2 - 3.8(1 + r)} - 1 \tag{10.6}$$

from which we may generate values of k corresponding to various $r° = r$ and plot the function (see Figure 10.3).

Note that $r°$ is a double-valued function of k. Since we cannot lose more than we have invested in the project,[2] values of $r < -100$ percent are not economically meaningful and may thus be ignored. We cannot lose more than 100 percent of what we invest in the project, because the cash flows reflect the total effect of the project on the firm; *all* costs and revenues attributable to the project are incorporated in the cash flows. At 10 percent, a double root to the IRR equation, it is interesting that the function touches, but does not cross, the $r° = k$-axis. This project is acceptable for $0 \leq k < 10$ percent and 10 percent $< k < 60$ percent, the same as by the NPV criterion. The NPV function is shown in Figure 10.4.

---

[2] We are still assuming project independence in this chapter.

124 SPECIAL TOPICS AND METHODS

Figure 10.3 r^* as function of k.

Figure 10.4 NPV function.

Example 10.5

Let us now solve for the RIC of a project having cash flows in six periods:

$t = 0$	$t = 1$	$t = 2$	$t = 3$	$t = 4$	$t = 5$
$-\$100$	$+\$600$	$-\$1509$	$+\$2027$	$-\$1436$	$+\$418$

This project has real IRR values of 0 percent, 10 percent, and 90 percent. The IRR equation also has complex roots of $0 + i$ and $0 - i$.

I. Find $r_{\min}$:
(1) $-100(1 + r) + 600 = 0$
$r_1 = r = 5$ or 500%

(2) $-100(1 + r)^2 + 600(1 + r) - 1509 = 0$
$$r = \frac{-600 \pm \sqrt{(600)^2 - (4)(-100)(-1509)}}{-200}$$

Since r is a complex root, skip r_2.

(3) We can approach this in two ways. First, we could solve the equation:
$$-100(1 + r)^3 + 600(1 + r)^2 - 1509(1 + r) + 2027$$

after setting it equal to zero. This is a laborious process, conducive to errors in calculations, unless we use a computer program. Even in this case there may be time lost in accessing a computer and waiting for results. Once we did find r we would set $r_3 = r$. The second approach may save us this trouble.

Let us substitute the r_{min} thus far obtained—$r_1 = 500$ percent. If this equation value is less than zero for r_1, we do not need to solve for the value of r_3. Using this approach, we find the equation value is -32.53, so we need not solve for r_3.

(4) As in (3), we could solve for r in the equation:
$$-100(1 + r)^4 + 600(1 + r)^3 - 1509(1 + r)^2 + 2027(1 + r) - 1436$$

after setting it equal to zero. But again, let us first try the second approach. We obtain a value of -33.64; so again we need not solve for r_3.

We have found that $r_{min} = r_1 = 500$ percent, since for this rate, and no lesser rate, all project balance equations are less than or equal to zero.

II. Evaluate $s_n(r_{min})$:
$$s_n(r_{min}) = -100(6)^5 + 600(6)^4 - 1509(6)^3 + 2027(6)^2 - 1436(6) + 418$$
$$= -33.59 < 0$$

So this is a mixed project.

III. Let k be the firm's cost of capital:
$s_0 = a_0 = -100$
$s_1 = -100(1 + r) + 600 = 0$ at $r = r_{min}$
$s_2 = -100(1 + r)(1 + k) + 600(1 + k) - 1509 < 0$
$s_3 = -100(1 + r)^2(1 + k) + 600(1 + r)(1 + k) - 1509(1 + r) + 2027 < 0$
$s_4 = -100(1 + r)^3(1 + k) + 600(1 + r)^2(1 + k) - 1509(1 + r)^2 + 2027(1 + r) - 1436 < 0$
$s_5 = -100(1 + r)^4(1 + k) + 600(1 + r)^3(1 + k) - 1509(1 + r)^3 + 2027(1 + r)^2 - 1436(1 + r) + 418$

IV. Solve for $r° = r$.

Because this involves solution of a fourth degree equation, we will present the solutions for $k = 15$ percent and $k = 25$ percent. At $k = 15$ percent, $r° = r = 15.08$ percent, and the project is marginally acceptable. At $k = 25$ percent, $r° = r = 25.28$ percent, and again the project is marginally acceptable.

THE UNIQUE, REAL INTERNAL RATE OF RETURN: CAVEAT EMPTOR![3]

The internal rate of return (IRR), even when unique and real, may nevertheless be an incorrect measure of the return on investment. All projects characterized by negative flows occurring only at the beginning and the end will be mixed investments for which the IRR, whether unique and real or not, is not a correct measure of investment return.

Several years ago, W. H. Jean [5] proved that for capital-budgeting projects in which only the first and last cash flows were negative that there would be a unique, real, positive internal rate of return or no positive IRR. J. Hirschleifer [4] subsequently showed that if the sum of cash flows beyond the first was less than or equal to the first cash flow, the multiple IRRs can exist for the project. This prompted Professor Jean [6] to extend his treatment, and further specify the conditions for unique IRR for such cases as Hirschleifer cited.

Although Jean's results are mathematically interesting, they do not take into account the way in which such projects violate the assumption of independence between the IRR and the firm's cost of capital, which destroys the economic meaningfullness of the resulting IRR. The conditions under which the IRR of a project may not be independent of the firm's cost of capital have been widely ignored in the literature, one noteworthy exception being Mao's text [9]. Jean's article and examples are cited here for purposes of illustration, since his article is mathematically rigorous.

However, mathematical uniqueness of a real root to the traditional IRR equation is, although a *necessary* condition, nevertheless not a *sufficient* condition to insure that one has obtained a rate independent of the firm's cost of capital, and thus a measure of investment return "internal" to the cash flow of the project. In fact, we shall prove that in the case of a project with negative flows only at beginning and end, for which Professor Jean proved a unique, positive IRR can always be found, that the IRR will *never* (excluding rare events in which the firm's cost of capital is the same as the rate r_{min}, which is discussed later) be independent of the firm's cost of capital.

The TRM Algorithm Applied to Jean and Hirschleifer Cases

A theorem will be proved later that has two corollaries relating to the discussion of Professors Jean and Hirschleifer. First, however, the examples provided by Jean [5] and Hirschleifer [4] will be analyzed within the framework provided by TRM. A cost of capital $k = 10$ percent will be assumed for all cases.

Case 1 Cash flows are $-1, 5, -6$ (Hirschleifer; in Jean [5], case 2a).
  IRR = $-100\%, 200\%$
  $r_{min} = 400\%$

---

[3]Reprinted with permission of *Journal of Financial and Quantitative Analysis,* Copyright ©1978. With Corrections.

$$s_n(r_{min}) = -6 < 0$$

Hence this is a mixed investment.

$$s_0 = a_0 = -1 < 0$$
$$s_1 = s_0(1 + r°) + a_1$$
$$= -1(1 + r°) + 5 = 0 \quad \text{(using } r_{min} \text{ for } r°)$$
$$s_2 = s_1(1 + k) + a_2$$
$$= -1(1 + r°)(1 + k) + 5(1 + k) - 6$$

Therefore $r° = -145.45\%$, the rate for which $S_2 = 0$

Case 2 First m inflows are negative (in Jean, case 1a). Cash flows are $-5, -1, 2, 2$.

$$\text{IRR} = -15.9\%$$
$$r_{min} = -45.9\%$$
$$s_n(r_{min}) = +2 > 0$$

Hence this is a pure investment and the IRR is a unique, real measure of project return, independent of k.

Case 3 In middle life, m inflows are negative (in Jean, case 3a). Cash flows are $-1, 2, -4, 2$.

$$\text{IRR} = -36.0\%$$
$$r_{min} = 100\%$$
$$s_n(r_{min}) = -6 < 0$$

Hence this is a mixed project.

$$s_0 = a_0 = -1 < 0$$
$$s_1 = s_0(1 + r°) + a_1$$
$$= -1(1 + r°) + 2 = 0 \quad \text{(using } r_{min} \text{ for } r°)$$
$$s_2 = -1(1 + r°)(1 + k) + 2(1 + k) - 4 < 0$$
$$s_3 = s_2(1 + r°) + a_3$$
$$= -1(1 + r°)^2(1 + k) + 2(1 + r°)(1 + k) - 4(1 + r°) + 2$$
$$r° = -24.09\%, \quad \text{the rate for which } s_3 = 0$$

Of the three cases considered, only Case 2 has a return "internal" to the project. Case 1 has two IRRs and thus the IRR is not only an incorrect measure of investment return, but also ambiguous. Case 3 has a unique, real IRR. However, it is not a proper measure of return on investment. *This is a crucial criticism of the IRR—even though it may be unique and real in the mathematical sense, this in itself is not a sufficient condition for it to be a correct measure of return on investment.*

An example presented by Professor Mao [9] vividly emphasizes this point in Case 4.

Case 4 Cash flows are $-10, +40, -40$.

$$\text{IRR} = 100\%$$
$$r_{min} = 300\%$$
$$s_n(r_{min}) = -40 < 0$$

Hence this is a mixed project.

$$s_0 = a_0 = -10 < 0$$
$$s_1 = s_0(1 + r°) + a_1$$

$$= -10(1 + r°) + 40 = 0 \quad (\text{using } r_{\min} = r°)$$
$$s_2 = s_1(1 + k) + a_2$$
$$= -10(1 + r°)(1 + k) + 40(1 + k) - 40$$
$$r° = -63.64\%, \quad \text{the rate for which } s_2 = 0$$

This is a mixed investment with return on invested capital of *minus* 63.64 percent, even though the project has a unique, real, positive IRR of 100 percent. Thus, use of the IRR would lead to acceptance of the project for any cost of capital $k < 100$ percent—a very undesirable consequence for a firm with normal financial management goals.

A NEW THEOREM

To generalize our findings, we now present a theorem that has significant implications on the class of investment projects with negative cash flows only at the beginning and the end.

THEOREM
Given that $a_0 < 0$, $a_n < 0$, $a_t \geq 0$ for $t = 1, \ldots, n-1$ with some $a_t > 0$ for a project, *the project will always be a mixed investment* (a mixed financing project[4] if $a_0 > 0$, $a_n > 0$, and $a_t \leq 0$ for $t = 1, \ldots, n-1$ with some $a_t < 0$).

Proof Since $a_0 < 0$, and $a_t \geq 0$ for $t = 1$ to $n - 1$, if we look only at the cash flows a_0 through a_{n-1}, they form in themselves a *simple investment* that TRM have proved has a unique, real rate r for which all the $s_t \leq 0$ for $t = 1, 2, \ldots, n-1$. In particular, $s_{n-1} = 0$. Therefore, this r is the $r_{\min}$ of the project, for any larger r would cause all s_t to be less than zero for $t \leq n - 1$.

In evaluating s_n at rate $r = r_{\min}$, we simply add a_n, which is less than zero to $(1 + r_{\min})s_{n-1}$, which is equal to zero. Then, since $s_n < 0$, we have a mixed investment as defined by TRM, and the project rate $r°$ is *not* independent of the firm's cost of capital.

COROLLARY I
If
$$a_t < 0 \quad \text{for } m < n - 1$$
and
$$a_n < 0$$
with
$$a_t \geq 0 \quad \text{for } m \leq t \leq n \quad \text{and some} \quad a_t > 0$$
then the project will be a mixed investment.

[4] In this case we negate all cash flows before applying the TRM algorithm.

Proof By similar argument to that of the theorem.

COROLLARY II
If

$$a_t < 0 \quad \text{for } t < m$$
$$a_t < 0 \quad \text{for } t > p$$

with

$$a_t \geq 0 \quad \text{for } m < t < p \quad \text{and some} \quad a_t > 0$$

where

$$0 < m < p < n$$

then the project will be a mixed investment.

Proof By similar argument to that of the theorem.

Strong Points of TRM Method

1. It is conceptually superior to the IRR and encompasses IRR as a special case.
2. Like other discounted cash flow (DCF) methods, the TRM method takes into account the time-value of funds and does not ignore any cash flows of the project.
3. It recognizes that some projects are neither entirely investments nor entirely financing endeavors.
4. It is consistent with the basic valuation model expressed in Chapter 2.
5. It provides a unique rate of return that management can examine and make judgment about when k is not known with confidence.

Weak Points of TRM Method

1. Like other DCF methods, it requires an estimate of the organization's cost of capital.
2. It is perhaps the most difficult method to apply because of the great computational burden.
3. The author's experience with computer programs that implement the algorithm indicates it is sensitive to even small rounding errors. In applications to large-scale practical problems, these errors may propagate to become serious errors that affect both final and intermediate results. Checking problems by hand that have large numbers of cash flows may not be feasible.
4. It does not distinguish between projects of different size and/or different economic lives.

130 SPECIAL TOPICS AND METHODS

QUESTIONS

1. What are the differences and the similarities between the IRR and the TRM return on investment?
2. How would you explain the concept of return on invested capital to operating management already familiar with the IRR?
3. Can the TRM method be applied to analysis of loans as well as investments? If so, must we make any modifications?
4. What relationship can be observed between the net present value and return on invested capital? (*Hint:* Look at corresponding graphs of the two functions.)

PROBLEMS

10.1 In the problems to Chapter 6 there was a project having cash flows (in $) of:

$t=0$	$t=1$	$t=2$
-10	50	-50

(a) Calculate the $r°$ of this project.
(b) Graph the function for $r°$ in terms of k.

10.2 A famous problem in capital-budgeting literature is that originally proposed by J. H. Lorie and L. J. Savage, and now known as the "Lorie and Savage 'pump' project." The cash flows (in $) are:

$t=0$	$t=1$	$t=2$
-1600	$10,000$	$-10,000$

(a) Calculate the $r°$ of this project
(b) Graph $r°$ as a function of k.

10.3 If a firm has 15 percent annual cost of capital, should it accept this capital-budgeting proposal? The cash flows (in $) are:

$t=0$	$t=1$	$t=2$	$t=3$
-1000	800	-900	1500

Explain your recommendation.

10.4 Calculate the rates of return on the investments having the following dollar cash flows, with $k = .15$:

	$t=0$	$t=1$	$t=2$	$t=3$	$t=4$
I.	-100	150	200	150	100
II.	-100	150	-50	150	-50

Is either project acceptable?

10.5 Consider the project for which the dollar cash flows are:

$t=0$	$t=1$	$t=2$	$t=3$	$t=4$
-1000	2000	2000	2000	-5000

(a) At a cost of capital of 10 percent is this project acceptable by the return on invested capital criterion? By the net present value criterion?

(b) Plot the net present value and return on invested capital functions for this project.
(c) What, if anything, can you generalize from your results in parts (a) and (b)?

10.6 The capital-budgeting project with dollar cash flows of

$t = 0$	$t = 1$	$t = 2$
−1,000,000	5,650,000	−12,647,500
$t = 3$	$t = 4$	$t = 5$
14,005,875	−7,662,600	1,653,919

has five roots to the internal rate of return equation, but has only three distinct roots. The percentages and corresponding roots are: −25 percent (.75), 10 percent (1.10), and 35 percent (1.35). The roots .75 and 1.35 are double roots; they have multiplicity two.
(a) Plot the NPV function for this project.
(b) Can you make a tentative generalization about the effect of a double root on the NPV function?
(c) Is this project acceptable for any positive cost of capital?

10.7 A project has dollar cash flows:

$t = 0$	$t = 1$	$t = 2$
−1000	6750	−16,375
$t = 3$	$t = 4$	$t = 5$
17,375	−7875	1250

(a) Find the return on investment for cost of capital 0, 10, 20, 30, . . . , 130 percent. (Use a computer program such as CITROMA unless you have unlimited time!)
(b) Graph the return on investment function and the NPV function over the range −30 percent $\leq k \leq$ 130 percent. (Negative k is only for mathematical completeness.)
(c) Compare the NPV and return on investment functions you have obtained.

Bibliography

1. Beedles, William L., "Evaluating Negative Benefits," *Journal of Financial and Quantitative Analysis*, Vol. XIII, No. 1 (March 1978), pp. 173–176.
2. Herbst, A. F. "A FORTRAN IV Procedure for Determining Return on Invested Capital," *Management Science* (February 20, 1974).
3. ———, "The Unique, Real Internal Rate of Return: Caveat Emptor!," *Journal of Financial and Quantitative Analysis*, Vol. 13, No. 2 (June 1978).
4. Hirschleifer, J., "On Multiple Rates of Return: Comment," *The Journal of Finance*, Vol. XXIV, No. 1 (March 1969).
5. Jean, W. H., "On Multiple Rates of Return," *The Journal of Finance*, Vol. XXIII, No. 1 (March 1968).
6. ———, "Reply," *The Journal of Finance*, Vol. XXIV, No. 1 (March 1969).
7. Lorie, J. H., and L. J. Savage, "Three Problems in Rationing Capital," *Journal of Business*, Vol. 28 (October 1955), pp. 229–239.

8. Mao, J. C. T., "Financing Urban Change in the Great Society: Quantitative Analysis of Urban Renewal Investment Decisions," *The Journal of Finance*, Vol. XXII, No. 2 (May 1967).
9. ———, *Quantitative Analysis of Financial Decisions* (New York: MacMillan, 1969).
10. Teichroew, D., *An Introduction to Management Science* (New York: Wiley, 1964).
11. ———, A. Robichek, and M. Montalbano, "Mathematical Analysis of Rates of Return Under Certainty," *Management Science*, Vol. II (January 1965).
12. ———, "An Analysis of Criteria for Investment and Financing Decisions Under Certainty," *Management Science*, Vol. 12 (November 1965).

Chapter 11
The Problem of Mixed Cash Flows: II

In the previous chapter the problem of mixed cash flows was introduced, and a particular method of analysis, that of Teichroew, Robichek, and Montalbano (TRM), was discussed. Although the theoretical merits of the rigorously developed TRM approach may be superior, other methods are more widely used in practice to deal with projects having mixed cash flows. The question of which, if any, of the existing methods is universally "best" may be unresolvable. The appropriateness of any of the methods to a given situation depends on the extent to which the method's underlying assumptions match the particular situation and the goals of the enterprise's management. Different circumstances may require different analytical assumptions, and these in turn may imply different methods of analysis.

The methods examined in this chapter are the *Wiar method* and the *sinking fund family of methods*. Because it is substantially different in nature from the others, the Wiar method is discussed first.

THE WIAR METHOD

Robert Wiar [6] developed this method for analysis of the investment returns on leases,[1] for which he asserted it is inappropriate to analyze directly the net cash

---

[1] Leveraged leases are covered in detail in a later chapter. The characteristic of leveraged leases of concern to us now is that they generally have mixed net, after-tax cash flows to equity.

flows to equity. His approach was to employ that aspect of the Keynesian theory that states that the supply cost of funds cannot exceed the imputed income stream yield. In other words, analysis must be handled by simultaneous treatment of three components: (1) positive cash inflows; (2) mortgage bond amortization flows; and (3) the required equity investment. This analysis can be stated in two equivalent ways:

$$E_0(1 + r_e)^t = \sum_{i=1}^{t} R_i(1 + r°)^{t-1} - \sum_{i=1}^{t} M_i(1 + r_b)^{t-1} \quad (11.1)$$

or

$$R_0(1 + r°)^t = M_0(1 + r_b)^t + E_0(1 + r_e)^t \quad (11.2)$$

where

M_0 is the amount financed by bonds
M_i is the fixed amortization payment
r_b is the effective yield to the bond holders
E_0 is the equity investment
r_e is the return on equity, ignoring bond service
R_0 is the initial outflow—investment—equity plus bond financing
$r°$ is the overall return on aggregate investment
R_i is the future income stream

In the case of capital-budgeting projects it will normally be appropriate to consider the supply cost of funds as the firm's overall marginal cost of capital k.[2] Let us examine Eq. (11.2), letting $M_0 = 0$, $k = r_e$, and $R_0 = E_0$. Then

$$R_0(1 + r°)^t = R_0(1 + k)^t \quad (11.3)$$

and it is clear that $r° = k$. This means that the imputed income stream yield, $r°$, equals the supply cost of funds k. This is what we would expect, in equilibrium, at the cut-off point, for a firm not constrained by capital rationing, and it is consistent with the IRR criterion or Keynesian marginal efficiency of capital (MEC).[3]

Example 11–1. An Application of the Wiar Method

Consider a project costing $10 million that is expected to yield net, after-tax cash flows of $1.5 million at the end of each year of its useful lifetime of ten years. There is expected to be a salvage value of zero.

The firm's existing capital structure is 25 percent debt, 75 percent equity, and is

---

[2] This is because of risk considerations. No individual capital-budgeting project, unless independent of the firm's existing assets, can be properly considered in isolation and without regard to its effect on the firm's risk characteristics that affect the firm's cost of capital.

[3] The Keynesian term "MEC" is normally used in macroeconomic discussions concerning the aggregate investment return curve for an entire national economy, whereas IRR is normally used by noneconomists to refer to the return on individual projects.

Table 11-1. CASH FLOWS FOR WIAR METHOD EXAMPLE

Year	Project Cash Flow	For Bond Service	Net Cash Flow to Equity
0	−$10,000,000	$2,500,000	−$7,500,000
1	1,500,000	−250,000	1,250,000
2	1,500,000	−250,000	1,250,000
3	1,500,000	−250,000	1,250,000
4	1,500,000	−250,000	1,250,000
5	1,500,000	−250,000	1,250,000
6	1,500,000	−250,000	1,250,000
7	1,500,000	−250,000	1,250,000
8	1,500,000	−250,000	1,250,000
9	1,500,000	−250,000	1,250,000
10	1,500,000	−2,750,000	−1,250,000
IRR of cash Flow stream =	8.14%	10.00%	7.03%

considered optimal. The project, if accepted, will be financed by a private placement of $2.5 million in bonds yielding 10 percent and maturing in ten years, and the balance by equity.

Assuming the bonds are sold at par value, the payment (assumed to be made at year end) will be $250,000. The entire $2.5 million must be retired in the tenth year, the year of maturity for the bond.

The overall cash flow stream is composed of two component streams, as shown in Table 11-1. It is the return on *equity* we are interested in. The equity cash flow stream has mixed cash flows. Applying the Wiar method, we obtain from (11.2) the equation to be solved for r_e:

$$.75(1 + r_e)^{10} = 1.0(1.0814)^{10} - .25(1.1000)^{10}$$

and

$$r_e = 7.45\%$$

which is greater than the IRR of 7.03 percent on the equity stream. The ordinary IRR on the mixed equity stream is unique in this particular problem, but it need not be so. The previous chapter showed that, when mixed cash flows are considered, even a unique IRR does not measure return on investment.

The r_e obtained is then compared with the required return on equity. If it is greater than the required rate, the project will be acceptable.

The Wiar method will be discussed again in Chapter 13, which deals with leveraged leases. For now we recognize that for capital-budgeting projects as a class, the method reduces to the IRR method already treated in detail, and that it is inadequate for analyzing projects having mixed cash flows.

SINKING FUND METHODS

Sinking fund methods, as a class, are characterized by some adjustment being made to the original cash flows series, aimed at making the adjusted cash flow series amenable to treatment by internal rate of return analysis. To apply any of them, we first follow some procedure for systematically modifying the cash flow series to remove all negative flows except those at the beginning,[4] which represent the initial cash outlay or outlays. All negative cash flows beyond the initial outlay sequence are forced to zero. Next, because the adjusted cash flows have only one sign change, the internal rate of return procedure is applied. Under this definition, the Teichroew, or Teichroew, Robichek, and Montalbano method discussed in the previous chapter can also be considered a sinking fund method.

To avoid, or perhaps clear up some semantic difficulties, let us state here that (at least) three sinking fund methods have been used in practice. One is the *initial investment method* (IIM), another is the *sinking fund method* (SFM), the third is the *multiple investment sinking fund method* (MISFM). A possible semantic problem exists because *the* SFM, although a *particular* method, carries the name of the *entire class* of methods. In other words, the sinking fund method is really only one of several methods, all of which can be characterized as sinking fund methods. As a class they include all of these methods as well as the TRM method. To avoid confusion, we shall refer to "the" sinking fund method as the *traditional sinking fund method* (TSFM).

The *sinking fund earnings rate* refers to the assumed rate at which funds that are set aside in a (hypothetical) sinking fund will accrue interest earnings. The *sinking fund rate, sinking fund rate of return*, or *sinking fund return on investment* refers to the internal rate of return on the adjusted cash flow sequence. Similarly, the *initial investment rate*, and so on, refers to the analogous internal rate of return on the adjusted cash flow series with the initial investment method.

To avoid complicating matters, we rule out the possibility of early project abandonment in this chapter. That is, we assume all projects will be held until the end of their economic lives. Furthermore, a uniform period-to-period sinking fund earnings rate is assumed in order to simplify and streamline exposition.

The Initial Investment Method

The initial investment method (IIM) is a type of sinking fund method. In the standard, conservative IIM it is assumed that an additional amount is invested, at the beginning of the project, specifically for the purpose of accumulating funds exactly sufficient to cover all negative cash flows occurring after the first positive flow.[5] Such *initial investment* is assumed to earn at some rate of return compounded

---

[4] The multiple investment sinking fund method is an exception to this because not all negative cash flows are removed beyond the initial negative flow or flows.

[5] A series of *m* negative cash flows followed by a series of positive flows would cause no problem in determining return, for we could use the IRR directly in such cases.

from period to period. The rate of return is calculated on the revised initial investment and the subsequent positive cash flows. Negative flows are zeroed inasmuch as they are assumed to be exactly offset by the additional initial investment. Another way of applying the IIM is to assume that the *earliest* positive cash flows are set aside into a sinking fund earning just sufficiently to match exactly later negative cash flows.

To gain an understanding of the IIM, it will help to analyze an example. However, in order that the two similar methods may be compared together, this will be postponed until after the following discussion of the traditional sinking fund method.

The Traditional Sinking Fund Method

The traditional sinking fund method (TSFM), like the initial investment method, assumes that positive cash flows can be invested at some nonnegative rate of return so that later negative cash flows may be exactly covered. Unlike the IIM, however, the TSFM assumes that the most proximate positive cash flows preceding the negative flow will be put into a sinking fund to the extent required to offset the negative flow or flows. The TSFM, therefore, can be considered a much less conservative method than the IIM, to the extent it delays investment for some time and thus does not provide the benefit of having at least some accumulated earnings should the actual available earnings rate decline later in the project life.

INITIAL INVESTMENT AND TRADITIONAL SINKING FUND METHODS

The initial investment and traditional sinking fund methods are based on similar assumptions. Both the IIM and the TSFM are based on a technique that modifies the cash flows of a project having mixed cash flows (and thus often a mixed project in the TRM sense) to produce a simple, pure project that has zeros where the original had negative flows, in all but the initial outlays.[6] In fact, the TRM algorithm of the preceding chapter is closely related, with the earning rate on "sinking fund" equal to k, the firm's cost of capital. However, with the TRM method the timing and the amount of investment in a "sinking fund" are perhaps obscured by the nature and the complexity of the algorithm, with the cash flows "compressed"[7] prior to the solution for return on invested capital. With the IIM and TSFM, cash flows that had been negative are zeroed prior to solution for rate of return. Thus, the order of the polynomial that will be solved for a unique, real root will be less for the TRM than for the IIM or TSFM. This will be clarified by using two of the same examples that were used in the previous chapter with the TRM algorithm, but this time with the IIM and TSFM.

---

[6] The nonpositive cash flows preceding the first positive cash flow.
[7] Compressed in the sense that the polynomial that must be solved for the return on invested capital, $r°$, is of lesser degree than the IRR polynomial would be for the same project.

Figure 11.1 Initial investment method applied to Example 11.2 cash flows.

Example 11-2

This example is the same as Example 10-1 used in Chapter 10. The cash flow is:

$t = 0$	$t = 1$	$t = 2$
$-\$100$	$+\$320$	$-\$240$

As stated in Chapter 10, this project has two IRRs: 20 percent and 100 percent. The NPV reaches a maximum of $4.49 at 31.25 percent cost of capital. The return on invested capital for this project, for $k = 10$ percent, is 1.82 percent. Figure 11.1 indicates the procedure used in applying the initial investment method to the cash flows. The IIM rate of return on investment is 7.26 percent for this example. Figure 11.2 suggests the procedure followed in applying the traditional sinking fund method. It is assumed that the applicable sinking fund's earning rate is 10 percent.

The essence of application of the TSFM to this project is to set aside sufficient cash, at some earnings rate, to accumulate to an amount exactly sufficient, one period later, to match the negative cash flow.

Thus, for any positive cost of capital above 1.82 percent, the project would be unacceptable for investment under either method. Like the IRR method or that of TRM, we compare the project yield to the enterprise's cost of capital and reject the project if the yield rate is less than the cost of capital. For this project, if the

THE PROBLEM OF MIXED CASH FLOWS: II 139

Figure 11.2 Traditional sinking fund method applied to Example 11.2 cash flows.

earnings rate on the funds set aside[8] is 10 percent, and the cost of capital is $k = 10$ percent, then $r_{TSFM} = 1.82$ percent—the same as that obtained with the TRM method in Chapter 10. In general, they will not be the same. However, it is indicative of the relationship between the methods.

Let us next examine another example, this one the same as Example 10-2.

Example 11-3

Figure 11.3 displays the net cash flows for this project and indicates the application of the initial investment method.

Note that positive cash flows are compounded forward in time. They are not discounted back to an earlier point in time with the various sinking fund methods.[9] Otherwise, the $1936 positive cash flow at the end of year three could have been discounted back one year to offset partially the negative flow of $4730 at the end of year two.

The cash flow sequence that must be solved for r_{IIM} is: $-(\$1000 + x)$ at $t = 0$; $3800 at $t = 1$; 0 at $t = 2$; and $1936 at $t = 3$. The value of x depends on the assumed earnings rate on the sinking fund. It is equal to $\$4730/(1 + k)^2$, where i is

---

[8] In practice, it will be rare to find an investor actually depositing or setting aside cash to meet outflows later in the life of a project. Rather, the firm will usually employ the positive cash flows in its operations. To be conservative, we could assume that a zero earnings rate is applicable. However, it would be normally appropriate to assume that funds earn at the firm's cost of capital.

[9] An exception to this general rule is to be found in what Brennen [1] refers to as the modified sinking fund method (MSFM). We shall not discuss this method here, since it is a straightforward variation of the TSFM in which later positive cash flows may be discounted to pay off earlier negative flows.

140 SPECIAL TOPICS AND METHODS

Figure 11.3 Initial investment method: Application to Example 11.3.

Figure 11.4 Traditional sinking fund method: Application to Example 11.3.

the applicable rate. For $i = 10$ percent, we obtain $x = \$3909.10$ and $r_{IIM} = 10$ percent.

Figure 11.4 illustrates application of the traditional sinking fund method to the same project. The adjusted cash flows from which we find the r_{TSFM} are: $-\$1000$ at $t = 0$; $\$3800 - x$ at $t = 1$; 0 at $t = 2$; and $\$1936$ at $t = 3$. The value of x is $\$4730/(1 + i)$, where i is the sinking fund earnings rate. For $i = 10$ percent, we obtain $r_{TSFM} = 10$ percent.

Example 11-4

The cash flows for this project are illustrated in the time diagram of Figure 11.5. This project has two positive cash flows at the end of the years preceding the final cash flow of minus $22 at the end of year three.

Figure 11.6 shows the procedure involved in applying the traditional sinking fund method to Example 11-4. At an assumed earnings rate of 10 percent on the sinking fund, a set-aside of $20 (out of the $90 cash flow) at the end of year two will increase to $22 a year later. The sinking fund amount of $20 plus $2 interest will exactly offset the negative cash flow at the end of year three. After set-aside of $20

THE PROBLEM OF MIXED CASH FLOWS: II

Figure 11.5 Original cash flow series for Example 11.4.

Figure 11.6 Traditional sinking fund method; adjusted cash flows for Example 11.4 with $i = 10$ percent.

Figure 11.7 Initial investment method: Adjusted cash flows for Example 11.4 with $i = 10$ percent.

at end of year two, $70 remains for other uses. The yield on the adjusted cash flows is 25.7 percent $= r_{\text{TSFM}}$.

Application of the initial investment method to Example 11-4 is illustrated in Figure 11.7. Again, the assumed earnings rate on funds set aside is 10 percent. With this method we must invest an extra $16.53 at $t = 0$ to offset the negative $22 cash flow at $t = 3$. The r_{IIM} on the adjusted cash flow series is 22.91 percent.

The initial investment method, a special case of the sinking fund method, may be considered more conservative than the traditional sinking fund method. This difference relates to the manner of selecting the timing and amounts to be set aside.

One might argue that it is extreme conservatism to assume that sufficient extra funds must be put into a sinking fund at $t = 0$ to cover the later negative cash flows. The initial investment method so far discussed is the limiting case on the conservative end of the spectrum (especially so if the assumed earnings rate were to be zero). As an alternative initial investment approach, we could assume that sufficient funds are set aside from the *earliest positive* cash flows to offset later negative flows. Figure 11.8 illustrates this variation of the IIM. The r_{IIM} in this case is 24.25 percent.

142 SPECIAL TOPICS AND METHODS

$$\begin{array}{r}\$70.00\\-18.18\,(1.10)^2\\\hline\$51.82\end{array}$$

Figure 11.8 Initial investment method: Adjusted cash flows for Example 11.3 with $i = 10$ percent.

Figure 11.9 Original cash flow series for Example 11.5.

Example 11-5

Now let us consider a somewhat more complex project than those in the previous examples of this chapter. Consider, for instance, a replacement chain of one capital investment following another. Let us assume we have a mine, which will cost $100 initially to develop and which will provide net, after-tax cash flows of $150 at the end of each year of its three-year economic life. Furthermore, assume that undertaking this mining project commits our organization to a project for secondary mineral recovery costing $350 to initiate and providing net, after-tax cash flows of $100 at the end of each year of its three-year useful life. Finally, at the end of the secondary recovery, our organization will have to pay out $350 to close down operations and rehabilitate the land on which the mine is situated to comply with environmental legislation. Since we have some positive cash flows from the projects at the end of years three and six, the overall net outlays in those years are not $350, but are $200 and $250, respectively. Figure 11.9 contains a time diagram illustrating the cash flows for this example.

This project has two positive internal rates of return: 10.23 percent and 85.47 percent. From Chapter 10 we know that neither is a correct indication of the return on investment. The net present value function for the project is plotted in Figure 11.10. Note that under the net present value criterion the project would be considered acceptable for values of cost of capital k, such that 10.23 percent $< k <$ 85.47 percent.

Since this project is more complex than those considered previously in this chapter, application of the traditional sinking fund and initial investment methods is

Figure 11.10 Net present value as a function of cost of capital for Example 11.5.

illustrated in the tables. Table 11-2 shows, for a 10 percent traditional sinking fund earnings rate, the adjustment to the cash flows that will be made employing the traditional sinking fund method. The traditional sinking fund method yield rate can be seen by inspecting the adjusted cash flows to be 9.27 percent. Figure 11.11 contains a time diagram showing the adjusted cash flows.

Table 11-3 shows, for a 10 percent sinking fund earnings rate, the procedure employed for adjusting the cash flows with the less conservative variation of the initial investment method. Figure 11.12 contains the time diagram corresponding to the adjusted cash flows. The initial investment method yield rate cannot be obtained by inspection (in contrast to the sinking fund yield rate). By calculation we find it to be 9.84 percent.

Figure 11.13 and Table 11-4 contain sensitivity analyses of the (less conservative) initial investment, traditional sinking fund, and TRM rates of return associated with various cost of capital percentages (traditional sinking fund earnings rates). Note that for $k = 0$ there is no real solution to the TRM return on investment equation.

THE MULTIPLE INVESTMENT SINKING FUND METHOD

The final sinking fund variant we shall discuss in this chapter is the multiple investment sinking fund method (MISFM). The idea underlying the MISFM is to adjust the cash flow sequence to obtain two distinct, nonoverlapping investment sequences having identical internal rates of return. For example, the project having a five-year useful life can be decomposed as follows into adjusted cash flows plus sinking fund. We assume the sinking fund earns at 15 percent per period.

The adjusted cash flows can be considered to be two nonoverlapping investments, each having a unique, positive internal rate of return of 50.0 percent. For this particular project the r_{IIM} is 28.93 percent, r_{TSFM} is 40.95 percent, and the RIC is 52.24 percent.

144 SPECIAL TOPICS AND METHODS

Table 11-2. TRADITIONAL SINKING FUND METHOD ADJUSTMENT TO ORIGINAL CASH FLOWS FOR EXAMPLE 11.5.

Time Period	$t=0$	$t=1$	$t=2$	$t=3$	$t=4$	$t=5$	$t=6$
Original Cash Flows	$-100	$150	$150	$-200	$100	$100	$-250
Step 1						$-100 \times (1.1) \longrightarrow$	110
Step 2					$-100 \times (1.1)^2 \longrightarrow$		121
Step 3			$-12.98 \times (1.1)^4 \longrightarrow$				19
Step 4			$-137.02 \times (1.1) \longrightarrow$	150.72			
Step 5		$-40.73 \times (1.1)^2 \longrightarrow$		49.28			
Sinking Fund Method Cash Flows	−100	109.27	0	0	0	0	0

Figure 11.11 Traditional sinking fund method: Adjusted cash flows for Example 11.5 with $i = 10$ percent.

Table 11-3. MODIFIED INITIAL INVESTMENT METHOD ADJUSTMENT TO ORIGINAL CASH FLOWS FOR EXAMPLE 11.5.

Time Period	$t=0$	$t=1$	$t=2$	$t=3$	$t=4$	$t=5$	$t=6$
Original Cash Flows	$-100	$150	$150	$-200	$100	$100	$-250
Step 1		$-150 \times (1.1)^2 \longrightarrow$		181.50			
Step 2			$16.82 \times (1.1) \longrightarrow$	18.50			
Step 3			$-133.18 \times (1.1)^4 \longrightarrow$				194.99
Step 4					$-46.46 \times (1.1)^2 \longrightarrow$		55.01
Initial Investment Method Adjusted Cash Flows	−100	0	0	0	54.54	100	0

THE PROBLEM OF MIXED CASH FLOWS: II 145

Figure 11.12 Modified initial investment method: Adjusted cash flows for Example 11.5 with $i = 10$ percent.

Table 11-4. SENSITIVITY ANALYSIS OF EXAMPLE 11.5 PROJECT

k%	TRM(1)%	TRM(2)%	IIM%	TSFM%
0	—	—	−3.42	−50.00
10	51.64	10.44	9.83	9.27
20	60.74	2.80	23.16	39.68
30	67.07	− 2.40	35.81	54.85
40	71.94	− 6.40	47.50	64.25
50	75.87	− 9.66	58.01	70.89
60	79.14	−12.40	67.25	76.08
70	81.90	−14.77	75.26	80.28
80	84.29	−16.86	82.14	83.79
90	86.38	−18.72	88.02	86.76
100	88.21	−20.39	93.02	89.31
110	89.85	−21.91	97.29	91.53
120	91.31	−23.30	100.94	93.49
130	92.63	−24.58	104.06	95.22

Figure 11.13 Sensitivity analysis of Example 11.5 project.

146 SPECIAL TOPICS AND METHODS

	$t=0$	$t=1$	$t=2$	$t=3$	$t=4$	$t=5$
Original Cash Flows	−$1000	765	2500	−3500	1000	3000
Adjusted Cash Flows	−$1000	500	1500	−2000	1000	3000
Sinking Fund		265	1000	−1500		

The MISFM is much more difficult to apply than the IIM or TSFM, because it requires that the original cash flows be adjusted so that one, two, or several nonoverlapping subsequences remain, all of these having the same unique, real IRR, which is the r_{MISFM}. The method has been used by several major organizations in their leveraged lease analysis. Limited experience with results of the MISFM suggests that the rate is generally close to the TRM RIC rate. This suggests that the RIC could be used as a first approximation to the r_{MISFM}.

Strong Points of the Methods

1. Both the traditional sinking fund and initial investment methods are based on theoretically defensible assumptions.
2. The methods take into account the time-value of money and do not exclude any cash flows.
3. The methods are much easier to apply than the Teichroew, Robichek, and Montalbano algorithm, except for the MISFM.
4. Both methods assure a unique, real measure of return on investment.
5. Application of the methods is not difficult and can be easily learned.

Weak Points of the Methods

1. Both the traditional sinking fund and initial investment methods may require, in addition to an estimate of the organization's cost of capital, an estimate of the sinking fund rate at which cash may be invested. For reinvestment of funds within the firm this rate could be the same as the cost of capital.
2. Both methods are more difficult to apply without a computer than the net present value method.
3. The methods do not distinguish between projects of different size and/or different economic lives. However, adjustment may be made for this.
4. In general, the methods may not adequately reflect the interrelated nature of investment and financing imbedded within mixed projects.

QUESTIONS

1. Explain the reasoning behind the method developed by Robert Wiar. What limits are there on its application to capital-budgeting projects?
2. Explain the traditional sinking fund and initial investment methods, and contrast with that developed by Teichroew.
3. Why do the adjustments to cash flows with the sinking fund methods assure there will be a unique rate of return on the adjusted series?

4. In what sense is the initial investment method more conservative than the sinking fund method?
5. How might adjustments be made to the sinking fund methods to resolve the problems of unequal project size and unequal project life?
6. Why is it the TRM method sometimes has more than one RIC value for a given value of k? Is not the algorithm supposed to yield a unique, real rate $r°$?

PROBLEMS

11.1 Apply the traditional sinking fund and initial investment methods to Problem 10.2, the Lorie and Savage "pump" project. (a) Calculate the r_{TSFM} and r_{IIM} in terms of k (assume k is the sinking fund earnings rate). (b) Graph r_{TSFM} and r_{IIM} as functions of k.

11.2 Assuming a 15 percent annual cost of capital, apply the traditional sinking fund and initial investment methods to Problem 10.3.

11.3 Solve Problem 10.4 for the traditional sinking fund and initial investment methods yield for $k = .15$.

11.4 Solve Problem 10.5 by applying the traditional sinking fund and initial investment methods.

11.5 For $k = 5, 10, 15, 20, 25$ percent (a) solve for the NPV, the TRM return on investment, the traditional sinking fund, and initial investment rates of return. (b) Plot your results. (c) What generalization can you make? The cash flows are:

$t = 0$	$t = 1$	$t = 2$	$t = 3$	$t = 4$
−$100	100	100	100	−100

Bibliography

1. Brennan, Edward P., "Will the Real Yield Please Stand Up?," *MA Monitor*, Vol. 1, No. 3 (July 1974). (Published by Malloy Associates in Haverford, Pa.)
2. Champion, Robert, and Gary Koenig, "A Comparison of Sinking Fund Methods," *ITEL Corp.*, San Francisco, Cal. (February 15, 1977).
3. Childs, C. Rogers, Jr., and William G. Gridley, Jr., "Leveraged Leasing and the Reinvestment Rate Fallacy," *The Bankers Magazine*, Vol. 156 (Winter 1973), pp. 53–61.
4. Hichens, Antony, "The Cost of Equipment Leasing," *The Investment Analyst* (December 1966).
5. Robertson, James, *The Leveraged Lease: Determining the Benefits to the Lessor*, Industrial Leasing Corporation, Providence, R.I., undated.
6. Wiar, Robert C., "Economic Implications of Multiple Rates of Return in the Leveraged Lease Context," *Journal of Finance*, Vol. XXVIII (December 1973), pp. 1275–1286.

Appendix to Chapter 11
The Problem of Mixed Cash Flows—III: A Two-Stage Method of Analysis

INTRODUCTION

The two preceding chapters present the Teichroew, Robichek, and Montalbano method and other methods classifiable as sinking fund approaches to obtaining a unique, real rate of return measure on those investments having mixed cash flows. It was shown in Chapter 10 that even a mathematically unique, real internal rate of return is no assurance, under the TRM assumptions, of a measure of return on investment independent of the enterprise's cost of capital. This chapter presents an alternative, developed by the author, to the various sinking fund methods.

The algorithm, or method of analysis, presented here is designed to separate explicitly the analysis of investments with mixed cash flows into two separate but related decision phases, or stages. The method yields two measures by which investments with mixed cash flows, such as leveraged leases, may be evaluated:

1. The *time* required to recover the initial investment *plus* the opportunity cost associated with the funds committed to the project.
2. The implicit "borrowing" *rate* contained within the cash flows occurring beyond the capital recovery time.

Together the two measures provide a decision rule: If the capital recovery period is acceptable *and* the implicit borrowing rate less than the rate at which the firm can acquire funds (the firm's cost of capital), or reinvest the second stage cash flows, the project is acceptable.

RELATIONSHIP TO OTHER METHODS

The net present value (NPV) method assumes that the enterprise cost of capital is the appropriate rate at which to discount the cash flows, whether they be positive or negative. The NPV itself is a measure of monetary return over and above the investment outlay. Although it is implicit in the NPV, the method and the measure provide no information pertaining to the timing of recovery of the funds invested in the project. The NPV method relates directly to the basic valuation model of modern financial management and is generally preferred by academic writers to other capital-budgeting methods. It will be shown in this chapter that the two-stage method is, unlike the internal rate of return (IRR), perfectly compatible with the NPV. The two-stage method yields identical accept/reject decisions to those obtained with the NPV, when the acceptable time span to recover the invested funds is unconstrained.

The two-stage method, although yielding results identical to NPV, provides decision measures in the separate stages that are in terms of time and percentage rate. Thus, the first stage, by providing a time measure, relates to the ubiquitous payback method. As shall be seen, however, it does not suffer from the well-known shortcomings of the payback method. The second stage relates to the IRR, except that the rate found will be a cost rate rather than a return rate.

THE TWO-STAGE METHOD

That business people employ the payback method very heavily, much to the dismay of academics who have dwelt upon and publicized its shortcomings, has been documented by many authors, among them Lewellan [9], Durand [6], Klammer [8], Christy [5], Mao [10], and Soldofsky [11]. The major shortcomings of the payback method are that it ignores the time-value of money and ignores cash flows beyond the end of the payback period. Or, equivalently, a zero opportunity cost rate is assigned during the payback period, with an infinite rate thereafter.

In stage one of the method proposed here, a payback period for the initial investment is determined. However, this payback period takes the time-value of money into account by requiring not only that the initial investment be recovered but, in addition, the opportunity cost of the unrecovered funds remaining invested in the project. This is related to Durand's unrecovered investment: At this payback, and not before, unrecovered investment is zero. Unrecovered investment is discussed in Chapter 14. Because the time-value of funds is taken into account, this payback measure is economically justifiable.[1]

In stage two, the cash flows remaining beyond the payback are analyzed, in the "negative investment" or "loan" phase of the project. Thus the second major objec-

---

[1]For the remainder of this chapter "payback" will refer to this time-value-of-money-adjusted payback—"traditional payback" to the method as it is usually applied.

tion to the traditional payback method is of no consequence. In the second stage, an imputed rate is determined that can be compared to the enterprise's cost of capital or the investment opportunity rate available to the firm over the periods remaining in the project life from payback to the end of the project life.[2] If the "loan" rate is less than the firm's cost of capital, or rate the firm expects to be able to earn on the cash flows from the project, it is acceptable on the rate basis. Since the firm's cost of capital would be less than or equal to the reinvestment rate offered by future acceptable projects,[3] we shall assume that comparison will be with the cost of capital. Otherwise, it could be possible to accept a project with an implicit cost greater than the enterprise cost of capital because the reinvestment rate of return is greater.

The two-stage method can perhaps be best explained by detailed treatment of examples.

Example 11A-1

We shall analyze the cash flows to equity on a leveraged lease discussed by Childs and Gridley [4] and treated by others, such as Bierman [1], in subsequent articles. Chapter 13 examines leveraged leases in detail, and this same leasing project is examined further. For now it will suffice to take the net cash flows to equity as given and note that our purpose here is to illustrate the two-stage method of project analysis and not to discuss leveraged leases. Table 11A-1 contains the original net cash flows and the adjusted cash flow series. We assume a cost of capital $k = 10$ percent.

The project (lease) requires an initial equity outlay of $20. With $k = 10$ percent the enterprise must recover $20 plus 10 percent of $20, $20(1 + k)$, at the end of the following year. The enterprise will be no better off nor worse off if it can recover the capital committed to the project along with the cost of those funds; its capital will still be preserved. Because the cash flow at $t = 1$ is only $13.74, with $8.26 of the $22 remaining to be recovered a year later, which with opportunity cost amounts to $9.09. The cash flow of $5.89 at $t = 2$ cannot quite suffice, and therefore $3.52 must be recovered at $t = 3$. Figure 11A.1 illustrates the procedure.

By allowing a noninteger value for payback, we violate the assumption that cash flows occur only at the end of each period. To be consistent with this assumption we would take three years as the payback period required to recover the initial investment plus opportunity cost of funds. However, if we recognize that the assumption of end-of-period cash flows is only to facilitate calculations, and that cash flows do, in fact, occur more or less uniformly over time, we will be comfortable with the fractional result as calculated.

---

[2] Or, if abandonment is to be considered, rates can be found corresponding to abandonment at any time prior to the end of the project's economic life.

[3] If the "loan" rate is less than the cost of capital, the project is providing funds at a cost less than the combined total of other sources. Such funds can be invested as they are received to earn the opportunity rate available to the firm. In the idealized construct of a world without capital rationing, the enterprise would be expected to invest funds up to the point at which the marginal rate of return equaled the marginal cost of capital.

Table 11A-1. ASSUMED PER-ANNUM OPPORTUNITY COST OF FUNDS (COST OF CAPITAL) IS 10%.

t	Original Investment Plus Opportunity Cost	Original Net After-Tax Cash Flows	Adjusted Cash Flow Series°	
0	0	$-20.00	$-20.00	2.698
1	$-22.00	13.74	-8.26	Year
2	-9.09	5.89	-3.20	Payback
3	-3.52	5.04	1.52	
4		4.19	4.19	
5		3.32	3.32	
6		2.43	2.43	
7		1.54	1.54	
8		.63	.63	
9		-.51	-.51	
10		-2.68	-2.68	
11		-2.90	-2.90	
12		-3.16	-3.16	
13		-3.41	-3.41	
14		-3.70	-3.70	
15		-3.90	-1.72	
16		+2.40	0	

°The payback is in 2.7 years. The $1.52 remaining after payback in year three is assumed to occur at the end of the period, just as the original flow of $5.04 is.

Before solving for the implicit loan rate, the last flow of +$2.40 is discounted back at the opportunity cost rate, using a sinking fund approach until absorbed by the negative flows. This may be interpreted as assigning, at discount, the last positive flow to the project—in other words, using it to prepay a portion of the loan.

The residual $1.52 after investment recovery, or capital recovery, is the first nonzero cash flow in the adjusted series. If it were not for the final cash flow of +$2.40 at $t = 16$ we would have, in the remaining cash flows, the series of a simple *financing* project with only one sign change in the cash flows. Before applying stage II of the method, we must first get rid of this last cash flow. One approach, a conservative one, would be to ignore the +$2.40, to assume it will not be received. A better approach, in the author's opinion, is to assume that funds can be borrowed at rate k, and the loan proceeds used to offset one or more of the immediately preceding negative cash flows. The +$2.40 would be used at $t = 16$ to repay the loan. Equivalently, we may assume the +$2.40 is assigned (at discount of k) to a creditor. This latter approach is the one that will be used. Figure 11A-2 illustrates the method.

The enterprise has recovered its initial investment and the associated cost of the unrecovered funds remaining committed by the end of the first 2.7 years. The remaining adjusted cash flows occurring subsequent to that time are gratuitous to capital recovery of the initial investment. They are characteristic of a loan, and therefore we are interested in the rate implied by these cash flows. This "loan" rate is determined to be 3.9 percent, much less than our assumed 10 percent cost of

152 SPECIAL TOPICS AND METHODS

Original Cash Flows

```
t = 0           t = 1           t = 2           t = 3
               +$13.74
                                 5.89
                                                 5.04
```

$-\$20(1 + k) \rightarrow -22.00$
$ - 8.26(1 + k) \rightarrow -9.09$
$ -3.20(1 + k) \rightarrow -3.52$
$ +1.52$

Adjusted Cash Flows

```
t = 0      t = 1      t = 2      t = 3
  0          0          0        +1.52
```

The payback is thus $2 + 3.52/5.04$ years, or 2.7 years.

Figure 11A.1 Stage I analysis.

Original Cash Flows

```
       t = 14              t = 15              t = 16
                          +2.18  ←——— + 2.40 ÷ (1 + k)

        -3.70              -3.90
                           -1.72
```

Adjusted Cash Flows

```
       t = 14              t = 15              t = 16
                                                 0

                           -1.72
        -3.70
```

Figure 11A.2 Preparation for Stage II analysis.

capital. If we can obtain funds at a rate lower than our cost of capital, we should do so,[4] and the project is acceptable on this basis.

As will become apparent in the formal development of the two-stage method, *if a project is not rejected on the basis of an unacceptable payback, the accept/reject decision obtained from stage II will be identical to that obtained with the NPV method.* This is an important result. Although the stage II results are perfectly compatible with the NPV, the stage I payback may mark a project as unacceptable because capital recovery takes longer than is considered acceptable.

Before getting into the formal, mathematical treatment of the two-stage method, it will be useful to analyze one more example. This is the same as Example 10–2 from Chapter 10.

Example 11A-2

This project has cash flows:

$t = 0$	$t = 1$	$t = 2$	$t = 3$
−$1000	+$3800	−$4730	+$1936

Again assuming $k = 10\%$, the $1000 initial investment plus cost of the funds committed (a total of $1100) is fully absorbed by the large positive cash flow at $t = 1$. The stage I payback for this project is $1100/3800 = .289$ or $.3$. The adjusted cash flows are:

$t = 0$	$t = 1$	$t = 2$	$t = 3$
0	+$2700	−$4730	+$1936

Before finding the stage II rate, we assume the $1936 is assigned to a creditor, at a discount of k percent, and the proceeds received at $t = 2$. Thus, the adjusted cash flow at $t = 2$ is $-\$4730 + (\$1936/1.10) = -\$2970$. To find the stage II rate, r_B, we solve for the IRR of the cash flow series:

$t = 0$	$t = 1$	$t = 2$	$t = 3$
0	+$2700	−$2970	0

And

$$\$2700(1 + r_B) = \$2970$$

so that

$$r_B = 10 \text{ percent}$$

Since $r_B = k$ the project is not acceptable. This project, not coincidentally, as will be shown, has a zero NPV for $k = 10$ percent. Figure 11A.3 contains a plot of the two-stage method results and NPV for various values of k.

---

[4] Even if we recognize that risk considerations may alter this conclusion, the effect of the project itself on k could have been incorporated into the rate itself prior to this analysis.

Figure 11A.3 NPV and two-stage measures for Example 11A.2.

FORMAL DEFINITION AND RELATIONSHIP TO NPV

It was stated earlier in this chapter that the two-stage method yields results identical to those obtained with the NPV provided that time for full capital recovery is unimportant. To make the two-stage NPV relationship explicit and at the same time provide a formal definition of the two-stage method, we first write the formula for NPV as:

$$\text{NPV} = \sum_{t=0}^{n} \frac{R_t(1+r_r)^{n-t}}{(1+k)^n} \tag{11A.1}$$

where R_t are the net, after-tax cash flows, r_r the reinvestment rate.

$$\text{NPV} = \sum_{t=0}^{n} \frac{R_t}{(1+k)^t} = \sum_{t=0}^{n} R_t(1+k)^{-t} \tag{11A.2}$$

also by reduction of (11A.1).

Similarly, the two-stage method may be written as the following:

Payback Stage

$$\sum_{t=0}^{P} \frac{R_t(1 + r_r)^{P-t}}{(1 + k)^P} = 0 \to P \tag{11A.3}$$

$$\sum_{t=0}^{P} \frac{R_t}{(1 + k)^t} = \sum_{t=0}^{P} R_t(1 + k)^{-t} = 0 \to P \tag{11A.4}$$

Multiplying Eq. (11A.4) by $(1 + k)^n$ yields the equivalent form actually employed in the problem treated earlier:

$$\sum_{t=0}^{P} R_t(1 + k)^{n-t} = 0 \to P \tag{11A.5}$$

"Borrowing" Rate:

$$\sum_{t=P+1}^{n} \frac{R_t(1 + r_B)^{n-t}}{(1 + r_B)^{n-P}} = \sum_{t=P+1}^{n} R_t(1 + r_B)^{-t} = 0 \to r_B \tag{11A.6}$$

where r_B is the implicit cost of funds inherent in the flows remaining after payback.[5] Formula (11A.6) assumes the opportunity cost rate equals the implicit cost of funds. If necessary, the last cash flow at the end of the project can be forced to zero as illustrated earlier.

Formula (11A.6) can be modified to incorporate the firm's cost of capital and to obtain a present value formulation:

$$\sum_{t=P+1}^{n} \frac{R_t(1 + r_B)^{n-t}}{(1 + k)^{n-P}} = \text{present value} \tag{11A.7}$$

Now, adding (11A.3) and (11A.7), we obtain:

$$\sum_{t=0}^{n} \frac{R_t(1 + r_r)^{P-t}}{(1 + k)^P} + \sum_{t=P+1}^{n} \frac{R_t(1 + r_B)^{n-t}}{(1 + k)^{n-P}} \tag{11A.8}$$

which, for reinvestment rate $r_r =$ "borrowing" rate $r_B = r$, reduces to:

$$\sum_{t=0}^{n} \frac{R_t(1 + r)^{n-t}}{(1 + k)^n} \tag{11A.9}$$

which is identical to the NPV formulation of (11A.1).

In this chapter we have so far considered projects with mixed cash flows. What

---

[5] The rates r_r, r_B, and k are assumed to be greater than or equal to zero in order that they have a meaningful economic interpretation.

if we now apply the two-stage method to a simple investment? Consider the cash flows in the following example.

Example 11A-3

$t = 0$	$t = 1$	$t = 2$	$t = 3$	$t = 4$
−$1000	1000	1000	1000	1000

If we again let $k = 10$ percent, the stage I payback is 1.11 periods and the revised cash flow series is:

$t = 0$	$t = 1$	$t = 2$	$t = 3$	$t = 4$
0	0	+$890	1000	1000

There is no real rate that satisfies the second stage rate equation. However, because the remaining cash flows are all positive, they constitute in themselves a "loan" that does not have to be repaid, or a gift to the firm, and the project is acceptable on this basis. The two-stage method may be used for simple investments as well as those with mixed cash flows. It is generally applicable, which was to be expected from what is basically a special formulation of the NPV.

CONCLUSION

The NPV method of analysis has been largely ignored by those decision makers who have shown continuing preference for the traditional payback method and to a lesser extent the (internal) rate of return. The two-stage method discussed in this chapter presents the NPV in terms decision makers are accustomed to: payback and percentage rate. The payback, however, takes into account the time-value of funds at the enterprise's cost of capital; the percentage rate, for nonsimple investments, is a cost rate implicit in the cash flows after payback. If payback is not constrained, the two-stage method will always yield the same accept/reject decision as the NPV method.

Because decision makers have shown long-standing tenacity for the traditional payback method, the two-stage algorithm may find better acceptance by practitioners than the NPV method has received. And the two-stage method makes explicit, in the payback measure, the time required to recover the capital committed to a project. This is something the NPV method does not do, as it is usually stated.

A BRIEF DIGRESSION ON UNCERTAINTY

Up to this point we have considered the environment in which capital investment decisions are to be made one of certainty. If we relax this assumption, as we do in the next section, we are compelled to admit that, to the extent that cash flow estimates become increasingly tenuous and subject to error the further they occur from the present, a project that returns the initial investment early is to be preferred to one that does not, *ceteris paribus*. This is particularly so during times of economic, political, and social instability, the combined effects of which may cause cumulative exogenous effects to the enterprise that are impossible to predict far in advance.

Some years ago the distinction was often made between risk and uncertainty. Today it seems the distinction is often ignored, perhaps because the theory of finance in general and investments in particular have been developed to their present state by assuming risk rather than the more intractable uncertainty. The distinction is this: With risk we take as known the probability distributions of the variables; with uncertainty we assume ignorance of the distributions of the variables.

The two-stage algorithm for investment analysis provides, in its payback measure, a means of addressing uncertainty. *Two investments with identical NPV may have substantially different capital recovery paybacks and, in a world characterized by uncertainty, the investment with the shorter payback is to be preferred.* Because the two-stage method provides a capital recovery measure, it allows management to determine whether or not the capital recovery is swift enough. Because capital preservation may be a goal that overrides possible investment returns, the payback should be of interest.

QUESTIONS

1. Explain the difference between the traditional payback period and the payback of stage I of the two-stage algorithm.
2. How can the two-stage measures be used to choose between two projects with identical NPVs? Explain why such choice should be made.
3. Can you suggest modification of the two-stage procedure to obtain measures corresponding to the profitability index or uniform annual equivalent that stem from NPV?
4. Discuss the distinction that may be made between risk and uncertainty. Which is likely to prevail for the typical capital-budgeting project? (Remember that for most projects, unlike common stock shares, we have no statistical history.) What is it that makes errors in estimation become greater the further into the future that estimates are made?
5. Why is it that projects with a negative NPV have no stage I payback? What of projects with zero NPV?
6. Explain how the stage I payback is related to unrecovered investment by looking ahead to Chapter 14.
7. Can you propose a project for which the cash flows for stage II analysis are not those of a loan but rather an investment? If so, what decision rule involving the cost of capital k should be used?

PROBLEMS

11A.1 Assuming $k = 15$ percent, calculate the NPV and the two-stage algorithm measures for the following projects. Which is preferable?

	$t = 0$	$t = 1$	$t = 2$	$t = 3$	$t = 4$
Project AAA	−$1000	500	600	700	1000
Project BBB	−$1000	800	700	600	526

158 SPECIAL TOPICS AND METHODS

11A.2 After finding the stage I payback measures in Problem 11A.1, find the present value of the adjusted cash flow series. Compare to the NPV results you obtained.

11A.3 Calculate for $k = 5, 10, 15, 20,$ and 25 percent the NPV and the two-stage measures, and plot the results, for the project with these cash flows:

$t = 0$	$t = 1$	$t = 2$	$t = 3$	$t = 4$	$t = 5$	$t = 6$
$-\$10,000$	7000	3000	2000	2000	2000	-1000

11A.4 Calculate the NPV and the two-stage measures for the following projects for $k = 15$ percent. Comment on any difficulties that you encounter.

Project	$t = 0$	$t = 1$	$t = 2$	$t = 3$	$t = 4$	$t = 5$	$t = 6$
CCC	$\$-1000$	1150	1150	1150	1150	1150	-2500
DDD	-1000	200	200	200	200	200	200
EEE	-1000	1150	1150	1150	1150	1150	1150
FFF	-1000	1150	-1000	200	200	200	200
GGG	-1000	450	805	1000	1000	1000	-2000

12.5 This is the well-known Lorie and Savage "pump" project previously presented in Problem 10.2. Apply the two-stage analysis to it, and plot the results along with the NPV for $k = 0, 10, 20, 30, 40,$ and 50 percent. What do you observe?

$t = 0$	$t = 1$	$t = 2$
-1600	10,000	$-10,000$

Bibliography

1. Bierman, Harold, Jr., "Leveraged Leasing: An Alternative Analysis," *The Bankers Magazine*, Vol. 157 (Summer 1974).
2. Campanella, Joseph A., "Leveraged Lease Analysis and the Commercial Bank," Unpublished Masters Thesis, The Stonier Graduate School of Banking, Rutgers University, 1974.
3. Carlson, C. Robert, Michael L. Lawrence, and Donald H. Wort, "Clarification of the Reinvestment Assumption: The Discounted Cash Flow Techniques." Paper presented October 1972 at the annual meetings of the Financial Management Association.
4. Childs, C. Rogers, Jr., and William G. Gridley, Jr., "Leveraged Leasing and the Reinvestment Rate Fallacy," *The Bankers Magazine*, Vol. 156 (Winter 1973).
5. Christy G. A., *Capital Budgeting: Current Practices and Their Efficiency*, University of Oregon, Bureau of Business Research, 1966.
6. Durand, David, "Time as a Dimension of Investment," Proceedings of the Eastern Finance Association (April 1973).
7. Hichens, Antony, "The Cost of Equipment Leasing," *The Investment Analyst* (December 1966).
8. Klammer, T. P., "Empirical Evidence of the Adoption of Sophisticated Capital Budgeting Techniques," *Journal of Business* (July 1972).
9. Lewellen, Wilbur G., Howard P. Lanser, and John J. McConnell, "Payback Substitutes for Discounted Cash Flow," *Financial Management*, Vol. 2, No. 2 (Summer 1973).

10. Mao, James C. T., "Survey of Capital Budgeting: Theory and Practice," *The Journal of Finance*, Vol. XXV, No. 2 (May 1970).
11. Soldofsky, Robert M., "The What, Why, and How of Capital Budgeting for Smaller Businesses," *Iowa Business Digest* (January 1966).
12. Teichroew, D., A. Robichek, and M. Montalbano, "Mathematical Analysis of Rates of Return Under Certainty," *Management Science* (January 1965).
13. ————, "An Analysis of Criteria for Investment and Financing Decisions Under Certainty," *Management Science*, Vol. 12 (November 1965).
14. Weingartner, H. Martin, "Some New Views on the Payback Period and Capital Budgeting Decisions," *Management Science*, Vol. 15 (August 1969).
15. Wiar, Robert C., "Economic Implications of Multiple Rates of Return in the Leveraged Lease Context," *Journal of Finance*, Vol. XXVIII (December 1973).

Chapter 12
Leasing

A lease is a contract under which the user (lessee) receives use of an asset from its owner (lessor) in return for promising to make a series of periodic payments over the life of the lease. A lease separates use from ownership. The two basic types of leases are operating and financial. *Operating leases* have relatively short terms, provide less than full payout,[1] and may be canceled by the lessee. A hotel room, or home telephone, water or electrical service may thus be considered forms of operating lease. In contrast, a *financial lease* is for a long term, provides for full payout, and is not cancelable without penalty by the lessee. We shall not be concerned with operating leases, but instead focus on financial leases.

Financial leases may be separated into two main categories: ordinary and leveraged. This chapter is concerned with ordinary financial leases. Chapter 13 considers leveraged leases and their unique attributes and problems. Both kinds of financial leases have assumed increasing importance in recent years and we may expect growth in leasing to continue over the next decade, barring major changes in tax laws that apply to them.

---

[1] Full payout for a lease requires that the total of payments be sufficient for the lessor to recover, in addition to the capital investment, the cost of funds and profit.

ALLEGED ADVANTAGES TO LEASING

Many advantages over conventional financing have been attributed to leasing. Although some have genuine value, others may have advantages only to certain firms in particular circumstances, and still others may have dubious value altogether. Among the claimed advantages are the following:

1. *Off-Balance-Sheet Financing* This is of dubious value, since the existence of financial leases must be footnoted and analysts will treat a lease as if its capitalized value were a listed liability.
2. *Provides 100 Percent Financing* This may be advantageous when other financing is not available or available only under unacceptable terms.
3. *Longer Maturity Than Debt* For a long-lived asset this may be a significant advantage. Financial leases generally run for the life of the asset. Loan terms, on the other hand, are generally set by the policy of the lender and maturity may be much shorter than the asset life.
4. *Entire Lease Payment Tax Deductible* This can be advantageous if land is involved since it is not depreciable if owned.
5. *Level of Required Authorization* Leases may sometimes be authorized by plant managers, whereas purchase of the same asset may require approval higher in the organization.
6. *Avoids Underwriting and Flotation Expense* Leasing also avoids the public disclosure associated with sale of securities.
7. *Front-End Costs Reduced* Delivery and installation costs are spread over the life of the lease.
8. *Lease Payments Fixed Over Time* Both the lessee and the lessor know the costs over the life of the lease.
9. *Less Restrictive, Quicker, More Flexible.*
10. *May Conserve Available Credit* Possibly, but consider comment under number 1.
11. *Lease May "Sell" Depreciation* The lessee, if unable to use depreciation and investment tax credit directly because of losses, in essence "sells" them to the lessor for more favorable leasing terms and thus gains from what would otherwise be lost.
12. *Leased Assets Provide Own Collateral* The lessee does not have to pledge other assets that might have to be pledged to secure debt financing for the same leased equipment. Because the lessor owns the leased asset, he can recover it in the event the terms of the lease are broken.

ANALYSIS OF LEASES

The analysis of ordinary financial leases in the literature has focused almost exclusively on lease evaluation from the viewpoint of the lessee, the user of the equipment. Very little has been written on lease analysis from the lessor's view until recently. Evaluation by the lessor is in itself a capital-budgeting problem that, depending on the terms of the lease and the quality of the lessee, may approach a certainty environment in many respects. In this chapter the analysis of leases will be considered from both the lessee and the lessor viewpoints. First, the traditional analysis from the lessee's position will be considered. Then an integrated treatment of the lessee's and the lessor's positions will be discussed.

It should be made clear at the outset that lease analysis itself does not address the question of whether a particular asset should be acquired or not. Rather, *lease analysis starts with the premise that the asset should be acquired by the lessee.*[2] The question that lease analysis tries to answer is whether the asset in question should be purchased or leased. This is often expressed as "lease or buy" or "lease or borrow." The traditional analysis, through the lessee's eyes, involves finding the least cost alternative to acquiring an asset: the minimum of the lease cost and the alternative financing cost. The alternative financing is generally assumed to be 100 percent debt financing, since leasing commits the lessee to making periodic payments just as a fully amortized bond would do. And contrary to alleged advantages 1 and 10 above, it has become widely recognized that leases do displace debt.

Traditional Analysis

Many approaches to the valuation of leases have been proposed. The one proposed by Bower [2] is representative of a broad class of net present value (NPV) models, and thus will be discussed first. The Bower model (in this author's notation) is:

$$\text{NAL} = C - \sum_{t=1}^{H} \frac{L_t}{(1+r_1)^t} + \sum_{t=1}^{H} \frac{TL_t}{(1+r_2)^t} - \quad (12.1)$$

$$\sum_{t=1}^{H} \frac{TD_t}{(1+r_3)^t} - \sum_{t=1}^{H} \frac{TI_t}{(1+r_4)^t} +$$

$$\sum_{t=1}^{H} \frac{O_t(1-T)}{(1+r_5)^t} - \frac{S_H}{(1+r_6)^H}$$

where

$\quad$ NAL = Net Advantage to Leasing
$\quad\quad C$ = Asset Cost if Purchased
$\quad\quad H$ = Life of the Lease
$\quad\quad L_t$ = Periodic Lease Payment
$\quad\quad T$ = Marginal Tax Rate on Ordinary Income
$\quad\quad D_t$ = Depreciation Charged in Period t
$\quad\quad I_t$ = Interest Portion of Loan Payment
$\quad\quad O_t$ = Operating Maintenance Cost in Period t
$\quad\quad S_H$ = Realized, After-Tax Salvage Value
$\quad\quad r_i$ = Applicable Discount Rate

---

[2] This question having been answered by the capital-budgeting methods generally applied to determine project acceptance.

This model allows for discount rates that are different for each of the terms. However, Bower concludes that the appropriate discount rate is the firm's cost of capital. With this in mind, we drop the term containing I_t since the interest tax shelter is implicitly contained in the cost of capital. The model then becomes:

$$\text{NAL} = C - \sum_{t=1}^{H} \frac{L_t}{(1+k)^t} + \sum_{t=1}^{H} \frac{TL_t}{(1+k)^t} - \qquad (12.2)$$

$$\sum_{t=1}^{H} \frac{TD_t}{(1+k)^t} + \sum_{t=1}^{H} \frac{O_t(1-T)}{(1+k)^t} -$$

$$\frac{S_H}{(1+k)^H}$$

or, by combining terms:

$$\text{NAL} = C - \sum_{t=1}^{H} \frac{L_t(1-T) + TD_t - O_t(1-T)}{(1+K)} - \qquad (12.3)$$

$$\frac{S_H}{(1+k)^H}$$

At this point let us consider a numerical example.

Example 12–1

A firm with 12 percent overall marginal cost of capital has decided to acquire an asset that, if purchased, would cost $100. This same asset may be leased for five years at an annual lease payment of $30. Operating maintenance is expected to be $1 a year, and straight-line depreciation to a zero salvage value would be used if the asset were to be purchased. The prospective lessee is in the 48 percent marginal tax category.

Applying Eq. (12.3) we obtain:

$$\text{NAL} = 100 - \sum_{t=1}^{5} \frac{30(1-.48) + (.48)20 - (1-.48)}{(1.12)^t}$$

$$= 100 - \sum_{t=1}^{5} \frac{15.60 + 9.60 - .52}{(1.12)^t}$$

$$= 100 - \sum_{t=1}^{5} \frac{24.68}{(1.12)^t}$$

$$= \$11.03$$

Since $11.03 > 0, the leasing alternative is preferable to purchase of the asset. But what if the net, realized after-tax salvage was estimated to be $20? In this case the last term of (12.3) would be −$11.35 and the lease would be marginally less attractive than purchase.

Alternative Analysis[3]

The discussion so far has been limited to the case of the *lessee*. Also, the impact of the lease on the lessee's debt capacity has not yet been considered. Myers, Dill, and Bautista [19] (MDB) developed a model that allowed for the impact of the lease on the lessee's debt capacity. The MDB model assumes that the lessee borrows 100 percent of the tax shields created by interest payments, lease payments, and depreciation. This debt constraint is used to eliminate the debt displacement term normally used in the lease valuation equation, assuming that a dollar of debt is displaced by a dollar of lease. Myers, Dill, and Bautista generalize their model by removing the constraint that a dollar of lease displaces a dollar of debt. However, they constrain the proportion of debt displaced by a dollar of the lease, λ, to be equal to the proportion of the tax shields the lessee borrows against, γ.

Here the effects of allowing λ to vary from 1.0 are examined. At the same time it is assumed that the lessee borrows 100 percent of the tax shields ($\gamma = 1.0$) in order to maintain an optimal capital structure. The generalized model, using MDB's model as the starting point, is:[4]

$$V_0 = 1 - \sum_{t=1}^{H} \frac{P_t(1-T) + Tb_t}{(1+r-\gamma rT)^t} + \sum_{t=0}^{H-1} \sum_{\tau=t+1}^{H} \frac{rTP_\tau(\gamma-\lambda)}{(1+r-\gamma rT)^{t+1}(1+r)^{\tau-t}} \quad (12.4)$$

where

V = Value
P_t = Lease Payment in Period t (normalized by dividing by the purchase price of the asset leased).
b_t = The Normalized Depreciation Foregone in Period t If the Asset Is Leased Instead of Purchased
r = Lessee's Borrowing Rate
T = Lessee's Marginal Tax Rate on Income
H = Life of the Lease
λ = Proportion of Debt Displaced by a Dollar of the Lease
γ = Proportion of the Tax Shields the Lessee Borrows Against

Equation (12.4) follows MDB's notation except for the inclusion of γ. Salvage value and foregone investment tax credit are assumed to be zero to simplify the model, and operating maintenance expenses absorbed by the lessor are also assumed to be zero.

The valuation model in (12.4), once again *is for the lessee*. To determine the value of the lease to the lessor may be somewhat more controversial if for no other

---

[3]This section is based on the extension to the MDB work by Perg and Herbst [21].
[4]The derivation is contained in the appendix to this chapter.

reason than little work in this area has been published. The claim of MDB [19, p. 806] is that the lessor's valuation is the lessee's valuation model multiplied by -1.0 to reflect the reverse direction of the cash flow. And for the lessor they claim that λ is the proportion of debt *supported by* the lease, because the lease is an investment to the lessor. (Remember that for the lessee, λ represents the proportion of debt *displaced by* the lease.) The lessor's λ will very likely be different from the lessee's; so may the tax rate, T.

If λ were to be the proportion of the lessor's debt *supported by* the lease [in (12.4) multiplied by -1.0 and with $\lambda = \gamma$], however, then r would be the lessor's borrowing rate, *not* the lessee's borrowing rate. This presents a problem. If the lessor acts as financial intermediary, then the lessor's borrowing rate will generally be less than the lessee's borrowing rate, because the debt obligations of the lessor are less risky. This lower risk is due to the lessor's equity cushion, the likely more liquid nature of the lessor's obligations, and the diversification through holding many different leases. Financial intermediaries also tend to keep the maturity of their obligations shorter than their assets in order to take advantage of a yield curve, that is, an average, upward sloping. Myers, Dill, and Bautista made a valuable contribution to the literature on leasing. The problem, however, of two different discount rates (the lessee's and the lessor's) make the MDB approach to determining the lessor's valuation of the lease unsuitable. We will now look at an alternative model for the lessor.

We base our approach to determining the value of a lease to the lessor on the fact that, *to the lessor, the lease is an investment*. The NPV of the lease is equal to the present value of its after-tax cash flows, valued at the after-tax discount rate appropriate for the level of risk associated with investment in the lease, less the purchase price of the asset to be leased. It is assumed that the lessor is also a lender, a share value maximizer, and financial markets are competitive. From this we can say that the lessor will invest in bonds, including those of the lessee, until their after-tax return is equal to the lessor's after-tax cost of capital appropriate to the risk associated with holding the bonds.

If the lease is equivalent in risk[5] to the lessee's bonds, then the cost of capital associated with investing in the lease is equal to the cost of capital associated with investing in those bonds: the after-tax borrowing rate of the lessee. If the risk is *not* equal, then the lessor's cost of capital for the lease equals X times the after-tax borrowing rate of the lessee, where $X > 1.0$ if the lease is riskier than the lessee's bonds, and $X < 1$ if the lease is less risky than the bond. Recognizing this we obtain the model for the value of the lease to the lessor:

$$V_0 = \sum_{t=1}^{H} \frac{P_t(1-T) + Tb_t}{[1 + Xr(1-T)]^t} - 1 \qquad (12.5)$$

---

[5] Strictly speaking, this section deals with a certainty environment. However, in discussing analysis of leases it is necessary to bring risk into consideration. The awkward alternative would be either to deal with leases under certainty here and bring in risk in a later chapter or to postpone treatment of leasing until later, and out of this author's desired sequence of topics. Risk treatment *in a formal sense* is deferred, however, until later chapters.

Here P_t, b_t, and r are the same as in (12.4). But T now represents the *lessor's* marginal tax rate, not the lessee's, and X is a risk adjustment factor. The factor X can be reasonably expected to be related to the debt displacement factor λ in (12.4). For example, if leases have financial characteristics similar to subordinated debt, then the lessor's cost of capital for the lease will exceed his cost of capital for the bonds ($X > 1$), and a dollar of lease will displace *less than* a dollar of bonds ($\lambda < 1$). On the other hand, if leases possess financial characteristics that make them senior to the firm's bonds, we would expect $X < 1$ and $\lambda > 1$. These possible relationships are discussed in the following analysis.

ANALYSIS

The factors that enter into the possible superiority of leasing over conventional financing are (1) the marginal tax rates (T) of the lessor and the lessee and (2) the relationship between λ and X. In order to explore the effects of the interactions of these variables on the value of a lease, we compute the breakeven lease payment of the lessee for various combinations of the lessee's tax rate and λ. The breakeven lease payment is then used to compute the value of the lease to the lessor for various combinations of the lessor's tax rate and X. The patterns of the results are of major interest. They are not affected by varying H, r, or the use of accelerated depreciation since these factors are common to both the lessee's and the lessor's valuation models. Therefore, only the results for $H = 15$, $r = 10\%$, and straight-line depreciation are presented in Table 12-1. In calculating the values for Table 12-1 the value of γ is kept equal to 1.0 because it is thought the results will be more meaningful if the lessee always maintains an optimal capital structure.

The topmost section of Table 12-1 confirms the conventional results that hold when leases are financially equivalent to loans. Thus, if a dollar of lease displaces a dollar of debt (that is, $\lambda = 1$) and leases have the same risk as loans ($X = 1$), then leasing is advantageous if, and only if, the lessee's marginal tax rate is less than that of the lessor. The advantage occurs because the lease is tantamount to the sale of depreciation tax shields by the lessee to the lessor. If the lessor has a higher tax rate, then the value of the tax shields is greater to the lessor than the cost to the lessee for giving up the tax shields. The lower the lessee's tax rate, and the higher the lessor's, the more mutually advantageous leasing becomes.

Results change dramatically once the assumption of financial equivalency is dropped. The second and third panels of Table 12-1 illustrate what happens if a dollar of lease displaces only 80 cents of debt ($\lambda = .8$). With this value of lambda the lessee's breakeven lease payment actually *increases* as the tax rate increases, rather than decreasing as we might have expected from the standard result at the top of the table. To understand this we refer to an important point made by MDB [19, p. 802]. The lessee's lease valuation rests upon the well-known Modigliani and Miller assumptions, which imply (among other things) that the only advantage to borrowing is the interest tax shield. If $\lambda = 1.0$, then leasing decreases the present value of the available tax shields because depreciation tax shield is surrendered. Therefore, as the lessee's tax rate rises, his breakeven lease payment falls. But if λ is sufficiently less than one ($\lambda = .8$ is sufficiently less), then leasing actually *increases* the present value

Table 12-1. $H = 15$, $r = .10$, STRAIGHT-LINE DEPRECIATION $\gamma = 1$

Lessee's Marginal Tax Rate		Lessee's Breakeven Lease Payment	Value of Lease to Lessor		
	$\lambda = 1$			$X = 1$	
			$T = 0$	$T = .25$	$T = .50$
$T = 0$		.1314738	0	.0175207	.0283163
$T = .25$		.1288274	−.0201286	0	.0145813
$T = .50$		.1260179	−.0414979	−.0185998	0
	$\lambda = .8$			$X = 1.2$	
			$T = 0$	$T = .25$	$T = .50$
$T = 0$		.1314738	−.1045497	−.0708275	−.0378043
$T = .25$		.1337616	−.0889678	−.0569969	−.0266946
$T = .50$		.1410994	−.0389911	−.0126358	.0089385
	$\lambda = .8$			$X = 1$	
			$T = 0$	$T = .25$	$T = .50$
$T = 0$		.1314738	0	.0175207	.0283163
$T = .25$		.1337616	.0174014	.0326661	.0401897
$T = .50$		.1410994	.0732132	.0812453	.0782708
	$\lambda = 1.2$			$X = .8$	
			$T = 0$	$T = .25$	$T = .50$
$T = 0$		.1314738	.1253474	.1195513	.1015017
$T = .25$		.1242443	.0634667	.0668896	.0613131
$T = .50$		.1138490	−.0255119	−.0088307	.0035225
	$\lambda = 1.2$			$X = 1$	
			$T = 0$	$T = .25$	$T = .50$
$T = 0$		.1314738	0	.0175207	.0283163
$T = .25$		.1242443	−.0549879	−.0303416	−.0092031
$T = .50$		.1138490	−.1340555	−.0991614	−.0631539

of the tax shields available since the increase in debt capacity—and therefore interest tax shields—more than outweighs the loss of depreciation tax shield. Because of this the lessee's breakeven lease payment rises as the tax rate rises.

It follows that if λ is sufficiently less than one, the value of leasing is a positive function of the tax rates of *both* the lessor *and* the lessee. How high the tax rates must be for lessor and lessee to make leasing advantageous depends on how much riskier these debt-capacity-increasing leases are than the lending/borrowing alternative. If they are no more risky than lending (that is, $X = 1$), leasing is then advantageous for *all positive tax rates*, regardless of whether the lessee's or lessor's tax rate is higher.

The two panels at the bottom of Table 12-1 show the case in which $1 of lease displaces $1.20 of debt. In this case the lessee's breakeven lease payment falls even faster as his or her tax rate rises than it does when $\lambda = 1$. The reason this happens is that the lessee gives up the present value of reduced interest tax shields as the lessee's debt capacity falls, in addition to the present value of the depreciation tax shield.[6] Here the lessee's marginal tax rate must be as low as possible if leasing is to be advantageous. However, it does not follow that it is necessarily best for the *lessor's* tax rate to be as high as possible to make the lease most advantageous. When the debt-capacity-reducing effect of the lease (perhaps as a result of its senior claim on the leased asset or assets) is reflected in lower risk and a lower cost of capital for the lessor (for example, $X = .8$), the greatest gain to leasing occurs if both the lessee and the lessor were to have zero tax rates.

IMPLICATIONS

From the foregoing it is clear that the conventional condition for leasing to be advantageous—that the lessee's tax rate be less than the lessor's—applies only if leasing and borrowing are financially equivalent (that is, both $\lambda = 1.0$ and $X = 1.0$). In the literature it has become traditional to argue that financial equivalency should hold. However, for such equivalency to prevail would require that product differentiation of financial instruments not influence their sales. Whether or not product differentiation can affect sales may not be settled to everyone's satisfaction. But until empirical evidence refuting parallel effects to those among consumer goods are published and confirmed, it would seem reasonable to expect differentiation to apply. If there really were no marketable differences between debentures, mortgage bonds, leases, and so on, one would be hard-pressed to explain why different financial instruments and arrangements persist.

If λ and X may differ from 1.0, we may ask how they may do so. First, let us consider a lessee in sound financial condition; all debt is on an unsecured basis. A lease, however, is a highly secured form of debt.[7] This extra security—actual ownership of the physical asset—makes the lease senior to the firm's debt and impairs the security of the other debt.[8] It follows that if the riskiness of this debt is not going to increase (and it cannot if γ, the cost of capital, is to stay constant), total borrowings—including the obligation on the lease—must fall, and this means $\lambda > 1$. The senior claim of the lease makes it somewhat less risky than the lessee's debt. To the extent that proceeds from the sale or re-lease of the asset, if it were to be seized from the delinquent lessee, would be insufficient to cover the unpaid rentals and expenses caused by the default, the lessor becomes a general creditor. Altogether, this implies that $X < 1$.

Now, in contrast, let us consider a highly leveraged firm whose debt is virtually all secured. In such a case existing creditors would not perceive themselves as being harmed by leasing, relative to financing the asset with debt, because the new debt

---

[6] Note that for $T = 0$ the lessee's breakeven lease payment is not affected by λ since the value of the tax shields is zero.

[7] The lessor holds title to the asset and thus may recover it more easily than if title were held by the lessee.

[8] If the asset were purchased, the title would be held by the firm that otherwise would be the lessee and it would serve to secure all that firm's debt along with all its other assets.

would have been secured in any case. But prospective creditors might find themselves more willing to make new leases than new secured loans because of their superior position with respect to recovering the asset they hold title to if the lessee were to encounter financial difficulty. This enhanced recovery ability may cause such prospective creditors to be more willing to make leases rather than loans ($\lambda < 1.0$) even though risk were to be increased ($X > 1.0$).

PRACTICAL PERSPECTIVE

It is probably reasonable to assume that much, if not most, leasing is done in situations where $\lambda \neq 1.0$ and $X \neq 1.0$. For high-quality, low-risk lessees it is likely that $\lambda > 1.0$ and $X < 1.0$. From the bottom two panels of Table 12.1 we see that a low tax rate for the lessee is of the greatest importance in this situation. It is also in the lessee's vital interest to negotiate terms for the lease that reflect the low risk associated with the lease. Because most standardized leases are set up to protect the lessor from the higher risk lessees, this would tend to limit low-risk prospective lessee's to large, negotiated, and (usually) leveraged leases. Leveraged leases are discussed in the following chapter.

In high-risk leases, $\lambda < 1.0$ and $X > 1.0$. As shown by the middle two panels of Table 12–1, it may make leasing advantageous if the lessee were to have a high tax rate, *provided* that λ is sufficiently less than one. In this case expansion of his or her debt capacity is of prime concern to the lessee; the foregoing analysis may understate the value of leasing because the value of additional debt capacity to the lessee may well exceed the present value of the tax shields since the future of the firm as a viable, going concern may well lie in the balance.

SUMMARY AND CONCLUSION

A financial lease is a financing arrangement in which the lessee purchases the use of an asset owned by the lessor. Asset use is separate from asset ownership. Lease analysis does not determine whether or not an asset should be acquired; it starts with the premise that the asset should be acquired and attempts to determine if leasing provides an attractive alternative for financing the asset. The associated question is normally phrased as "lease or buy" or "lease or borrow."

Traditional analysis of leases has focused almost exclusively on the problem of the lessee. However, to the lessor the lease is even more of a capital-budgeting decision; it is an investment. The lessor's decision is not simply the mirror image of the lessee's decision, because of different tax rates and different risk implications of the same lease to each of them. Traditional analysis has assumed that leases were substitutes for debt, but it did not address the impact of leasing on the lessee's debt capacity, or the measure of substitutability.

Myers, Dill, and Bautista [19] extended the traditional analysis of leases to take into account the effect of leasing on the debt capacity of the lessee. Perg and Herbst [21] extended the analysis to the lessor and integrated the analysis of lessee and lessor.

QUESTIONS

1. What is the difference between an operating lease and a financial lease? What is payout and how can it help in the distinction?
2. In analyzing financial leases, what is meant by tax shields? How is it there are depreciation tax shields and interest tax shields (and investment tax credit tax shields)? What role do they play in analyzing a lease?
3. Operating maintenance is generally borne by the lessor. What effect does this have on analysis of a lease.
4. Salvage value in this chapter was treated as a constant or assumed to be zero. However, salvage would seldom be known with anything like certainty. How does this complicate lease analysis? Can it make a measurable difference in whether a lease is worthwhile or not?
5. If the income tax on corporations were to be abandoned and replaced by a value-added tax, what effect would this likely have on the use of leasing as a form of financing?
6. Discuss the advantages to leasing that may be found by a firm that has losses that prevent it from taking advantage of depreciation or investment tax credit. What advantage is there in leasing when land is the asset involved?
7. In light of this chapter's integration of the leasing financing interaction, discuss the alleged advantage of leasing that it "provides 100 percent financing."
8. Is the "off-balance-sheet financing" alleged for leasing genuine? If it is genuine, what does this imply for market efficiency?
9. How can leasing reduce front-end costs for the lessee? Under what circumstances is this likely to be particularly advantageous?
10. If leases can be authorized by a plant manager, whereas purchase of the same equipment would require approval by a committee of executives reporting to the president or board of directors, is this an advantage of leasing or a defect in the organization? Discuss critically.
11. What is meant when we say that leases provide their own collateral?
12. In the case of a lease, the asset is used by the lessee but owned by the lessor. In the case of secured credit, the asset is both owned and used by the debtor and the creditor has a lien on the asset. What difference does this distinction make in the case of default?

PROBLEMS

12.1 Using the model of Eq. (12.1) determine whether a firm with 15 percent marginal cost of capital and 48 percent tax rate, should finance a machine costing $10 million by leasing or borrowing. The firm has decided to acquire the machine, that is expected to last seven years and have a salvage value of $3 million. Straight-line depreciation is used, and there is a 10 percent investment tax credit. Maintenance costs are estimated to be $100,000 annually. The firm may lease the asset for seven years for $1.3 million each year. What difference would it make to the decision if salvage was estimated to be zero?

12.2 Assume that in Problem 12.1 the potential lessee has tax loss carry-forwards that prevent it from immediately benefiting from depreciation, interest, or investment tax credit. Modify Eq. (12.1) and solve again for the advantage to leasing. Should this be taken into account in negotiating the terms on the lease?

(Remember, if depreciation and interest deductions have no immediate benefit neither will lease cost write offs.)

12.3 Demonstrate how the model of Eqs. (12.1) through (12.3) may be related to that of (12.4) by normalizing with the purchase cost, C. What is the difference between (12.3) and (12.4) if the lessee borrows exactly 100 percent of the debt displaced by the lease?

12.4 Solve Problem 12.1 assuming that the lessee would borrow 120 percent of his tax shields ($\gamma = 1.20$) and that a dollar of lease would displace less than a dollar of debt ($\lambda = .8$). What difference do you observe in the value of the lease?

12.5 Solve Problem 12.1 for the *lessor*, assuming less risk ($X = .9$) and a tax rate for the lessor of .48.

12.6 The Aye Company will lease a machine to the Bye Company for $200,000 a year. If purchased, the machine would cost Bye $500,000. The machine has an economic lifetime of five years and will be depreciated to zero salvage using straight-line depreciation. The basic cost of capital, r, is 10 percent and both firms have 48 percent tax on earnings. Evaluate the lease, using Eqs. (12.4) and (12.5) and with (a) $X = 1.5$, $\lambda = 1.3$, $\gamma = .8$ and (b) $X = .9$, $\lambda = .8$, $\gamma = 1.2$. What do you find?

12.7 Evaluate for the lessee, for all combinations of γ and λ, the lease over five years ($H = 5$) having normalized payment $P_t = \bar{P} = .2548796$ if $r = 10$ percent and $T = 50$ percent. Gamma can take on values of 0.8 and 1.0, and λ values of 0.8, 1.0, and 1.2. The values of b_t are .400, .240, .180, .120, and .060.

12.8 Evaluate the lease in Problem 12.7 for the lessor, with X having values of 0.8, 1.0, and 1.2, $T = 50$ percent and $r = 10$ percent, $r = Xr(1 - T) = 4$ percent, 5 percent, and 6 percent.

Appendix

The derivation of the generalized lease valuation equation for the lessee uses MDB's notation except for introducing γ to represent the proportion of the tax shields that the lessee borrows against. The starting point of the derivation is the debt constraint of the lessee. Y_t is the total debt of the firm in period t, L is the initial dollar value of the leased asset, D_t is the debt displaced in t per dollar of asset leased ($D_t \equiv \partial Y_t / \partial L$), S_t is the lessee's total tax shield due to book depreciation on all assets owned in t, and $\widehat{Z}$ is optimal borrowing excluding any contribution to debt capacity made by depreciation and interest tax shields.

$$Y_t = \lambda \sum_{\tau=t+1}^{H} \frac{P_\tau L}{(1+r)^{\tau-t}} = \widehat{Z} + \gamma \left\{ \sum_{\tau=t+1}^{\infty} \frac{S_\tau + rTY_\tau}{(1+r)^{\tau-t}} + \sum_{\tau=t+1}^{H} \frac{TP_\tau L}{(1+r)^{\tau-t}} \right\} \quad \text{(A.1)}$$

Differentiating Y_{H-1} with respect to L and solving for D_{H-1}:

$$D_{H-1} = \frac{-P_H(\lambda - \gamma T) - \gamma T b_H}{1 + r - \gamma r T} \quad \text{(A.2)}$$

Substituting D_{H-1} into the expression for V_{H-1} and simplifying,

$$V_{H-1} = \frac{-P_H(1-T) - Tb_H}{1 + r - \gamma rT} + \frac{rTP_H(\gamma - \lambda)}{(1+r)(1+r-\gamma rT)} \quad \text{(A.3)}$$

Going back to the debt constraint, (A.1), for Y_{H-2}, differentiating with respect to L, and solving for D_{H-2}:

$$D_{H-2} = \frac{-P_{H-1}(\lambda - \gamma T) - \gamma Tb_{H-1}}{1 + r - \gamma rT} + \frac{D_{H-1}}{1 + r - \gamma rT} \quad \text{(A.4)}$$

Substituting (A.2) into (A.4) and then substituting (A.4) into the expression for V_{H-2} and simplifying:

$$V_{H-2} = \frac{-P_{H-1}(1-T) - Tb_{H-1} + V_{H-1}}{1 + r - \gamma rT} + \sum_{\tau=H-1}^{H} \frac{rTP_\tau(\gamma - \lambda)}{(1 + r - \gamma rT)(1+r)^{\tau-H+2}} \quad \text{(A.5)}$$

Clearly, this reasoning repeats and in general (except for $t = 0$):

$$V_t = \frac{-P_{t+1}(1-T) - Tb_{t+1} + V_{t+1}}{1 + r - \gamma rT} + \sum_{\tau=t+1}^{H} \frac{rTP_\tau(\gamma - \lambda)}{(1 + r - \gamma rT)(1+r)^{\tau-t}} \quad \text{(A.6)}$$

For $t = 0$,

$$V_0 = 1 + \frac{-P_1(1-T) - Tb_1 + V_1}{1 + r - \gamma rT} + \sum_{\tau=1}^{H} \frac{rTP_\tau(\gamma - \lambda)}{(1 + r - \gamma rT)(1+r)^\tau} \quad \text{(A.7)}$$

By successive substitution, $V_1, V_2, \ldots, V_{H-1}$ are eliminated to obtain:

$$V_0 = 1 - \sum_{t=1}^{H} \frac{P_t(1-T) + Tb_t}{(1 + r - \gamma rT)^t} + \sum_{t=0}^{H-1} \sum_{\tau=t+1}^{H} \frac{rTP_\tau(\gamma - \lambda)}{(1 + r - \gamma rT)^{t+1}(1+r)^{\tau-t}} \quad \text{(A.8)}$$

Bibliography

1. American Institute of Certified Public Accountants, Accounting Principles Board, *Opinion 5*, "Reporting of Leases in Financial Statements of Lessee" (September 1965), and *Opinion 31*, "Disclosure of Lease Commitments by Lessees," (June 1973).
2. Bower, Richard S., "Issues in Lease Financing," *Financial Management* (Winter 1973), pp. 25–34.
3. Chamberlin, Douglas C., "Capitalization of Lease Obligations," *Management Accounting*, Vol. 57, No. 6 (December 1975), pp. 37–38, 42.
4. Clark, R., J. Jantori, and R. Gann, "Analysis of the Lease-or-Buy Decision: Comment," *Journal of Finance*, Vol. XXVIII (September 1973), pp. 1015–1016.
5. Cooper, K., and R. H. Strawser, "Evaluation of Capital Investment Projects Involving Asset Leases," *Financial Management* (Spring 1975), pp. 44–49.
6. Doenges, E. C., "The Cost of Leasing," *Engineering Economist*, Vol. 17 (Winter 1971), pp. 31–44.

7. Findlay, M. Chapman, "A Sensitivity Analysis of IRR Leasing Models," *Engineering Economist* (Summer 1975), pp. 231–240.
8. Gant, Donald R., "Illusion in Leasing Financing," *Harvard Business Review*, Vol. 37 (March-April 1959), pp. 121–142.
9. Gordon, Myron J., "A General Solution for the Buy or Lease Decision: A Pedogogical Note," *Journal of Finance*, Vol. XXIX (March 1974), pp. 245–250.
10. Johnson, Robert W., and Wilbur G. Lewellen, "Analysis of the Lease-or-Buy Decision," *Journal of Finance*, Vol. XXXVIII (September 1972), pp. 815–823.
11. Johnson, Robert W., and Wilbur G. Lewellen, "Reply," *Journal of Finance*, Vol. XXVIII (September 1973), pp. 1024–1028.
12. Kim, E. Hon, Wilbur G. Lewellen, and John J. McConnell, "Sale-and-Leaseback Agreements and Enterprise Valuation," *Journal of Financial and Quantitative Analysis*, Vol. XIII, No. 5 (December 1978), pp. 871–884.
13. Lev, B., and Y. Orgler, "An Analysis of the Lease-or-Buy Decision: Comment," *Journal of Finance*, Vol. XXVIII (September 1973), pp. 1022–1023.
14. Lewellen, Wilbur G., Michael S. Long, and John J. McConnell, "Asset Leasing in Competitive Capital Markets," *Journal of Finance*, Vol. XXXI (June 1976), pp. 787–798.
15. Mao, James C. T., "Lease or Borrow: A Synthetic View," *Cost and Management*, Vol. 38 (February 1964), pp. 46–52.
16. ———, *Quantitative Analysis of Financial Decisions* (New York: Macmillan, 1969).
17. Miller, Merton H., and Charles W. Upton, "Leasing, Buying, and the Cost of Capital Services," *The Journal of Finance*, Vol. XXXI (June 1976), pp. 761–786.
18. Moyer, R. Charles, "Lease Evaluation and the Investment Tax Credit: A Framework for Analysis," *Financial Management* (Summer 1975), pp. 39–43.
19. Myers, Stewart C., David A. Dill, and Alberto J. Bautista, "Valuation of Financial Lease Contracts," *Journal of Finance*, Vol. XXXI (June 1976), pp. 799–820.
20. Nantell, T. J., "Equivalence of Lease versus Buy Analysis," *Financial Management*, Vol. 2, No. 3 (Autumn 1973), pp. 61–65.
21. Perg, Wayne F., and Anthony F. Herbst, "Lease vs. Conventional Financing: Integrating the Lessor's Gains and Losses," *Proceedings of the 1980 Meeting, Eastern Finance Association*.
22. Roenfeldt, Rodney L., and James B. Henry, "Lease vs. Debt Purchase of Automobiles," *Management Accounting*, Vol. 58, No. 4 (October 1976), pp. 49–54.
23. Roenfeldt, Rodney L., and Jerome S. Osteryoung, "Analysis of Financial Leases," *Financial Management* (Spring 1973), pp. 74–87.
24. Sartoris, W., and R. Paul, "Lease Evaluation—Another Capital-Budgeting Decision," *Financial Management*, Vol. 2, No. 2 (Summer 1973), pp. 46–52.
25. Schall, L., "The Lease-or-Buy and Asset Acquisition Decisions," *Journal of Finance*, Vol. XXIX (September 1974), pp. 1203–1214.
26. Vancil, Richard F., "Lease or Borrow—New Method of Analysis," *Harvard Business Review*, Vol. 39 (September–October 1961), pp. 138–159.

Chapter 13
Leveraged Leases

DEFINITION AND CHARACTERISTICS

Analytical techniques discussed in previous chapters are applicable to analysis of the lease versus purchase decision and to lease analysis in general. This chapter is concerned with the analysis of a particular category of financial lease termed *leveraged leases*.

Leveraged leases are tax-sheltered financial leases in the sense that some of the returns to the lessor are attributable to the tax legislation that was enacted to encourage capital investment. The investment tax credit, for example, has its raison d'être in encouraging capital investment. However, as Campanella [4, p. 1] points out, those companies that could benefit from new capital often could not benefit from the investment tax credit. Such firms might not have been producing taxable income, for instance, or carry-over from previous tax shelter may have made the credit useless. Those firms found it advantageous to find a lessor who could use the tax benefits, and then arrange a lease in return for a lease cost lowered by those tax benefits. Leveraged leasing grew rapidly during the 1960s and is still significant. Changes in the tax laws have not, as some thought they might, negated the advantages of leveraged lease arrangements.

In terms of setting up a leveraged lease, it is typically done through a trust arrangement. The lessor contributes a small percentage (20 to 40%) of the capital equipment cost, and the trust then borrows the balance from institutional investors on a nonrecourse basis to the owner. The loans to the trust are secured by a first lien on the equipment along with an assignment of the lease and the lease payments. According to Campanella [4, p. 94], "a leveraged lease is a direct lease wherein the lessor, through a trust, has borrowed a portion of the equipment cost to help finance the transaction. Under the 'true' lease concept, the lessor retains a material equity and ownership in the leased property and no option to purchase, other than a fair market value option at the expiration of the lease term, is given to the lessee." This is an important point because, with the similar railroad trust certificate leases, the lessee is treated as the owner for tax purposes, and no tax advantage exists.

The trust is usually administered by a commercial bank, called the *owner trustee*. This trustee takes title to the capital equipment and enters into the lease arrangement with the actual user, the lessee. The lease is a long-term, full-payment "true" lease. With a true lease the lessor retains a material equity ownership interest in the capital equipment and no option to purchase the equipment is provided to the lessee, at any price other than "fair market value." The tax treatment on which leveraged leases are predicated rests on their being true leases. After first servicing principal and interest on debt, the trustee remits any remaining funds, pro rata, to the equity investors. It is the profitability of the leasing arrangement to the equity investors that we are primarily concerned with in this chapter.

Although the returns to the creditors of the trust normally may be straightforwardly calculated as the yield on a fully amortized note, and the cost to the lessee may similarly be found, calculating the return to equity is much more troublesome. The reason for this difficulty is in the mixed cash flows to equity that is characteristic of leveraged leases. A number of methods for computing the attractiveness of returns to equity on leveraged leases have been proposed. Unfortunately, instead of resolving the issue, the various proposals themselves may have added to the confusion. When one applies the methods to the typical leveraged lease, the results may seemingly be contradictory. Leveraged leases provide us with an interesting application of analytical techniques that have been proposed for dealing with mixed cash flows. Furthermore, the assumption of certainty is not so unreasonable as it may be with most capital investment projects because the returns are governed by the contractual terms of the lease.

METHODS OF LEVERAGED LEASE ANALYSIS

The methods of analysis we shall consider are the net present value, the Wiar method, the sinking fund methods (including the Teichroew, Robichek, and Montalbano (TRM) approach), and the two-stage method. Since these methods have been introduced in previous chapters, the reader is already familiar with the basic application of each. We shall therefore analyze several example problems to provide a structure for comparing the various methods.

176   SPECIAL TOPICS AND METHODS

Figure 13.1   Bierman example. Plot of investment characteristics.

APPLICATION OF THE METHODS

Example 13-1

This example was proposed by Bierman to illustrate the superiority of the net present value (NPV) method of analysis. The project has cash flows of $-\$400$, $\$1100$, and $-\$700$ at the end of years $t = 0, 1$, and 2. Figure 13.1 contains plotted results of NPV for different values of k, the cost of capital. The NPV function reaches a maximum at 27.0 percent. The project has IRR at 0 percent and 75 percent, and between these values the NPV is positive. This suggests that for 0 percent $< k <$ 75 percent the project is acceptable.

That this is a mixed project is apparent if we decompose the cash flows into two subsequences as follows:

	$t=0$	$t=1$	$t=2$	
(a)	−400	+400		Return = 0%
(b)		+700	−700	Cost = 0%

or

	$t=0$	$t=1$	$t=2$	
(c)	−400	700		Return = 75%
(d)		400	−700	Cost = 75%

Subprojects (a) and (c) are investments, whereas (b) and (d) are financing projects. In the particular subproject above, the investment returns are exactly offset by the corresponding financing costs. At rates between 0 percent and 75 percent the investment return dominates the financing cost. Consider the decomposition corresponding to 10 percent cost of capital, for example:

	$t=0$	$t=1$	$t=2$
(e)	−400	463.64	
(f)		636.36	−700

Figure 13.2 Bierman example. Plot of investment characteristics.

Figure 13.3 NPV-RIC Conflict. Plot of investment characteristics.

The "loan" implicit in cash flow sequence (f) is at 10 percent. The NPV of sequence (e) is 21.49 and has an IRR of exactly 16 percent.

The TRM return on invested capital (RIC = $r°$) is plotted against k in Figure 13.2. The $r°$ values for $r° > k$ are for 0 percent $< k <$ 75 percent—the same as obtained with the NPV approach. The initial investment method (IIM) yields r_{IIM} values of 0 percent and 75 percent for corresponding cost of capital percentages. Furthermore, the traditional sinking fund method (TSFM) yields r_{TSFM} values of 0 percent and 75 percent. The two-stage method yields results consistent with these. Next let us consider a project that has two more cash flows.

Example 13-2

This project has cash flows at end of years 0, 1, 2, 3, and 4 of $-$1000, $2000, $2000, $2000, and $-$5000, respectively. The NPV is positive between 0 and 400 percent as shown in the NPV versus k graph in Figure 13.3. The corresponding RIC or $r°$

Figure 13.4 NPV-RIC conflict.

plot is contained in Figure 13.4. Note that the $r°$ is a double-valued function of k. In this case the plot of interest is for positive values of $r°$. We reject the negative values on the basis that the adjusted cash flow series from which we find $r°$ for a given k value sums to greater than zero. In other words, the simple sum of the adjusted cash flows is positive, so we do not admit negative returns even though mathematically they are acceptable. Table 13–1 contains an outline of the TRM solution and some selected dual values of $r°$ for corresponding k. As we have noted before, returns of less than -100 percent have no economic significance because it is not possible to "lose more than we lose" with a project.

In contrast to the Bierman project in Example 13–1, for this case the NPV and the RIC are not totally in agreement. In fact, the RIC conflicts with the other, NPV-compatible methods also, as is to be expected. The NPV is greater than zero between the IRR boundary values of 0 percent and 400 percent. The $r°$ (RIC) is greater than k over much of the same range but not all of it. As a k value of 200 percent, for instance, the $r°$ is 176.65 percent whereas the NPV is still positive. One could dismiss this conflict as irrelevant in a world where k cannot be so great, since the $r°$ and NPV do agree over the range of k values that firms could, in fact, be expected to have. However, because they *are* different over part of the range of k, we should abandon any complacency generated by the Bierman example and other examples involving only two cash flows beyond the initial outlay. The Bierman example underscores the hazards lurking in the shadows for those who would try to generalize from the three-cash-flow case to the N-cash-flow case.

The conflict between the NPV and the RIC for large values of k is attributable in this case to the assumption implicit in the NPV that the investment and financing rates are both equal to the cost of capital, whereas the RIC requires only that the financing rate be equal to k.

Table 13-1. TRM ANALYSIS OF EXAMPLE 13.2

Original Cash Flows	Solution to Project Balance Equation[a]
−1000	
2000	100.00000%
2000	173.20508
2000	191.96396 = r_{min}
−5000	

Some solution values are:

k	$r°$	$r°$
−5	− 90.93%	124.50%
0	−100.00	130.25
5	−107.75	135.25
10	−114.55	139.25
20	−126.10	145.50
30	−135.73	150.25
40	−144.00	154.34
50	−151.29	157.55
100	−178.96	167.73
400	—	183.12

[a]This is a mixed project, for which, to find $r°$ for a given k, we must solve the equation:

$$-(1 + k)(1 + r°)^3 + 2(1 + k)(1 + r°)^2 + 2(1 + k)(1 + r°) + [2(1 + k) - 5] = 0$$

Let us next apply the Wiar method (WM), the initial investment method (IIM), traditional sinking fund method (TSFM), and the two-stage method (TSM) to this example and summarize the results obtained in Table 13–2.

The various methods are in agreement that for k values of 10, 20, and 30 percent the project is acceptable. The Wiar method could not properly be applied because it is predicated on overall debt service and equity-return cash flow streams. Since no debt was assumed for this example, the method could not yield results other than the IRR values of 0 and 400 percent. This would not be a proper test of the method.

ANALYSIS OF A TYPICAL LEVERAGED LEASE (CHILDS AND GRIDLEY)

Example 13-3

This example was first proposed by Childs and Gridley [5] and since discussed extensively in the literature. Table 13–3 contains the salient data for the Childs and Gridley leveraged lease. A 7 percent investment tax credit applies to the equipment. Depreciation was calculated using sum-of-the-years' digits method and an 11-year

180 SPECIAL TOPICS AND METHODS

Table 13-2. SUMMARY OF ANALYTICAL RESULTS FOR EXAMPLE 13.2 PROJECT

FOR $k = 10\%$		
NPV Method	$558.64	Accept
TRM RIC	39.25%	Accept
Wiar Method Equity Return	Inapplicable	
IIM Return	17.06%	Accept
TSFM Return	71.45%	Accept
Two-Stage Measures	.55 years, 4.58%	Accept[a]
FOR $k = 20\%$		
NPV Method	$801.70	Accept
TRM RIC	45.50%	Accept
Wiar Method Equity Return	Inapplicable	
IIM Return	34.57%	Accept
TSFM Return	109.09%	Accept
Two-Stage Measures	.60 years, 9.05%	Accept[a]
FOR $k = 30\%$		
NPV Method	$881.59	Accept
TRM RIC	50.25%	Accept
Wiar Method Equity Return	Inapplicable	
IIM Return	52.01%	Accept
TSFM Return	125.70%	Accept
Two-Stage Measures	.65 years, 13.47%	Accept[a]

[a] Assumes management's requirement for capital recovery is not less than these fractions of a year.

lifetime. The equipment was depreciated to a salvage-for-tax amount of 5 percent of the original depreciable value. The depreciation for $t = 9$ (year ten) is shown as $4.09; the calculated amount was $4.55. This difference is due to the requirement that $5 remain for write-off at $t = 15$ (year 16). The column of data of most concern to the equity investor is the "Net-After-Tax Cash Flow" column. It is this column on which our analysis will focus, although the Wiar method incorporates additional information.

This series of cash flows is a mixed project in the TRM sense. The r_{min} can be calculated from the series by taking the cash flows for $t = 0$ through $t = 8$ and solving for the IRR. Verification that the result obtained, 28.5038 percent, is, in fact, the project r_{min} can be obtained by evaluating the project balance equations corresponding to the preceding cash flows at this rate; they will all be less than or equal to zero.

The Wiar analysis can be carried out by evaluating the equation:

$$20(1 + r_W)^{16} = 100(1.045220)^{16} - 80(1.0416)^{16}$$

to find that $r_W = 5.80736$ percent after tax (or 11.16799 percent pretax). The rate of 4.52220 percent is the return on the *overall* cash flow to the leveraged lease, whereas the 4.16 percent rate is the *after-tax* interest on the debt financing. The overall cash flows to this lease are displayed in Table 13–4. Note that the Wiar rate

Table 13-3. CHILDS AND GRIDLEY LEVERAGED LEASE EXAMPLE—A LA WIAR'S ANALYSIS BORROW $80 AT 8% FOR 15 YEARS, INVEST $20 EQUITY, TAX RATE 48%

t	Year	Lease Payment	Deprec.	Mortgage Interest Payment	Effect on Earnings Before Taxes	Effect on Taxes	Effect on Earnings After Taxes	Mortgage Principal Payment	Net After-Tax Cash Flow (To equity)
0		0	0	0	0	0	0	0	−20.00
1	1	9.64	16.67	6.40	−13.43	−13.45[a]	.02	2.95	13.74[a]
2	2	9.64	15.15	6.16	−11.67	−5.60	−6.07	3.19	5.89
3	3	9.64	13.64	5.91	−9.91	−4.75	−5.16	3.44	5.04
4	4	9.64	12.12	5.63	−8.11	−3.90	−4.21	3.72	4.19
5	5	9.64	10.61	5.34	−6.31	−3.03	−3.28	4.01	3.32
6	6	9.64	9.09	5.02	−4.47	−2.14	−2.33	4.33	2.43
7	7	9.64	7.57	4.67	−2.60	−1.25	−1.35	4.68	1.54
8	8	9.64	6.06	4.29	−.71	−.34	−.37	5.06	.63
9	9	9.64	4.09	3.89	1.66	.80	.86	5.46	.51
10	10	9.64	0	3.45	6.19	2.97	3.22	5.90	−2.68
11	11	9.64	0	2.98	6.66	3.19	3.47	6.37	−2.90
12	12	9.64	0	2.47	7.17	3.45	3.72	6.88	−3.16
13	13	9.64	0	1.92	7.72	3.70	4.02	7.43	−3.41
14	14	9.64	0	1.33	8.31	3.99	4.32	8.02	−3.70
15	15	9.64	0	.68	8.96	4.30	4.66	8.56	−3.90
	Total	144.60	95.00	60.14	−10.54	−12.06	1.52	80.00	−3.48
16	Residual	0	5.00	0	−5.00	−2.40	−2.60	0	2.40
	Total	144.60	100.00	60.14	−15.54	−14.46	−1.08	80.00	−1.08

[a]Includes 7% investment tax credit on the $100 investment.

Table 13-4. ANALYSIS OF CHILDS AND GRIDLEY LEVERAGED LEASE EXAMPLE—A LA WIAR

t	Year	Lease Payment	Deprec.	Effect on Earnings Before Taxes	Effect On Taxes	Effect on Earnings After Taxes	Net After-Tax Cash Flow (Overall lease)
0		0	0	0	0	0	−100.00
1	1	9.64	16.67	−7.03	−10.37[a]	−3.34[a]	20.01[a]
2	2	9.64	15.15	−5.51	−2.64	−2.87	12.28
3	3	9.64	13.64	−4.00	−1.92	−2.08	11.56
4	4	9.64	12.12	−2.48	−1.19	−1.29	10.83
5	5	9.64	10.61	−.97	−.47	−.50	10.11
6	6	9.64	9.09	.55	.26	.29	9.38
7	7	9.64	7.57	2.07	.99	1.08	8.65
8	8	9.64	6.06	3.58	1.72	1.86	7.92
9	9	9.64	4.09	5.55	2.66	2.89	6.98
10	10	9.64	0	9.64	4.63	5.01	5.01
11	11	9.64	0	9.64	4.63	5.01	5.01
12	12	9.64	0	9.64	4.63	5.01	5.01
13	13	9.64	0	9.64	4.63	5.01	5.01
14	14	9.64	0	9.64	4.63	5.01	5.01
15	15	9.64	0	9.64	4.63	5.01	5.01
	Total	144.60	95.00	49.60	16.82	32.78	7.78
16	Residual	0	5.00	−5.00	−2.40	−2.60	2.40
	Total	144.60	100.00	44.60	14.42	35.38	10.18

[a] Includes 7 percent investment tax credit on the $100 investment.

Figure 13.5 Several measures on the Childs and Gridley leveraged lease returns.

does not depend on the lessor's cost of capital. The decision to accept the leasing project as an investment or not is made by comparing the r_W with the lessor's cut-off or hurdle rate.

The TRM-RIC function for the Childs and Gridley leveraged lease is plotted in Figure 13.5, along with the initial investment, traditional sinking fund, and two-stage measures. The functions are plotted on the same graph to illustrate the consistency of the methods: All but the Wiar equity return would mark the project acceptable for values of $k < 25$ percent, and unacceptable for $k > 25$ percent. The apparent symmetry of the "loan" phase measure of the two-stage method with the traditional sinking fund method is interesting. The lease is acceptable for $k < 25$ percent with the two-stage method, provided that the payback (recovery of investment plus opportunity cost) is acceptable, since the implicit loan embedded in the later cash flows is at a rate less than k in this range. The fact that the two-stage payback goes to infinite value after k reaches 28.5 percent is noteworthy, for that is the value of $r_{\min}$ in the TRM solution. An infinite value of the two-stage payback means that the initial investment and opportunity cost of the funds committed will never be fully recovered. Any such payback beyond the project's economic life may be similarly interpreted.

CONCLUSION

Leveraged leases provide perhaps the closest "real-world" approximation to the certainty environment we have considered to exist for capital-budgeting analysis to this point. Furthermore, growth in the use of leveraged leasing and the magnitude of funds involved make leveraged lease profitability analysis a significant area for investigation.

In this chapter we have examined leveraged leases as an interesting and practical application of analytical methods designed to deal with mixed cash flows. The results obtained suggest that accept/reject decisions may be correctly reached by several of the methods: NPV; two-stage method; initial investment method; traditional sinking fund method; and the TRM approach.

The Wiar method would reject projects acceptable under the other criteria. In fact, the Wiar rate is truly internal to the project—the cost of capital does not enter into its calculation at all. It is solely a function of the internal rate of return to the overall lease cash flows and the interest rate on the debt component of the lease. Because of this the Wiar rate, r_W, plotted on a straight-line parallel to the k-axis.

Analysis of leveraged leases involves a sufficient number of cash flows to uncover a cause of some concern with the TRM algorithm—it can sometimes conflict seriously with other methods.

QUESTIONS

1. Explain why leveraged leases normally have mixed cash flows to equity, whereas the overall cash flows to the lease are not mixed.
2. Are methods suitable for analysis of leveraged leases also suitable for general capital-budgeting project analysis and vice versa? Is there any exception?
3. What is the main difference between a railroad trust certificate lease and a leveraged lease?
4. Can the Wiar method be applied to projects financed entirely with equity?
5. Why may it be appropriate to talk in terms of separate debt and equity costs with a leveraged lease? Is this appropriate for capital investments in general? Why or why not?

PROBLEMS

13.1 The following *quarterly* cash flows are from a leveraged lease discussed by Campanella [4]. Analyze this project in terms of net present value, initial investment method, traditional sinking fund method, and two-stage method for $k = 0$ percent, 10 percent, and 20 percent annually.

$t =$	Cash Flow	$t =$	Cash Flow	$t =$	Cash Flow
0	−130,000	15	5,429	30	−2,074
1	19,259	16	4,433	31	−2,316
2	19,127	17	2,614	32	−2,563
3	18,993	18	2,430	33	−2,816
4	17,256	19	2,242	34	−3,073
5	13,916	20	1,395	35	−3,336
6	13,773	21	−112	36	−3,605

t =	Cash Flow	t =	Cash Flow	t =	Cash Flow
7	13,627	22	−312	37	−3,880
8	12,197	23	−516	38	−4,160
9	9,485	24	−775	39	−4,446
10	9,329	25	−938	40	−7,360
11	9,171	26	−1,156		
12	7,984	27	−1,378		
13	5,771	28	−1,606		
14	5,601	29	−1,838		

13.2 Assume that in Problem 13.1 the total equipment cost was $1 million, equity participation $200,000, and debt at 8.5 percent annual rate fully amortized over the 40 quarters (ten years). Assume the IRR (annualized) on the overall lease cash flows is 12 percent. What is the Wiar rate?

13.3(a) The following quarterly cash flows are from a leverage lease discussed by Hichens [7]. Calculate the NPV, two-stage measures, initial investment, traditional sinking fund, and TRM rate for $k = 15$ percent.

t =	Cash Flow	t =	Cash Flow
0	−$651.50	10	− 11.10
1	98.50	11	98.50
2	98.50	12	−170.00
3	98.50	13	0.00
4	78.50	14	−117.60
5	98.50	15	0.00
6	219.70	16	0.00
7	98.50	17	0.00
8	78.50	18	17.20
9	98.50		

13.3(b) If these cash flows to equity are for a lease 20 percent equity financed, find the Wiar rate if the rate on debt is 9 percent and the overall return on the leased equipment is 12 percent. Assume annual data.

13.4 Show formally why for $k > r_{min}$ the payback of the two-stage method becomes infinite—the investment plus opportunity cost is never recovered.

13.5 Show why the initial investment method return is lower than the traditional sinking fund method return.

13.6 As an approximation to the rate of return on a leveraged lease, how good is the profitability index based on the ratio of the uniform annual equivalent of NPV to the initial outlay?

13.7 Show that the initial investment method is analogous to the NPV procedure since it assumes initially invested amounts earn at rate k percent. Also, initial investment is increased by only enough to cover later cash flows; the original initial investment is the amount on which the rate of return is based. The extra investment at $t = 0$ is only to cover later negative cash flows and earns only at rate k percent.

Bibliography

1. Barone, Robert, "Some Theoretical and Practical Problems in Leveraged Lease Analysis," *Business Economics* (September 1973), p. 5.

2. Bierman, Harold Jr., "Leveraged Leasing: An Alternative Analysis," *The Bankers Magazine,* Vol. 157 (Summer 1974), pp. 62–65.
3. Brown, Norman M., "Return on Investment and Book Accounting for Leveraged Lease Transactions," *Journal of Commercial Bank Lending* (August 1972), pp. 26–28.
4. Campanella, Joseph A., "Leveraged Leasing Financing and the Commercial Bank," Masters Thesis, the Stonier Graduate School of Banking, Rutgers University, June 1974.
5. Childs, C. Rogers, Jr., and William G. Gridley, Jr., "Leveraged Leasing and the Reinvestment Rate Fallacy," *The Bankers Magazine,* Vol. 156 (Winter 1973), pp. 53–61.
6. Dyl, Edward A., and Stanley A. Martin, Jr., "Setting Terms for Leveraged Leases." Paper presented at the Seventh Annual Meeting of the Financial Management Association, Seattle, Washington, October 1977.
7. Hichens, Antony, "The Cost of Equipment Leasing," *The Investment Analyst* (December 1966).
8. Myers, Stewart C., David Dill, and Alberto Bautista, Jr., "Valuation of Financial Lease Contracts," *Journal of Finance* (June 1976), pp. 799–819.
9. Packham, Richard E., "An Analysis of the Risks of Leveraged Leasing," *Journal of Commercial Bank Lending* (March 1975), pp. 2–29.
10. Perg, Wayne R., "Leveraged Leasing: The Problem of Changing Leverage," *Financial Management* (Autumn 1978), pp. 47–51.
11. Reed, Edward W., Richard V. Cotter, Edward K. Gill, and Richard K. Smith, *Commercial Banking* (Englewood Cliffs, N.J.: Prentice-Hall, 1976), pp. 244–248.
12. Robertson, James, *The Leveraged Lease: Determining the Benefits to the Lessor* (Providence, R.I.: Industrial Leasing Corporation, undated), p. 34.

Chapter 14
Alternative Investment Measures

The purpose of this chapter is to introduce several additional measures that may be applied to capital-budgeting projects. These include the geometric mean rate of return, the average rate of return, Boulding's time spread, and Macaulay's duration.

In this chapter, in order to simplify the exposition, capital outlays will be restricted to the initial outlay, and subsequent net cash flows will be assumed to be nonnegative. All cash flows are assumed to occur at the end of the corresponding time periods. In other words, only simple investments in the sense defined in Chapter 10 will be considered.

ADDITIONAL RATE OF RETURN MEASURES

Geometric Mean Rate of Return

In contrast to the more generally known arithmetic mean, the geometric mean is obtained by taking the nth root of the product of the n items, rather than dividing their sum by the number n. When considering the average of interest or growth rates over a period of time, the geometric mean is considered more appropriate than the arithmetic mean because it takes into account the effects of period-to-period compounding that the arithmetic mean ignores. Because of the time-value of money, it is, for example, not correct to say that a deposit of $1000 that earns 4 percent the first year, 8 percent the second year, and 9 percent the third year has earned an average rate of 7 percent over the three-year period. The amount earned is $224.29 on the $1000 principal. The uniform, average annual rate for which $1000 will grow to $1224.29 over three years is not 7 percent but 6.98 percent. For a three-year period, this is not a great difference, but the error of the arithmetic mean over the geometric mean becomes greater the longer the time span covered. For example, if a principal amount can earn 4 percent for ten periods, 8 percent for the next ten periods, and 9 percent for the last ten periods of a 30-year investment life, the geometric mean rate is 6.16 percent, whereas the arithmetic mean is 7 percent.

The *geometric mean rate of return* on an investment, r_g, may be defined by:

$$r_g = \left[\prod_{t=1}^{n}(1+y_t)\right]^{1/n} - 1 \tag{14.1}$$

where

$$y_t = \frac{E_t - E_{t-1} + R_t}{E_{t-1}} \tag{14.2}$$

with R_t the cash flow at end of period t and the E_t representing the market value of the investment at end of period t. Note that this formulation measures the period-to-period changes in equity value over the life of the investment even though the overall change in equity value is not realized until disposition of the asset at the end of its useful life.

Average Discounted Rate of Return

The *average discounted rate of return*, r_a, may be defined as:

$$r_a = \frac{\sum_{t=1}^{n} y_t(1+r_a)^{-t}}{\sum_{t=1}^{n}(1+r_a)^{-t}} \tag{14.3}$$

where y_t is as defined in Eq. (14.2). Since r_a is defined recursively, it would appear difficult and time consuming to compute. However, existing computer programs for finding internal rate of return can be used.

Equation (14.3) is equivalent to:

$$1 - (1+r_a)^{-n} = \sum_{t=1}^{n} y_t(1+r_a)^{-t}$$

since

$$\sum_{t=1}^{n}(1+r_a)^{-t} = \frac{1-(1+r_a)^{-n}}{r_a}$$

which is the equation for $a_{\overline{n}|r_a}$, the present value of an annuity of one for n periods at rate r_a.

Rearranging the terms, we obtain:

$$1 = \sum_{t=1}^{n-1} y_t(1 + r_a)^{-t} + (1 + y_n)(1 + r_a)^{-n} \tag{14.4}$$

To solve for r_a in Eq. (14.4), we need only recognize that this is the equation for an "investment" of \$1, returning $y, \ldots, y_{n-1}$, and a final return of $1 + y_n$ at time n, and apply any computer program for finding IRR. This equation is the same as that for finding yield to maturity for a variable-payment bond that sells for its par value of \$1, and at maturity returns the \$1 with the final payment of interest.

Robert R. Trippi illustrated the application and usefulness of geometric mean return and average-discounted rate of return for measuring the returns on investments that undergo changes in market value over their useful lives.[1] Trippi employed 12 illustrative examples in his exposition. Here we will examine several similar examples to demonstrate the techniques and compare r_g with r_a and the IRR, which is denoted by r_c for "conventional" rate of return in Trippi's notation.

To illustrate the meaning and calculation of r_g and r_a, let us consider the following example, which requires a \$1000 initial investment and returns the net, after-tax cash flows indicated. In addition, the market value of the asset changes from period to period.

Example 14-1

	$t=1$	$t=2$	$t=3$	$t=4$	$t=5$
Cash Flow	\$ 200	200	300	400	200
Market Value	\$1100	1200	1250	1300	1325

Assuming the asset will be disposed of at the end of year five, the \$1325 market value will be realized as a positive salvage value and the total cash flow increased by this amount to \$1525. For simplicity we assume that the market values are the after-tax proceeds that would be realized if the asset were to be disposed of at the end of any indicated year. The internal rate of return (here denoted r_c) is 28.5044 percent, on the cash flow series $-\$1000, \$200, \$200, \$300, \$400$, and \$1525.

To calculate r_g we employ Eq. (14.2) $n = 5$ times, substituting into Eq. (14.1). Thus

$$y_1 = \frac{E_1 - E_0 + R_1}{E_0} = \frac{1100 - 1000 + 200}{1000} = .3000$$

$$y_2 = \frac{E_2 - E_1 + R_2}{E_1} = \frac{1200 - 1100 + 200}{1100} = .2727$$

$$\vdots$$

and so on

---

[1] Robert R. Trippi, "Conventional and Unconventional Methods for Evaluating Investments," *Financial Management*, Vol. 3 (Autumn 1974), pp. 31–35.

And applying Eq. (14.1), we obtain:

$$r_g = [(1.3)(1.27273)(1.29166)(1.36)(1.17308)]^{1/5} - 1$$
$$= 27.8024 \text{ percent}$$

Now, to find r_a we employ Eq. (14.4). This results in the following series to which we apply the procedure for finding the internal rate of return:

$$-1 \quad .3 \quad .27273 \quad .29167 \quad .36 \quad 1.17308$$

Note that this is identical to the series for a hypothetical bond that sells for $1, yields the various amounts defined by Eq. (14.2), and returns the original investment in a balloon payment of one at $t = 5$. Thus we find that:

$$r_a = 28.6193 \text{ percent}$$

For this example, $r_a > r_c > r_g$. This, however, will not always be the case. In fact, several cases were identified by Trippi. Table 14–1 displays the relationship between r_g, r_a, and r_c for some different patterns of cash flow and market value. It is important to note that the internal rate of return, r_c, depends only on the pattern of *cash flows*, whereas both r_g and r_a depend on the pattern of changes in market value in addition to cash flows. Thus many projects having the same IRR will have different r_g and still different r_a.

Trippi had proposed the average discounted rate of return as an alternative to the geometric mean rate of return for incorporating the change in equity value and its pattern in measuring the return on investment. This is something that heretofore has received more attention in the area of securities analysis and portfolio management than in capital budgeting. However, the concept is as equally applicable to capital investment projects as it is to investments in securities.

Shortly after the appearance of Trippi's paper, Peter Bacon, Robert Haessler, and Richard Williams[2] found an interesting counterintuitive example in an asset that produces no cash flow prior to its sale, doubles in value in the first year, and then in the second year declines to its original value. To quote Bacon, Haessler, and Williams: "The marginal return in year 1 is 100% and year 2 is −50%. Calculating the geometric mean and the internal rate of return or just relying on intuition all indicate that the true return is zero. . . . However, when . . . r_a is computed, the result is 36%."[3] As they go on to point out, the problem with Trippi's r_a is that it discounts the marginal returns in addition to averaging them. Since percentage increases are weighted the same as percentage decreases, the problem is not readily apparent with those investments that only increase or decrease in market value. However, with assets that first increase and then decrease, or vice versa, the investment return is misrepresented by r_a. The fact that early marginal percentage changes are discounted less than those occurring later further contributes to the problem.

---

[2] Peter Bacon, Robert Haessler, and Richard Williams, comment on Trippi's "Conventional and Unconventional Methods for Evaluating Investments," *Financial Management*, Vol. 5 (Spring 1975), p. 8.
[3] Ibid.

Table 14-1. EXAMPLES OF r_g, r_a, AND r_c FOR VARIOUS CASES, EACH REQUIRING $1000 INITIAL OUTLAY

Case No.		1	2	3	4	5	r%	r%	r (IRR)%
1	Cash Flow	0	100	200	300	400			
	Market Value	1000	1000	1000	1000	1000	19.1956	16.9082	16.9082
2	Cash Flow	200	200	200	200	200			
	Market Value	1000	1000	1000	1000	1000	20.0000	20.0000	20.0000
3	Cash Flow	400	300	200	100	0			
	Market Value	1000	1000	1000	1000	1000	19.1956	24.2573	24.2573
4	Cash Flow	0	0	0	0	0			
	Market Value	1000	1100	1300	1600	2000	14.8698	13.6208	14.8698
5	Cash Flow	0	0	0	0	0			
	Market Value	1200	1400	1600	1800	2000	14.8698	15.5507	14.8698
6	Cash Flow	0	0	0	0	0			
	Market Value	1400	1700	1900	2000	2000	14.8698	19.1003	14.8698
7	Cash Flow	200	200	200	200	200			
	Market Value	1000	900	700	400	0	−10.7682	−10.5832	0.0000
8	Cash Flow	200	200	200	200	200			
	Market Value	800	600	400	200	0	0.0000	0.0000	0.0000
9	Cash Flow	200	200	200	100	200			
	Market Value	1000	600	300	200	0	9.8561	12.7813	0.0000
10	Cash Flow	200	200	200	200	200			
	Market Value	1000	1100	1200	1300	1400	25.0228	24.9019	24.8848
11	Cash Flow	200	200	200	200	200			
	Market Value	1000	1400	1400	1400	1400	23.4399	27.0023	24.8848
12	Cash Flow	200	200	200	200	200			
	Market Value	1000	1000	1000	1000	1400	27.1069	24.8848	24.8848

192 SPECIAL TOPICS AND METHODS

In his reply to Bacon, Haessler, and Williams, Trippi emphasized that his "primary intent . . . was not to advocate universal acceptance of one measure over the others, but rather to demonstrate the general difficulties and frequent lack of conformity of each of the measures. . . . Clearly some nonunity marginal rate of substitution of present for future undistributed wealth is likely to apply . . . this phenomenon being totally lost with the conventional measures."[4]

Thus, although caution must be exercised, the geometric mean rate of return and average discounted rate of return may be considered adjuncts in the process of investment evaluation, particularly where there is unrealized (monotonic) increase or decrease over the life of the investment. Problem 14.1 at the end of this chapter serves to illustrate why the methods yielding r_g and r_a should perhaps not be used at all for investments characterized by nonmonotonically changing market value.

A subsequent chapter takes up the topic of abandonment value in capital budgeting. There it may be seen that an alternative to r_a exists. For now, we shall go on to finish this chapter with the topics of unrecovered investment, duration, and time spread.

TIME-RELATED MEASURES IN INVESTMENT ANALYSIS

Although the literature has generally concentrated on other aspects of the topic of capital budgeting, time-related measures are useful and may provide additional insight. Here we shall consider two time-related measures: Macaulay's *duration* and Boulding's *time spread*. The latter, although identical to the modern actuaries' *equated time*, was proposed in 1936.

Boulding's Time Spread

Kenneth E. Boulding[5] proposed *time spread* (TS) as a measure of the average time interval elapsing between sets of capital outlays and returns. For investments having a single initial outlay at time $t = 0$, Boulding's time spread is defined by:

$$\sum_{t=1}^{N} R_t = \sum_{t=1}^{N} R_t (1 + r)^{TS-t} \tag{14.5}$$

Since $(1 + r)^{TS}$ is constant for a given r and TS,

$$\sum_{t=1}^{N} R_t = (1 + r)^{TS} \sum_{t=1}^{N} R_t (1 + r)^{-t} \tag{14.5a}$$

---

[4] Robert R. Trippi, "Reply," *Financial Management*, (Spring 1975), pp. 8–9.
[5] K. E. Boulding, "Time and Investment," *Economica*, Vol. 3 (1936), pp. 196–220.

so that

$$(1 + r)^{TS} = \frac{\sum_{t=1}^{N} R_t}{\sum_{t=1}^{N} R_t(1 + r)^{-t}} \qquad (14.5b)$$

and

$$TS = \log\left\{\frac{\sum_{t=1}^{N} R_t}{\sum_{t=1}^{N} R_t(1 + r)^{-t}}\right\} \div \log(1 + r) \qquad (14.6)$$

In the case of $r = r°$ (the internal rate of return), it can be shown (as Boulding did) that:

$$TS = \log\left\{\frac{\sum_{t=1}^{N} R_t}{R_0}\right\} \div \log(1 + r) \qquad (14.7)$$

where R_0 is the initial (and only) capital outlay for the project. The proof of this involves the recognition that for the internal rate of return (IRR) the initial outlay is equal to the sum of the discounted cash flows at discount rate $r°$.

When used with the internal rate of return, time spread shows how long the initial investment remains invested on average at rate $r°$ (the IRR). Time spread provides the point in time at which a *single* amount, equal to the undiscounted sum of cash flows, would be equivalent to the individual cash flows at intervals over the life of the investment, at a given rate of interest. It is a measure of the average time between capital outlays and net cash receipts. In cases in which the only cash outlay is at $t = 0$, time spread therefore measures the average time elapsed to receive the net cash flows over the interval $t = 1$ through $t = N$. The following example will clarify this and set the concept.

Consider case 1 in Table 14–1. This project, costing $1000, yields total cash flows of $2000 over its life, including $1000 realized on disposition of the asset at $t = 5$. Time spread for this project is $TS = 4.4370$ years, and the internal rate of return is $r_c = 16.9082$ percent. The individual net cash flows could be replaced by a single cash flow of $2000 (equal to the undiscounted sum of cash inflows) at $t = TS$: the equation

$$R_0 = \sum_{t=1}^{N} R_t(1 + r°)^{-TS} = (1 + r°)^{-TS} \sum_{t=1}^{N} T_t \qquad (14.8)$$

follows directly from Eq. (14.7). Substituting the parameters of case 1, we obtain

$$\$1000 = (1.169082)^{-4.4370} \quad \$2000 = \$1000$$

Thus the entire cash flow series beyond the initial outlay may be replaced by a single amount equal to its sum at $t = TS$. Similarly, rates other than the IRR may be used, with the same interpretation, although for different rates different values for TS will be obtained.

Macaulay's Duration

Following soon after Boulding, Frederick R. Macaulay[6] developed the concept of *duration* as an alternative to the conventional time measure for bonds—the term to maturity. For those investments with a single cash outlay at $t = 0$, duration is a weighted average of repayment times (or dates) with weights equal to the present values of the cash flows at their respective dates. Equation (14.9) defines duration:

$$D = \frac{\sum_{t=1}^{N} t R_t (1 + r)^{-t}}{\sum_{t=1}^{N} R_t (1 + r)^{-t}} \quad (14.9)$$

For $r = r°$, the internal rate of return, the denominator, by definition of the IRR, is equal to R_0, the initial outlay. Therefore, for $r°$:

$$D = \frac{\sum_{t=1}^{N} t R_t (1 + r°)^{-t}}{R_0} \quad (14.10)$$

Calculation of duration is straightforward, even if tedious. As Durand has pointed out,[7] even though different, D converges to the same value as TS when N is finite and the discount rate approaches zero. It might be added that, when the only cash flow is at $t = N$, $D = TS = N$.

The history of development and application of duration has been very well described by Weil, who, among other things, points out that Hick's elasticity of capital with respect to discount factors is equivalent to duration,[8] although apparently developed independently and somewhat later. Weil also mentions Tjalling C. Koopmans' 1942 (unpublished) paper on matching life insurance assets and liabilities to "immunize" the company against effects of interest rate changes. At the time Koopmans was employed by Penn Mutual Life Insurance Company.[9] Credit for the

---

[6] Frederick R. Macaulay, *Some Theoretical Problems Suggested by the Movement of Interest Rates, Bond Yields and Stock Prices in the United States Since 1856* (New York: National Bureau of Economic Research, 1938).
[7] David Durand, "Time as a Dimension of Investment," *Proceedings of the Eastern Finance Association* (April 1973), pp. 200–219.
[8] Roman L. Weil, "Macaulay's Duration: An Appreciation," *Journal of Business*, Vol. 46 (October 1973), p. 590.
[9] Ibid., p. 591.

seminal idea on immunization is often awarded to Redington[10] for his later contribution, which appears to be the earliest published paper on the topic although appearing a decade after Koopmans' paper was written.

Like time spread, duration provides a useful adjunct measure to be used in capital budgeting, although it was developed for another purpose, as stated earlier. For case 1 of Table 14–1, $D = 4.3696$. This provides the "average" time that elapses for a dollar of present value to be received from this project. This is somewhat less than the time spread value. It may be shown that $D \leq TS$.

Unrecovered Investment

The *unrecovered investment* of a capital-budgeting project is defined by:

$$U = R_0(1 + r)^T - \sum_{t=1}^{T} R_t(1 + r)^{T-t} \tag{14.11}$$

With the internal rate of return it is implicitly assumed that the IRR rate, $r°$, is earned on the unrecovered principal as measured at the beginning of each period over the project life. This was made explicit in the treatment of conflicting IRR—net present value rankings in Chapter 8. With $r°$, the unrecovered investment will be exactly zero at $t = N$. For $t < N$ and with $r = r°$, $U > 0$; the unrecovered investment will be positive prior to the end of the project life. For $t < N$ and $r < r°$, U becomes negative prior to $t = N$. Figure 14.1 shows the graphs for U as a function of t and r. Since it is assumed that cash flows occur only at the end of each period, discontinuities occur at these points. For $r = r°$ the unrecovered investment becomes zero after the end of period four. At a higher rate, $r = 30$ percent, for example, the cash flows were not even adequate for paying the "interest" on the unrecovered investment by $t = 5$, so that the investment is not fully recovered by that time. In fact, at $t = 5$ the unrecovered investment is greater than the initial investment at $t = 0$. For rates less than $r°$ the investment is fully recovered prior to $t = 5$.

Table 14–2, which employs the same type component breakdown used in Chapter 8, serves to illustrate the concept of unrecovered investment. The table displays the unrecovered investment under the heading "Ending Principal" for the beginning-of-period points. Table 14–2 treats the investment case 1 of Table 14–1 as though it were a loan, and unrecovered investment is seen to be the "loan principal."

Unrecovered investment, U, is related to payback period P, which was discussed in Chapter 5. The point at which U becomes zero corresponds to the time

---

[10] F. M. Redington, "Review of the Principles of Line-Office Valuations," *Journal of the Institute of Actuaries*, Vol. 78 (1952).

196 SPECIAL TOPICS AND METHODS

Figure 14.1 Unrecovered investment at end of time period indicated.

Table 14-2. COMPONENT BREAKDOWN OF CASH FLOWS (AMOUNTS ROUNDED TO NEAREST CENTS) FOR $r = r^*$

	Beginning Principal	Interest on Beginning Principal	Principal Repayment	Total Payment	Ending Principal
1	$1000.00	169.08	0	0	$1169.08
2	1169.08	197.67	0	100	1266.75
3	1266.75	214.18	0	200	1280.93
4	1280.93	216.58	0	300	1197.51
5	1197.51	202.48	1400	1400	0

Note: It is assumed that end-of-period payments are composed of interest at $r° = 16.9082$ percent on beginning-of-period principal plus (if there is an excess over the interest) principal repayment.

when the investment has been fully recovered. For $r = 0$, the conventionally defined payback period is obtained.[11]

---

[11] With the conventional calculation of payback, the assumption that cash flows occur only at the end of each period is violated; once the payback period has been bracketed, the end-of-period cash flow at the further time period is treated as if it occurred uniformly over the period. The formula for U does not violate the assumption of end-of-period cash receipts, and to this extent there is a difference with payback calculation.

The concept and measure of unrecovered investment are useful as an adjunct to other capital-budgeting measures. It serves to focus attention on the nature of the process of investment recovery implicit within other measures, as was done in Chapter 8.

SUMMARY AND CONCLUSION

The additional investment measures presented in this chapter provide useful *adjuncts* to other capital-budgeting measures. They illustrate that factors other than cash flow alone may be of interest; as, for instance, Trippi's average rate of return that, to some extent, incorporates the appreciation in asset value that is not realized until the end of the project life. Used alone they are not especially useful; but used with other measurements of capital-budgeting project characteristics they can provide additional insight, thereby facilitating better decision making.

Perhaps Durand states the case as well as anyone when he says:

> From all this I conclude that we need to take a far broader view of capital budgeting than we have in the past. We have squandered altogether too much effort on a futile search for that elusive will-O'-the-wisp the one and only index of profitability; and we have lost valuable perspective thereby.[12]

QUESTIONS

1. An alternative definition of duration was used by J. B. Yawitz, G. H. Hempel, and W. J. Marshall, "Is Average Maturity a Proxy for Risk?," *Journal of Portfolio Management* (Spring 1976). They defined duration as the period of time that elapses before a stream of payments generates one-half its present value: a measure of median time rather than mean time. Compare with Macaulay's duration.
2. Describe the difference between Macaulay's duration and Boulding's time spread. What does each measure?
3. Is average discounted rate of return appropriate or useful for projects that experience an appreciation in market value followed by a decrease? Explain.
4. What specific advantage, if any, does average discounted rate of return offer vis-a-vis conventional internal rate of return?
5. Explain the concept of unrecovered investment, and relate to the problem of conflicting net present value-internal rate of return discussed in Chapter 8. Why does unrecovered investment for $r = 0$ percent, as defined in this chapter, usually not correspond exactly to the payback period calculation?
6. Explain why, other factors being equal, we would prefer an investment with a low, positive, unrecovered investment at $t = N$ to one with a high recovered investment.

---

[12] David Durand, "Time as a Dimension of Investment," *Proceedings of the Eastern Finance Association* (April 1973), p. 191.

7. What is meant by the term *immunization* that was used in this chapter? How might it be related to capital budgeting: to the maturity of liabilities and equity versus the "maturity" of capital assets?
8. Durand [5] suggested that the only financial assets with exceptionally long durations were growth stocks and that organizations with long-duration liabilities would wish to reduce risk of loss due to interest rate fluctuations by holding growth stocks. Analyze this in light of the concept of immunization.
9. Irving Fisher showed that $dV/di = -DV$, where V is the present value of a series of payments, D the duration, and i the interest rate compounded (discounted) continuously. What is the significance of this finding in applying the Newton-Raphson method for finding rates of return?

PROBLEMS

14.1 You are provided the following information for two capital investment projects, each costing $1000 and having five-year useful lives:

Project		Time Period				
		1	2	3	4	5
A	Cash Flow	$ 200	200	200	200	200
	Market Value	1000	1250	1500	1250	1000
B	Cash Flow	$ 200	200	200	200	200
	Market Value	1000	750	500	750	1000

(a) Calculate for each project r_g, r_a, and $r_c = $ IRR.
(b) Compare the results.
(c) What conclusions do you draw regarding r_g and r_a for such projects having nonmonotonically increasing or decreasing market value?

14.2 Prove that for the IRR, $r°$, that:

$$C_0(1 + r°)^{TS} = \sum_{t=1}^{N} R_t$$

14.3 You are given the following information about the net, after-tax cash flows for two mutually exclusive capital investment projects each costing $1000 at $t = 0$:

Project	$t = 1$	$t = 2$
C	$ 700	1500
D	1500	500

The appropriate cost of capital is 12 percent.
(a) Calculate the NPV and the IRR for each project.
(b) Calculate duration, D, and time spread, TS. In addition, develop a schedule of the type shown in Table 14–2.
(c) With the additional information obtained in part (b) interpret the results obtained in part (a).

14.4 For the following two capital investment projects, calculate r_g, r_a, $r_c (= $ IRR),

D, and TS. Compare results and discuss anything unusual you may observe. Both projects require the same initial outlay: $1000. Use 15 percent cost of capital:

Project		$t=1$	2	3	4	5
E	Cash Flow	$200	200	200	200	200
	Market Value	600	300	100	100	100
F	Cash Flow	$200	200	200	200	200
	Market Value	600	300	100	0	0

14.5 Show that, if the only cash flow beyond the initial investment outlay is one at $t = N$, $D = TS = N$.

Bibliography

1. Bacon, Peter, Robert Haessler, and Richard Williams, comment on Trippi's "Conventional and Unconventional Methods for Evaluating Investments," *Financial Management*, Vol. 5 (Spring 1975), p. 8.
2. Bernhard, Richard H., "A Comprehensive Comparison and Critique of Discounting Indices Proposed for Capital Investment Evaluation," *Engineering Economist*, Vol. 16 (1971), pp. 157-185.
3. Bernhard, Richard H., and Carl J. Norstrom, "A Further Note on Unrecovered Investment, Uniqueness of the Internal Rate, and the Question of Project Acceptability," *Journal of Financial and Quantitative Analysis*, Vol. XV, No. 2 (June 1980), pp. 421-423.
4. Boulding, K. E., "Time and Investment," *Economica*, Vol. 3 (1936), pp. 196-220.
5. Durand, David, "Growth Stocks and the Petersburg Paradox," *Journal of Finance*, Vol. 12 (1957), pp. 348-363.
6. ———, "Time as a Dimension of Investment," *Proceedings of the Eastern Finance Association* (April 1973), pp. 187-192.
7. ———, "Indices of Profitability as Aids to Judgment in Capital Budgeting," *Journal of Bank Research*, Vol. 3 (1973), pp. 200-219.
8. Fisher, Lawrence, "An Algorithm for Finding Exact Rates of Return," *The Journal of Business of the University of Chicago* (January 1966), pp. 111-118.
9. Fisher, Lawrence, and Roman L. Weil, "Coping with the Risk of Interest-rate Fluctuations: Returns to Bondholders from Naive and Optimal Strategies," *Journal of Business*, Vol. 44 (1971), pp. 408-433.
10. Hicks, John R., *Value and Capital* (Oxford: Clarenden Press, 1939; also 2nd ed., 1946).
11. Lintner, John, "Corporate Growth Under Uncertainty," in Robert Marris, ed., *The Corporate Economy* (London: Macmillan Press, 1971).
12. Macaulay, Frederick R., *Some Theoretical Problems Suggested by the Movement of Interest Rates, Bond Yields and Stock Prices in the United States Since 1856* (New York: National Bureau of Economic Research, 1938).
13. Redington, F. M., "Review of the Principles of Line-Office Valuations," *Journal of the Institute of Actuaries*, Vol. 78 (1952), pp. 286-340.
14. Solomon, Ezra, "The Arithmetic of Capital-Budgeting Decisions," *Journal of Business*, Vol. 29 (1956), pp. 124-129.
15. Trippi, Robert R., "Conventional and Unconventional Methods for Evaluating Investments," *Financial Management*, Vol. 3 (Autumn 1974), pp. 31-35.

16. ———, "Reply," *Financial Management*, Vol. 4 (Spring 1975), pp. 8–9.
17. Vanderhoof, I. T., "The Interest Rate Assumption and the Maturity Structure of the Assets of a Life Insurance Company," *Transactions of the Society of Actuaries*, Vol. 24 (1972), pp. 157–205.
18. Wallas, G. E., "Immunisation," *Journal of the Students Society, Institute of Actuaries*, Vol. 12 (1959), pp. 345–357.
19. Weil, Roman L., "Macaulay's Duration: An Appreciation," *Journal of Business*, Vol. 46 (October 1973), pp. 589–592.
20. Weingartner, H. Martin, "Some New Views on the Payback Period and Capital Budgeting Decisions," *Management Science*, Vol. 15 (1969), pp. B594–B607.
21. Whittaker, John, "The Relevance of Duration," *Journal of Business Finance*, Vol. 2 (1970), pp. 1–8.

Chapter 15
Project Abandonment Analysis

Up to this point it has been implicitly assumed that capital-budgeting projects, if accepted for investment, would (for better or for worse) be held until $t = N$. This is unduly restrictive. Furthermore, it violates the realities of capital-budgeting practice; capital investments are often abandoned prior to termination of their theoretical useful lives. In this chapter the topic of abandonment analysis is taken up.

THE ROBICHEK-VAN HORNE ANALYSIS

In a paper published in 1969, Alexander A. Robichek and James C. Van Horne (R-VH) presented an algorithm for determining if and when a capital investment project should be abandoned prior to the end of its useful life at $t = N$.[1] The original procedure was modified somewhat[2] after Edward A. Dyl and Hugh W. Long[3] showed that the original algorithm could, in some circumstances, break down.

---
[1] Alexander A. Robichek and James C. Van Horne, "Abandonment Value and Capital Budgeting," *The Journal of Finance*, Vol. 22 (December 1967), pp. 577–589.
[2] Alexander A. Robichek and James C. Van Horne, "Abandonment Value and Capital Budgeting: Reply," *The Journal of Finance*, Vol. 24 (March 1969), pp. 96–97.
[3] Edward A. Dyl and Hugh W. Long, "Abandonment Value and Capital Budgeting: Comment," *The Journal of Finance*, Vol. 24 (March 1969), pp. 88–95.

The R-VH paper has become widely known and cited, perhaps because it was the first paper in a major journal in recent years to have dealt with the subject of abandonment value. It provided an important prod in the process of awakening academics to a problem that in practice has always been a factor to be considered, but for which little mention has been made in the literature.

R-VH assumed, in order to facilitate analysis, that (1) an adequate estimate of the firm's cost of capital exists; (2) there is no capital rationing; and (3) a unique internal rate of return exists for the projects considered. Assumption (3) may be satisfied by considering only simple investments, in the sense defined in Chapter 10.

The R-VH algorithm (corrected to satisfy the Dyl-Long critique) is stated as:

(a) Compute $PV_{\tau \cdot a}$ for $a = n$, where

$$PV_{\tau \cdot a} = \sum_{t=\tau+1}^{a} \frac{EC_{t \cdot \tau}}{(1+k)^{(t-\tau)}} + \frac{AV_{a \cdot \tau}}{(1+k)^{(a-\tau)}}$$

(b) If $PV_{\tau \cdot n} > AV_{\tau}$,
continue to hold project and evaluate it again at time $\tau + 1$, based upon expectation at that time.

(c) If $PV_{\tau \cdot n} \leq AV_{\tau}$,
compute $PV_{\tau \cdot a}$ for $a = n - 1$.

(d) Compare $PV_{\tau \cdot n-1}$ with AV_{τ} as in (b) and (c) above. Continue procedure until either the decision to hold is reached or $a = \tau + 1$.

(e) If $PV_{\tau \cdot a} \leq AV$ for all $\tau + 1 \leq a \leq n$, then abandon project at time τ. . . .
$EC_{t \cdot \tau}$ = expected cash flow in year t as of year τ.
AV_t = abandonment value in year t.
AC_t = "actual" simulated cash flow in year t.[4]

This algorithm as it is stated appears to have been written to deal with the timing of abandonment for a project after it had been accepted. However, R-VH suggested that their rule might be extended to *ex ante* project analysis. This chapter is primarily concerned with such *ex ante* capital investment project analysis. This emphasis, however, should not be construed to imply that continued project review, such as that suggested in the R-VH algorithm, is any less important.

Step (a) of the R-VH algorithm defined the present value *at time reference point* τ as the discounted sum of all cash flows occurring from the period immediately following τ to the end of the project life *plus* the present value at τ of the expected salvage value to be received at the end of the project life.

Step (b) states we should keep the project if the present value of continuing to do so as defined in step (a) is greater than the present value of salvage. Note that these present values are *at time* $= \tau$. Present values are normally calculated for $t = 0$.

Step (c) requires that we perform additional calculation and analysis before

---

[4] Robichek and Van Horne, "Abandonment Value and Capital Budgeting: Reply," op. cit., p. 96.

abandoning the project, even though the salvage at time τ is greater than or equal to the present value of expected cash flows from time $\tau + 1$ to the end of the project's maximum useful life at $t = N$. This step is necessary in order to avoid premature abandonment of the project; the NPV may possibly be increased by holding the project for one or more additional time periods even though it will not be held all the way to $t = N$.

Step (d) specifies that the analysis in steps (a) through (c) inclusive be repeated until a period is found for which, in light of the expected returns as of *today*, the decision is to hold on to the project, or else we get to $a = \tau + 1$. In the latter case the decision is to hold on for the current period, then abandon.

Finally, step (e) prescribes that if the salvage value at any point in time τ exceeds the present values that are potentially to be obtained by holding on to the project, it should be abandoned at time τ.

As quoted above, the R-VH algorithm seems particularly designed for ongoing, periodic analysis of capital investments with a view as to whether they should be abandoned or kept in service for another time period. However, although it may not be clear from the wording of the procedure, the R-VH approach is suitable for analyzing capital-budgeting projects *ex ante* (prior to acceptance) as well as the *ex post*, which the R-VH paper appears to stress. In such cases it could be used to help answer these questions. (1) What is the optimal period to keep the project if it is accepted? (2) What is the expected present value if the project were to be accepted and held for the optimal period and no longer?

The R-VH paper was useful in calling attention to the problem of project abandonment. However, it is equivalent to a "dual" formulation of the Terborgh-MAPI method discussed in Chapter 9. Such formulation yields, instead of the MAPI "adverse minimum," a "propitious maximum" NPV, if NPV is the measure of project acceptability or desirability employed. Associated with this maximum is the optimum number of years over which the project, if accepted, would be held. To develop the methodology, we need, in addition to the R-VH assumptions, the assumption that we have or can obtain reliable estimates of salvage values for time periods between the adoption of the project and the end of its useful life at $t = N$. For those fairly standard types of equipment for which there is a well-developed secondary market, this should be a reasonable assumption.[5] On the other hand, for plant and for custom-made equipment this assumption will in general lack the reliability associated with the former category. For a thorough treatment of the problems associated with extraction of such estimates, the reader is referred to Terborgh's *Dynamic Equipment Policy* [11].

The following two sections illustrate application of the modified MAPI procedure to three capital-budgeting projects and compare results with the R-VH method.

---

[5] For example, we could develop estimates of salvage value deterioration gradients by careful, systematic analysis of trade publications carrying advertisements for used equipment and by consulting with dealers specializing in such equipment.

AN ALTERNATE METHOD: A PARABLE[6]

To highlight the points presented an example will be employed.

The capital project committee of Typical Manufacturing Company is considering which of three mutually exclusive production machines it should purchase to perform certain operations on a new product that the company has decided to add to its line. The machines are all of standard design, and hundreds of various vintages are in use across the nation. The following information has been presented to the committee:

	Purchase Price	\multicolumn{7}{c}{For the Year Indicated Net After-Tax Cash Benefits}						
Machine A	$2,000	$600	$600	$600	$600	$100	$100	$100
Machine B	2,000	700	600	500	400	300	200	100
Machine C	1,000	100	200	300	400	300	200	100

All three machines have useful lives of 7 years. Machine A has an estimated salvage value of $419.43, B $419.43, and C $478.30 at the end of 7 years.

The recommendation provided to the committee is that machine C be purchased since, at the firm's 10 percent cost of capital, it has a net present value of $350.69, while A and B have, respectively NPVs of $286.99 and $346.75. Since most members of the committee are well versed in the traditional finance literature concerned with capital budgeting, C is chosen for purchase with little discussion. Of course, there is some argument over the significance of the slight edge in NPV that C has over B, but A is out of the running from the beginning.

Has the committee selected wisely? No! "But," the reply will be, "by selecting the project with the highest net present value we are assuring the maximum increase in the value of equity." However, there is more to the story. In the approach to project selection that was followed, no attention was paid to salvage value *prior to* the end of each machine's useful life. In the example presented here the salvage values for A and B represent 20 percent per annum declines from the prior year's value, beginning with the purchase price paid for each, while that for C represents a 10 percent per annum decline.

Tables 1-A, 1-B, and 1-C present alternative calculations that might have been performed for machines A, B, and C. Readers familiar with the MAPI method for replacement evaluation presented by Terborgh [11] will note some similarity in that his method also considers intermediate salvage values. However, the MAPI method was developed primarily for replacement decisions, and is based on minimum cost (adverse minima) rather than maximum benefit considerations. The method presented here might be considered the dual to Terborgh's method. Like the MAPI method, that shown in Tables 1-A, 1-B, and 1-C uses the concept of time-adjusted annual averages, or level annuities. However, instead of finding adverse minima, we instead find what might be called "propitious maxima." In this instance these are employed to present matrices representing the continuum of net present value opportunities of each project, assuming that the projects may be abandoned at the end of years 1, 2, 3, ..., n where "n" represents the last year in the useful life of the project.

---

[6] The following pages are reprinted with permission from *The Engineering Economist*, Vol. 22, No. 1 (Fall 1976). Copyright © American Institute of Industrial Engineers, Inc., 25 Technology Park/Atlanta, Norcross, GA. 30092.

Table 1-A. CAPITAL-BUDGETING PROJECT WITH SALVAGE VALUE AT END OF EACH YEAR

(Initial outlay = $2000; estimated useful life = 7 Years;
decline in salvage value from beginning of period value—20%/year)

Year	1 Return	2 Present Value Factor— 10%	3 P.V. of Return = (1)×(2)	4 Accum. P.V. = (3) Acc.	5 Capital Recovery Factor— 10%	6 Level Annuity = (4)×(5)	7 Level Annuity = Cost $2000×(5)
1	$600	.9091	545.46	545.46	1.1000	600.00	−2200.00
2	600	.8264	495.84	1041.30	.5762	600.00	−1152.40
3	600	.7513	450.78	1492.08	.4021	600.00	− 804.20
4	600	.6830	409.80	1901.88	.3155	600.00	− 631.00
5	100	.6209	62.09	1963.97	.2638	518.10	− 527.60
6	100	.5645	56.45	2020.42	.2296	463.89	− 459.20
7	100	.5132	51.32	2071.74	.2054	425.54	− 410.80

Year	8 Salvage Value at Year End	9 P.V. of Salvage = (2)×(8)	10 Level Annuity = (9) = (5)×(9)	11 (6)+(7) +(10)	12 P.V. of Annuity— 10%	13[a] N.P.V. of (11) = (11)×(12)	14 Internal Rate of Return
1	1600.00	1454.56	1600.00	0.0	.909	0.0	.1000
2	1280.00	1057.79	609.50	57.10	1.736	99.13	.1311
3	1024.00	769.33	309.35	105.15	2.487	261.51	.1609
4	819.20	559.51	176.53	145.53	3.170	461.33	.1881
5	655.36	406.91	107.34	97.84	3.791	370.89	.1680
6	524.28	295.96	67.95	72.64	4.355	316.35	.1565
7	419.43	215.25	44.21	58.95	4.868	286.97	.1502

[a] Column 13 will generally be very slightly different than if NPV were calculated directly, due to rounding.

Table 1-B. CAPITAL-BUDGETING PROJECT WITH SALVAGE VALUE AT END OF EACH YEAR
(Initial outlay = $2000; Estimated useful life = 7 Years; decline in salvage value from beginning of period value—20%/year)

Year	1 Return	2 Present Value Factor— 10%	3 P.V. of Return = (1)×(2)	4 Capital Accum. P.V. = (3) Acc.	5 Level Recovery Factor— 10%	6 Level Annuity = (4)×(5)	7 Level Annuity = Cost $2000×(5)
1	$700	.9091	636.37	636.37	1.1000	700.00	−2200.00
2	600	.8264	495.84	1132.21	.5762	652.38	−1152.40
3	500	.7513	375.65	1507.86	.4021	606.31	− 804.20
4	400	.6830	273.20	1781.06	.3155	561.92	− 631.00
5	300	.6209	186.27	1967.33	.2638	518.98	− 527.60
6	200	.5645	112.90	2080.23	.2296	477.62	− 459.20
7	100	.5132	51.32	2131.55	.2054	437.82	− 410.80

Year	8 Salvage Value at Year End	9 P.V. of Salvage = (2)×(8)	10 Level Annuity = (9)× (5)×(9)	11 (6)+(7)+(10)	12 P.V. of Annuity Factor— 10%	13[a] N.P.V. of (11) = (11)×(12)	14 Internal Rate of Return
1	1600.00	1454.56	1600.00	100.00	.909	90.90	.1500
2	1280.00	1057.79	609.50	109.48	1.736	190.06	.1602
3	1024.00	769.33	309.35	111.46	2.487	277.20	.1668
4	819.20	559.51	176.53	107.45	3.170	340.62	.1699
5	655.36	406.91	107.34	98.72	3.791	374.25	.1696
6	524.28	295.96	67.95	86.37	4.355	376.14	.1662
7	419.43	215.25	44.21	71.23	4.868	346.75	.1599

[a]Column 13 will generally be very slightly different than if NPV were calculated directly due to rounding.

Table 1-C. CAPITAL-BUDGETING PROJECT WITH SALVAGE VALUE AT END OF EACH YEAR
(Initial outlay = $1000; estimated useful life = 7 Years; decline in salvage value from beginning of period value—10%/year)

Year	1 Return	2 Present Value Factor— 10%	3 P.V. of Return = (1) × (2)	4 Accum. P.V. = (3) Acc.	5 Capital Recovery Factor— 10%	6 Level Annuity = (4) × (5)	7 Level Annuity = Cost $1000×(5)
1	$100	.9091	90.91	90.91	1.1000	100.00	−1100.00
2	200	.8264	165.28	256.19	.5762	147.62	− 576.20
3	300	.7513	225.39	481.58	.4021	193.64	− 402.10
4	400	.6830	273.20	754.78	.3155	238.13	− 315.50
5	300	.6209	186.27	941.05	.2638	248.25	− 263.80
6	200	.5645	112.90	1053.95	.2296	241.99	− 229.60
7	100	.5132	51.32	1105.27	.2054	227.02	− 205.40

Year	8 Salvage Value at Year End	9 P.V. of Salvage = (2) × (8)	10 Level Annuity = (9) × (9)	11 (6)+(7) +(10)	12 P.V. of Annuity Factor— 10%	13[a] N.P.V. of (11) = (11) × (12)	14 Internal Rate of Return
1	900.00	818.19	900.00	−100.00	.909	− 90.90	.0000
2	810.00	669.38	385.70	− 42.88	1.736	− 74.44	.0562
3	729.00	547.70	220.23	11.77	2.487	29.27	.1120
4	656.10	448.12	141.38	64.01	3.170	202.91	.1637
5	590.49	366.64	96.72	55.76	3.791	211.39	.1821
6	531.44	300.00	68.88	81.27	4.355	353.93	.1858
7	478.30	245.46	50.42	72.04	4.868	350.69	.1812

[a]Column 13 will generally be very slightly different than if NPV were calculated directly, due to rounding.

Column 6 in the tables gives the level annuity having the same accumulated value at the end of the indicated year as the values in Column 4. Column 7 gives the level annuities for the number of years indicated that are equivalent to the initial outlay. Column 10 gives the uniform annual equivalent to the salvage value in each indicated year. By summing across Columns 6, 7, and 10 and then multiplying by the appropriate factors for the present value of an annuity, the NPVs of Column 13 are obtained. The figures in Column 13 are the NPVs of the projects if they are abandoned and sold for salvage at the end of the year indicated. Column 13 could have been calculated directly, of course, and to a somewhat greater precision in the trailing digits.

Armed with the information contained in Tables 1-A, 1-B, and 1-C the committee probably would have selected project A and not project C. If project A were selected, and then abandoned at the end of the fourth year of service, it would provide an NPV of $461.33. This is higher than that of B, which reaches a peak of $376.14 in the sixth year, and C, which must also be kept for 6 years if its peak NPV of $353.93 is to be realized.

Since the projects reach maximum NPV with different timing, we have a situation tantamount to that of projects with unequal economic lives. Thus, it may appear necessary to adjust the Table 1 figures to reflect the different timing of optimal abandonment for each project. Ordinarily, the easiest means for adjusting for different economic lives is to find the uniform annual equivalent of the NPVs by multiplying them by the corresponding capital recovery factor. However, we already have these results in Column 11.

Over a 12-year time horizon, the least common denominator of 4 and 6 year lives, projects A, B, and C have NPVs of $991.78, $588.46, and $553.71, respectively. These figures may be obtained by multiplying the uniform annual equivalents for optimal abandonment by the present value of annuity factor for twelve periods. Note that since the same present value of annuity factor is used, the comparison could have been directly between the uniform annual equivalents.

Comparison to R-VH[7]

This section is concerned with comparison of the method illustrated in the foregoing section with the revised Robichek-Van Horne algorithm.

Let us begin by applying the R-VH rule to the machines that were considered by TMC. Employing the R-VH procedure with fixed, point estimates of cash returns in each period results in the values displayed in Table 2. The values in row 1 for projects A, B, and C are identical (except for rounding errors in the trailing digits) to the values in column 13 of Table 1.

In row 5 of Table 2-A we see that the first figure is negative. The interpretation of this value is that, if at the end of year 4 project A is not abandoned, the company will incur an opportunity cost with present value *as of the end of year 4*, of $132.51 during year 5.

The figure of −$212.35 that follows in row 5 is the present value as of the end of year 4, of the cumulative opportunity cost if project A is held through years 5 and 6. The figure of −$255.39 in the last column in row 5 is the present value, as of the end of

[7] Ibid., pp. 63–71.

Table 2. PRESENT VALUE IN ROW YEAR 1, OF SALVAGE IN COLUMN YEAR J PLUS CUMULATIVE RETURNS THROUGH COLUMN YEAR J LESS SALVAGE VALUE AT START OF COLUMN YEAR J

A

	1	2	3	4	5	6	7
1	0.00	99.17	261.46	461.45	370.94	316.41	287.01
2		109.09	287.60	507.59	408.03	348.05	315.71
3			196.36	438.35	328.84	262.86	227.28
4				266.18	145.72	73.14	34.01
5					−132.51	−212.35	−255.39
6						−87.82	−135.17
							−52.08

B

	1	2	3	4	5	6	7
1	90.91	190.08	277.24	340.62	374.30	376.22	346.82
2		109.09	204.96	274.68	311.73	313.84	281.50
3			105.46	182.15	222.90	225.22	189.65
4				84.36	129.19	131.74	92.62
5					49.31	52.12	9.08
6						3.09	−44.26
7							−52.08

C

	1	2	3	4	5	6	7
1	−90.91	−74.38	29.30	202.92	307.72	353.96	350.73
2		18.18	132.23	323.22	438.50	489.35	485.80
3			125.45	335.54	462.34	518.29	514.38
4				231.09	370.58	432.11	427.82
5					153.44	221.12	216.40
6						74.46	69.26
7							−5.72

year 4, of the cumulative opportunity cost that will be suffered if project A is held from the end of year 4 through the end of year 7.

Thus, in terms of the figures of Table 2, each project should be abandoned at the end of the year prior to that corresponding to the row in which the figures become negative. In terms of opportunity cost, the interpretation is that a project should be abandoned when continued retention results in an opportunity cost, from loss in salvage value, greater than revenues in subsequent periods.

The figures in Table 2 could have been generated entirely by the procedure implicit in Table 1, simply by shifting the time reference point forward one period for each new row of figures generated. However, in Table 2, for project A the values in Column 4 are greater than any values in their corresponding rows. Therefore, at $t = 0$ there is no need to generate any more than the first row of values for each project. However, once a particular project has been selected, it may be useful to re-evaluate it at the end of subsequent periods to determine if the optimal time of abandonment has shifted under changing estimates of cash flow and abandonment value. Such a procedure is equivalent to the R-VH approach.

SPECIAL TOPICS AND METHODS

Table 15-1. CALCULATION OF OPTIMAL ABANDONMENT DECISION AND PRESENT VALUE FOR THREE EXAMPLE MACHINES (DYNAMIC PROGRAMMING APPROACH)

Project A (Machine A)

End of Year t	Return R_t	Abandonment Value (AV_t)	Discounted Return $(DR_t) =$ $max\{AV_t; (.9091) DR_{t+1}\} + R_t$	Decision
7	$100	$ 419.43	$ 519.43	—
6	100	524.28	624.28	Abandon
5	100	655.36	755.36	Abandon
4	600	819.20	1419.20	Abandon
3	600	1024.00	1890.19	Keep
2	600	1280.00	2318.37	Keep
1	600	1600.00	2707.63	Keep
0	—	—	2461.51	—

Project B (Machine B)

End of Year t	Return R_t	Abandonment Value (AV_t)	Discounted Return $(DR_t) =$ $max\{AV_t; (.9091) DR_{t+1}\} + R_t$	Decision
7	$ 100	$ 419.43	$ 519.43	—
6	200	524.28	724.28	Abandon
5	300	655.36	958.44	Keep
4	400	819.20	1271.32	Keep
3	500	1024.00	1655.76	Keep
2	600	1280.00	2105.25	Keep
1	700	1600.00	2613.88	Keep
0	—	—	2376.28	Keep

Project C (Machine C)

End of Year t	Return R_t	Abandonment Value (AV_t)	Discounted Return $(DR_t) =$ $max\{AV_t; (.9091) DR_{t+1}\} + R_t$	Decision
7	$100	$478.30	$ 578.30	—
6	200	531.44	731.44	Abandon
5	300	590.49	964.95	Keep
4	400	656.10	1277.24	Keep
3	300	729.00	1461.14	Keep
2	200	810.00	1548.32	Keep
1	100	900.00	1489.40	Keep
0	—	—	1354.00	—

A DYNAMIC PROGRAMMING APPROACH[8]

The solutions shown in Table 15-1 were obtained by using a dynamic programming approach, which provides a useful alternative to that described in the preceding section and also to the R-VH algorithm. Note that this dynamic programming formulation and solution employs the "backward searching" algorithm.[9] This is what

---

[8] The solutions to the preceding examples, which are shown in Table 15-1, were offered by an anonymous referee, who reviewed the paper for *The Engineering Economist*.

[9] This is described in the chapter on dynamic programming by Daniel Teichroew, *An Introduction to Management Science: Deterministic Models* (New York: Wiley, 1964), pp. 610-621.

James L. Pappas used in his contribution on project abandonment,[10] which was published simultaneously with the paper from which the preceding section was extracted.

Application of dynamic programming to equipment repair and replacement problems is covered by A. O. Converse,[11] who cites the earlier work of R. E. Bellman and S. E. Dreyfus.[12] The problem of abandonment value reduces to a special case of replacement, one in which an existing asset may be replaced by a hypothetical asset that does not exist, and therefore has a value of zero for the parameters of cost, cash flows, and so on, associated with it.

Since the methodology may not be familiar to many readers, a few words about Table 15-1 are in order. Starting with the year seven values for project A, the value $519.43 is the sum of that year's return and salvage value. Subsequent returns do not have to be considered since the machine lasts only seven years. For year six, the value $624.28 is obtained by adding the $100 return in year six to $524.28, which is the year six's abandonment value. Since the abandonment value is $524.28, which is a greater amount than the discounted future returns ($519.43 × .9091 = $472.21), the decision is to abandon. The decision to abandon holds until year three, where the $1024 abandonment value is less than $1290.19 (= $1419.20 × .9091).

SUMMARY AND CONCLUSION

It has been shown that consideration of abandonment values can change the selection from among alternatives that would otherwise be made if only final salvage values were considered.

The possibility of abandoning a capital investment at a point in time prior to the estimated useful or economic life has important implications for capital budgeting. Although we have not yet considered the effects of risk and uncertainty, the possibility of abandonment expands the options available to management and subsequently reduces the risk associated with decisions based on holding assets to the end of their lives. We must recognize that in a world clouded with great economic and political uncertainties, abandonment analysis synchronizes with the array of techniques that fall under the topic broadly termed *contingency planning*. To neglect the meaning and impact of abandonment and intermediate salvage values would be to refuse a most valuable instrument for gaining additional insight into the process of capital investment evaluation.

The origins of abandonment analysis are implicit in writings going back at least as early as Terborgh's *Dynamic Equipment Policy* published in 1949. Actually, the adverse minimum of the Terborgh-MAPI method does identify the optimal project life. The methods illustrated in this chapter will no doubt be supplemented, modi-

---

[10] James L. Pappas, "The Role of Abandonment Value in Capital Asset Management," *The Engineering Economist*, Vol. 22 (Fall 1976), pp. 53–61.
[11] A. O. Converse, *Optimization* (New York: Holt, Rinehart and Winston, 1970), pp. 121–129.
[12] R. E. Bellman and S. E. Dreyfus, *Applied Dynamic Programming* (Princeton, N.J.: Princeton University Press, 1962), p. 116.

fied, argued, and discussed much more over the years to come. Some may prefer the R-VH algorithm, some the tabularized procedure, some the dynamic programming technique. Since the methods presented in this chapter yield equivalent results, the question of which one should be employed is largely a matter of personal preference.

QUESTIONS

1. Explain how consideration of intermediate salvage value may cause a different (mutually exclusive) project to be selected than by assuming all projects to be held to the end of their economic lives.
2. How does the backward searching procedure of dynamic programming work?
3. Describe how explicit consideration of abandonment value greatly expands management options. Assuming that without such explicit consideration, projects would be held until the end of their useful lives, how would risk be reduced?
4. The discussion and illustrations used in this chapter employed net present value. Explain how other measures of project acceptability could be used in economic analysis of abandonment value.
5. In what sense was the *original* Terborgh-MAPI method of Chapter 9 a method that took into account abandonment value? Discuss in terms of the original method, not the dual formulation of this chapter.
6. Explain how analysis of abandonment value may be used instead of the average rate of return r_a, defined in Chapter 14 for investments that have changes in market value over their economic lives.

PROBLEMS

15.1 Assuming a 12 percent cost of capital, and the year-end salvage values shown, which of the two following mutually exclusive capital investments is preferable by the NPV criterion when abandonment value is considered? Present your solution systematically. Both projects cost $1000.

Project		1	2	3	4	5
A	Cash Flow	200	200	250	250	300
	Salvage Value	750	562	422	316	237
B	Cash Flow	225	235	290	290	340
	Salvage Value	725	526	381	276	200

(Time Period)

15.2 Using the tabular, MAPI-dual method presented in this chapter, analyze the following two mutually exclusive capital investment projects. For cost of capital of 14 percent, which is preferred with the NPV criterion? In what year should it be abandoned? Each project requires a $1000 initial outlay.

Project		1	2	3	4	5
A	Cash Flow	400	400	400	200	200
	Salvage Value	1100	880	616	370	−500
B	Cash Flow	500	500	250	250	250
	Salvage Value	1000	667	267	66	0

(Time Period)

15.3 Show how the optimum abandonment period would change for the assumption that salvage value declines by 10 percent per year versus 25 percent per year for this project, which costs $1000. Use cost of capital, k, of 11 percent per year.

	Time Period				
	1	2	3	4	5
Cash Flow	300	300	400	400	500
Salvage Value (10%)	900	810	729	656	590
Salvage Value (25%)	750	562	422	316	237

15.4 What would happen if, in Problem 15.3, the following salvage values applied?

	Time Period				
	1	2	3	4	5
Salvage	900	600	200	−300	−600

Under what circumstances can *negative* salvage values be expected to occur?

Bibliography

1. Bellman, R. E., and S. E. Dreyfus, *Applied Dynamic Programming* (Princeton, N.J.: Princeton University Press, 1962).
2. Converse, A. O., *Optimization* (New York: Holt, Rinehart and Winston, 1970).
3. Dyl, Edward A., and Hugh W. Long, "Abandonment Value and Capital Budgeting: Comment," *The Journal of Finance*, Vol. 24 (March 1969), pp. 88–95.
4. Gaumnitz, Jack E., and Douglas R. Emery, "Asset Growth Abandonment Value and the Replacement Decision of Like-for-Like Capital Assets," *Journal of Financial and Quantitative Analysis*, Vol. XV, No. 2 (June 1980), pp. 407–419.
5. Herbst, Anthony F., "An Algorithm for Systematic Economic Analysis of Abandonment Value in Capital Budgeting," *The Engineering Economist*, Vol. 22 (Fall 1976), pp. 63–71.
6. Pappas, James L., "The Role of Abandonment Value in Capital Asset Management," *The Engineering Economist*, Vol. 22 (Fall 1976), pp. 53–61.
7. Robichek, Alexander A., and James C. Van Horne, "Abandonment Value and Capital Budgeting," *The Journal of Finance*, Vol. 22 (December 1967), pp. 577–589.
8. Robichek, Alexander A., and James C. Van Horne, "Abandonment Value and Capital Budgeting: Reply," *The Journal of Finance*, Vol. 24 (March 1969), pp. 96–97.
9. Shillinglaw, Gordon, "Profit Analysis for Abandonment Decisions," *Journal of Business* (January 1957). Reprinted in Ezra Solomon, ed., *The Management of Corporate Capital* (Chicago: Graduate School of Business, University of Chicago, 1959), pp. 269–281.
10. Teichroew, Daniel, *An Introduction to Management Science: Deterministic Models* (New York: Wiley, 1964).
11. Terborgh, George, *Dynamic Equipment Policy* (Washington: Machinery and Allied Products Institute, 1949).

Chapter 16
Multiple Project Capital Budgeting

Preceding chapters considered various means for measuring the acceptability of individual capital-budgeting projects under conditions of certainty and no risk. Ranking of projects was limited to the problem of choosing which one, and only one, of mutually exclusive projects that should be selected when all the candidates meet at least the minimum criterion for adoption. The problem of capital rationing was not considered, although actually no firm has unlimited capital, and most have funds limitations, at least periodically, that preclude investment in all projects meeting their minimum criteria. Neither, to this point, were the effects of other constraints considered, whether economic, technical, or of management policy.

BUDGET AND OTHER CONSTRAINTS

In this chapter we shall continue to assume a world of certainty in order not to let considerations relating to risk and uncertainty obscure the development of basic principles and methodologies. However, we *shall* deal explicitly with the implications of those factors that constrain management to choose a subset of the total array of projects that would *individually* be acceptable in the absence of restrictions.

To simplify exposition, a single measure of investment worth will be employed here. Throughout this chapter the net present value (NPV) will provide the measure

Table 16-1.

Project	Cost	NPV
A	$60,000	$30,000
B	30,000	20,000
C	40,000	25,000

Table 16-2.

Budget	Accepted	Total NPV
≥$130,000	A,B,C	$75,000
100,000	A,C	55,000
90,000	A,B	50,000
70,000	B,C	45,000
60,000	A	30,000

of individual project desirability. The NPV was chosen as the single measure to be used primarily because it relates more directly and unambiguously to the basic valuation model of financial management, which was introduced at the outset of this book, than other measures do. Alternatively, if preferred, the profitability index, internal rate of return, payback, or a composite function of measures could be used.[1]

Consider the three capital investment projects in Table 16-1. If the projects are not mutually exclusive *and* there are no limits on funds that may be invested, all three projects would be undertaken by the firm. However, once we begin to consider capital rationing, it becomes clear that a method is needed for selecting from among the candidate projects. For example, various budget limitations yield differing selections and total NPV for the capital budget (see Table 16-2). Here we have only three projects, and the only constraint is the one on funds available for investments—capital rationing. Other constraints are common and complicate the selection process.

GENERAL LINEAR PROGRAMMING APPROACH

Additional constraints may be of several types. For example, suppose that one project is to construct a new assembly facility a short distance from our existing plant, and another project is to build an overhead conveyer from our existing plant to the new facility. Obviously, we should not even consider building the conveyor unless the construction project has first been accepted. Another type of constraint is that of mutual exclusivity. An example are the two projects: (1) repair the existing facility now and the mutually exclusive alternative being (2) to destroy the existing facility now and replace it with something new. Still another type of constraint is the requirement that if two projects are both accepted, a third project will also be accepted. Depending upon whether our objective is to maximize a value (such as

---

[1] We would hope, however, that the payback measure would not be adopted as the *sole* criteria by anyone who has read this far.

NPV) or minimize a value (such as cost), the general *linear programming* problem may be specified as:

$$\begin{aligned}
\text{Maximize} \quad & p_1 x_1 + p_2 x_2 + \cdots + p_n x_n \\
\text{Subject to} \quad & a_{11} x_1 + a_{12} x_2 + \cdots + a_{1n} x_n \leq b_1 \\
& a_{21} x_1 + a_{22} x_2 + \cdots + a_{2n} x_n \leq b_2 \\
& \quad \vdots \\
& a_{m1} x_1 + a_{m2} x_2 + \cdots + a_{mn} x_n \leq b_m \\
& \text{and for all } i \quad x_i \geq 0
\end{aligned}$$
(16.1)

or

$$\begin{aligned}
\text{Minimize} \quad & b_1 u_1 + b_2 u_2 + \cdots + b_m u_m \\
\text{Subject to} \quad & a_{11} u_1 + a_{21} u_2 + \cdots + a_m u_m \geq p_1 \\
& a_{12} u_1 + a_{22} u_2 + \cdots + a_{m2} u_m \geq p_2 \\
& \quad \vdots \\
& a_{1n} u_1 + a_{m2} u_2 + \cdots + a_{mn} u_m \geq p_n \\
& \text{and for all } i \quad u_i \geq 0
\end{aligned}$$

which, in matrix algebra notation, becomes:

$$\begin{array}{ll}
\text{Maximize} \quad p \cdot x & \qquad \text{Minimize} \quad b'u \\
\text{Subject to} \quad A \cdot x \leq b \quad \text{or} & \qquad \text{Subject to} \quad A'u \geq p' \\
\quad x_i \geq 0 \quad \text{for all } i & \qquad \quad u_i \geq 0 \quad \text{for all } i
\end{array}$$
(16.2)

By adding the requirement that x_i be integer-valued for all i, we have made this into a linear integer programming problem. Further restriction on the x_i, specifically the requirement that they take on only the values zero or one, produces a *zero-one integer programming* problem.

We formally specify the following two frequently encountered and important constraints.

Mutual Exclusivity

A set of n projects, from which at most one may be selected, yields the constraint:

$$\sum_{i=1}^{n} x_i \leq 1$$
(16.3)

Since we already have a nonnegativity constraint on all the xs, this means that only one of the x_i may have a nonzero value, namely a value of one. However, the constraint allows for none being accepted, since zero values for all the x_i satisfy the constraint.

Contingent Projects

Project B is said to be contingent on project A if it can be accepted only if A is accepted. This yields the constraint:

$$x_b \leq x_a \tag{16.4}$$

which is equivalent to:

$$x_b - x_a \leq 0 \tag{16.5}$$

or

$$x_a - x_b \geq 0$$

This last constraint form allows project A to be accepted, yet does not force its acceptance. However, an attempt to accept B with A not accepted produces a value of -1, which is less than zero and violates the constraint. Therefore this constraint accomplishes what we want and no more.

As the number of projects increases, the difficulty of selecting a subset that is in some sense "best" increases. When constraints in addition to budget limitations apply to the selection problem, it quickly becomes unmanageable without a systematic procedure for carrying out the selection process.

We have used the method of linear programming to illustrate how a subset of projects may be selected. Linear programming facilitates the handling of constraints, but its use in capital budgeting is limited. Capital investment projects are not infinitely divisible. We either accept a project or reject it; for example, we do not choose to invest in .763 or 1.917 of a project. This means that we invest in 0, 1, 2, or some other *integer* number of projects of the particular type. In fact, it often will be the case that we have a unique project, so that the relevant values are 0 (reject the project) or 1 (accept the project). For such projects there is no option of accepting a second, a third, and so on, because they do not exist. When there are multiples of a particular project, for example, construction of one warehouse, construction of a second warehouse, and so on, then each may be considered to be a separate project, identical to the others.

Linear programming may be made appropriate to capital-budgeting applications by modifying, for example, the well-known simplex method,[2] to incorporate Gomory's cutting-plane approach.[3] The result of such modification is an *integer linear programming* algorithm. However, because most capital-budgeting proposals involve one or a few projects of a particular type, and because the problem setup and constraint system are similar, the approach that will be taken here is that of 0-1 (zero-one) integer programming. The 0-1 terminology is useful since a project is either selected (1) or it is rejected (0) and thus can be assigned a numerical value of either 0 or 1 as the algorithm proceeds.

---

[2] For applications of the simplex method and a useful FORTRAN implementation, see Hans G. Daellenbach and Earl J. Bell, *User's Guide to Linear Programming* (Englewood Cliffs, N.J.: Prentice-Hall, 1970).
[3] R. E. Gomory, "All-Integer Programming Algorithm," in Muth and Thompson, eds., *Industrial Scheduling* (Englewood Cliffs, N.J.: Prentice-Hall, 1963), chap. 13.

ZERO-ONE INTEGER PROGRAMMING

Two similar approaches to 0-1 integer programming are those of Balas[4] and of Lawler and Bell.[5] Both rest on the concept of vector partial ordering as a heuristic for systematically searching out the optimal solution (if one exists) to an array of n projects in m constraints, without the necessity of evaluating each and every one of the 2^n possible combinations of projects.[6] The discussion that follows is patterned on that of Lawler and Bell. Development of new zero-one solution algorithms and refinements on existing methods continues because methods developed so far have their individual idiosyncrasies and none is clearly superior to the others for all problems. The Lawler and Bell algorithm, for purposes of illustration, is as useful as any. However, in terms of computational efficiency, there seem to be marked differences between alternative solution algorithms. For instance, Pettway examined the efficiency of several, and found wide differences among them.[7] So has Horvath [9], who has developed a FORTRAN program for using the algorithm that he found the most efficient and reliable.

A vector x is said to be a binary vector if each element is either 0 or 1. The vector may then be looked upon as a binary number. For two binary vectors, x and y, vector partial ordering means that $x \leq y$ if, *and only if*, $x_i \leq y_i$ for all i. For example, $x \leq y$ for $x = (0\ \ 0\ \ 1\ \ 0\ \ 1)$ and $y = (0\ \ 0\ \ 1\ \ 1\ \ 1)$. For a particular vector x, there may or may not exist a vector or vectors x' such that $x \leq x'$.

Lawler and Bell denote by $x°$ the vector following x in numerical (binary number) ordering for which $x \not\leq x°$. The vector $x°$ can be calculated by treating the vector x as a binary number. There are three steps involved. First, subtract 1 from x. Next, apply the logical "or" operation[8] to x and $x - 1$ to obtain $x° - 1$. Finally, add 1 to $x° - 1$. The alert reader will note that these three steps are equivalent to binary addition of "1" to the rightmost "1" in x.

Applying the notion of vector partial ordering to the problem of:

$$\begin{aligned}\text{Minimize} \quad & g_0(x) \\ \text{Subject to} \quad & -g_1(x) \geq 0 \\ & g_2(x) \geq 0\end{aligned}$$

where $x = (x_1, x_2, \ldots, x_n)$ and $x_1 = 0$ or 1, Lawler and Bell have developed an optimization algorithm containing only three decision rules. The vector $\widehat{x}$ denotes the best solution so far obtained.

---

[4] Egon Balas, "An Additive Algorithm for Solving the Linear Programs with Zero-One Variables," *Operations Research*, Vol. 13 (July–August 1965), pp. 517–546.

[5] E. L. Lawler, and M. D. Bell, "A Method for Solving Discrete Optimization Problems," *Operations Research*, Vol. 14 (November–December 1966), pp. 1098–1112.

[6] The number 2^n rapidly becomes very large as n increases. For example, $2^{25} = 33{,}554{,}432$, and $2^{35} = 34{,}359{,}738{,}368$.

[7] Richard H. Pettway, "Integer Programming in Capital Budgeting: A Note on Computational Experience," *Journal of Financial and Quantitative Analysis* (September 1973), pp. 665–672.

[8] The logical "or" means here that if *both* the jth element of x and the jth element of $x - 1$ are 0, then the jth element of $x° - 1$ is set to 0, or else it is set to 1.

Figure 16.1 Flow chart for Lawler and Bell 0-1 integer algorithm.

Rule 1. If $g_0(x) \geq g_0(\hat{x})$, replace x by $x°$.
Rule 2. If x is feasible, replace x by $x°$. Feasibility means that $-g_1(x) \geq 0$ and $g_2(x) \geq 0$, or that $g_{i1}(x) - g_{i2}(x) < 0$.
Rule 3. If for any i, $g_{i1}(x° - 1) - g_{i2}(x) \not\geq 0$, replace x by $x°$.

If no rule is applicable, replace x by $x + 1$ and continue.[9]

A flow chart for the algorithm with a sample problem and solution is shown in Figure 16.1. In using the algorithm to solve problems, it is suggested, following the experience of Lawler and Bell, that those variables that *a priori* would seem to be least significant be placed so as to occupy the rightmost positions in the solution vector. This should serve to reduce the number of iterations required, and hence the requisite solution time.

This algorithm is minimizing, and is predicated on monotonically nondecreas-

---

[9] It is strongly recommended that the reader refer to the original article by Lawler and Bell for a much more detailed explanation of the algorithm, and for examples of how problems involving nonbinary integer coefficients and quadratic objective functions may be handled.

ing functions for the objective equation and the constraints. However, maximization problems can be handled by negating the objective function and the constraint equations and objective function made monotonically nondecreasing by substituting $x' = 1 - x$ in the original problem. After the optimal solution to the minimization problem has been obtained, reverse substitution for the x' will provide the optimal array of projects for the maximum problem.

Since zero-one programming problems of practical scale do not lend themselves to manual calculation, and since computer programs are available for application of zero-one integer programming algorithms, the steps involved in solving a specific problem will not be illustrated here. Even small problems, although easily solvable on a computer, involve too many iterations for the methods to be considered suitable for manual application. The important thing, since problem setup is similar or identical with all the methods, is an understanding and mastery of the *problem setup and constraint specification*. This is vital, because an incorrectly specified constraint will often cause an incorrect problem solution. In practice, it may be useful to have the same problem set up independently by two or more persons or teams to provide a check on results.

Example 16-1

To illustrate the type of problem amenable to solution by zero-one integer algorithms and the formulation of the constraints, consider the following problem faced by the management of Tangent Manufacturing Company. Tangent is a small firm engaged in light manufacturing. The company has recently experienced a substantial increase in demand that is expected to continue for several years. The company currently owns a dilapidated warehouse that has 7000 square feet of space, and a small building for assembling its product. The condition of the existing warehouse is such that it cannot be used much longer in its current state of disrepair.

The executive committee has decided that next year the company will require at least 3000 square feet of warehouse floor space and, in the three following years, 7000, 8000, and 11,000 square feet of space. In none of these years, however, do they want more than 20,000 square feet of warehouse space.

The company also wants to expand its assembly operations by either renovating its current plant or by constructing another building for its assembly operations. Outlays for capital improvements are to be limited to $55,000 the first year, and to $45,000, $35,000, and $20,000 in the following three years.

The treasurer of the company has developed information on the present value of returns and on the required outlays for alternatives available to the firm. This information is presented in Table 16-3.

Management will not allow both project 1 and project 2 to be undertaken. Furthermore, adoption of project 7 is dependent on the prior adoption of project 3; project 8 is dependent on the prior adoption of project 4. Lastly, management requires that there be some expansion in assembly capacity, so either project 5, or project 6, or both must be adopted. Table 16-4 contains the system of constraints.

MULTIPLE PROJECT CAPITAL BUDGETING

TABLE 16-3.

Project	Present Value	\$ Thousands Required Outlays			
		Year 1	Year 2	Year 3	Year 4
1. Construct New Warehouse (10,000 sq. ft.) in Year 1	$50	$25	$ 7	$ 0	$ 0
2. Renovate Existing Warehouse (7000 sq. ft.) in Year 1	27	10	5	5	5
3. Lease Warehouse for 2 Years (3000 sq. ft.) in Year 1	15	6	6	0	0
4. Lease Second Warehouse for 2 Years (3000 sq. ft.) in Year 1	15	6	6	0	0
5. Construct New Assembly Plant in Year 1 (3000 unit capacity)	35	20	5	0	0
6. Renovate Existing Plant for Expanded Production (1500 unit increase in capacity)	25	12	3	0	0
7. Lease Warehouse for 2 Years (3000 sq. ft.) in Year 3	13	0	0	6	6
8. Lease Second Warehouse for 2 Years (3000 sq. ft.) in Year 3	13	0	0	6	6
9. Construct New Warehouse (10,000 sq. ft.) in Year 3	40	0	0	25	7
Outlay Constraints		≤55	≤45	≤35	≤20
Warehouse Space Constraints (thousands of sq. ft.)		≤20 >3	≤20 >7	≤20 >8	≤20 >11

Notice that the last constraint may be stated in two alternative ways. Also, constraints 5, 6, 9, and 10 are redundant in the presence of constraints 7, 8, 11, and 12, respectively, and can be eliminated.

Since the Lawler and Bell algorithm is predicated on monotonically decreasing functions, we must substitute $x' = 1 - x$ for x in the objective function and in the constraints as follows:

Case	Original Constraint	Modified Constraint
I.	$a_i x_i \leq b$	$a_i x_i' \geq +a_i - b$
II.	$a_i x_i \geq b$	$-a_i x_i' \geq -a_i + b$

After substitution, the modified constraint coefficients are ready to be punched on computer cards for the program. The modified constraint system is contained in Table 16-5. Note that all constraints are now in the "≥" form.

According to the computer solution to this problem, acceptance of all projects but 1, 5, 7, and 8 yields an objective function value of 122. In other words, the optimum feasible solution to this problem yields a total NPV of $122. The solution is

Table 16-4.

		x_1	x_2	x_3	x_4	x_5	x_6	x_7	x_8	x_9	b
Financial Constraints	1.	25	10	6	6	20	12	0	0	0	≤ 55
	2.	7	5	6	6	5	3	0	0	0	≤ 45
	3.	0	5	0	0	0	0	6	6	25	≤ 35
	4.	0	5	0	0	0	0	6	6	7	≤ 20
Warehouse Space Constraints Yr. 1	$\{$5.	10	7	3	3	0	0	0	0	0	≤ 20
	6.	10	7	3	3	0	0	0	0	0	> 3
Yr. 2	$\{$7.	10	7	3	3	0	0	0	0	0	≤ 20
	8.	10	7	3	3	0	0	0	0	0	> 7
Yr. 3	$\{$9.	10	7	0	0	0	0	3	3	10	≤ 20
	10.	10	7	0	0	0	0	3	3	10	> 8
Yr. 4	$\{$11.	10	7	0	0	0	0	3	3	10	≤ 20
	12.	10	10	0	0	0	0	3	3	10	> 11
Projects 1 and 2 Mutually Exclusive	13.	1	1	0	0	0	0	0	0	0	≤ 1
Project 7 Dependent on Prior Adoption of Project 3	14.	0	0	1	0	0	0	-1	0	0	≥ 0
Project 8 Dependent on Prior Adoption of Project 4	15.	0	0	0	1	0	0	0	-1	0	≥ 0
Assembly Facilities Must Be Expanded	16.	0	0	0	0	3	1.5	0	0	0	≥ 1.5
or	16'.	0	0	0	0	1	1	0	0	0	≥ 1

Table 16-5.

Constraint	x_1	x_2	x_3	x_4	x_5	x_6	x_7	x_8	x_9	$\geq$	b
1.	25	10	6	6	20	12	0	0	0		24
2.	7	5	6	6	5	3	0	0	0		−13
3.	0	5	0	0	0	0	6	6	25		7
4.	0	5	0	0	0	0	6	6	7		4
5.	−10	7	3	3	0	0	0	0	0		3
6.	−10	−7	−3	−3	0	0	0	0	0		−20
7.	10	7	0	0	0	0	3	3	10		13
8.	−10	−7	0	0	0	0	−3	−3	−10		−25
9.	1	1	0	0	0	0	1	0	0		1
10.	0	0	−1	−1	0	0	0	1	0		0
11.	0	0	0	−1	0	0	1	0	0		0
12.	0	0	0	0	−1	−1	0	0	0		−1

223

Table 16-6. SAMPLE PROBLEM TO ILLUSTRATE PROGRAM USAGE—9 VARIABLES, 12 CONSTRAINTS (Objective function maximum equals 122.0000)

Project Number	Decision Value	Decision Action
1	0.	Reject
2	1.	Accept
3	1.	Accept
4	1.	Accept
5	0.	Reject
6	1.	Accept
7	0.	Reject
8	0.	Reject
9	1.	Accept

Constraint Number	Actual Value	Constraint Constants
1	.54000E 02	≤ 55
2	.25000E 02	≤ 45
3	.30000E 02	≤ 35
4	.12000E 02	≤ 20
5	.13000E 02	≤ 20
6	$-$.13000E 02	< -3
7	.17000E 02	≤ 20
8	$-$.17000E 02	< -8
9	.10000E 01	≤ 1
10	$-$.10000E 01	≤ 0
11	$-$.10000E 01	≤ 0
12	$-$.20000E 01	≤ -1.5

All constraints are satisfied.

feasible since no constraint is violated. Table 16–6 illustrates the foregoing results.

These results could not have been obtained by ordinary linear programming methods. Integer linear programming could have been used, provided that additional constraints were added to restrict the number of each project accepted to the number available.

GOAL PROGRAMMING

In Chapter 2 the goal of maximization of shareholder wealth was singled out as *the* goal of modern financial management. And use of the NPV criterion for project selection serves to move the firm toward this goal when capital markets are approximately perfect and there is certainty with respect to project parameters. These, however, are abstractions from the reality that typically prevails; capital markets are less than perfect and uncertainty does prevail. Situations are often encountered in which management has more than one objective. In fact, this is probably the norm rather than an exception. Management recognizes that the market takes into account more information than the NPV of accepted capital investment projects could provide. Accounting profits, earnings, and dividend stability and growth, market share, total assets, and so on, affect the value of shareholder wealth.

Management may have compatible goals, goals for which the achievement of one does not prevent achievement of the others. On the other hand, goals may be incompatible; steps to reach one goal may require moving further from other goals. Ordinary linear programming can lead to less satisfactory results than can be obtained with what is known as *goal programming*. And in cases for which there is no solution when target values are treated as constraints in ordinary linear programming, goal programming can provide feasible solutions.

Goal programming is an extension of ordinary linear programming. In fact, the basic simplex algorithm and its computerized implementations are suitable in those instances in which integer solutions are not required. The general goal programming problem may be specified as:

$$\text{Minimize } f = (M_1 y_1^+ + N_1 y_1^-) + (M_2 y_2^+ + N_2 y_2^-) + \cdots \quad (16.6)$$
$$+ (M_n y_n^+ + N_n y_n^-)$$

$$\text{Subject to } \quad a_{11}x_1 + a_{12}x_2 + \cdots + a_{1n}x_n - y_1^+ + y_1^- = b_1$$
$$a_{21}x_1 + a_{22}x_2 + \cdots + a_{2n}x_n - y_2^+ + y_2^- = b_2$$
$$\vdots$$
$$a_{m1}x_1 + a_{m2}x_2 + \cdots + a_{mn}x_n - y_m^+ + y_m^- = b_m$$
$$\text{and for all } i \quad x_i, y_i^+, y_i^- \geq 0$$

In the more compact form obtained by using matrix notation for the constraint system this becomes:

$$\text{Minimize } f = \sum_{i=1}^{m} (M_i y_i^+ + N_i y_i^-) \quad (16.7)$$

$$\text{Subject to } \quad A \cdot x - y^+ + y^- = b$$

Several things should be noted about the goal programming model. First, many of the y^+ and y^- will be unimportant; in this case they will not appear in the objective function and may be ignored. Second, the normal linear programming constraints are present. These represent technological, economic, legal, or other requirements that must not be violated. Third, since the y_i^+ and y_i^- represent underachieving or overachieving the same goal, one of them must be zero.

The M_i and N_i provide for different weights to be assigned to under- or overachieving a goal. If either is zero it means that no importance is attached to that particular deviation from goal. The M_i and N_i also allow priority levels to be established. For instance, if goal i must be achieved before goal j can be considered, this may be specified by defining the *priority level coefficients*. The relationship:

$$M_i >>> M_j$$

denotes M_i to be a very large value in comparison with M_j, so large that goal i will be given *absolute* preference to goal j.

If M_i is to take absolute preference over M_j, but M_j is only twice as important as M_k, this can be stated as:

$$M_i >>> M_j = 2M_k$$

Thus, we can (1) define a hierarchical structure of goals, in which each level is fixed in relation to the others and (2) define *trade-off functions* between goals within a particular hierarchical stratum. When we state that goal j is twice as important as goal k, we are defining a trade-off function. Absolute priority is accomplished by making the trade-off too costly to be considered.

A goal programming problem formulation requires three main items:

1. An objective function. In this function, the weighted deviations from the target or goal levels are minimized according to specified priority rankings. This is in contrast to the ordinary linear programming formulation, in which an aggregate value objective function is maximized or, equivalently, the opportunity costs (shadow prices) are minimized.
2. The normal linear programming constraints reflecting economic, technological, legal, and other constraints.
3. The goal constraints that incorporate one or both of y_i^+ and y_i^-, the *deviational variables*.

The objective function must specify (1) the priority level of each goal, (2) the relative weight of each goal, and (3) the appropriate deviational variables. The deviational variables are viewed as penalty costs associated with under- or overachieving a particular target, or goal.

The specification of deviational variables in the objective function determines whether a particular goal is to be reached as exactly as possible, whether either under- or overachievement is to be avoided, or whether it is desired to move as far from some target level as possible. Specification of these goals is summarized in Table 16-7.

A great advantage of goal programming is that it can handle both complementary and conflicting goals as long as a *trade-off function* is specified that links the conflicting goals. Since management must make decisions in a world of risk and imperfect capital markets, project characteristics beyond NPV may have to be factored into the decision process. Interactions between the value of the firm and capital investments may have to be recognized. For example, large capital projects may require borrowing that could affect the firm's capital structure and its cost of capital for several years. Also, accounting profits may be important to the extent they influence the markets for the firm's shares and debt instruments. Goal programming is particularly useful, because it allows management perceptions and policies, and some interrelationships between the firm and the prospective capital investments to be handled simultaneously. It enables management to obtain insight into the implicit costs of its goals and trade-off functions if sensitivity analysis is carried out to show the effects of changing goal and trade-off parameters.

Table 16-7. GOAL SPECIFICATION

Reach at Least a Specified Minimum Level:	Minimize y^-
Do Not Exceed a Specified Maximum Level:	Minimize y^+
Approach Specified Target as Closely as Possible:	Minimize $(y^+ + y^-)$
Achieve Specified Minimum Level, Then Move as Far Above as Possible:	Minimize $(-y^+ + y^-)$
Achieve Specified Maximum Level, Then Move as Far Below as Possible:	Minimize $(y^+ - y^-)$

Goal programming allows the objective of maximizing shareholder wealth—enterprise value—to be approached by setting lesser goals that, if reached, contribute to the major objective. In other words, goal programming provides a means for disaggregating a strategic objective into a series of tactical goals that, taken together, move the firm toward that objective. And the tactical goals themselves may be interrelated by trade-off relationships.

Three difficulties affect using goal programming, particularly in capital budgeting. *One,* in capital-budgeting projects indivisibility is the rule rather than the exception. This means that ordinary linear programming computer codes are generally not suitable and one must resort instead to integer programming algorithms that are not as generally available. *Two,* specification of goals is often based on conjecture or "hunches" about empirical questions. Thus, different managers will generally make different subjective assessments of reality, based on individual experience, perception, and bias. This means that solutions obtained will depend on whose goals are achieved in the goal programming formulation. There is nothing necessarily wrong with this. In fact, since goals must be clearly specified, an added benefit may result when managers must articulate goals in a form amenable to programming solution. What goal programming can provide is an objective procedure for systematically and accurately reaching goals—goals that themselves may have been subjectively determined. *Three,* conflicting goals require that trade-off relationships be defined. This often requires that noncommensurables be compared, that exchange rates between "apples and oranges" be defined even though the trade-off function may involve less tangible factors than these. A further difficulty in this vein is that trade-off functions may not be linear, but may change over a range of values. This third difficulty means that one of the strengths of goal programming, its ability to deal with conflicting goals, is also potentially one of its greatest weaknesses if not approached with care.

SUMMARY AND CONCLUSION

Selection of which (if any) capital investments out of an array of candidates should be accepted requires a systematic approach. The indivisible nature of most capital investment projects means that ordinary linear programming may not produce correct results. Integer linear programming may be used, but requires constraints that reflect the number of each project available for adoption. Zero-one integer programming provides a very useful means of selection, and requires fewer explicit constraints.

Several methods of zero-one integer programming have been developed, and likely there will be further refinements and new developments. Experimentation has suggested that some methods are more generally useful than others. However, since problem specification will be identical, or at least very similar, for all existing zero-one integer programming algorithms, and probably for new developments as well, we have concentrated on specification of the problem and constraints.

Programming solution to multiple project selection is particularly useful because many constraints beyond that imposed by capital rationing may be handled easily. Great care must be exercised, however, in specifying all constraints. A seemingly minor error in one constraint may cause an entirely incorrect solution to be obtained.

QUESTIONS

1. Why do we require integer solutions to multiple project capital-budgeting problems?
2. What is the difference between integer linear programming and zero-one integer programming?
3. If we may invest in any number from zero to five of a particular project, such as identical delivery trucks, how would this be handled with zero-one integer programming? With integer linear programming?
4. Explain why, even with large, high-speed electronic computers, enumeration of all combinations of projects is not feasible or desirable as a selection method.
5. What criteria should be used in comparing two or more different zero-one integer programming algorithms?
6. Provide examples of projects that would yield constraints such as Problem 16.2 contains.

PROBLEMS

16.1 (a) Using a noninteger linear programming code, solve the sample problem of this chapter. Try first without constraints to limit solution values to ≤ 1, and then with such constraints. Compare results with the 0-1 integer programming solution. (b) If available to you, use an integer linear programming code to solve the problem. What additional constraints to those used with the 0-1 setup do you need?

16.2 Formulate the following constraints in terms of greater than or equal to inequalities:
(a) If project a is accepted, then project b must be accepted.
(b) If c is not accepted, then d must be accepted.
(c) Project g may be accepted only if both projects e and f are accepted.
(d) Project h cannot be accepted if either project i or j is accepted.

16.3 Given a vector $\bar{x} = 0\ 1\ 0\ 1\ 1\ 1\ 0$, and the Lawler and Bell algorithm:
What does $\bar{x}$ represent in terms of tangible quantities, in the $x' = 1 - x$? In other words, what does it tell us about the accept/reject decision for the projects? What is the $x°$ corresponding to $\bar{x}$?

16.4 Given a list of projects corresponding to $x_1 \ldots x_9$,
  (a) Set up the constraints in terms of the xs, an inequality of the form "$\geq$", and a constant for the following restrictions. Consider each restriction independently of the others for this question.
  (b) Convert your answers in part (a) to "$\leq$" inequalities in $x_i' = 1 - x_i$, with the constant to the right of the inequality symbol.
  (i) Projects x_1, x_2, and x_3 are mutually exclusive.
  (ii) Project x_2 must be selected before x_4 can be considered.
  (iii) Both x_5 and x_6 must be selected.
  (iv) If both x_2 and x_4 are selected, then x_7 must be selected.
  (v) If both x_1 and x_8 are selected, then x_9 cannot be selected.
  (vi) At least one of the projects x_1, x_2, or x_3 must be selected.

16.5 The Elenem Wydget Company is studying proposals for modernization and expansion. The following projects, with associated outlays, net present values, and contribution to expanded Wydget production (ΔW) are under consideration:

	NPV	W	Required Outlays Year 1	Required Outlays Year 2
1. Renovate existing plant	$15	50	$40	$40
2. Replace existing plant with new and larger building.	25	140	70	30
3. Construct warehouse building.	10	35	20	5
4. Construct building for assembly.	12	80	30	10
5. Build power conveyor system to assembly building from warehouse.	8	60	3	18

Management requires that no more than $130 be invested in year one and $90 in year two. Also required is that Wydget capacity be increased by at least 200. To determine the selection of projects that maximizes NPV: (a) set up the objective function and system of constraints, (b) convert to a system in x_i', and (c) solve the optimum selection.

16.6 Let the increase in Wydget capacity of 200 units in Problem 16.5 be a *goal* rather than a constraint. Try to set up the problem as one in goal programming. What prevents you from using a zero-one integer program to solve the goal problem?

16.7 The municipality of Oz owns 1280 acres of land that, years before, had supported a strip mine. The city council has directed the city manager's office to submit a plan for optimum use of the land. Several alternative, and to some extent conflicting, uses are possible. Optimum use has been defined by the city fathers to be maximization of net present value. Spending constraints apply in the initial year and the year following. In the first year ($t = 0$) no more than $75 million may be invested and at least $60 million must be invested. To spend less may jeopardize future state and federal government funding for Oz, because it may be thought that appropriations to Oz should be reduced if the city cannot spend the money on capital improvements. The corresponding amounts for the following year are $54 million and $48 million. The projects that are being considered, with associated NPVs and costs (in $ millions), are:

Project	Acres Required	NPV	Required Outlays $t=0$	Required Outlays $t=1$
1. Construct a park.	50	$-2.5	$ 5	$ 3
2. Build a golf course.	160	2	10	2
3. Build high-density housing for low-income families.	190	−3	15	20
4. Construct a commercial airport.	320	3	12	8
5. Develop an industrial park.	160	7	12	10
6. Construct stockyards & cattle feedlot facilities and lease them out.	120	1	4	2
7. Construct a sewage treatment-methane gas generation facility.	100	5	8	2
8. Dredge low areas to create lakes.	240	−1	6	0
9. Establish a zoological park and botanical garden.	300	4	10	4
10. After rehabilitation set land aside for a wildlife preserve.	240	0	4	0

For political reasons, at least one project out of 1, 3, 9, and 10 must be undertaken. For aesthetic reasons, neither 6 nor 7 may be undertaken unless two projects out of 4, 5, and 10 are first accepted in order to have a buffer zone between 6 and 7 and the remaining projects.

(a) Set up the objective function and system of constraints for this problem.
(b) Convert into the system of x_i' as illustrated in this chapter.
(c) If you have access to a zero-one integer program on a computer, find the optimum selection of projects.

16.8 The North Bay Harbor Authority (NBHA) is considering several interrelated investments due to rapid economic and population growth in the bay area. The following sketch illustrates the situation. Points A and B may currently be reached by automobile only by driving over bridges at D to E and G to F and connecting roads. This causes traffic problems along the various routes (in Old Towne) because of the increasing number of motorists. The existing bridges at D to E and G to F are suffering increased damage from loads in excess of what they were designed for; they cannot carry more traffic. If points A and B are connected by bridge or tunnel, then bridge or tunnel connections from B to C and A to C would be redundant. As an alternative to these bridges and tunnels, the two existing bridges may be replaced or augmented and an expressway built between them. The expressway would be built along the edge of Moribund Swamp, which is ecologically beyond saving. The swamp is destined for future heavy industrial development. The Harbor Authority is limited to spending $100 million. For simplicity, assume all investment outlays will occur only in the first year. The minimum increase in traffic has been set at 20,000 cars per day (includes round trips).

Given the following projects and associated values, (a) set up the objective function and system of constraints. Since funds for the investments will be raised by sale of revenue bonds, the Harbor Authority wishes to minimize the cost of the construction. (b) What combination of projects should be selected?

Project	Δ Cars/Day (thousands)	Required Investment ($millions)
1. Tunnel from A to B	14	$75
2. Bridge from A to B	10	60
3. Bridges from B to C and C to A	8	45
4. New bridges D to E and F to G (old bridges not destroyed)	10	20
5. Expressway E to F	13	29
6. New bridges D to E and F to G (old bridges destroyed)	12	25

16.9 The C. B. Breaker Trucking Company wants to solve the problem of which route its trucks should take between Steerville and Motown. In fact, Breaker Trucking management wants the problem solved for two different objective functions: (1) maximum fuel economy (that is, minimum fuel consumption) and (2) minimum time.

The following map illustrates those feasible all-year routes open between the two cities. (a) Set up the system of constraints and both objective functions. (b) If the trade-off between time of travel and fuel consumption is ten gallons for one hour, what is the objective function that incorporates both time and

16B

fuel economy constraints? (c) What is the optimum route with the objective function of part (b)?

Bibliography

1. Balas, Egon, "An Additive Algorithm for Solving the Linear Programs with Zero-One Variables," *Operations Research*, Vol. 13 (July–August 1965), pp. 517–546.
2. Balinski, M. L., "Integer Programming: Methods, Uses, Computation," *Management Science*, Vol. 12 (November 1965), pp. 253–309.
3. Charnes, A., W. W. Cooper, and Y. Ijiri, "Breakeven Budgeting and Programming to Goals," *Journal of Accounting Research*, Vol. 1 (Spring 1963), pp. 16–43.
4. Daellenbach, Hans G., and Earl J. Bell, *User's Guide to Linear Programming* (Englewood Cliffs, N.J.: Prentice-Hall, 1970).
5. Dyer, James S., "Interactive Goal Programming," *Management Science* (September 1972), pp. 62–70.
6. Geoffrion, A. M., "An Improved Implicit Enumeration Approach for Integer Programming," *Operations Research*, Vol. 17 (May–June 1969), pp. 437–454.
7. Gomory, R. E., "All-Integer Programming Algorithm," in Muth and Thompson, eds., *Industrial Scheduling* (Englewood Cliffs, N.J.: Prentice-Hall, 1963), chap. 13.
8. Hawkins, Clark A., and Richard A. Adams, "A Goal Programming Model for Capital Budgeting," *Financial Management* (Spring 1974), pp. 52–57.
9. Horvath, P. A., "A High Quality Heuristic for the Resolution of Zero-One Quadratic Programs with Interdependence Constraints," a working paper, June 1978.
10. Hughes, John S., and Wilbur G. Lewellen, "Programming Solutions to Capital Rationing Problems," *Journal of Business Finance and Accounting*, Vol. 1 (Spring 1974), pp. 55–74.
11. Ignizio, J. P., *Goal Programming and Extensions* (Lexington, Mass.: Lexington Books, 1976).
12. Ijiri, Y., *Management Goals and Accounting for Control* (Chicago: Rand-McNally, 1965).

13. Lawler, E. L., and M. D. Bell, "A Method for Solving Discrete Optimization Problems," *Operations Research*, Vol. 14 (November–December 1966), pp. 1098–1112.
14. Lee, Sang, *Goal Programming for Decision Analysis* (Philadelphia: Averback, 1972).
15. Lee, Sang, and A. J. Lerro, "Capital Budgeting for Multiple Objectives," *Financial Management* (Spring 1974), pp. 58–66.
16. Lemke, C. E., and K. Spielberg, "Direct Search Algorithms for Zero-One and Mixed-Integer Programming," *Operations Research*, Vol. 15 (September–October 1967), pp. 892–914.
17. Mao, James C. T., *Quantitative Analysis of Financial Decisions* (New York: Macmillan, 1969).
18. Metzger, Robert W., *Elementary Mathematical Programming* (New York: Wiley, 1958).
19. Pettway, Richard H., "Integer Programming in Capital Budgeting: A Note on Computational Experience," *Journal of Financial and Quantitative Analysis* (September 1973), pp. 665–672.
20. Rychel, Dwight F., "Capital Budgeting with Mixed Integer Linear Programming: An Application," *Financial Management*, Vol. 6, No. 4 (Winter 1977), pp. 11–19.
21. Salkin, Harvey M., *Integer Programming* (Reading, Mass.: Addison-Wesley, 1975).
22. Weingartner, H. Martin, "Capital Budgeting of Interrelated Projects: Survey and Synthesis," *Management Science*, Vol. 12 (March 1966), pp. 485–516.

Part IV
CAPITAL BUDGETING UNDER RISK—WITHOUT DIVERSIFICATION

Chapter 17
Utility and Risk Aversion

In this chapter, the first one to consider the matter of risk, we examine the concept of utility and how a utility function may be calculated, various ways of estimating risk, and problems associated with the probability of ruin. This last topic is of some importance to the enterprise (perhaps a small firm) for which candidate capital investment projects are large in relation to its financial resources.

The concept of utility is essential if we are to develop a rationale by which a decision may be reached for a capital investment that has a range of possible outcomes, each with an associated probability. Some of the possible outcomes may be large losses, whereas others are large gains.

In a world of certainty we would be able to say whether or not a project was acceptable based on objective criteria, such as the profitability index. Once risk is introduced, however, we must take into account the decision maker's[1] attitude toward risk in order to reach an economically rational decision. Two different persons are likely to disagree about accepting risky projects if they have different attitudes toward risk. One may take risk in stride, whereas the other is considerably bothered by it.

---
[1] We shall avoid the problem of whose attitude specifically is to be taken into account by using the term "decision maker" or "management."

THE CONCEPT OF UTILITY

Economists developed the concept of utility many years ago, and it is the foundation upon which microeconomic analysis rests. Utility is a reflection of personal satisfaction. Something that provides more feeling of pleasure than something else (or, equivalently, less pain) is said to have greater utility.

In this work we measure project traits in currency units—dollars. Because of this our task is much easier than it would be otherwise. We do not have to compare the respective utility of oranges and that of apples—only that of more dollars versus fewer.

The utility of more dollars is assumed to be greater than the utility of fewer dollars, so that the utility function we will be working with is monotonically nondecreasing in dollars, at least over the range of values we will be considering. A second dollar may have the same utility value of the first (constant marginal utility), greater value (increasing marginal utility), or lesser value (decreasing marginal utility).

When risk is introduced, we recognize that there is a trade-off between possible dollar gain (and thus utility) and risk. Projects promising the greatest return are also normally the riskiest projects. Otherwise others would have snapped them up before now.

The classic article on risk as it relates to utility is that of Tobin [9]. The following section follows his terminology.

Attitudes Toward Risk

Individual attitudes toward risk are revealed in the curvature of utility functions. Before going into the determination of an individual utility function, it will be useful to examine these attitudes toward risk. First, in Figure 17.1 we have a utility function corresponding to a *risk averse* individual, a risk averter. Here the utility function is concave from below. This means that each additional monetary gain, while contributing to increased utility, contributes less than the same amount when the individual has less to begin with. In other words, the function depicts *diminishing marginal utility*. An extra dollar offers less additional utility to given risk averse individuals when they have $100,000 than it does when they have $10,000. Diminishing marginal utility means that the loss of a dollar causes more disutility (negative utility, or loss of utility) than the gain of a dollar offers. For example, consider a person with $10,000 in cash savings, which may have taken many years to accumulate. An extra $1000 would increase utility, but not as much as a loss of $1000 would decrease it. If this person were offered a "fair bet," one with zero expected value based on equal probabilities of gaining or losing a large amount, the bet would be rejected. It would be rejected because the expected utility is negative, even though the expected monetary gain is zero.

For *small* amounts of monetary gain or loss, a risk averse individual may take "fair bets" or even bets where the expected monetary gain is negative. This may be explained on the basis that the negative utility of the small loss is dominated by the utility provided by the entertainment provided, or the utility provided by the hope, however remote, of a large monetary gain (as in a lottery).

Figure 17.1 Relationship of money gain to utility for a risk averter.

Figure 17.2 Relationship of money gain to utility for a risk neutral person.

Figure 17.2 corresponds to a *risk neutral*, or a risk indifferent individual. Each additional dollar, no matter at what point on the function, offers the same utility.

The utility function of a risk indifferent individual is a straight line. The slope is constant and therefore the marginal utility of monetary gain does not change over the curve. A large loss would reduce this person's utility by the same amount of utility as would be gained by winning an identical dollar amount. A risk indifferent individual could be expected to take fair bets, even those involving large amounts of possible gain or loss.

The final utility curve is that of a *risk lover*. This is illustrated in Figure 17.3. Tobin concluded that there are no 100 percent risk lovers. Such individuals, on reflection, would have to have a self-destructive compulsion to prefer the riskier of any two propositions. The utility curve has the property of increasing marginal utility, suggesting greed. The important thing about such utility function is that most individuals have utility functions that exhibit properties of risk aversion, risk neutrality, or risk seeking for different ranges of monetary values. This is illustrated in Figure 17.4.

For the individual whose utility function is shown in Figure 17.4 we can observe that the person is risk averse for amounts less than m_1 and greater than m_3. This individual is essentially risk neutral for amounts between m_2 and m_3, and is a

240 CAPITAL BUDGETING UNDER RISK—WITHOUT DIVERSIFICATION

Figure 17.3 Relationship of money gain to utility for a risk lover.

Figure 17.4 Overall utility of money for an individual.

risk lover or risk seeker for values between m_1 and m_2. The next section will show you how to estimate your own utility function or that of someone else. Do not be surprised if it is similar to the one in Figure 17.4, nor should you be bothered if it is not. The benefit you derive through plotting points along your utility function is that you gain a better understanding of how you react to risk. Your attitude toward risk influences your performance as a decision maker evaluating capital investments. And it is likely that your attitude toward risk changes as the dollar magnitude of the potential gain or loss changes.

CALCULATING PERSONAL UTILITY

This section presents a method for estimating an individual's utility function. The method could also be used to try to determine a composite utility curve for a group.

The treatment here parallels the presentation contained in Teweles, Harlow, and Stone [8]. Their purpose was to illustrate how the individual commodity futures trader could obtain his or her personal utility function for the risks found in such

Table 17-1. COMPUTATION OF DECISION MAKER'S UTILITIES FOR VARIOUS MONETARY GAINS

(1) Best Result	(2) Worst Result	Probability of (3) Computed Utility[a]	(4) Dollar Cash Equivalent	
1.0	0.0	1.0	$2,000,000	Best Result
.9	.1	.9	1,200,000	
.8	.2	.8	950,000	
.7	.3	.7	750,000	
.6	.4	.6	550,000	
.5	.5	.5	400,000	
.4	.6	.4	−100,000	
.3	.7	.3	−300,000	
.2	.8	.2	−400,000	
.1	.9	.1	−450,000	
0.0	1.0	0.0	−500,000	Worst Result

[a] $1.0 \times$ column 1 $+ 0.0 \times$ column 2. The utility of the best result is arbitrarily assigned a value of 1.0, the worst result, a value of 0.0. Other values could be used if desired.

activity.[2] The principle is applicable here also. However, consider that you are asked to put yourself in the role of manager here, and not one who is risking your own personal funds. That this is a distinction that a sole proprietor cannot make will not be argued. Because most managers in various enterprises do have different attitudes about their own money vis-à-vis that of their employers, try to make this distinction to the extent it is possible.

After assuming the "managerial frame of mind," the next step is to determine the largest dollar gains your capital investment decisions have regularly made and the largest dollar losses that have similarly resulted. This may be impossible for many readers. Thus students and managers who have not made such decisions will have to *imagine* what the amounts would be, and try to be perfectly honest about it. This is not a test; there are no right or wrong answers. It is not necessary to do any calculations in reaching your answers, although you may if you prefer. Calculation of the reader's personal utility function for monetary gains is included in Problem 17.1. For now we shall only illustrate the procedure.

Let us begin by developing the utility function for an entrepreneur who tells us that he (individually) has regularly made decisions that have resulted in gains of as much as $2 million and losses of as much as $500,000. We shall not concern ourselves here with whether these are gains and losses over the entire project life, or with other details of the timing of the amounts. The procedure would not be materially different anyway. Having established the largest regular gains and losses, we write them down as shown in Table 17–1, column 4. The value $2 million is associated with utility of 1.0 and the loss of $500,000 with utility 0.0. Other values could

[2] Their book is highly recommended for the many insights provided and its interesting style of presentation.

Figure 17.5 Plotted utility function of entrepreneur, From Table 17-1 dollar cash equivalents.

have been used for the utilities, such as $+1.0$ and -1.0, but the scaling is unimportant and by assigning zero utility to the worst outcome the calculations are a little easier.

Having established utilities of 1.0 for a gain of $2 million with probability 1.0, and 0.0 for loss of $500,000 with probability 1.0, we now need to find intermediate values. Suppose now we ask our entrepreneur to tell us if he would accept an investment offering a gain of $2 million with probability .9 and loss of $500,000 with probability .1; in other words, nine chances in ten of gaining $2 million and one chance in ten of losing $500,000. He answers "yes," certainly he would accept such investment. Now we ask if he would pay us $1 million for the opportunity to make such an investment. Yes, he would. $1.5 million? No, not this much. How about $1.2 million? Maybe. At $1.2 million he is not sure. For $50,000 more he will not take the investment, for $50,000 less he will. Thus in Table 17-1 we write in the second row, rightmost column, the amount $1,200,000.

We repeat the process for gain of $2 million with probability .8 and loss of $500,000 with probability .2. Our entrepreneur will pay up to $950,000 but no more for an investment offering these prospects. For each missing value we repeat the process until column 4 is completed. Then we can plot the results obtained, as shown in Figure 17.5, and fit an approximate curve to the points.

In constructing his or her own utility curve for monetary gains and losses, the reader can perform a self-interview or work with someone who will perform the function of interviewer. Further insight into the process is found in Teweles et al., cited earlier.

The curve obtained and plotted in the graph of Figure 17.5 is reasonably satisfactory, except that we do not have enough data points between $-\$100,000$ and $+\$400,000$ to be confident in the shape of the curve in that range. We can obtain more information by continuing the interview process. Let us begin by con-

UTILITY AND RISK AVERSION

Table 17-2. COMPUTATION OF REFINED UTILITY OF DECISION MAKER'S MONETARY GAINS

Best Outcome		Worst Outcome			
(1)	(2)	(3)	(4)	(5)	(6)
Utility	Probability	Utility	Probability	Computed Utility[a]	Dollar Cash Equivalent
.5	1.0	.4	0.0	.50	$400,000
.5	.9	.4	.1	.49	360,000
.5	.8	.4	.2	.48	350,000
.5	.7	.4	.3	.47	325,000
.5	.6	.4	.4	.46	280,000
.5	.5	.4	.5	.45	250,000
.5	.4	.4	.6	.44	180,000
.5	.3	.4	.7	.43	160,000
.5	.2	.4	.8	.42	50,000
.5	.1	.4	.9	.41	0
.5	0.0	.4	1.0	.40	−100,000

[a] Computed utility is obtained as best outcome times best outcome probability plus worst outcome times worst outcome probability.

Figure 17.6 Plot of refined utility of decision maker's monetary gains from Table 18-2.

structing Table 17-2 with best result now $400,000 and worst result −$100,000. The associated utilities are, respectively, .5 and .4.

Values between $400,000 gain and $100,000 loss are obtained as before. The decision maker is asked if he would accept an investment project offering $400,000 gain with .9 probability and $100,000 loss with .1 probability. Yes. Would he pay $380,000? No. $370,000? No. $360,000? Maybe. Don't know. $350,000? Yes. We write $360,000 in column 6 of Table 17–2. The process is repeated until column 6 is filled and then the results are plotted. Figure 17.6 contains the graph for the section of utility curve between −$100,000 and +$400,000. The scale is enlarged

Figure 17.7 Revised decision maker's utility of monetary gain.

from that used in Figure 17.5. After combining the information contained in Table 17-2 with that of Table 17-1, and plotting the results, we obtain Figure 17.7. The additional detail for utility between −$100,000 and +$400,000 enables a more refined approximation. The tentative judgment that our entrepreneur is a risk seeker for monetary gains seems to be vindicated by the additional information over the range of about $0 to $400,000. Because of the rather wide spread between utility values for dollar amounts in the ranges −$300,000 to −$100,000 and $1.2 million to $2 million, we might want to repeat the procedure for obtaining detail over these ranges, if our entrepreneur's patience has not been exhausted. We shall not do this here, however, since the procedure has been illustrated.

The plotted results obtained from our entrepreneur do not deviate very widely from the fitted curve. In fact, they are very close to it, thus indicating a high degree of consistency in evaluating alternatives over the range of values regularly experienced by the decision maker. We should not have been surprised if the points were much more scattered about the fitted curve. What happens if we now attempt to obtain utility values for dollar gains and losses beyond the range of the decision maker's regular experience? If we attempt to do this, we will most likely find that the decision maker becomes increasingly inconsistent as the monetary values become further and further removed from the domain of his experience.

To compute the utility of larger monetary gains, the formula used is:

$$U(\text{Gain}) \times Pr(\text{Gain}) + U(\text{Loss}) \times Pr(\text{Loss}) = U(\text{Cash Equivalent}) \quad (17.1)$$

which is equivalent to:

$$U(G)p + U(L)(1 - p) = U(C) \quad (17.2)$$

By rearranging the terms, we obtain formulas for computing the utilities of gains and losses outside the range of the decision maker's experience:

$$U(G) = \frac{U(C) - U(L)(1-p)}{p} \qquad (17.3)$$

and

$$U(L) = \frac{U(C) - U(G)p}{1-p} \qquad (17.4)$$

In calculating the utility of gains and losses for extended amounts for commodity traders, Teweles, Harlow, and Stone [8] suggest computing them three times. The reason behind repeating the procedure is to find out how consistent the decision maker is in making decisions outside the range of his or her experience. The reader is referred to the excellent discussion by Teweles et al. for a detailed treatment.

The main reason for concern about the decision maker's consistency for larger gains and losses than he or she has regularly experienced is this: If judgments do become increasingly inconsistent for larger gains and losses, then the decision maker should either exercise greater caution (something the person will probably do anyway) in evaluating such prospects, or else avoid them entirely if possible. Otherwise it is likely that decisions will be made for which the perceived *a priori* and *a posteriori* utilities are different and the decision maker regrets the decision after making it, even before the results are in.

In the next chapter we shall examine capital investments with stochastically determined characteristics. The returns from such projects cannot be known ahead of time with certainty. It will be shown, however, that the probable outcomes can be estimated, and such estimates evaluated by comparison with the decision maker's utility function.

Whose Utility?

In the foregoing discussion of utility it was assumed that the utility function of interest was that of an individual decision maker. An entrepreneur with sole responsibility for capital investment decisions in one's proprietorship provides a clear example. For the entrepreneur it is reasonable to assume that the utility function for monetary gains and losses to the enterprise is none other than that of the entrepreneur.

But what is to be done for a partnership, in which each partner shares personally in the gains and the losses? Can we still obtain a meaningful estimate of the utility of monetary gain? We can certainly repeat the procedures illustrated earlier, and in so doing obtain a curve relating cash equivalents to risky alternatives. This author chooses to dodge the question of whether the curve obtained is really a utility curve or whether an aggregate utility function exists. Instead, let us refer to the curve obtained for all partners in a partnership as the enterprise's *investment curve*.

More complex conceptual considerations enter the scene when we begin to examine the situation for enterprises in which ownership is largely separated from management. For such enterprises (in which we would include public sector undertakings), the utilities of money gain and loss on investments may cover a wide spectrum just among the owners. Those who make the capital investment decisions may (and most likely do) have personal utility curves that are substantially different from their decisions *as managers* would indicate. What managers must do is to surmise the enterprise's *investment curve*, the composite of the aggregated owner's preferences. This may be linked to the personal utilities of individual high-ranking managers inasmuch as their job security, bonuses, reputations, and the like may reflect how well or poorly they serve the owners. Thus, monetary gains and losses to the enterprise may be associated with a manager's personal utility.

To conclude this section, we adopt the operational guideline that the required utility function or investment curve is that of the person or persons who, individually or collectively, are responsible for making investment decisions of the magnitude with which we are concerned. In corporations this may mean the board of directors itself for large projects. Once the individual or the group responsible for decisions on capital investments has been identified it is theoretically possible to derive an investment curve along the lines illustrated for an individual. However, in practice, there may be considerable difficulty in getting a group to cooperate fully over a long enough time to obtain enough data points to be useful.

MEASURES OF RISK

As mentioned earlier, in a risk environment variables are not known with certainty but follow probability distributions. With risk, the outcome of a capital investment decision is a particular value, but the value cannot be known *a priori*. When risk is present, we may be able to predict with statistical confidence the range of values within which the outcome may be expected to occur.

For experiments that may be repeated a number of times we can generally estimate the empirical parameters. However, capital investment projects are usually one-of-a-kind undertakings; we will not have the opportunity to repeat them. Therefore, empirical estimation of the parameters is not possible and we must instead make subjective judgments about the governing probability distributions. Past experience with *similar* projects may be helpful. For example, we may have determined that the useful or economic life of capital investments is, in general, Poisson distributed, or that it is negative-exponentially distributed.

When "risk" is discussed in relation to the overall return on an investment, the word has come to mean the potential variability of the actual return from its expected value. Other things being equal, the investment with the greatest range of possible results is said to be the riskiest. The most widely used measure for risk is the *variance*. Figure 17.8 illustrates the concept. Projects R_A and R_B are both risky; both have a range of possible outcomes associated with them. The possible outcomes are distributed around the most likely values $\bar{V}_A$ and $\bar{V}_B$, which are defined as the expected values of returns on the projects. Project R_B is the riskier project because the range of possible outcomes is much wider than for R_A. If we were able to say with 95 percent (statistical) confidence that project R_A would have a value in the range R_{AL} to R_{AH} and project R_B a value in the range R_{BL} to R_{BH}, then

Figure 17.8 Comparative riskiness.

$R_{AH} - R_{AL} < R_{BH} - R_{BL}$. Therefore, R_B is riskier. Since the range of values, for any particular statistical level of confidence, is a function of the distribution's variance (or standard deviation), we can say that for projects whose outcomes follow the same type of probability distribution, the project having the larger variance of outcome is the riskier.

There is a problem with using the variance alone as risk measure, however, although it is easily adjusted for: The variance does not distinguish between projects of different size. A large investment undertaking may have a larger variance than a smaller undertaking simply because it is larger. This problem is readily resolved by substituting for the variance the *coefficient of variation*. The coefficient of variation is a "risk relative" measure defined as the ratio of variance to expected value. The investment having coefficient of variation 2.3 is relatively riskier than the investment with coefficient 1.9.

Occasionally, we may want to analyze the pattern of net, after-tax cash flows for past projects in order to estimate the cash flows for similar projects under consideration now. Such endeavor is predicated on a stable relationship of the cash flows to one or more variables that presumably can be accurately forecast. If we fit a regression for cash flows to the independent variables, one of the pieces of information obtained is the *standard error of the estimate*. This measures the variability of actual values from predicted values of the regression equation. In other words, the standard error of estimate is analogous to the standard deviation, but is calculated from deviations of actual values around the computed regression line. Estimation of values from a regression equation with large standard error is riskier than from a regression with small standard error.

The question has been raised as to why we use variance to measure risk when people do not feel the same about bad results as they do about better-than-expected results. This asymmetry of attitude toward deviation above and below expected values can be explained in terms of diminishing marginal utility; the increase in utility from a gain above the expected value is less than the utility loss from an outcome with the same dollar amount below the expected value. Consider Figure 17.9.

In Figure 17.9 outcomes less than the value $\bar{V}_T$ are considered undesirable. On the other hand, outcomes above $\bar{V}_T$ are considered fortuitous. Yet the variance does not distinguish between deviations above the expected value and those below it. Mao [7] and others have suggested that decision makers are sensitive to, and influenced much more by outcomes with values less than the expected value. In other

Figure 17.9 Risk perception for results better and worse than expected value.

words, when decision makers speak of risk, they mean the distribution of outcomes that are worse than anticipated. This is not measured by the variance but by the *semivariance*. The semivariance is calculated like the variance, but only for values less than the targeted value.[3] For an empirical distribution this means summing the squares of the deviations equal to or below the target and dividing by the number of such observations. For a theoretical distribution it means integrating or summing the density function up to the target value. Above this value deviations are ignored.[4]

A conceptual problem with the semivariance is that fortuitous outcomes are ignored in risk considerations (although they may enter determination of the target value nevertheless). We might expect that instead of ignoring better-than-expected results, they should to some extent counteract the worse-than-average outcomes that are possible. If we were to use utility weights instead of dollar NPV or other value weights, this problem might be alleviated. Although the variance may leave much to be desired as a risk measure, the semivariance offers a debatable advantage to it, and a generalized utility-based distribution may not be obtainable.

In subsequent chapters the variances and covariances of returns are used to illustrate portfolio selection approaches to investment and the capital asset pricing model. Although the semivariance could, in principle, be substituted, it is not. The reason for this would seem to be that the mathematical calculations are much less tractable for the semivariance. This serves to explain why development of the literature on investments has employed the variance or coefficient of variation almost exclusively. To the extent efforts have been made to use the semivariance, it has been by those who have attempted to modify results obtained originally with variance as the risk measure for a specific application. General substitution of the semivariance has not been successful.

---

[3] It is necessary to say "targeted value" rather than "expected value" because an arbitrary value may be used in calculating the semivariance. The arbitrary value could be the expected value of the distribution of outcomes, as is the case with the variance, but it may just as well be some critical value established by management policy.

[4] Mao [7, p. 353] describes the semivariance as follows:

Consider investment return R, as a random variable with known probability distribution. If h stands for a critical value against which the actual values of R are compared, and $(R - h)^-$ stands for $(R - h)$ if $(R - h) \leq 0$ and for zero if $(R - h) > 0$, then S_h (semi-variance with h the reference point) is given by the formula:
$S_h = E[(R - h)^-]^2$
where E is the expectation operator.

```
                    +              +
                    +              +
          A         +              +
                    +              +              B
                    +              +
                    +              +
           +        +              +
           +        +              +             +
                    +              +             +
    |----+----+----+----+----+----+   |----+----+----+----+----+----+
    -2   0    2    4    6         0    2              6    8
```

Figure 17.10 Mao's test distributions.

J. C. T. Mao's Survey Results

Mao [7], in a survey based on personal interviews with managers of eight medium and large companies in electronics, aerospace, petroleum, household equipment, and office equipment firms found that decision makers do indeed think of risk as being related to outcomes that are worse than expected, and that the possibility of a bad outcome significantly influences the capital investment decision. To verify the relevance of semivariance he designed a test in which the decision makers were asked to choose between two (hypothetical) mutually exclusive investments, each costing the same amount and returning after one year the cost plus profit or loss. The probability distributions of the returns were as shown in Figure 17.10.

The reader may readily verify an interesting property of the distributions of projects A and B: They both have expected value of 3 and variance of 4. Since they require the same investment outlay, their coefficients of variation are identical, and therefore their risk as conventionally measured. But are they equally risky? Mao's respondents did not think so. Their answers were consistent with the semivariances (using zero in each as the critical value) that were .2 for project A and 0 for project B. Note also that there is a nonzero probability that project A could actually *lose* money.

To summarize Mao's findings, they are that:

> Executives seemed more likely to choose A if their businesses accustomed them to that degree of risk, if they personally preferred risky ventures, and if they could control the loss possibility in A through diversification. When these conditions are absent, the executive is more likely to pick B because the absence of loss possibility makes it a more secure investment. . . .
>
> The previous analysis was concerned with a choice between two individual investments. It is equally important to examine the risk concept from the portfolio viewpoint. The executives were asked to imagine the same alternatives on a larger scale, where X represented the total company investment, and questioned as to which portfolio they would select. The answer was unanimously B, and their reasons were most succinctly voiced by the statement of one executive:
>> "The key is survival. We take a chance on evaluating individual projects rather optimistically, but we will not take a chance on the main company. One of our obligations is to sustain this company in life and every time we put it in a minus position, it dies a little bit if not in total."
>
> This evidence is consistent with semi-variance as a concept of risk. . . .[5]

[5] Ibid., p. 355.

RISK OF RUIN

If all capital investments were small relative to the enterprise's financial resources, this section would not be necessary. However, capital investments are often large in terms relative to the enterprise's size as well as absolutely. Because of this an adverse investment result may impair the firm's capital; several such adverse investments with one after another destroy the firm. Therefore, in addition to analysis of individual projects, it will be useful to examine the relationship of project size relative to firm size within the context of the risk affecting the probabilities of return on investment.

Risk of ruin, like many useful concepts, has its origins in gambling. It is applicable to other situations in which a series of losses (adverse outcomes) can result in ruin (loss of equity). Teweles, Harlow, and Stone [8] have illustrated application of the concept to an individual who undertakes the trading of commodity futures. This is a very risky venture because of the small margin requirements, usually around 10 percent of the commodity contract value. Their discussion is highly recommended to readers who wish to reinforce their understanding of the concept and its application. Here we shall focus attention on risk of ruin as it applies to capital investment decisions.

The probability of eventual ruin (loss of equity, bankruptcy) is given by:

$$R = \left(\frac{1-A}{1+A}\right)^C \tag{17.5}$$

where A is the investor's advantage in decimal form and C is the number of investment units with which the investor starts.[6] For capital investments we may define the investor's advantage as the probability of a favorable outcome minus the probability of an unfavorable outcome resulting in monetary loss.[7] If P is the probability of a favorable outcome, this means that the advantage is $P - (1 - P)$ or $2P - 1$. To obtain C we divide the required investment outlay into the enterprise's total equity.[8]

To illustrate, let us take the case of a company considering an investment of $40 million in a project that is thought to offer .60 chance of returning 100 percent and a .40 chance of loss of the entire investment. The firm has equity of $160 million. Translating these numbers into risk of ruin, we get:

$$R = \left(\frac{1-.2}{1+.2}\right)^4 = .198 \tag{17.6}$$

or about one chance in five of *eventual* ruin.

This one project cannot by itself ruin the firm. However, there is .40 chance that the entire investment will be lost. The significance of the risk of ruin is this: If

---

[6] William Feller, *An Introduction to Probability Theory and Its Applications* (New York: Wiley, 1957).
[7] Ruin, in the sense we are using the word here, rests upon the probability of actual out-of-pocket money losses, if ruin would be considered to result from its loss.
[8] If desired, a lesser amount may be used.

the firm makes a habit of undertaking investments of similar risk, cost, and return, there is one chance in five that the firm will go bankrupt as a result. Thus, risk of ruin relates to the firm's ongoing policy with respect to investments. Should the firm regularly undertake investments for which the probability of eventual ruin is one-fifth? Is this an exceptional case? If so, how does it relate to the firm's investment policy?

Examination of the formula for risk of ruin yields some principles that may be useful in policy formulation. Of major significance is the fact that by reducing the size of investments that may be considered, the risk of ruin may be greatly reduced, other things being constant. In the example just considered, reducing the size of the investment to $20 million reduces risk of eventual ruin to .039 or four chances in 100. Halving the size of investment outlay in this case reduced the risk of ruin by 80 percent. Although one chance in five would be considered an unacceptable risk of ruin by many executives, four chances in 100 might well be considered good odds.

Risk of ruin as presented above is somewhat an abstraction. Firms do not have continuing opportunity to undertake a series of identical capital investments over the time continuum. Furthermore, enterprise policy is not immutable; it tends to change to adjust to circumstances. If a firm has a run of losses on its investments, sooner or later it will review its investment policies, objectives, and procedures in order to correct its errors.

Nevertheless, risk of eventual ruin provides a gauge for measuring the enterprise's approach to risky investments. It indicates management's attitude toward the ultimate investment risk—that of financial ruin, bankruptcy. The measure itself could be incorporated into the decision process as a constraint. For instance, a policy could be adopted constraining investments to risk of ruin of X chances in 100 (based on the calculation above, which assumes the same investment outlay and success/failure probabilities to be repeated over time).

SUMMARY

Risk, in the context of this chapter, was considered without regard to portfolio effects. This chapter introduced the subject of risk and the notion that risk cannot be adequately handled without reference to utility. We saw that the utility function governs the investor's attitude toward risky investments, and that diminishing marginal utility of monetary gain leads to risk aversion.

Risk is normally measured by the variance or coefficient of variation of the outcome variable. Professor Mao's interviews with executives who make capital investment decisions yielded attitudes congruent with semivariance as a measure of risk actually representative of management thought.

Even though capital investments are typically one of a kind, the concept of risk of eventual ruin was introduced. By calculating the probability of ruin it is possible to assess more fully than otherwise managements' attitudes toward risky investments. Risk of ruin also ties in well with one of Mao's survey respondents who put survival of the enterprise ahead of any profit aspirations.

QUESTIONS

1. Explain why risk aversion depends on diminishing marginal utility.
2. How can risk of eventual ruin have any bearing on capital investment when projects are one of a kind?
3. Discuss why risk of ruin may be of more concern to the executives of a small firm than to those making similar capital investment decisions for a large firm.
4. Using the concept of risk of ruin, discuss how a series of capital investment losses may be more likely for a government unit than for a private firm.
5. Outline how you would estimate the composite investment (utility of monetary gain) function for a firm that is run by its four founders. Assume a history of frequent gains and losses of $1 million and $200,000, respectively.
6. Discuss how the matter of obtaining an investment function for a large corporation might be approached. Assume the management owns a small portion of the total shares issued.
7. What is semivariance? Why has it not been used to build modern financial theory if it is superior as a risk measure to variance?

PROBLEMS

17.1 Using the following forms, determine your own personal utility curve for monetary gains and losses. It may be helpful if you have someone assist you. If you have not regularly experienced reasonably large gains or losses on investment decisions, you will have to try to imagine what they might be.

Form 17-1. COMPUTATION OF DECISION MAKER'S UTILITIES FOR VARIOUS MONETARY GAINS

Probability of (1) Best Result	(2) Worst Result	(3) Computed Utility	(4) Dollar Cash Equivalent	
1.0	0.0	1.0	_____	Best Result
.9	.1	.9	_____	
.8	.2	.8	_____	
.7	.3	.7	_____	
.6	.4	.6	_____	
.5	.5	.5	_____	
.4	.6	.4	_____	
.3	.7	.3	_____	
.2	.8	.2	_____	
.1	.9	.1	_____	
0.0	1.0	0.0	_____	Worst Result

Form 17-2. COMPUTATION OF REFINED UTILITY OF DECISION MAKER'S MONETARY GAINS

Best Outcome		Worst Outcome		Computed	Dollar Cash
Utility	Probability	Utility	Probability	Utility	Equivalent
_____	_____	_____	_____	_____	_____
_____	_____	_____	_____	_____	_____
_____	_____	_____	_____	_____	_____

Form 17-2. COMPUTATION OF REFINED UTILITY OF DECISION MAKER'S MONETARY GAINS *(continued)*

Best Outcome		Worst Outcome		Computed	Dollar Cash
Utility	Probability	Utility	Probability	Utility	Equivalent
____	____	____	____	____	____
____	____	____	____	____	____
____	____	____	____	____	____
____	____	____	____	____	____
____	____	____	____	____	____
____	____	____	____	____	____
____	____	____	____	____	____

17.2 Calculate the expected values, variances, coefficients of variation, and semivariances for the following series. Use zero as reference point in calculating the semivariance.

Series A	10	10	10	10	10	50	−100
Series B	−100	10	100				
Series C	−10,000	0	100	500	100,000		
Series D	−100,000	200,000	900,000				
Series E	1,000	0	999,000				

17.3 Calculate the risk of eventual ruin, R, for investments with the characteristics that follow for investment outlays of 5 percent, 10 percent, 20 percent, and 40 percent of the firm's capital. The investments will return either a 100 percent gain or a 100 percent loss after one year.

Investment EKS   Probability Advantage of .05
Investment WYE   Probability Advantage of .20
Investment ZEE   Probability Advantage of .60

17.4 Calculate the variance and semivariance for the following two projects. Which is preferable if a large portion of the firm's resources must be committed to the investment? Which is preferable if the investment outlay is small relative to the firm's total capital resources? (*Hint:* Refer to Professor Mao's survey results.)

Project A-ONE:

$Outcome	Probability
−10,000	.2
20,000	.7
100,000	.1

Project A-TWO

$Outcome	Probability
3,500	.4
20,000	.6

Bibliography

1. Allen, R. G. D., *Mathematical Economics*, 2nd ed. (London: Macmillan Company, 1965).
2. Bernado, John J., and Howard P. Lanser, "A Capital Budgeting Model with Subjective Criteria," *Journal of Financial and Quantitative Analysis*, Vol. XII, No. 2 (June 1977), pp. 261–275.
3. Copeland, Thomas E., and J. Fred Weston, *Financial Theory and Corporate Policy* (Reading, Mass.: Addison-Wesley, 1979).
4. Feller, William, An *Introduction to Probability Theory and Its Applications* (New York: Wiley, 1957).
5. Knight, Frank H., *Risk, Uncertainty and Profit* (Boston: Houghton Mifflin, 1921).
6. Mao, James C. T., *Corporate Financial Decisions* (Palo Alto, Cal.: Pavan, 1976).
7. ———, "Survey of Capital Budgeting: Theory and Practice," *The Journal of Finance*, Vol. XXV, No. 2 (May 1970), pp. 349–360.
8. Teweles, Richard J., Charles V. Harlow, and Herbert L. Stone, *The Commodity Futures Game* (New York: McGraw-Hill, 1977).
9. Tobin, James, "Liquidity Preference as Behavior Towards Risk," *The Review of Economic Studies*, Vol. 67 (February 1958), pp. 65–86.
10. Vinso, Joseph D., "A Determination of the Risk of Ruin," *Journal of Financial and Quantitative Analysis*, Vol. XIV, No. 1 (March 1979), pp. 77–100.
11. Von Neumann, John, and Oskar Morgenstern, *The Theory of Games and Economic Behavior* (Princeton, N.J.: Princeton University Press, 1947).

Chapter 18
Single Project Analysis Under Risk

This chapter considers methods that have been used to analyze capital investment projects when one or more project characteristics are random variables. Independence of projects (with respect to the existing assets of the firm as well as one another) is assumed throughout this chapter in order to concentrate on risk considerations without the added complexities introduced by portfolio effects. Project analysis with diversification and project interdependence is covered in the next section.

Chapter 17 considered those factors that influence our attitudes toward risk and the concept of risk of ruin. In this chapter we shall examine means of measuring risk and dealing with it. Among the matters to be covered are the payback as a risk-coping method, the certainty equivalent approach, the risk-adjusted discount rate approach, and computer simulation.

THE PAYBACK METHOD

The payback has been rationalized as a method for coping with risk. If we recognize that considerable importance may be attached to capital preservation, it is understandable that some measure of solace may be gained from the knowledge that a particular investment project promises a quick return of the funds invested in it.

The longer the time required to recover a project's investment cost, the more uncertain we are about the recovery. The more time that passes between the present and an anticipated event, the more unanticipated influences can spring up to render our forecast results worthless.

The shortcomings of the payback criterion are well known; an earlier chapter discusses them. As a means of dealing with risk or uncertainty, payback does favor those projects that promise early recovery of investment. It does not make much sense to use the payback as the sole criterion or even major criterion, but, used as an adjunct to the discounted cash flows, it provides an unequivocal, if crude, means of screening projects to eliminate those that take what management considers too long to recover their investment and therefore too likely to fail to help the enterprise's capital preservation efforts.

To an extent, reliance on the payback may be tantamount to an admission of forecasting impotence. That is, if we feel it is not at all possible to make usefully reliable forecasts, then we may adopt the project that exposes our capital to the ravages of time the least. After having gotten back our investment, if the project offers further returns, that is all to the good; if not, we still have our funds to invest in something else. In relatively stable economic times the payback may have little to recommend it. In times like the present, with forecasting made all the more difficult by one crises after another, coupled with chronic inflation, preservation of capital is not a trivial matter, if it ever was. It is understandable that the payback holds a prominent position among the methods of capital asset selection used by those who must make decisions with their firm's resources and be held accountable for results. And if a project selected on the basis of payback does not perform according to expectations, it will be recognized early, within the payback period, and appropriate measures taken—no need to wait years for a return only to find it is a will-o-the-wisp that vanishes as approached.

CERTAINTY EQUIVALENTS: METHOD I

In the previous chapter it was shown how a utility curve could be estimated by determining the (certain) cash amount that was considered equivalent to two different amounts, each with a probability attached. The cash was considered equivalent to the risky investment, which could have yielded either more or less than the cash equivalent. This is the essence of the certainty equivalent approach to capital investment analysis. If amount A may be received with probability $P(A)$ and amount B with probability $P(B) = 1 - P(A)$, and the events are mutually exclusive,[1] then amount C is said to be a certainty equivalent to the investment that could result in outcome A or outcome B, and $P(C) = 1.0$. This can be generalized to investments with more than two outcome possibilities.

For investments with more than two outcome possibilities, the certainty equivalent, C, may be defined as the (certain) cash amount for which the investor is

---

[1] Mutually exclusive may be defined in terms of the conditional probabilities as $P(A|B) = 0$ and $P(B|A) = 0$.

Figure 18.1 Risk-return tradeoff curve for the enterprise.

indifferent to the risky investment for which the dollar returns are described by the probability distribution $P(A)$, where A is a vector. It is important to note that C is *not* the expected value of the investment, $E[A]$. Rather, C is the certain cash amount with utility equivalent to the investment. In other words, if U denotes utility, then:

$$U(C) = E[U(A)] \tag{18.1}$$

Because it is the utility of the returns vector A that determines investor attitudes toward the investment, it is unimportant in determining certainty equivalents whether A is the vector of net present values (NPVs), internal rates of return (IRR), or other measure of investment returns. In this chapter we use the NPV as a matter of convenience only, noting that the certainty equivalent may be based on any measure for which the investor can make consistent choices.

Although utility itself is a personal matter, we may, as suggested in the previous chapter, estimate a composite investment curve for the decision makers of a particular organization.[2] To illustrate the use of certainty equivalents, in Figure 18.1 a risk-return trade-off curve for a given enterprise is illustrated. All points of the curve have equal utility, so we could refer to it as an iso-utility curve. Different organizations may be expected to have different curves. Figure 18.1 is consistent with risk aversion because expected returns must rise more rapidly than risk (however risk is measured) for the utility to remain constant.

Example 18-1

The Ajax Company is evaluating a production mixer that costs $25,000. The mixer is expected to produce cash flows of $10,000, $15,000, $20,000, and $20,000 at the end of each year of its four-year economic life. The firm's management feels that the cash flows become riskier the further into the future they are expected to occur.

---

[2] Some authors have suggested that the equal market valuation curve be employed in calculating certainty equivalents. Although such an approach may be useful in securities investment analysis, it is questionable within the context of capital investment analysis for an individual firm.

Certainty equivalents are calculated at .982, .930, .694, and .422 of the expected cash flows. Since certainty equivalents are used, we discount at the risk-free rate[3] that is assumed to be 8 percent. The NPV of the mixer is:

$$NPV = -\$25,000 + \frac{(.982)(\$10,000)}{1.08}$$
$$+ \frac{(.930)(\$15,000)}{(1.08)^2} + \frac{(.694)(\$20,000)}{(1.08)^3}$$
$$+ \frac{(.422)(\$20,000)}{(1.08)^4} =$$
$$-\$25,000 + \$9092.59 + \$11,959.88$$
$$+ \$11,018.39 + \$6203.65 = \underline{\$13,274.51}$$

which is positive; thus the project is acceptable under the NPV criterion.

CERTAINTY EQUIVALENTS: METHOD II

The previous section showed one way in which certainty equivalents may be found and used to calculate a project's certainty-equivalent NPV. Another method that is sometimes used is first to calculate the project's NPV at the risk-free interest rate. The next step is to convert to a "certainty" equivalent by subtracting an allowance for risk, usually taken to be $V[NPV]$, the variance of NPV. To illustrate, assume the variance of the NPVs of the cash flows in Example 18–1 is $V[NPV] = \$14,422.07$. First calculate the NPV of the expected cash flows at the risk-free rate (again assumed to be 8 percent):

$$NPV = -\$25,000 + \frac{\$10,000}{(1.08)^1} + \frac{\$15,000}{(1.08)^2} + \frac{\$20,000}{(1.08)^3} + \frac{\$20,000}{(1.08)^4} =$$
$$\$25,000 + \$9259.26 + \$12,860.08 + \$15,876.64$$
$$+ \$14,700.60 = \underline{\$27,696.58}$$

Next, subtract the variance to obtain the certainty equivalent:

$$NPV = \$27,696.58$$
$$-V(NPV) = -14,422.07$$
$$\$13,274.51 \quad \text{Certainty Equivalent}$$

In this case the certainty equivalent is identical to that obtained with method I; this is because the variance was chosen to make the results identical.

In general, it is unlikely that this method will yield results close to those obtained with method I. Although this is empirically questionable, we can say *a priori* that for this method to yield the same results as method I, it is necessary that the variance measure adequately risk in the same way that calculation of certainty

---

[3] Here risk free means free of default risk. The rate is generally taken to be the rate on U.S. government securities of the same future maturity as the cash flow's receipt.

equivalents for the individual period cash flows does. Considering that the certainty equivalents of the individual cash flows are based on utility, and the variance is based on dollars alone, the two methods will not yield comparable results except for investment curves of a most particular type.[4]

Despite the conceptual problems imbedded in method II, it is sometimes used, and it is then necessary to have equations for calculating the expected value of NPV, $E[NPV]$, and the variance of NPV, $V[NPV]$. The expected value of NPV is found from:

$$E[NPV] = \sum_{t=0}^{N} \frac{E[R_t]}{(1+i)^t} \tag{18.2}$$

where R_0 is the required investment outlay. The variance is found from the relationship:

$$V[NPV] = \sigma_0^2 + \frac{\sigma_1^2}{(1+i)^2} + \frac{\sigma_2^2}{(1+i)^4} + \cdots + \frac{\sigma_N^2}{(1+i)^{2N}} \tag{18.3}$$

if the cash flows are independent of one another (uncorrelated). If the cash flows are perfectly correlated, the variance is defined by:

$$V[NPV] = \sigma_0^2 + \frac{\sigma_1^2}{(1+i)^2} + \frac{\sigma_2^2}{(1+i)^4} \tag{18.4}$$
$$+ 2\left\{ \frac{\text{Cov}(0,1)}{(1+i)^1} + \frac{\text{Cov}(0,2)}{(1+i)^2} + \frac{\text{Cov}(1,2)}{(1+i)^3} \cdots \right\}$$

For the general case with three cash flows that are random variables, X_0, X_1, X_2 with weights a, b, c, the variance is given by:

$$\begin{aligned}V[NPV] &= V[aX_0 + bX_1 + cX_2] \\ &= a^2 V[X_0] + b^2 V[X_1] + c^2 V[X_2] \\ &\quad + 2ab\,\text{Cov}[X_0, X_1] + 2ac\,\text{Cov}[X_0, X_2] \\ &\quad + 2bc\,\text{Cov}[X_1, X_2]\end{aligned} \tag{18.5}$$

where $a = (1+i)^{-0} = 1$, $b = (1+i)^{-1}$, $c = (1+i)^{-2}$. The complexity of this expression suggests why Hillier [8] considered the special cases of zero correlation and perfect correlation, for which the considerably simpler equations apply.

RISK-ADJUSTED DISCOUNT RATE

Another method used for dealing with risky cash flows is that of risk-adjusted discount rate. Although the certainty equivalent method essentially adjusts the cash

---

[4] The assumption that the distribution of returns is normally distributed means that the distribution is fully described by two parameters: mean and variance. This implies that utility may be maximized by appropriate selection of assets according to a function of mean and variance, provided we know the equation for the investor's utility in terms of these parameters. Certainty equivalent method II, by subtracting the unweighted variance of returns, assumes a very special type of utility function in addition to normally distributed returns.

flows or the NPV of the unadjusted flows, the risk-adjusted discount rate makes the adjustment to the discount rate for each cash flow period prior to calculating the NPV.

In an earlier chapter the NPV method was discussed in the context of a certainty environment. There it was assumed that the enterprise's cost of capital was the appropriate rate of discount,[5] and that this was constant from period to period over the asset's economic lifetime. Now, assuming a risky environment in which the cash flows differ both in futurity and in uncertainty, it is no longer reasonable to assume that a constant discount rate is appropriate. *Ceteris paribus*, the riskier an investment return occurring sometime in the future, the greater the required rate of return—discount rate—that investors will apply to it.

Example 18–2

To illustrate the method of risk-adjusted discount rate let us again consider the Ajax Company mixer examined in Example 18–1. The cost of the mixer is $25,000 and the cash flows expected at the end of each year of its four-year economic life are $10,000, $15,000, $20,000, and $20,000.

The NPV, using the risk-adjusted discount rate approach with rates $k = 9.98$ percent, $k_2 = 11.99$ percent, $k_3 = 21.98$ percent, and $k_4 = 33.40$ percent, is:

$$\text{NPV} = -\$25{,}000 + \frac{\$10{,}000}{(1.0998)^1} + \frac{\$15{,}000}{(1.1199)^2} + \frac{\$20{,}000}{(1.2198)^3} + \frac{\$20{,}000}{(1.3340)^4} =$$

$$-\$25{,}000 + \$9092.56 + \$11{,}960.04 + \$11{,}019.56 + \$6315.48 = \underline{\$13{,}387.64}$$

which is within 1 percent of the certainty equivalent approach result. The difference is due to rounding errors in this case because the risk-adjusted discount rates were chosen to yield identical results.

If α is the constant that relates the certainty equivalent to its expected value of cash flow, and i the risk-free rate, then the relationship between these variables, as Mao [11, p. 146] has shown, is:

$$\underbrace{\frac{\alpha E[R_t]}{(1+i)^t}}_{\text{Certainty Equivalent}} = \underbrace{\frac{E[R_t]}{(1+k_t)^t}}_{\text{Risk-Adjusted Discount Rate}} \qquad (18.6)$$

which, after rearranging terms, yields:

$$k_t = \frac{1+i}{\alpha^{1/t}} - 1 \qquad (18.7)$$

---

[5] Some would argue that the cost of common equity is the appropriate rate since the net, after-tax cash flows accrue to the common shareholders. See, for example, James C. T. Mao, *Corporate Financial Decisions* (Palo Alto, Cal.: Pavan, 1976), p. 138.

An investor who is perfectly consistent in applying this method and the certainty equivalent method should obtain identical results (except for rounding errors). Whether or not decision makers are consistent in applying the methods is an empirical question, as is the question as to which method is preferred (if either is) by the same decision makers.

COMPUTER SIMULATION

Although the foregoing methods for dealing with risk can be useful, they have some shortcomings. Neither the certainty-equivalent nor the risk-adjusted discount rate provides more than a single, point estimate of the returns on a capital investment. Neither is suited to risky investments for which characteristics other than the cash flows themselves may be random variables. For example, the project life itself may be a random variable, or at least we may wish to examine the implications if it is treated as one. Circumstances may exist that compel us to treat the discount rate itself as a random variable, and we may have reason to want to treat the related cash flows according to a more complex relationship than simple correlation allows for. And we may want to examine the effect of having a particular policy that requires the asset to be abandoned if certain conditions are met; or to examine the effects of random shocks, such as a sudden increase in petroleum price.

Computer simulation (also referred to as Monte Carlo experimentation) enables us to analyze complex investments for which direct mathematical methods either do not exist or are inadequate for our purpose. Because of the speed with which modern digital computers can perform complex, repetitive calculations, we can examine the simulated outcome of hundreds of iterations that taken together provide a profile of the investment. Through analysis of the simulated profile, within the context of management's investment curve (as developed in the previous chapter), a rational decision may be reached to accept or reject the project.

The topic of computer simulation is covered thoroughly in texts devoted exclusively to the subject. For those who desire a detailed development we recommend the works listed in the bibliography. It is not our purpose here, however, to become sidetracked into a detailed discussion of computer simulation. For our purposes it should suffice to state that three basic things are required: (1) a computer; (2) a (pseudo-) random number generator; and (3) a mathematical model of the thing we wish to simulate. Since random number generators are often an integral part of the software provided by the computer manufacturer to perform a simulation analysis, we need to specify carefully our model, then translate it into suitable form for the computer. Special simulation "languages" have been developed to facilitate the task such as GPSS, SIMSCRIPT, and DYNAMO, to mention only a few. The following example was analyzed with KAPSIM, a FORTRAN program written by this author to simulate single capital investment projects.

Example 18-3

An investment costs $2.5 million and is expected to last nine years. The project life is thought to be Poisson distributed, so the variance is also nine. Management pol-

262 CAPITAL BUDGETING UNDER RISK—WITHOUT DIVERSIFICATION

Table 18-1. EXAMPLE 18-3 PROBLEM DESCRIPTION (PART 1)

Item	Distribution	Parm 1	Parm 2	Parm 3
Initial Outlay	Constant	$2.50000E + 07$	0	$-0.$
Period 1 Return	Normal	$-5.00000E + 06$	$2.00000E + 06$	$-0.$
Period 2 Return	Normal	$5.00000E + 06$	$2.00000E + 06$	$-0.$
Period 3 Return	Normal	$6.00000E + 06$	$2.00000E + 06$	$-0.$
Period 4 Return	Normal	$7.00000E + 06$	$2.00000E + 06$	$-0.$
Period 5 Return	Normal	$8.00000E + 06$	$2.00000E + 06$	$-0.$
Period 6 Return	Normal	$9.00000E + 06$	$2.00000E + 06$	$-0.$
Period 7 Return	Normal	$1.00000E + 07$	$2.00000E + 06$	$-0.$
Period 8 Return	Normal	$8.00000E + 06$	$2.00000E + 06$	$-0.$
Period 9 Return	Normal	$6.00000E + 06$	$2.00000E + 06$	$-0.$
Period 10 Return	Normal	0	$2.00000E + 06$	$-0.$
Period 11 Return	Normal	0	$2.00000E + 06$	$-0.$
Period 12 Return	Normal	0	$2.00000E + 06$	$-0.$
Period 13 Return	Normal	0	$2.00000E + 06$	$-0.$
Period 14 Return	Normal	0	$2.00000E + 06$	$-0.$
Period 15 Return	Normal	0	$2.00000E + 06$	$-0.$
Period 16 Return	Normal	0	$2.00000E + 06$	$-0.$
Period 17 Return	Normal	0	$2.00000E + 06$	$-0.$
Period 18 Return	Normal	0	$2.00000E + 06$	$-0.$
Period 19 Return	Normal	0	$2.00000E + 06$	$-0.$

Note: Number of iterations equals 1000; expected value of project life is 9 with variance of 9 distribution Poisson; maximum project life is 20.

icy: is to dispose of such assets after 20 years; thus if the project should last that long, it would be abandoned then.

The variance of the net, after-tax cash flows is estimated to be ($2 million)^2 every year. The first year cash flow has expected value of $-$$5 million; that of the second year is $+$$5 million; from the third through the ninth year the returns are expected to grow by $1 million each year, starting at $6 million at the end of the third year. The returns in years ten on are zero because the project is expected to last only nine years.

A further complication is that, because of structural changes in the economy, the discount rate is expected to increase over time. The expected rate is 10.1 percent for the first year's cash flow, with variance (1.01 percent).^{2} Each subsequent year is expected to be .1 percent higher, and the standard deviation to be 10 percent of expected value.

Finally, because the project may be abandoned prior to the end of its economic lifetime, it is necessary to estimate salvage at the end of each year. Salvage value is assumed to decline from the original investment by 20 percent each year. However, the rate of decline is estimated to be Poisson distributed.

This information is summarized in Tables 18-1 and 18-2, which contain the provided information as part of the computer-printed simulation results. One thousand iterations are employed to obtain a sufficient sample of results, which are measured by the net present value. If too few iterations are used, we cannot draw conclusions from the scattered results, whereas too many iterations would waste

SINGLE PROJECT ANALYSIS UNDER RISK   263

Table 18-2. EXAMPLE 18-3 PROBLEM DESCRIPTION (Continued)

Item	Distribution	Parm 1	Parm 2	Parm 3
Period 1 Capital Cost	Normal	.101000	.010100	000000
Period 2 Capital Cost	Normal	.102000	.010200	000000
Period 3 Capital Cost	Normal	.103000	.010300	000000
Period 4 Capital Cost	Normal	.104000	.010400	000000
Period 5 Capital Cost	Normal	.105000	.010500	000000
Period 6 Capital Cost	Normal	.106000	.010600	000000
Period 7 Capital Cost	Normal	.107000	.010700	000000
Period 8 Capital Cost	Normal	.108000	.010800	000000
Period 9 Capital Cost	Normal	.109000	.010900	000000
Period 10 Capital Cost	Normal	.110000	.011000	000000
Period 11 Capital Cost	Normal	.111000	.011100	000000
Period 12 Capital Cost	Normal	.112000	.011200	000000
Period 13 Capital Cost	Normal	.113000	.011300	000000
Period 14 Capital Cost	Normal	.114000	.011400	000000
Period 15 Capital Cost	Normal	.115000	.011500	000000
Period 16 Capital Cost	Normal	.116000	.011600	000000
Period 17 Capital Cost	Normal	.117000	.011700	000000
Period 18 Capital Cost	Normal	.118000	.011800	000000
Period 19 Capital Cost	Normal	.119000	.011900	000000
Period 20 Capital Cost	Normal	.120000	.012000	000000

Note: Salvage assumed to decline from initial outlay by percent per period of: Poisson $2.00000E - 01$ $2.00000E - 01$ $0.$

some computer time. With the cost of computation being one of the few things that has actually come down in cost (thanks to improved technology), it may be best to err somewhat on the side of too many iterations rather than too few.

Tables 18–1 and 18–2 provide a record of the information we put into the computer simulation of the investment project. All simulations should be accompanied by such "echo" output for two reasons: (1) in order to find mistakes that may have been made in specification of the problems or preparation of the data and (2) in order to provide an organized record to accompany the simulated results. Simulation output for one case may look about the same as output for another. If the input data are attached to the computer printout, one can avoid the frustration and difficulty of trying to reconstruct the assumptions that produced a particular computer run's output.

Table 18–3 contains the frequency interval bounds, and frequency distribution of the simulated NPV results for Example 18–3. The frequency count for an interval is determined by the number of results that are greater than or equal to the lower bound and less than the upper bound.

The decision to accept or reject the investment may be made from the frequency distribution, which is clearly not normally distributed. The first 12 intervals contain only negative NPV results, whereas the thirteenth contains mixed results. If we may assume the distribution within the thirteenth interval to be uniformly spread over that interval, then 87 of the 105 observations (simulated results) in that interval are negative, and 18 are positive. Therefore, there is probability of

Table 18-3. EXAMPLE 18-3 NPV FREQUENCY DISTRIBUTION

Interval	Lower Bound	Upper Bound	Frequency $\geq$ = L.B., < U.B.
1	$-.308229000E + 08$	$-.284193447E + 08$	1.
2	$-.284193447E + 08$	$-.260157834E + 08$	4.
3	$-.260157834E + 08$	$-.236122341E + 08$	2.
4	$-.236122341E + 08$	$-.212086788E + 08$	6.
5	$-.212086788E + 08$	$-.188051235E + 08$	7.
6	$-.188051235E + 08$	$-.164015682E + 08$	20.
7	$-.164015682E + 08$	$-.139980129E + 08$	27.
8	$-.139980129E + 08$	$-.115944576E + 08$	20.
9	$-.115344576E + 08$	$-.919090230E + 07$	35.
10	$-.919090230E + 07$	$-.678734700E + 07$	43.
11	$-.678734700E + 07$	$-.438379170E + 07$	37.
12	$-.438379170E + 07$	$-.198023640E + 07$	74.
13	$-.198023640E + 07$	$.423318900E + 06$	105.
14	$.423318900E + 06$	$.282687420E + 07$	156.
15	$.282887420E + 07$	$.523042950E + 07$	176.
16	$.523042350E + 07$	$.763398480E + 07$	140.
17	$.763398480E + 07$	$.100375401E + 08$	101.
18	$.100375401E + 08$	$.124410354E + 08$	35.
19	$.124410954E + 08$	$.148446507E + 08$	9.
20	$.148446507E + 08$	$.172482060E + 08$	1.

Note: Avg. NPV = $.631806495E + 06$; std. dev. of NPV = $.762450328E + 07$; Low = $-.308229000E + 08$; high = $.172482060E + 08$; range = $.480711060E + 08$

363/1000, or .363 that this project, if accepted, would yield a negative NPV, or better than one chance in three.

Let us say that management will not accept any project for which the odds of losing more than the initial investment (in this case $2 million) exceed 1/10. If we may again assume results to be uniformly distributed over the twelfth interval, 22 of them in the interval are −$2.5 million or less. This means the odds are 224/1000, or .224 of losing more than the initial investment (a little less if we were to consider the negative cash flow at the end of the first year as part of the initial investment). This project would be unacceptable to management under this policy, even though the mean NPV is $6,318,065.

A virtually limitless number of management policies may be applied to the frequency distribution. The particular ones applied will depend on the enterprise's investment curve, which reflects the risk attitudes of its management. For instance, management might consider the project acceptable if the odds for an NPV exceeding $10 million were greater than the odds of NPV loss of more than −$20 million (on the assumption that management could and would intervene to prevent such loss actually occurring; that is, changing the odds during the game). Alternatives are limited only by one's imagination.

This example was not designed to represent necessarily a realistic project, but rather to illustrate how simulation analysis can facilitate the decision-making process for a complex project. No doubt the example may be made more realistic simply by changing some of the parameters. As it stands, this hypothetical project would

```
Frequency   1   4   2   6   7  20  27  20  35  43  37  74 105 156 176 140 101  35   9   1
         ___ ___ ___ ___ ___ ___ ___ ___ ___ ___ ___ ___ ___ ___ ___ ___ ___ ___ ___ ___
         EACH * EQUALS 4 POINTS
```

Figure 18.2 Frequency histogram for Example 18-3 computer simulation.

probably not be very attractive to a risk-averse, capital preservation-oriented management because there are fairly large odds that losses with NPV as large as minus $30 million could result from adopting this project. Unless management believed that the odds could be significantly improved by intervention as time went on, this project would be passed over by most executives if we may extrapolate from Mao's [11] survey findings cited in the previous chapter.

LEWELLEN-LONG CRITICISM

Wilbur G. Lewellen and Michael S. Long [10], in a very articulate and incisive comparison of simulation results with those obtained from point estimates, draw some thought-provoking conclusions. These should be considered carefully, because of implications that may limit the classes of investment projects that are suitable for Monte Carlo treatment. In summary, the Lewellen-Long conclusions are:

1. If the IRR is used in simulating a capital investment, the relationship between the cash flows and the IRR will cause the mean IRR to be *lower* than the IRR obtained by discounting the means of the respective cash flow distributions. This holds even if the cash flow distributions are symmetrical about their respective means.
2. By using NPV rather than IRR as the measure of a simulated investment, the bias is eliminated because the present value of a future cash flow is a *linear* function of the size of the cash flow, whereas the IRR is not.
3. The discount rate that should be used in present value simulations is the *risk-free* rate (free of default risk, such as federal government securities).
4. Even with the NPV, problems arise when the project lifetime is uncertain. Variable project life will, *ceteris paribus*, cause the mean of the resulting simulated NPV distribution to be slightly less than the NPV obtained by discounting the cash flows over the mean project life.
5. Further disparities can be caused by nonsymmetrical cash flow distributions. This problem is likely to arise when a "most likely," or modal value, is used in place of the mean in specifying the simulation.
6. Since, because of the cost and time required to properly perform a computer simulation, it will be limited to the larger and more important projects, most will be evaluated by other methods, using a point estimate of each cash flow. It is therefore important that expected values rather than modal values be employed.
7. If any elements of the cash flows depend on multiplicative combinations of stochastic variables, it is important to use the cash flows directly in obtaining the expected values. Only if the multiplicative components are completely independent can $E[p \cdot q]$ be treated as equal to $E[p] \cdot E[q]$; otherwise $E[p \cdot q] = E[p] \cdot E[q] + \sigma_{pq}$, where σ_{pq} is the covariance between p and q.

    For example, if p represents price and q quantity sold, we should recognize that in all but perfectly elastic or inelastic demand, price and quantity are correlated. Since price and quantity demanded are inversely related, indirect estimation obtained by multiplying $E[p]$ by $E[q]$ will overstate $E[p \cdot q]$. Because the correlation coefficient ρ is defined by:

$$\rho = \frac{\sigma_{p \cdot q}}{\sqrt{\sigma_p \sigma_q}}$$

the relationships are:

$$E[p \cdot q] > E[p] \cdot E[q] \quad \text{if } \rho > 0$$
$$E[p \cdot q] < E[p] \cdot E[q] \quad \text{if } \rho < 0$$

8. All the above problems are either artificial or avoidable, with the exception of the variable project life. Therefore, as an index of investment project

worth the point-estimate analysis should serve quite well. While not incorrect in determining a proposal's expected return, simulation is unnecessary.
9. The claim that a major benefit from simulation analysis is that it provides an improved appreciation of the risk the enterprise would assume may be misleading and even dangerous. It is not the riskiness of the individual investment (its "own" risk) which is important, but rather its risk within the context of a collection of assets to which its returns may be related. To quote Lewellen and Long:[6]

> ... the one irrelevant feature of an asset's prospective returns is its "own risk"—the outcome uncertainties unique to the asset itself. These can, and will, be diversified away by individual investors and by institutions in their securities portfolios, leaving only the degree of correlation between the asset's returns and those of the so-called "market portfolio" as relevant to value, since this connection and its implied risks *cannot* be extinguished via diversification.

And they conclude by stating that:[7]

> Simulated profiles of capital expenditure proposal outcomes are, perforce, chiefly descriptions of "own risk." They do not reveal a project's addition to ... *total* risk. Having simulated, therefore, the analyst still cannot legitimately compare and choose among alternatives, because nowhere in the information he obtains is the single most important criterion of investment worth—portfolio impact—addressed. However imperfectly, the cost-of-capital/single-point-expected value cash flow forecast approach does get at the issue of portfolio context. For that reason, ... not only is such an approach less onerous in execution but, paradoxically, also has a higher potential for relevant risk recognition. ...

Although portfolio effects and diversification are topics that are addressed in the following chapters, the Lewellen-Long criticism of simulation should cause us to reflect carefully on the facts and circumstances surrounding an investment proposal before boldly embarking on a simulation analysis. And there are circumstances under which a simulation analysis may be preferable to using the simplified analysis based on point estimates. These might include the following:

1. The proposal is under consideration by an entrepreneur who will be putting all his or her assets into the project if it is accepted.
2. It is not possible to obtain meaningful estimates of the proposal's correlation with the existing assets of the firm, or the project being considered is estimated to be uncorrelated with them.
3. The project is large in relation to the firm and has a potential for large loss that could threaten the firm's survival.
4. Possible pressure on executives to avoid investments in risky assets that

---

[6] Wilbur G. Lewellen and Michael S. Long, "Simulation versus Single-Value Estimates in Capital Expenditure Analysis," *Decision Sciences*, Vol. 3 (1972), pp. 19–33.
[7] Ibid., p. 31.

would reduce or leave unchanged the organization's overall risk. If such pressures have been responsible for portfolio managers generally avoiding "second-tier" securities, gold, and commodity futures then we may surmise that similar peer group or external pressures may act to constrain decisions to "own risk" more than portfolio considerations.
5. The cash flows may be governed by complex relationships which preclude analysis of point estimates. (The Lewellen-Long article did not deal with the problem of *simultaneous* variability in cash flows and project life of contingent cash flows, for example.) Although some fairly complex proposals may be analyzed with point estimates, considerable time may pass before the analyst develops the insight and inspiration that may be necessary. Contingent asset relationships of the type treated in a subsequent chapter, for example, may be impossible to deal with on a point-estimate basis.
6. The matter of risk in the public sector may require a different approach even if the CAPM were unequivocally and universally accepted for firms in the private sector.
7. The CAPM is built upon a set of restrictive assumptions that may not always apply, particularly for smaller firms.

For additional insight into the pros and cons of simulation for the analysis of risky investments, the article by Stewart Myers [13] is recommended. The matter remains controversial and is likely to remain so, at least until some additional questions about the CAPM can be unequivocally answered.

With the conclusion of this chapter we shall leave the domain of risk without diversification and enter that of capital investment in which project proposals are not independent and portfolio aspects must be considered.

QUESTIONS

1. If we distinguish between risk and uncertainty, explain why the payback may be so widely employed, especially in the case of uncertainty.
2. In this chapter it was assumed that proposals to be analyzed were independent of one another and the existing assets of the enterprise. Why is this assumption necessary if we accept the Lewellen-Long criticism of simulation analysis of capital investment proposals?
3. Why is the appropriate discount rate to use with the certainty-equivalent method the (so-called) risk-free rate? In what respect is the rate risk free?
4. Explain why the risk-adjusted discount rate should yield the same NPV as the method of certainty equivalents if the analyst is perfectly consistent.
5. What is the reason for point-estimate IRR to be greater than the mean of the simulated IRR for the same project, even if the distributions of the cash flows are symmetrical? Why is the NPV not similarly affected?
6. The Lewellen-Long article raised some serious questions about the correctness of using computer simulation. What are they? To what extent do they apply to proposed projects that are independent not only of other proposed projects but to the existing assets of the firm?
7. Assume you have the simulation results for an independent risky project before you.

Explain how they may be used to decide whether or not to accept the project. How should the simulated results be merged with the organization's investment or utility function in reaching a decision?

PROBLEMS

18.1 Given Eq. (18.7) and certainty equivalents in periods zero through three of $-\$1000$, $\$1200$, $\$1800$, and $\$2400$, and the following α coefficients, convert to a risk-adjusted discount formulation and show that the results are the same. Assume a 9 percent risk-free rate (a) for $\alpha = .3$ and (b) for $\alpha = .6$.

18.2 Generalize formula (18.5) to the case of N correlated cash flows.

18.3 Using the following data for a risky, independent project, simulate 1000 times with the discount rate a constant 10 percent to get the distribution of NPV. The initial outlay is $1500 (constant), and (normally distributed) salvage has expected value 0.0 with standard deviation $50. The project is expected to yield $1000 at the end of each year of its useful life with standard deviation $50. The project life is 15 years, a constant. The cash flows are independent of one another and normally distributed.

What are the mean NPV and standard deviation or variance of NPV? What is the probability that the NPV will actually be less than $6000? Would this project likely be acceptable to an executive concerned with capital preservation? Why?

Explain why the lower range frequencies of a simulation may never be reached if the project is accepted. How does this tend to bias simulated results? (*Hint:* If the project were to be accepted, are the actual cash flows that would be received independent of management action?)

18.4 Work out the expected NPV and standard deviation or variance of NPV for the problem specified in Problem 18.3 using as point estimates the expected values of the cash flows and salvage. Compare your results with those obtained in Problem 18.3 by simulation. Can you find the exact probability of an NPV less than $6000?

18.5 A friend wants your help in evaluating a business she is thinking of buying with her life savings. Most of her assets will be used if the purchase is made, so there is no question of diversification. The required rate of return on equity for similar businesses with publicly traded shares is approximately 18 percent. The current risk-free rate is 10 percent.

The business will cost $7500. Net returns to equity are expected to start at $2000 at the end of the first year and grow by $2000 a year for five years and then remain constant; the cash flows are otherwise independent. The cash flows are thought to be normally distributed with standard deviations 10 percent of their respective expected values. It is believed that the business can be sold after ten years for a net capital gain of $20,000.

What will you advise your friend? How will you relate this investment proposal to her utility function?

Bibliography

1. Blatt, John M., "Investment Evaluation Under Uncertainty," *Financial Management*, Vol. 8, No. 2 (Summer 1979), pp. 66–81.
2. Brennan, M. J., "An Approach to the Valuation of Uncertain Income Streams," *The Journal of Finance*, Vol. XXVIII, No. 3 (June 1973), pp. 661–674.
3. Everett, James E., and Bernhard Schwab, "On the Proper Adjustment for Risk Through Discount Rates in a Mean-Variance Framework," *Financial Management*, Vol. 8, No. 2 (Summer 1979), pp. 7–23.
4. Forrester, Jay W., *Industrial Dynamics* (Cambridge, Mass.: M.I.T. Press, 1969).
5. Hertz, David B., "Risk Analysis in Capital Investment," *Harvard Business Review*, Vol. 42, No. 1 (January–February 1964), pp. 95–106.
6. ————, "Investment Policies That Pay Off," *Harvard Business Review*, Vol. 46, No. 1 (January–February 1968), pp. 96–108.
7. Hess, S. W., and Quigley, H. A., "Analysis of Risk in Investments Using Monte Carlo Techniques," *Chemical Engineering Symposium Series 42: Statistics and Numerical Methods in Chemical Engineering* (New York: American Institute of Chemical Engineers, 1963).
8. Hillier, Frederick S., "The Derivation of Probabilistic Information for the Evaluation of Risky Investments," *Management Science*, Vol. 9 (April 1963), pp. 443–457.
9. Kryzanowski, L., P. Lusztig, and B. Schwab, "Monte Carlo Simulation and Capital Expenditure Decisions—A Case Study," *Engineering Economist*, Vol. 18 (February 1972).
10. Lewellen, Wilbur G., and Michael S. Long, "Simulation versus Single-Value Estimates in Capital Expenditure Analysis," *Decision Sciences*, Vol. 3, No. 4, October 1972, pp. 19–33.
11. Mao, James C. T., *Quantitative Analysis of Financial Decisions* (New York: Macmillan, 1969).
12. ————, "Survey of Capital Budgeting: Theory and Practice," *The Journal of Finance*, Vol. XXV, No. 2 (May 1970), pp. 349–360.
13. Myers, Stewart C., "Postscript: Using Simulation for Risk Analysis," *Modern Developments in Financial Management* (Hinsdale, Ill.: Dryden, 1976), pp. 457–463.
14. Naylor, Thomas, *Computer Simulation Experiments with Models of Economic Systems* (New York: Wiley, 1971).
15. Naylor, Thomas, J. L. Balintfy, D. S. Burdick, and K. Chu, *Computer Simulation Techniques* (New York: Wiley, 1966).
16. Park, Chan S., and Gerald J. Thuesen, "Combining the Concepts of Uncertainty Resolution and Project Balance for Capital Allocation Decisions," *The Engineering Economist*, Vol. 24, No. 2 (Winter 1979), pp. 109–127.
17. Weingartner, H. Martin, "Some New Views on the Payback Period and Capital Budgeting Decisions," *Management Science*, Vol. 15 (August 1969).

Chapter 19
Multiple Project Selection Under Risk: Portfolio Approaches

In Chapter 16 we discussed the matter of investment selection from an array of individually acceptable independent[1] projects. The selection was constrained by conditions of capital rationing (that is, budget constraints), management policy, and technical considerations. Chapter 18 considered the analysis of individual risky projects within a framework of complete project independence. This chapter takes up the problem of capital investment analysis when we recognize stochastic dependence between project proposals themselves and between project proposals and the existing assets of the firm.

INTRODUCTION

When investment projects are statistically related to one another and/or to the currently existing assets of the firm, it is no longer appropriate to treat them as independent for purposes of analysis. When there is dependence, it is not unusual to

---

[1] We assume here that contingent project relationships do not necessarily reflect stochastic dependence. We shall reserve the term *stochastic dependence* for dependence between the cash flows of projects and not dependencies seen only at the initial accept-reject decision. Contingent relationships are often asymmetrical ("accept B only if A has been accepted," not vice versa), whereas stochastic dependence is generally taken to be symmetrical.

272 CAPITAL BUDGETING UNDER RISK—WITHOUT DIVERSIFICATION

Table 19-1. DATA FOR EXAMPLE 19-1

	Appliance Store (Existing assets)	Proposed Attached Laundromat and Equipment Rental Shop
Market Value/Cost	$1,000,000	$500,000
Expected Annual Return	$E[R_0] = \$100,000$	$E[R_1] = \$75,000$
Variance of Annual Return	$\sigma_0^2 = (\$10,000)^2$	$\sigma_1^2 = (\$15,000)^2$
Coefficient of Variation	$\sigma_0/E[R_0] = .100$	$\sigma_1/E[R_1] = .200$
Covariance	$\sigma_0^2,1 = -(\$12,000)^2$	

find that project A is preferable to project B, even though A has a greater variance and coefficient of variation in its returns than B has, and it is therefore more risky as an individual project. The reason that results such as these are obtained is that the covariance of project A makes it more favorable for selection than does the covariance of project B. Up to this point we have assumed that all project covariances to other projects and to the enterprise's existing assets to be zero—complete independence. We shall now drop the assumption of zero covariances. And because the covariance terms are no longer zero, we shall have to take them explicitly into account; we can no longer base decisions solely on a project's individual characteristics of risk and return as isolated factors.

To illustrate the effect of nonindependence between a project proposal and the firm's existing assets, let us examine the following example.

Example 19-1

The owners of Al's Appliance Store are considering a major expansion that, if undertaken, would mean construction of an attached laundromat and an equipment rental shop. The existing building would become one part of a triplex. The owners have investigated the natures of the businesses and have determined the data in Table 19-1 to be representative.

Although the return on investment is higher, the riskiness of the proposed expansion is greater in both absolute and relative terms than those of the firm's existing assets. If we were to treat the proposal as independent of the appliance store, it might well be more risky than the business to which the owners are accustomed. Analysis of the proposed expansion in isolation could be carried out with techniques suggested in previous chapters. *Here we are not interested in the proposal as an entire investment, but as an addition to an investment portfolio that already contains assets.* Therefore, it is not appropriate to analyze the expansion without reference to the combined, or portfolio, effect its acceptance would bring about.

Individually, the proposal is relatively twice as risky as the appliance store. However, the covariance between them is negative because it is expected that the proposal will respond differently to changing status of the economy than will the

Table 19-2. COMBINED ASSET CHARACTERISTICS, EXAMPLE 19-1

Value of Combined Assets	$1,500,000
Expected Combined Annual Returns	$E[R_c] = \$175,000$
Variance of Combined Returns	$\sigma_c^2 = (\$6083)^2$
Coefficient of Variation	$\sigma_c/E[R_c] = .035$

Table 19-3. RISK-RETURN RELATIONSHIPS FOR DIFFERENT RETURN CORRELATIONS BETWEEN EXISTING FIRM AND PROPOSED EXPANSION

σ	$Co(0,1)$	σ_c^2	$\sigma_c/E[R_c]$
-1.0	$-(\$12,247)^2$	$(5,002)^2$	.029
$-.5$	$-(\$ 8,660)^2$	$(13,229)^2$	.076
$.0$	0	$(18,028)^2$	.103
$+.5$	$(\$ 8,660)^2$	$(21,794)^2$	.125
$+1.0$	$(\$12,247)^2$	$(25,000)^2$	.143

existing business; in fact, it will respond oppositely. Table 19-2 contains data for the firm assuming the expansion has been undertaken.

Note that the relative riskiness as measured by the coefficient of variation has dropped far below what it was for the appliance store alone, which was less risky than the proposal. The variance of returns on the combined assets[2] is less than on the proposal alone or on the existing assets, so the absolute risk is also less than it would be without the expansion. This highlights the benefits to be gained by diversification among assets whose returns tend to move in opposite directions; the correlation in this case between the appliance store and the laundromat-cum-rental shop is $\rho = -.98$, an almost perfect negative correlation. So perfect is the relationship that 96 percent of the variation in the return on one may be statistically explained by variation in the other ($\rho^2 = .96$).

Generalizations

In this example the high negative correlation yielded dramatic results. But what if the correlation is not so strongly negative? And, what if, instead of negative correlation, there is positive correlation? Table 19-3 contains comparative figures.

Comparison of the coefficients of variation for the combined assets with the existing assets reveals the following:

1. As the correlation coefficient changes from perfect negative correlation to perfect positive, the riskiness of the combined enterprise increases.

---

[2]The variance of a linear combination of variables, with weights a, b, c, and so on, is given by:
$$\text{Var}(ax + by + cz + \cdots) =$$
$$a^2 \text{Var}(x) + b^2 \text{Var}(y) + c^2 \text{Var}(z) + \cdots$$
$$+ 2ab \text{Cov}(x, y) + 2ac \text{Cov}(x, z) + \cdots$$
$$+ 2bc \text{Cov}(y, z) + \cdots$$

2. For correlations $\rho < -.0625$, the acceptance of the proposal will reduce risk for the combined enterprise to less than that of the original assets (in this example the appliance store).
3. For correlation $\rho > -.0625$, acceptance of the proposal will increase risk above what it was for the original assets, but in all cases less than the risk of the proposal alone on a relative basis.
4. The case of $\rho = 0.0$ corresponds to covariance of zero and independence of the proposal and the existing firm.
5. Even with perfect positive correlation ($\rho = +1.0$) the relative risk for the combined assets is less than that of the proposed expansion alone.

Project Independence

An important implication of point 5 above is: Even if the proposed business expansion were independent of the existing assets of the firm, proper analysis cannot be done without reference to them. The coefficient of variation for the proposal is .200. Yet, the coefficient for the firm after undertaking the investment is .103, when $\rho = .0$. Thus, although the expansion itself is per se more risky than the existing firm, its acceptance would increase the risk of the firm very little. The point is that if the expansion is viewed separately, it may be rejected because it is relatively twice as risky as the firm as it exists without the investment. If, on the other hand, the accept/reject decision is based on the *riskiness of the firm before the investment to the firm after the investment* it is apparent that relative risk has increased by only 3 percent. The relevant comparison is not in the terms of the "own" risk of the proposal vis-à-vis the firm without the proposal, but rather the firm without the proposal to the firm with the proposal. This is not to say that techniques of analysis such as computer simulation of individual projects should be rejected, but that their use must be appropriately modified to take the foregoing into account *even when the project is statistically independent* of the existing assets of the enterprise.

Project Indivisibility

In portfolio selection applied to securities it is generally assumed that investments in any particular asset holding are infinitely divisible and, excluding short sales, the percentage of the portfolio committed to a particular asset is between 0 and 100 percent. In the case of securities such an assumption is reasonable because discontinuities are relatively small, amounting to no more than the smallest investment unit. With capital investments, however, the assumption of infinitely divisible investment units is seldom justified. In the foregoing example the question was not what proportion of the proposal should be invested in *between* 0 percent and 100 percent inclusive, but whether the investment would be rejected (0 percent) or accepted (100 percent). Only the extremes were considered because the project was considered indivisible.

Project indivisibilities are much more troublesome in capital budgeting than in (stock and bond) portfolio selection. Therefore, techniques that were originally developed for securities investment portfolio selection must be judiciously modified if correct decisions are to be made. Choices of percentage other than 0 percent (rejection) and 100 percent (acceptance) are generally not possible.

MULTIPLE PROJECT SELECTION

The formal model for optimal choice of risky assets for an investment portfolio is generally credited to Markowitz [4]. What is optimal for one investor will generally be different from what is optimal for another because of different attitudes toward risk-return relationships. The basic nature of risk and return within the framework of utility was covered in a preceding chapter for individual asset choice decisions. Here we shall extend the treatment of risk-return trade-off to the multiple asset case.

Let us denote the overall return from a portfolio, R, as a weighted average of the returns, R_i, with weights x_i as:

$$R = x_1 R_1 + x_2 R_2 + \cdots + x_n R_n \tag{19.1}$$

Each x_i is the proportion of the total invested in asset i, and R_i is the expected return from that asset. The R_i are random variables and therefore R, the portfolio return, is also a random variable. If we denote the expected values of the R_i by μ_i, the variance of asset i by σ_{ii}, and the covariance of asset i and asset j as σ_{ij}, we obtain for the portfolio:

$$E[R] = x_1 \mu_1 + x_2 \mu_2 + \cdots + x_n \mu_n \tag{19.2}$$

$$\begin{aligned} \text{Var}[R] = {} & x_1^2 \sigma_{11} + x_2^2 \sigma_{22} + \cdots + x_n^2 \sigma_{nn} \\ & + 2x_1 x_2 \sigma_{12} + 2x_1 x_3 \sigma_{13} + \cdots + 2x_1 x_n \sigma_{1n} \\ & + 2x_2 x_3 \sigma_{23} + \cdots + 2x_2 x_n \sigma_{2n}, \cdots = \\ & \sum_{i=1}^{n} \sum_{j=1}^{n} x_i x_j \sigma_{ij} \end{aligned} \tag{19.3}$$

Although the optimum portfolio for any particular individual depends on one's utility function, we can nevertheless narrow considerably the field of choice. We can, for instance, eliminate from consideration those portfolios that will not be selected by anyone regardless of utility function. For this we use the concept of *efficient portfolio*.

An *efficient portfolio* is one for which a higher return cannot be had without incurring higher risk or, equivalently, a portfolio for which one cannot reduce risk without a corresponding loss of return. A portfolio is inefficient if, by changing the proportions of the assets held, we can obtain a higher return with no more risk, or reduce risk without sacrificing some return. Alternatively, an efficient portfolio is the minimum variance portfolio among all portfolios with the same expected return and it is the portfolio with the maximum expected return among all with the same variance of return.

Markowitz suggested two steps in finding an investor's optimum portfolio.

Figure 19.1 Selection of optimal portfolio of risky assets.

First, identify the set of efficient portfolios. Second, select that efficient portfolio that best matches the investor's risk-return attitude, which maximizes the investor utility. The exact portfolio will vary from investor to investor, but all of them must be efficient portfolios. Figure 19.1 summarizes the procedure.

Line AB is the efficient set of portfolios. The U_i represents a particular investor's set of utility curves relating risk to returns.[3] The shaded area represents the set of all other portfolios that could be formed from the same assets (assuming infinite divisibility). The point of tangency between the highest indifference curve (U_0) and the efficient set corresponds to the optimum portfolio for this particular investor.

Markowitz considered several different possible forms of utility functions. It was the quadratic form that Farrar [2] employed to determine the coefficients of risk aversion for mutual funds; also the quadratic form of utility function has been widely employed by many other writers, in no small measure due to its consistency with diminishing marginal utility and other generally accepted aspects of preference theory. The discontinuous utility function used by Roy [5] provides a linkage to the notion that survival of the enterprise is an important investment objective.

Roy's utility function was of the form:

$$U(R) = 1 \quad \text{for } R \geq a$$
$$ = 0 \quad \text{for } R < a$$

which yields expected utility of:

$$E[U] = 1 \cdot Pr(R \geq a) + 0 \cdot Pr(R < a)$$
$$ = 1 - Pr(R < d)$$

for which maximization of utility means minimization of the probability that the portfolio return will fall below amount a. Graphically, this corresponds to selecting the portfolio determined by the tangency of a line through point a with the efficient set in Figure 19.1. Roy's model is consistent with the responses elicited in Mao's

---

[3] For investments of the size represented by this portfolio. Chapter 17 suggests that the utility function is related to the size of the required investment and to risk of ruin as well.

survey of executives cited in Chapter 17. Together, they suggest that where the survival of the enterprise itself is a factor in the decision process, the decision maker may apply a utility function distinct from that which is used in circumstances in which the enterprise's survival is not in question.

Finding the Efficient Set

Since the first step in the procedure for finding the optimal investment portfolio is to find the set of efficient portfolios, we require a systematic method. This may be formulated as a mathematical programming problem:

$$\text{Maximize} \quad \Phi = E[R] - \lambda \cdot \text{Var}[R] \quad (19.4)$$
$$= x\mu - \lambda\sigma^2 \quad \text{(in vector notation)}$$

$$\text{Subject to} \quad \sum_i x_i = 1.0 \quad (19.5)$$

$$\text{or} \quad x_i \geq 0$$
$$x_i = 0 \quad \text{or} \quad 1$$

Lambda (λ) is the coefficient of risk aversion, which we restrict to the range 0 to $+\infty$. To obtain the efficient set we must solve the above problem in Eq. (19.4) for different values of λ until we have enough points on the efficient set to define its curve. It is important to recognize that this model assumes that the investor's risk attitude is adequately reflected by the variance-covariance matrix of all candidate investments. The final constraint restricts us to either accepting a project entirely ($x = 1$) or else rejecting it entirely. This constraint is not necessary (under most circumstances) when we are considering securities portfolio investments. However, most capital investment projects are indivisible; we either accept or reject a particular project; we do not have the option of owning a partial share of it. In securities portfolio selection this constraint is replaced by the restriction that the x_i (the weights) sum to a value of 1.0 (100 percent).

If we measure the return on an investment by its net present value (NPV), then we can formulate the problem of finding a point in the efficient set as:

$$\text{Maximize} \quad F = p_1 x_1 + p_2 x_2 + \cdots p_n x_n \quad (19.6)$$
$$- \lambda(x_1^2 \sigma_{11} + x_1 x_2 \sigma_{12} + \cdots x_1 x_n \sigma_{1n}$$
$$x_2 x_1 \sigma_{21} + x_2^2 \sigma_{22} + \cdots x_2 x_n \sigma_{2n}$$
$$\vdots$$
$$x_n x_1 \sigma_{n1} + x_n x_2 \sigma_{n2} + \cdots + x_n^2 \sigma_{nn})$$

$$\text{Subject to} \quad a_{11} x_1 + a_{12} x_2 + \cdots a_{1n} x_n \leq b_1 \quad (19.7)$$
$$a_{21} x_1 + a_{22} x_2 + \cdots a_{2n} x_n \leq b_2$$
$$\vdots$$
$$a_{m1} x_1 + a_{m2} x_2 + \cdots a_{mn} x_n \leq b_m$$
$$\text{and for all } i \quad x_i = 0 \quad \text{or} \quad x_1 = 1$$

which, in matrix algebra notation, becomes:

$$\text{Maximize} \quad F = p \cdot x - \lambda(x \cdot V \cdot x) \quad (19.8)$$

Subject to $\quad A \cdot x \leq b$ (19.9)
$\quad\quad\quad\quad x_i = 0 \quad \text{or} \quad 1$

where V is the variance-covariance matrix of returns.

A point regarding problem setup that seems to be often ignored in attempts to transfer this model to capital investments is that existing assets of the enterprise need to be included in the formulation. In other words, we cannot look solely at the proposals under consideration and their interrelationships, but need to include their relationships to the firm as it is now. In the programming framework above this may be done by treating the existing enterprise as a "project" with zero required investment outlay. If divestiture is not to be considered, it will also be necessary to include a constraint that requires the existing enterprise to be included in the optimal solution. It may be interesting, however, to solve again without the constraint to determine if divestiture would be worthwhile.

This formulation may be compared to that of the problem of project selection under certainty in Chapter 16. In fact, certainty means that the elements of the variance-covariance matrix are all zero, and the problem specified in Eqs. (19.6) through (19.9) reduces to Eqs. (16.1) and (16.2).

Mao [3, pp. 291-294] shows how the Lawler and Bell zero-one integer programming algorithm (discussed in Chapter 16) may be modified to solve problems with objective functions of the form in Eqs. (19.6) and (19.8). However, Baum, Carlson, and Jucker [1] have shown that the Markowitz approach, when applied to problems with indivisible projects, "may result in either (1) a solution set that does not contain all solutions of interest to the decision maker or (2) a requirement that the (implicit) utility function describing the decision maker's preferences be a linear function of the mean and variance of return."[4] By examining all feasible solutions to a problem solved by Mao [3, pp. 295-296] Baum, Carlson, and Jucker show that no matter what the value of λ, the coefficient of risk aversion, an efficient point is missed by the Markowitz approach. Furthermore, the Markowitz approach to Mao's problem, although missing an efficient point, produced a dominated point.[5] "More generally . . . any efficient point which is not located at a corner point of the upper boundary of the convex hull of the complete set of efficient points would also be missed."[6]

The Baum, Carlson, and Jucker article is significant in that it demonstrates that incorrect results may be obtained when the Markowitz approach is employed with problems involving selection of indivisible assets. This is a serious problem and we may expect that researchers will provide suitable modifications to the solution algorithm or offer alternative methods of solution, such as finding only dominant points, for example.

---

[4] Sanford Baum, Robert C. Carlson, and James V. Jucker, "Some Problems in Applying the Continuous Portfolio Selection Model to the Discrete Capital Budgeting Problem," *Journal of Financial and Quantitative Analysis*, Vol. XIII, No. 2 (June 1978), pp. 333-344.
[5] A *dominated point* is one that is inferior to other asset combinations for all values of λ, the coefficient of risk aversion.
[6] Baum et al., p. 338.

Although problems involving complex constraints of the type illustrated in Chapter 16 do not lend themselves to solution by complete enumerations, an enterprise which has only a few fairly large investment proposals may be able to analyze them quite successfully without relying on the Markowitz approach per se. Baum et al. found the error in the Mao problem solution by evaluating all 32 possible selections of the five candidate projects.[7] Full evaluation can get out of hand quickly, however, as the number of projects considered increases. Nevertheless, with up to ten projects or so ($2^{10} = 1024$) evaluation of all combinations of proposals by modern digital computers is not only possible but not particularly costly. After about ten projects, however, the number of combinations becomes rapidly so great that full enumeration is not possible. In all but the very largest enterprises this should not be an insurmountable problem, particularly if minor projects may be aggregated together.

Another possibly rewarding substitute approach might be found in using a modified zero-one programming algorithm, such as that discussed in Chapter 16 to obtain the partial enumeration combinations that will need to be evaluated in terms of risk in a second step. In other words, if we can eliminate nonfeasible combinations before looking at risk, then the number of combinations to be examined will be reduced, often substantially, particularly where several proposals are mutually exclusive.

The Sharpe Modification

William Sharpe [7] is credited with a modified version of the Markowitz model that has far-reaching implications for the valuation of assets. Sharpe's model is the foundation of the capital asset pricing model (CAPM) discussed in Chapter 21. The Sharpe model is often referred to as the "diagonal model" of portfolio selection. His model assumes that returns on assets are related only through their correlations with some index. Returns are defined as:

$$R_i = A_i + b_i I + u_i \tag{19.10}$$

where I is a random variable denoting an index, and A_i and b_i are constants for asset i. The variable I is assumed to have finite mean and finite variance. The u_i are random errors due to independent, external causes, and satisfy the usual least-squares assumptions of zero expected value, finite variance, and independence (zero covariances).

With these specifications any investment can be split into two parts: (1) an investment in A_i and u_i, the asset's basic, or unique characteristics and (2) an investment in I, the external index. This means that the variance-covariance matrix for n securities plus the external index ($n + 1$ in total) has zero elements *except* on the diagonal containing the covariances between each of the n securities and the external index.

Elimination of the covariances between individual assets makes the Sharpe

---

[7]The number of possible selections is given by 2^n, where there are n candidate proposals.

Figure 19.2 Selection of optimal portfolio of risky indivisible assets.

model much more amenable to computer solution than the original Markowitz formulation, because the computational burden is substantially lessened. It has yet to be determined whether or not the Sharpe model suffers from similar shortcomings to those Baum et al. found for the Markowitz formulation when assets are indivisible.

RELATING TO INVESTOR UTILITY

After determining the set of efficient assets for various[8] coefficients of risk aversion (λ), the actual combination of projects selected will depend on the decision maker's utility function. Graphically, the optimum project selection is that which just touches the indifference curve (that is, constant utility curve) corresponding to the highest utility.

In the case of infinitely divisible assets as depicted in Figure 19.1, the point of tangency equates the marginal rates of substitution of the efficient set curve[9] and the tangent indifference curve. For indivisible assets, the optimum efficient point is the one lying on the highest indifference curve. Figure 19.2 illustrates this.

In practice, it may not be necessary to estimate the family of indifference curves; in fact, most managements will insist on making the final decision on which efficient set of capital investments will be undertaken. There is a marked tendency for executives to resist what they interpret as arrogation of their authority and responsibility by technicians armed with computers. It may suffice to present to the executives who have the decision authority those few efficient alternative combinations that are undominated by others. This will generally mean considering which one, two, or few projects will be either removed or entered into the final selection, because alternative efficient collections are often similar over a rather wide range of λ values, differing by only few individual included or excluded projects.

---

[8] If we knew λ in advance, we could solve directly for the optimal portfolio.
[9] The curve defined by all efficient points is called the "efficient frontier."

EPILOGUE

Subject to qualifications resulting from the article by Baum, Carlson, and Jucker, the quadratic programming approaches to asset selection used by Markowitz and by Sharpe yield useful insights into the process by which risk averse investors select investment portfolios. Extension from the domain of securities analysis, where individual investments may be considered as finely, if not infinitely, divisible to the domain of indivisible capital project investments, can yield incorrect results. This appears, however, to be more a mechanical problem with implementation of the procedure than it is a problem with the theoretical concepts. As such it is a flaw that should be amenable to correction by modification of the algorithm.

Of a more fundamental nature are questions arising from concerns relating to the choice of measure of return that is used[10] as well as questions about the adequacy of variance-covariance relationship to reflect all relevant risk-return attitudes, although numerous authors have defended this latter factor. Still further unresolved concerns stem from the nature of the trade-off function relating uncertainty and futurity, from considerations of abandonment prior to final project life maturity, and from complex intertemporal contingencies between today's projects and future candidate projects.

Estimation of project variances and covariances is a difficult problem. And the question of solution sensitivity to misspecification or misestimation of the variance-covariance structure and the stability of these parameters over time has not been resolved to everyone's satisfaction for securities investments, not to mention capital expenditure proposals.

These concerns and cautions have not been raised to disparage application of portfolio selection techniques to capital investments, but rather to alert the reader that there are unresolved and controversial matters that tend to be ignored by the more zealous advocates of portfolio selection techniques to capital investment expenditure analysis.

QUESTIONS

1. How would treatment of the problem of Example 19.1 need to be modified if the laundromat/rental shop were to be built by another firm and the owners of Al's Appliance Store were offered from 0 to 100 percent participation (that is, ownership) of it?
2. Explain why a coefficient of risk aversion of zero means that the investment with the highest expected return will be included in the investment portfolio. Relate this to the concept of risk aversion in Chapter 17.
3. Discuss the notion that the firm's existing assets can be used to provide the external index required for project selection under the Sharpe formulation.
4. Why is it inappropriate to try to determine the efficient set from an array of proposals

---

[10]Mao [3] used NPV. However, it may be desirable to use alternative criterion. For example, the well-known size and economic disparity problems may impel use of level annuities or profitability index measures based on level annuities.

without the firm itself being treated as a proposal (a proposal that usually will be constrained to be accepted)?
5. Explain the concept of dominance in terms of two assets with different expected return and variance of return and with zero covariance of returns.
6. Why is it that adjoining efficient points of the efficient set usually will include most of the same project proposals? What does this suggest about the need to estimate precisely a set of indifference curves for the organization in order to identify the one optimal set of proposals?
7. Why is it misleading to connect the efficient points obtained by varying the coefficient of risk aversion when working with capital investment selection?

PROBLEMS

19.1 Denote the existing firm by A, and proposed capital investments by B, C, D, and E. Given the following data estimates, find the set of efficient portfolios by enumeration of all combinations and plot your results. Projects D and E are mutually exclusive. Expenditures must be limited to no more than $100.

Project	Cost	E[NPV]	\multicolumn{5}{c}{V[NPV]}
			A	B	C	D	E
A	$ 0	500	1000	−200	450	−100	−50
B	75	120	−200	500	−300	0	10
C	35	50	50	−300	200	0	−50
D	20	30	−100	0	40	0	—
E	10	20	50	10	−50	—	150

19.2 Roger's Rent-All does well during normal economic times, and better when times are bad. Roger is considering the purchase of a liquor store on the premises adjoining his current facility. Analysis of the income statements for the two businesses reveals the following:

	Rent-All	Liquor Store
Market Value	$500,000	$300,000
Expected Earnings	75,000	60,000
Variance of Earnings	$(5,000)^2$	$(4,000)^2$
Earnings Covariance	$+(3,500)^2$	

(a) What would be the expected return and variance for Roger's enterprise if he buys the liquor store? The variance?
(b) Would acquisition of the liquor store increase or decrease the riskiness of Roger's business holdings? Why?
(c) It is possible that major work will be done in the near future on the road in front of the two businesses. If so, traffic will be disrupted for several months. What effect would this likely have on the business risk? What if

another road were being improved that would permanently divert traffic from the street in front?

19.3 As in the previous problem Roger is considering the purchase of an additional business. This time, however, it is a health-food store in a new shopping center on the other side of town. The data for the health-food store must be estimated from similar stores elsewhere because it has been in business only a short while.

	Rent-All	Average Health-Food Store
Market Value	$500,000	$200,000
Expected Earnings	75,000	24,000
Variance of Earnings	$(5,000)^2$	$(2,000)^2$
Earnings Covariance		$-(3,000)^2$

(a) What would be the expected return and variance on Roger's holdings if he purchases the health-food store instead of the liquor store?
(b) Assuming Roger already bought the liquor store, what would purchase of the health-food store (as his third business holding) have on the expected return and variance of his holdings, assuming the covariance is $-(\$3,700)^2$?
(c) Considering the possible road problems of part (c) in Problem 19.2, what additional advantage can there be in purchasing the health-food store?
(d) A rival shopping center is being planned that would make the shopping center where the health-food store is located unattractive in comparison to much of the public. It will contain a health-food store run by a national chain. How would this enter Roger's decision?

19.4 Our current business is unique. It is related to three possible acquisitions only through the general state of the economy, which we believe is adequately portrayed by a stock market index. The data we have put together show the following:

	Market Value	Expected Return	Variance of Return	Covariance with Stock Market Index
Current Business	$10,000,000	$2,500,000	$(\$500,000)^2$	$(\$300,000)^2$
Acquisition I	2,500,000	1,500,000	$(50,000)^2$	$-(100,000)^2$
Acquisition II	4,000,000	2,000,000	$(400,000)^2$	$-(500,000)^2$
Acquisition III	3,000,000	2,000,000	$(100,000)^2$	$(200,000)^2$

We cannot invest more than $7 million. Calculate the expected returns and variances for the various feasible combinations of assets.

Bibliography

1. Baum, Sanford, Robert C. Carlson, and James V. Jucker, "Some Problems in Applying the Continuous Portfolio Selection Model to the Discrete Capital Budgeting Problem," *Journal of Financial and Quantitative Analysis*, Vol. XIII, No. 2 (June 1978), pp. 333–344.

2. Farrar, Donald E., *The Investment Decision Under Uncertainty* (Englewood Cliffs, N.J.: Prentice-Hall, 1962).
3. Mao, James C. T., *Quantitative Analysis of Financial Decisions* (New York: Macmillan, 1969).
4. Markowitz, Harry M., *Portfolio Selection: Efficient Diversification of Investments* (New York: Wiley, 1962).
5. Roy, A. D., "Safety First and the Holding of Assets," *Econometrica*, Vol. 20 (July 1952), pp. 431–449.
6. Schall, Lawrence D., and Gary L. Sundem, "Capital Budgeting Methods and Risk," *Financial Management*, Vol. 9, No. 1 (Spring 1980), pp. 7–11.
7. Sharpe, William F., "Risk Aversion in the Stock Market: Some Empirical Evidence," *The Journal of Finance*, Vol. 20 (September 1963), pp. 416–422.
8. Weingartner, H. Martin, "Capital Budgeting of Interrelated Projects: Survey and Synthesis," *Management Science*, Vol. 12 (March 1966), pp. 485–516.

Chapter 20
Multiple Project Selection Under Risk: Computer Simulation and Other Approaches

The previous chapter considered capital investment selection under risk when projects and existing assets are not independent, and projects therefore cannot be evaluated in isolation. It was assumed that all relevant asset characteristics were contained in the expected returns and their variances and covariances. This enabled selecting efficient combinations of investments: those with maximum expected return for a given level of risk or, alternatively, those with minimum risk for a given level of return.

In this chapter we examine further the problem of capital investment selection. Now, however, we shall not require that returns be normally distributed or that the relationship between project returns and existing assets be constant intertemporally. Additionally, we shall consider the problem introduced by sequential, event-contingent decisions over time. Specifically, matters relating to parameters other than the mean and the variance-covariance are considered, as are simultaneous variability of project characteristics.

DECISION TREES

The decision tree approach is a widely employed analytical device for addressing investment projects that contain sequential, event-contingent decisions. Such projects, in other words, have certain chance-determined outcomes during their lifetimes and these outcomes may influence decisions made during the project lifetime and interact with them.

Magee's [6] paper is now a classic on the topic of decision trees, and was responsible for focusing attention on this important technique, which others subsequently built upon. Two years prior to Magee, Massé [7] criticized the view of investments as single-period decisions isolated from future events. He noted that future alternatives are conditioned by present choices. Because of this, investment evaluation cannot be reduced to a single decision, but must be viewed as a sequence of decisions over time.

Decision trees are similar in some respects to Markov chains. They differ in that they include imbedded decisions and not solely probabilistic event nodes. A Markov chain has the properties that (1) the possible outcome set is finite; (2) the probability of any outcome depends only on the immediately preceding outcome,[1] and (3) the outcome probabilities are constant over time. Markov chains are suitable to many types of problems and the mathematics for their analysis is well developed. For a very readable discussion of Markov chains and their mathematics, the reader is referred to Shamblin and Stevens [12].

Figure 20.1 contains the structure of a generalized decision tree. The letter D denotes a decision and C a chance event. At $D_{1,1}$ the decision maker is faced with two choices.[2] The first subscript number refers to the point in time at which the decision or chance event occurs. Time need not be cardinal. In other words, the actual time between $t = n$ and $t = n + 1$ may be either more or less than the time from $t = n - 1$ to $t = n$. The second subscript refers to the position of the event or decision from top to bottom in the diagram.

The problem illustrated in Figure 20.1 requires two decisions, one at the outset and one after a chance event has occurred. Although they are shown as possibly different events, $C_{2,1}$ and $C_{2,2}$ may refer to the same chance event. The effect on the enterprise, however, is different because of the decision made at $D_{1,1}$. Similarly, $D_{3,1}$, $D_{3,2}$, and so on, could refer to the same decision, tempered by different precedents. Alternatively, the decisions could be quite different.

To find the optimal decisions we examine the payoff utilities associated with a particular sequence of decisions and chance events. The final result, denoted by x and y, is determined by conditional probability of preceding events. The optimal decisions are found by backward induction, by looking at the most distant result, and tracing back from there to the very beginning at $D_{1,1}$. As an alternative to working with the utilities of each separate terminal point, it is possible to find the final monetary outcomes and their associated probabilities for each branch from the final decision nodes, then take the certainty equivalents of the uncertain outcomes.

An example will help clarify how decision trees may be applied to capital investment decisions.

---

[1]This is true only for first-order Markov chains. If the chain is second-order, then an outcome may depend on the two prior events, and so on.

[2]In general, there will be n decision choices, where n is a finite number. Our space limitations dictates that for illustrative purposes only two choices be used.

Figure 20.1 General structure of a Decision Tree.

Example 20-1

The Northern Lites Manufacturing Company has successfully produced and marketed home heating units for 30 years. The units are designed to use either gas or fuel oil, but not both. The engineers of the firm have now designed a new unit that can use interchangeably either gas, fuel oil, coal, or cord wood, and, with an optional adapter, peanut shells and other waste products. The marketing staff is enthusiastic about the sales prospects for the new multiple-fuel furnace that they are calling the "Hades Hearth Home Heater."

The new heating unit could be produced in the existing factory, but changeover would take at least a year, perhaps longer, and an inventory of replacement parts would have to be built up to meet the owners' needs for repairs of the current models. A new plant could be constructed and in operation within a year, and a nearby facility could be leased and readied for production in the same time span.

288 CAPITAL BUDGETING UNDER RISK—WITHOUT DIVERSIFICATION

Because of shortages and rising fuel oil and natural gas prices, sales are expected to be brisk. However, there is a 30 percent chance of a depression in a year that would be so severe that even though they would like to buy the new furnace, consumers will not have the money. If there is such a depression, the firm will lose $1000 with a new plant facility, $300 with the leased facility, and $100 if it delays its production by deciding to use the existing plant. A deep depression would mean a halt to production until the economy improved.

The new plant will allow maximum production. Delaying production to use the existing plant will allow competitors to take the lead and sales will therefore be less. In two years the engineering staff feels it will have a much improved design that may be required to keep sales up. There is some risk, however, that the improved design may not be as popular as anticipated because of competitive developments and the possibility of meaningful government incentives for fuel conservation.

Figure 20.2 illustrates the tree diagram for this problem. If a new plant is built, if there is no depression, and the design is changed and successfully received in the market, the present value to the firm is $900. If not well received, the present value is $360. The remaining results are similarly interpreted. Note that the expected values shown in Figure 20.2 are expected monetary values, not expected utilities or certainty equivalents. Table 20-1 shows the calculations corresponding to the expected monetary values of Figure 20.2 for finding the expected utilities.

Implicit in the approach illustrated in Table 20-1 is the assumption that the expected utility is the proper measure by which the optimum course may be determined. However, we should note that this approach does not take into account the distributions of the outcome utilities but only their expected values. It may well be the case that certainty equivalents corresponding to the monetary outcomes would yield a different ranking. Therefore, it may be important in practice to have management make its choices on the basis of the certainty equivalents that it assigns to the various choices.

As matters stand, the expected utilities in Table 20-1 favor leasing a plant for production of the multiple fuel furnace to either building a new plant or delaying and using the existing plant. Note that the spread of both dollar and utility outcomes is greater for leasing than for delaying until the current plant can be used, thereby making the lease arrangement more risky. By the same reasoning the building of a new plant would be both more risky and offer a lower expected utility than leasing; it is thus dominated by the leasing alternative.

An alternative to either choosing the path offering the highest expected utility or choosing the path offering the highest certainty equivalent is found in the next chapter. There the capital asset pricing model (CAPM) is discussed and it is shown that the optimal choice may be made by employing the risk/return trade-offs prevailing in the market.

OTHER RISK CONSIDERATIONS

In addition to the types of risk considerations introduced by sequential, event-contingent decisions and intervening stochastic events, there are other situations in

MULTIPLE PROJECT SELECTION UNDER RISK: COMPUTER SIMULATION   289

	Economic Conditions	Change Design?		Net Profit	P (Profit)*	Net Present Value	Expected Value
P (Prosperity) = .7				$1000	.8	$900	$504
P (Depression) = .3		Yes	E	400	.2	360	50
	Prosperity	D					
		No	E	800	.6	720	302
				200	.4	180	50
	Depression	Expected Value = −$1000 × .3 = −$300					
Build New Plant				700	.8	630	353
	Depression	E.V. = −$300 × .3 = −$90	E	300	.2	270	38
Lease Plant	Prosperity	Yes D					
		No	E	600	.6	540	227
				250	.4	225	63
Delay Production	Depression	Expected Value = −$100 × .3 = −$30					
				500	.7	450	220
	Prosperity	Yes	E	150	.3	135	28
		D					
		No	E	400	.5	360	126
				100	.5	90	32

* Conditional probability of profit given prosperity

Figure 20.2 Decision Tree for Example 20-1.

which portfolio approaches may not be employed to best advantage. Since portfolio approaches developed by Markowitz and Sharpe assume stable (or at least not suddenly changing) relationships between projects and the enterprise's existing assets, problems in which the relationships may change in response to some future chance event or events do not lend themselves to portfolio selection approaches as they currently exist.

Recognizing the shortcomings pointed out in Chapter 18 for computer simulation of single investment proposals, computer simulation may offer the most suitable approach to the analysis of certain multiple-project problems. One such application arises in the case of problems involving assets with useful lives not only governed by

Table 20-1. CALCULATION OF PAYOFF UTILITIES FOR EXAMPLE 20-1

BUILD NEW PLANT
.7 × .8 × U($900) = .56 × .80 = .448
.7 × .2 × U(360) = .14 × .50 = .070
.7 × .6 × U(720) = .42 × .73 = .307
.7 × .4 × U(180) = .28 × .30 = .084
.3 × 1.0 × U(−1000) = .30 × −.90 = −.270
                                                          .639

LEASE PLANT
.7 × .8 × U($630) = .56 × .68 = .381
.7 × .2 × U(270) = .14 × .40 = .056
.7 × .6 × U(540) = .42 × .63 = .265
.7 × .4 × U(225) = .28 × .35 = .098
.3 × 1.0 × U(−300) = .30 × −.32 = −.096
                                                          .703

DELAY PRODUCTION
.7 × .7 × U($450) = .49 × .57 = .279
.7 × .3 × U(135) = .21 × .24 = .048
.7 × .5 × U(360) = .35 × .49 = .172
.7 × .5 × U(90) = .35 × .18 = .063
.3 × 1.0 × U(−100) = .30 × −.14 = −.042
                                                          .520

their own unique characteristics but by the life of the aggregate as well. An example will serve to illustrate this type of problem. The following example is rather lengthy because of the nature of the problem and because it illustrates a way of analyzing multiple-project problems by means of computer simulation.

A Comprehensive Simulation Example

Example 20-2[3]

In oilfield primary recovery operations equipment deterioration and breakdown create problems over the lifetime of the field. These problems are of a reinvestment/abandonment type for which little theoretical guidance is to be found in texts on capital budgeting, engineering economy, or operations research. For instance: (1) when should a particular well be rehabilitated rather than abandoned? and (2) when should the entire field be abandoned for continuing primary recovery and secondary recovery operations be undertaken?

Discussion is limited in scope to consideration of decision algorithms for determining:

1. Whether a particular well should be repaired after equipment breakdown, or should instead be shut down.

[3]Extracted from a paper by Anthony F. Herbst and Sayeed Hasan, "A Simulation Analysis of Primary Recovery Oilfield Reinvestment Management," Proceedings of the American Institute for Decision Sciences, Eighth Annual Meeting, San Francisco, Cal., November 10–12, 1976, pp. 94–96. By permission of the Institute.

2. Under what circumstances the entire field should be abandoned as a primary recovery field.

We consider the related problem of replacement of primary recovery with secondary recovery (by means of gas or water injection) before primary recovery in itself becomes economically nonviable, though our emphasis is on the above two problems.

For purposes of classification we distinguish between two cases of primary recovery field abandonment. First, the weak case, in which the primary recovery operation is in itself still economically viable, but inferior to and economically dominated by a change in technology to secondary recovery methods. Second, the strong case, in which primary recovery is in itself economically non-viable regardless of secondary recovery operations.

A difficult but interesting feature of the problems considered in this section is interdependence between the maximum expected economic life of each well and that of the entire field. Abandonment of any given well or set of wells may result in the entire field becoming unprofitable with primary recovery. Adoption of the decision to abandon the entire field, of course, implies abandonment of all individual wells whether or not they are operating profitably at the time.

The decision to abandon the entire field for primary recovery (strong case) is relatively straightforward. The field should be shut down when variable cash revenue contribution of the field no longer exceeds variable cash cost. In other words, in the strong case the field should be abandoned when net cash contribution to fixed cost coverage and profits becomes zero.

The weak case decision to abandon primary recovery and replace it with secondary recovery technology should be made when the expected net present value (NPV) of investment in secondary recovery by gas or water injection exceeds the expected net present value of the remaining cash flows with primary recovery. We will not at this time get into the problem of determining the NPV of secondary recovery investment, as this appears to be amenable to the more standard capital budgeting-engineering economy analysis. We do, however, address the problem of estimating the NPV of the remaining cash flows with primary recovery.

The more difficult question than field abandonment for primary recovery is that of when any particular stripper well should be abandoned. At least two circumstances must be considered. First, under what circumstances should a given well be abandoned prior to equipment failure? Second, given an equipment failure of a particular type, when should repair or replacement be undertaken, and when should the well be shut down and abandoned for primary recovery?

Characteristics of the Problem

THE OILFIELD
Type of Recovery Process: We adopt the terminology that primary oil and gas recovery is that undertaken by use of pumps and secondary recovery is that undertaken by use of water or gas injection.[4] When pumps are employed to raise the oil to the surface, the wells are called stripper wells. Each stripper well will have its own pump, and

---

[4] Another classification scheme would relegate to primary recovery the removal of oil by employing the natural subsurface pressure that may exist, secondary recovery to the use of pumps, and tertiary recovery to the water or gas injection methods. Under this alternative classification a field may be taken from primary to tertiary recovery by omitting the use of pumps entirely.

therefore there will be a close correspondence between the number of wells and the amount of capital equipment required.

Secondary recovery with water or gas injection is accomplished by drilling wells around the field through which water or gas may be injected to drive out the oil ahead of it. Unlike primary recovery, the number and location of injection wells are not strictly determined by the number of oil wells and there is no one-to-one correspondence between injection sites and oil wells as there is between pumps and stripper wells.

Breakdown of Stripper Wells: Stripper wells are subject to a variety of breakdowns which require the decision be made to either repair the problem or else to abandon that well during primary recovery. Major types of breakdown include pump overhaul, need for condensate wash, broken pump rod, and rupture in production tubing. In addition to the normal costs of repair, a condensate wash involves several days lost production while it is being carried out. Periodic, scheduled maintenance may entail pump overhaul and condensate wash to prevent unscheduled breakdowns which may be more costly than planned preventive maintenance.

The probabilities associated over time with different major breakdowns may not be independent. For instance, a broken pump rod may do other damage to other well equipment, and a condensate wash may sometimes be required after another type of breakdown.

It is not our purpose to become involved in the technical details of the recovery process, but rather to deal with the methodology for determining the optimal reinvestment policy for the oil company. Therefore, after this brief introduction to the technology of recovery, we will move on to the financial, economic, and methodological consideration of our work.

Decision Required

There are three basic decisions which must be made continually over the life of the field:

1. Given a well breakdown, whether to repair or shut down (abandon) the well.
2. Whether to replace all well equipment with new equipment of the same type or switch to another extraction technology and equipment.
3. When to shut down the entire field to recovery with the currently employed technology.

The second decision, we propose, is amenable to more-or-less familiar approaches, such as the MAPI (Machinery and Allied Products Institute) method of replacement analysis.

Financial Measures of Investment Return

Modern financial management heavily favors the use of discounted cash flow (DCF) methods of evaluation, and favors the net present value approach over internal rate of return. While the DCF approach has been favored, the payback criterion has simultaneously been attacked for use in investment decisions. However, DCF methods require certain information and conditions which may not exist.

In the problem we consider, the economic lives of the oilfield and the individual wells are interdependent. We do not know the useful life of any individual well, as that life depends on the nature and frequency of required repairs and especially on the life of the entire field. Similarly, the life of the field depends on the lives of the individual wells. When all wells are shut down, obviously the field life, with the particular technology, has ended. When it has been decided to close the field all wells in it will be closed. It is not known *a priori* how long the useful lives of either the individual wells or the field will be.

Additionally, the DCF methods require that the cash flows for each period be known or estimated. However, in the case of well breakdown the cash flows will be affected by the pattern and types of breakdown experienced, which are stochastically determined. The DCF measures are known to be affected by the pattern of cash flows as well as their magnitudes, and although the expected value of the cash flows could be determined the pattern cannot be on an *a priori* basis.

The absence of *a priori* knowledge of useful lives and cash flow patterns, coupled with the interdependence of the well and field characteristics, negates the usefulness of ordinary DCF methods to the problem we consider.

Methodology

We are interested in determining a policy for repairs that will yield the maximum expected net discounted return, and in the absence of *a priori* information, use the approach of simulation experience with the field under alternative policies. The results of the simulation then provide information that can be converted to the DCF present value measure. In other words, we approach the problem by simulating the cash flows of the field under different repair policies. The cash flows are carried forward with compounding at the firm's cost of capital as *future values*. At abandonment or shutdown of the field the future values are then converted to present value equivalents. Choice of the proper policy will yield results that would be obtainable in ordinary circumstances by a direct DCF approach.

Since the payback criterion is already familiar and widely used in industry we adopt it as our policy variable for repair decisions.[5] If the net cash flow over n periods, where n is the payback policy, is insufficient to recover the repair cost, we shut down the well. If the cash flow is greater than the repair cost, we repair and continue to operate the well. After a representative number of simulations, employing different seed values for the generation of (pseudo-) random numbers, we propose adopting that payback policy that promises the highest net present value for the field.

We also consider as a secondary policy the shut down of the field when the rate of change in the cash revenues becomes less than the rate of change in cash costs (including repair costs) over m periods. This provides a means for determining when to shut down the entire field before all wells are shut down and before net cash flow becomes negative. We define shutdown under this secondary policy variable as "weak case" shutdown. Treatment of this policy is left to a subsequent paper, as results so far are inconclusive.

The field will be shut down to primary recovery whenever the net cash flow becomes negative. That is, when cash revenues are inadequate to cover cash costs, we

---

[5] We do, however, adjust the payback criterion to include the time-value of funds.

will shut down the field. We define shutdown of the field under this condition as "strong case" shutdown.

The Model

I. Net Per Period Cash Revenue for the Field in Period j
NR = Total Cash Revenue − Variable Cash Cost
   − Fixed Cash Cost[6]

$$= \text{PCFOIL} \sum_{i=1}^{\text{NWELLS}} \text{OILBBL}_{i,j}$$

$$+ \text{PCFGAS} \sum_{i=1}^{\text{NWELLS}} \text{GASMCF}_{i,j}$$

$$- (\text{ROALTO} + \text{PROCD}) \sum_{i=1}^{\text{NWELL}} \text{OILBBL}_{i,j}$$

$$- \text{CASHFC}$$

$$- \sum_{i=1}^{\text{NWELL}} \text{REPRC}_{i,j}$$

Strong Case Decision: If NR ≤ 0, shut down the entire field

where i denotes individual wells:

PCFOIL and PCFGAS	the price per barrel of oil and MCF of gas, respectively
OILBBL and GASMCF	the barrels of oil output and MCF gas output for the ith well, jth period
ROALTO and ROALTG	the royalty charges levied per barrel of oil and MCF of gas
PROCO and PROCG	processing costs per barrel of oil and MCF of gas
CASHFC	fixed cash expense per period while the field is open
REPRC	repair cost for the ith well and jth period if a breakdown occurs and is repaired

II. For a Given Well i:
Let $b_{k,j}$ be the number of breakdowns of type k in period j. Then the reinvestment cost for repairing the breakdown is $C_{i,j}$. Let P_k be the cost of repair for type k breakdown. Then $C_{i,j} = \sum_{k=1}^{\text{NTYPE}} b_{k,j} P_k$ where NTYPE is the total number of

---
[6]Cash costs that would not exist were the field to be closed.

major breakdown types. We require recovery of the cost with a payback period of n time periods.

If $C_{i,j} < \sum_{l=j+1}^{j+n} \text{OILBBL}_{i,l}(\text{PCFOIL-ROALTO-PROCO})/(1 + \text{RATE})^{l-j}$

$+ \sum_{l=j+1}^{j+n} \text{GASMCF}_{i,l}(\text{PCFGAS-ROALTG-PROCG})/(1 + \text{RATE})^{l-j}$

where RATE is the firm's per period cost of capital, we repair the well and continue operation. Otherwise we shut down the well.

III. Breakdowns Are Assumed To:
   1. Be Poisson distributed over time, and be
   2. Independent of previous breakdown history of the well.

Figures 20.3(a) and (b) contain a flow chart of the model.[7]

Estimating NPV of Remaining Cash Flows with Primary Recovery

Empirical experience with our model, which provides for application of production deterioration gradients and changes in price, processing costs, and so on, suggests how remaining field NPV may be estimated to any arbitrary point in time. Since the accumulated net future value is calculated for each time period prior to shutdown, the net present value of cash flows over any time span prior to shutdown may be calculated. Thus, if shutdown should occur in period 85, and we are interested in the NPV of flows between period 40 and 85, we can determine this easily with customary financial mathematics.

Analysis of the remaining value of net cash revenues over time will provide information useful in the decision of whether, and when, to switch to other technology for recovery.

Empirical Results

The model was tested with empirical data provided to one of the authors, for a stripper field in Western Canada. Results of a typical simulation run are summarized in Table 20–2. The condition of this field is such that the maximum NPV is obtained with a payback policy of four periods (one week equals one period in this run). Such a short payback meant that after a major breakdown of any type the well involved would be abandoned. This may be attributed to the low oil and gas yields of the wells in a declining old field in relation to the cost of repairs.

Breakdown probabilities were assumed to be independent of prior breakdown history of any well. This assumption may not be warranted, but the authors had no information to the contrary which would enable them to modify the breakdown probabilities for further breakdowns once a well had been repaired. Because of this, breakdowns of the same type could occur within the payback period. This meant that a repair could be carried out only to have the same type of breakdown result in abandonment before the cost of the first repair had been recovered.

---

[7] The paper published in the *Proceedings* did not contain this flow chart because of space limitations.

Figure 20.3(a) Flow chart of the Model

Figure 20.3(b) Continuation of flow chart of model.

Table 20-2. SIMULATION RESULTS

NPAOUT	All Wells Shut Down in Period No.	NPV by Waiting Until All Wells are Shut Down	Stron Case Shut Down in Period No.	NPV with Strong Case Shut Down
4	15	$10,888.50	15	$10,888.50
5	18	− 1,756.10	9	8,312.77
6	18	− 1,756.10	9	8,312.77
7	18	− 2,592.75	5	5,263.98
8	18	− 2,592.75	5	5,263.98
9	18	− 2,592.75	5	5,263.98
10	26	−18,184.30	5	5,263.98
11	26	−18,184.30	5	5,263.98
12	26	−18,184.30	5	5,263.98
13	26	−18,184.30	5	5,263.98

CONCLUSION

The aim of this chapter was to illustrate two approaches to capital investment decision-making under risk that may provide useful results when portfolio approaches are not applicable. The first approach shown was that of decision tree analysis. The second was computer simulation of multiple project problems.

In decision tree analysis the problem is characterized by a sequential decision-event-decision-event . . . chain over time. Because decisions are contingent on chance events, it may not be possible to specify *a priori* which decision beyond the first will be made. The goal of decision tree analysis is to identify the mixed decision-event sequence that promises the maximum expected utility. By doing so it is possible to identify the superior initial decision because it is determined by all that follows it. Decisions reached through application of the decision tree approach will often be different from those reached through viewing the problem as an isolated, period decision because this latter approach ignores future choices.

Computer simulation of multiple project capital investment problems can be used to reach optimal decisions where the interrelationships between projects are complex. It is difficult to generalize about the type of problem warranting the time and expense of computer simulation. However, problems involving many projects, where their relationships cannot be described by variance-covariance or correlation, will be candidates for simulation, especially if the particular problem represents large resource value to the enterprise. Computer simulation should be viewed not as a replacement for other methods of analysis in normal situations, but rather as a last line of defense when other approaches fail, and a powerful last defense it is. In normal circumstances the extra time, effort, and expense of computer simulation are difficult to rationalize when other, less arcane methods yield correct decisions.

QUESTIONS

1. What steps are necessary in applying decision tree analysis to a problem?
2. Explain why decision nodes at the same future time may represent the same decision. How could they represent different decisions?
3. Why will a different initial decision often be reached under the decision tree approach than with treating the problem as a single-period, isolated decision?
4. When decision tree analysis yields two branches with different expected utilities and variances of utilities, what problem does this create? Assume that branch 1 has utility U_1 and variance of utility V_1 and branch 2 has U_2 and V_2 and that $U_1 > U_2$, but $V_1 > V_2$. Discuss.
5. If it is not possible to describe the relationship between projects with variance and covariance, explain why computer simulation may be more suitable than portfolio selection algorithms.

PROBLEMS

20.1 Freddie Farmer owns 600 acres of fertile land in the midwestern United States that overlays a rich seam of coal. He has recently been approached by representatives of AXON International who offer to buy Freddie's land, on which he owns the mineral rights. If he sells to AXON now, he will receive $1.2 million. If he continues to farm his land, Freddie believes he can earn $200 an acre annually because of worldwide grain shortages over the next five years.

There is a .5 probability that AXON will offer $3 million for Freddie's farm in five years, .3 probability that the company will offer $2.5 million, and .2 probability that it will offer nothing because new laws will make it uneconomical to remove the coal under the farm. On the other hand, world political and economic conditions suggest that grain prices may increase. After five years the probability is .4 that Freddie will earn $250 per acre, .3 he will earn $300, and .1 he will earn $350 from year five forward. There is also .3 probability that the government will take Freddie's land for the coal at the end of five years, paying him $1.32 million for it.

Assuming the above data are in real terms (that is, there is no inflation) and the appropriate discount rate is 10 percent per annum, what should Freddie do if he is after the decision that leads to maximum expected monetary value? What should he do if his utility function is $U = .2E[M] - .02E[M]^{1.02}$ where M is the final monetary value that may be achieved?

20.2 In Example 20.1, Figure 20.2, change the probability of profit figures (from top to bottom) to .9, .1; .8, .2; .7, .3; .5, .5; .8, .2; and .6, .4 and calculate the expected utilities assuming the utility function is adequately represented by the equation $U = .5E[M] - .07E[M]$ and select the optimum decision path.

20.3 Use computer simulation to solve this problem: Albatross, Inc., has three large machines in its factory. The machines are engaged in production of unrelated products (sales are uncorrelated) and are considered independent. However, because Albatross is a marginal firm, failure of any one of the three product lines could severely strain the resources of the firm. Failure of any two would ruin the firm. We define failure of a product line to be annual sales more than 60 percent under its expected value or a major machine breakdown (lasting more than three weeks). However, failure of one product line or machine can be offset if the other two machines together achieve production and sales offsetting the decline of the third. Management is interested in determining the probability of bankruptcy given the following information (annual basis). The effect of a major machine breakdown is assumed to be equivalent to the 60 percent shortfall in sales.

Machine/ Product Line	Expected Production/ Sales	Standard Deviation	Probability of Major Breakdown
I	$1,000,000	$100,000	.10
II	2,000,000	300,000	.25
III	3,000,000	500,000	.05

Expected production and sales are normally distributed. Assume you have on your computer system a function that returns a normally distributed random number when supplied the mean and the standard deviation of: $X = N(\text{XBAR}, \text{SDX})$. Also, assume a function RAND(ISEED) that returns a random number from a uniform distribution over the range 0 to 1 when supplied with an initially defined integer seed value.

20.4 In Problem 20.3 assume that Albatross, Inc., can sell machine and product line III. The proceeds will be used to purchase machine and product line IV that has (normally distributed) expected annual sales of $2.5 million, standard deviation $200,000, and major breakdown probability .025. Sales of machine IV are thought to have correlation −.81 with machine II. The breakdown probabilities are independent, however. Machine III can be sold for $10 million. Machine IV would cost $15 million, and the firm's annual cost of capital is 15 percent. Should the firm sell machine III and buy machine IV?

Bibliography

1. Bierman, Harold, Jr., Charles P. Bonnini, and Warren H. Hausman, *Quantitative Analysis for Business Decisions*, 4th ed. (Homewood, Ill.: Irwin, 1973).
2. Cooper, D. O., L. B. Davidson, and W. K. Denison, "A Tool for More Effective Financial Analysis," *Interfaces*, Vol. 5, No. 2, Pt. 2 (February 1975), pp. 91–103.
3. Derman, C., G. J. Lieberman, and S. M. Ross, "A Renewal Decision Problem," *Management Science*, Vol. 24, No. 5 (January 1978), pp. 554–561.
4. Herbst, Anthony F., and Sayeed Hasan, "A Simulation Analysis of Primary Recovery Oilfield Reinvestment Management," *Proceedings of the Eighth Annual Meeting of the American Institute for Decision Sciences*, November 10–12, 1976, pp. 94–96.
5. Luken, Jack A., and David P. Stuhr, "Decision Trees and Risky Projects," *The Engineering Economist*, Vol. 24, No. 2 (Winter 1979), pp. 75–86.
6. Magee, John F., "Decision Trees for Decision Making," *Harvard Business Review*, Vol. 42 (July–August 1964), pp. 126–138.
7. Massé Pierre, *Optimal Investment Decisions* (Englewood Cliffs, N.J.: Prentice-Hall, 1962).
8. Mao, James C. T., *Quantitative Analysis of Financial Decisions* (New York: Macmillan, 1969).
9. Mao, James C. T., *Corporate Financial Decisions* (Palo Alto, Cal.: Pavan, 1976).
10. Miller, David W., and Martin K. Starr, *Executive Decisions and Operations Research*, 2nd ed. (Englewood Cliffs, N.J.: Prentice-Hall, 1969).
11. Salazar, Rodolfo, and Subrata K. Sen, "A Simulation Model of Capital Budgeting Under Uncertainty," *Management Science*, Vol. 15, No. 4 (December 1968), pp. B-161–B-179.
12. Shamblin, James E., and G. T. Stevens, Jr., *Operations Research* (New York: McGraw-Hill, 1974).
13. Stone, Bernell K., "A General Class of Three-Parameter Risk Measures," *The Journal of Finance*, Vol. XXVIII, No. 3 (June 1973), pp. 675–685.

Part V
CAPITAL BUDGETING UNDER RISK—WITH DIVERSIFICATION

Chapter 21
The Capital Asset Pricing Model

In Chapter 4 the capital asset pricing model (CAPM) was mentioned in relation to the firm's cost of equity capital. In Chapter 18 it was mentioned again in the discussion of the criticism of computer simulation of individual capital investment proposals. Here we shall examine the capital asset pricing model more closely, to see how it may enable the firm to rationalize the risk-return trade-off and how it may assist in estimating the firm's cost of equity capital and in assessing the interaction between capital investment and cost of capital.

Development of what is now generally referred to as the capital asset pricing model, can be attributed to several individuals. Sharpe [20,21] and Treynor [22] performed the pioneering work, having more or less simultaneously solved the basic economic problem of finding the market price of risk in the case of an individual asset. Lintner [11,12], Mossin [15], and Black [1], among others, developed the CAPM further, and additional insights continue to be gained as yet more work is done on the model. One can scarcely find an issue of any major finance journal nowadays without an article about some aspect of the CAPM.

The purpose of this chapter is to present the CAPM as a means for dealing with risk in capital investment. In keeping with this purpose the model is examined critically in terms of how well it facilitates making better decisions, as well as problems that affect application of the model to capital investment projects.

ASSUMPTIONS OF THE CAPM

The CAPM is based on several of the following assumptions, some of which do not conform well to the reality of capital investment projects:
1. Investors are risk-averse maximizers of the expected utility based on wealth at end-of-holding period.
2. Expectations about asset returns are homogeneous: Everyone agrees on the probability distributions governing returns.
3. Assets are fixed in number, marketable, and infinitely divisible.
4. A risk-free asset exists and investors may borrow or lend without limit at the rate of return paid by the risk-free asset.
5. The market is perfect: no taxes, no transactions costs, no restrictions.
6. All investors have the same planning horizon and holding period.
7. Investors do not distinguish between sources of returns. They are indifferent between dividends and interest of equal dollar amount.

THE EFFICIENT SET OF PORTFOLIOS

In Chapter 19 portfolio selection techniques were examined. They required that we first find the set of efficient portfolios, those that cannot be improved upon in this sense: An efficient portfolio is one that has maximum expected return for a given level of risk or, alternatively, has minimum risk for a given expected rate of return. In other words, if a portfolio is efficient, we cannot improve upon it by finding another portfolio that has the same (or greater) return and lower risk or the same (or less) risk and greater return.

Since the investor is assumed to be risk averse and utility maximizing, and since greater utility is associated with greater returns, the only portfolios he or she is interested in are efficient portfolios. In Figure 21.1 the section of curve II' above point 0 is the efficient frontier. Points on II' below point 0 represent nonefficient portfolios because for the same risk each has an alternate providing higher expected return on the segment above.

The risk-averse, utility maximizing investor we have assumed can be interested only in efficient portfolios; it remains to determine exactly which efficient portfolio is optimum. In Chapter 19 this was found as the point of tangency between the efficiency frontier and the investor's highest indifference curve. These indifference curves contain risk-return combinations which, to the particular investor, offer constant utility along a given curve. In Figure 21.1 the portfolio choices of three investors (A, B, and C) are depicted by points 1, 2, and 3. Investor C may be considered the most aggressive of the three because point 3, although corresponding to higher returns than the others, is also associated with proportionately greater risk. By similar reasoning, investor A may be considered the most conservative of the three. Minimum risk is at point 0, but the return of the portfolio corresponding to that point is also at a minimum.

So far, we have not admitted the existence of a *risk-free* asset into our portfolio

Figure 21.1 The efficient set and investor portfolio choices.

considerations. At this point we shall assume such an investment exists, and examine implications.

Enter a Risk-Free Investment

The foregoing assumed that the only assets that existed were risky. Now we shall assume there is a risk-free asset, paying a certain rate of return denoted by R_f. Because federal government securities are risk free in this sense, and they are bonds, we might alternatively use i to denote the fixed, certain rate of return. Those who are totally averse to risk would be expected to purchase only the risk-free asset for its certain return. Others would purchase combinations of the risk-free asset and the market portfolio.

The risk-free assumption, it should be noted, requires several subsidiary assumptions. Although the payment of a fixed, periodic money interest on federal government bonds is reasonable (except possibly in time of war or revolution that may bring to power new government that will repudiate the debt), it raises questions. Is the rate of return in nominal terms or in real terms? What about capital gains or losses brought about by changes in the market rate of interest? If there can be capital gains, then the rate of return is not fixed and certain.

In order for the risk-free return to be in fact risk-free, or certain, we need to require either that (1) we measure nominal returns, unadjusted for inflation or (2) we have constant inflation or know the rate of inflation over the holding period, or (3) the risk-free security is a floating rate bond that pays a certain *real* return, or (4) the holding period is short enough that the effects of inflation can be ignored. If both the risk-free return and the market portfolio return are equally affected by inflation, the problem diminishes and it is not necessary to do more than insure that returns are measured on the same basis in either nominal or real terms.

The problem posed by capital gains may be resolved in either of two ways. We can add the assumption of costless information, which is sometimes listed as one of

Figure 21.2 Risk-free asset, market portfolio, and capital market line (CML).

the required assumptions of the CAPM,[1] or we may instead assume a constant interest rate over the holding period or else a short holding period over which interest-induced capital gains and losses would be minimal, such as with three-month U.S. Treasury bills, for example.

For our purposes we need not be overly concerned about these questions about the risk-free asset. However, because such questions tend to arise from students of the CAPM, this seems an appropriate place to bring them into the open. We shall not dwell on this matter further, but continue, assuming that the risk-free rate is indeed risk free.

A risk-free asset in addition to the efficient set means that now every investor can have a portfolio composed of the risk-free asset plus an efficient portfolio of risky assets. Figure 21.2 illustrates this. Any point on the straight line may be obtained by the appropriate linear combination of the risk-free asset and the efficient portfolio at the point of tangency. If q is the proportion of the investor's wealth invested in the risk-free asset, then $1 - q$ is the proportion invested in the tangent portfolio, and $0 \leq q \leq 1$.

The line from R_f tangent to the efficient set is called the *capital market line* (CML). No longer are investors content to hold only risky assets in efficient portfolios. Now they want to hold some of the risk-free asset in combination with an efficient portfolio. And the one efficient portfolio they will hold in such combination is the *market portfolio*. Every other portfolio is inferior, because now investors can achieve higher returns for a given level of risk. In terms of indifference curves this means that such curves will not be tangent to the efficient set, but rather will be tangent to line $R_f R_f'$ that lies above the efficient set at every point except M, the point of tangency corresponding to the market portfolio.

The market portfolio must include every risky asset; otherwise the prices of

---

[1]Haley and Schall [8] claim the assumption of "costless availability of information" is not necessary in a footnote on their p. 144.

some would rise and others fall until all were included, and all assets must be owned by someone. A change in the risk-free return vis-à-vis the return on the market portfolio means that a new point of tangency will exist and risky asset prices will adjust until a new equilibrium is reached and there is a new market portfolio.

The line segment of $R_f R_f'$ above point M corresponds to margin purchases of the market portfolio. In other words, investors who seek a higher return, albeit with higher risk, can borrow at the risk-free rate[2] and invest the proceeds in the market portfolio. Therefore, linear combinations of the risk-free asset and the market portfolio are all that investors will want to hold above point M as well as below it. Again, above point M as well as below it, investors will want to stay on line $R_f R_f'$ because it offers greater utility.

The equation of the capital market line $R_f R_f'$ is:

$$E[R_M] = R_f + \lambda \sigma_M \tag{21.1}$$

or if we can denote $E[R]$ by $\bar{R}$:

$$\bar{R}_M = R_f + \lambda \sigma_M \tag{21.2}$$

The line slope, λ, is the "price of risk." The risk-free rate and market expectations may change over time and, accordingly, the price of risk may change as a new equilibrium is reached. Equilibrium is assumed to exist now and to reflect expectations over one period into the future. Lambda is defined by:

$$\lambda = \frac{\bar{R}_M - R_f}{\sigma_M} \tag{21.3}$$

Thus the price of risk is not simply the difference between the price of the risk-free asset and the expected return on the market portfolio, but must be adjusted for the standard deviation of the portfolio return.

THE SECURITY MARKET LINE AND BETA

The equilibrium conditions for efficient holdings of a risk-free asset and the market portfolio are given by the capital market line. But we are also interested in the return on inefficient holdings, whether portfolios or individual assets. Every asset is held in the market portfolio, as we have previously stated; otherwise its price would change until it was included. The capital market line provides a measure of the price of risk for the overall market portfolio. But what is the risk-return trade-off for a given asset or inefficient asset portfolio?

By equating the "price of risk" with the slope of the efficient frontier at point of tangency M (Figure 21.2), we obtain:[3]

$$\frac{\bar{R} - R_f}{\sigma_M} = \frac{E[R_j] - \bar{R}_M}{(\sigma_{jM} - \sigma_M^2)/\sigma_M} \tag{21.4}$$

---

[2] By assumption.
[3] See Copeland and Weston [2], pp. 162–163, for the detail of the efficient set slope derivation.

from which can be obtained the relationship usually called *the capital asset pricing model*:

$$E[R_j] = R_f + \frac{\sigma_{jm}}{\sigma_M^2}[\bar{R}_M - R_f] \tag{21.5}$$

which is usually written in the form:

$$\bar{R}_j = R_f + \beta_j[\bar{R}_M - R_f] \tag{21.6}$$

where β is defined as:

$$\beta_j = \frac{\text{Cov}(R_j, R_M)}{\text{Var}(R_M)} = \frac{\sigma_{jM}}{\sigma_M^2} \tag{21.7}$$

Beta can be thought of as the volatility of the *j*th asset and may be estimated (if data are available) by fitting an ordinary least-squares regression to the equation:

$$R_j = \alpha_j + \beta_j R_M \tag{21.8}$$

Several investment services publish calculated betas for U.S. common stocks. However, because market returns would have to be based on a market portfolio including every asset weighted according to its importance, and because this would be impossible to achieve and prohibitively costly to try to approach, the "market" portfolio is in fact a portfolio of New York Stock Exchange listed common stocks or some more restricted list such as the Standard and Poors 500.

If we define total risk of any asset as *systematic risk* plus *unsystematic risk*, then the beta is the systematic risk. The actual return on any asset *j* is given by:

$$R_j = \alpha_j + \beta_j R_M + \mu_j \tag{21.9}$$

with variance

$$\sigma_j^2 = \beta_j^2 \sigma_M^2 + \sigma_\mu^2 \tag{21.10}$$

where μ represents an independent random error term, and R_j and R_M are random variables.

Since in (21.10) the variance is the total risk, the right-hand side contains the two component risks. The unsystematic risk is σ_μ^2, and this can be eliminated by diversification. Because unsystematic risk can thus be eliminated, the market will not pay to avoid it. However, systematic risk is another matter entirely. Investors will pay to avoid systematic risk, and *in equilibrium every asset must fall on the security market line*. Figure 21.3 illustrates the security market line. The market portfolio itself has $\beta = 1$, as indicated.

Although *the capital market line related a risk-free asset to the market portfolio, the security market line relates risk and return for individual securities*. These same individual assets are included in the market portfolio. Each has its own systematic, nondiversifiable risk associated with it and therefore its own rate of return that the marketplace will require of it. If the return is higher than necessary, investors will want to add more of it to their holdings, bidding up the price until, in equilibrium, it

Figure 21.3 The security market line.

Figure 21.4 Empirical security market line.

lies on the security market line. On the other hand, if the return is lower than necessary, holders will want to sell and the price will decline until it rests on the security market line.

If we plot data points for risk (that is, beta) and return on securities, we will obtain a scattergram such as that shown in Figure 21.4, to which an empirical security market line may be fitted by least-squares regression. We shall not address here the question of how well historical data reflect expectations about future performance, the stability of β, and so on. These significant questions have been formally considered by Fama and MacBeth [6], Miller and Scholes [13], Roll [19], and others.

An important property of the CAPM stated here without proof is:[4] The β of a portfolio is a linearly weighted average of the individual constituent assets. If a

---
[4] For detailed proof of these properties, see Copeland and Weston [2], pp. 166–169, and Fama [4], p. 270.

portfolio is composed of x percent asset A, y percent asset B, and z percent asset C, then the portfolio β is:

$$\beta = x\beta_A + y\beta_B + z\beta_C \qquad (21.11)$$

This is *a very important result because it means that the risk of a portfolio may be found without resort to quadratic programming to determine the efficient set.*

THE CAPM AND VALUATION

The CAPM (through the security market line) provides the relationship between risk and required return imposed by the interactions of all investors in the market. Expected return is determined by price paid for an investment. The return is determined as the ratio of earnings return (dividend or interest) plus (or minus) the price change in the asset over the holding period to the price paid for the asset. If we assume a single-period holding, the return is then:

$$R_i = \frac{D + (P_1 - P_0)}{P_0} \qquad (21.12)$$

where D is the income return component and $(P_1 - P_0)$ the capital gain or loss. Combining D with P_1 and calling it P_1', this becomes:

$$R_i = \frac{P_1' - P_0}{P_0} \qquad (21.13)$$

Equating this to the CAPM of Eq. (21.5) and taking expectations of both sides, we get:

$$\frac{\bar{P}_1' - P_0}{P_0} = R_f + \frac{\sigma_{jm}}{\sigma_M^2}[\bar{R}_M - R_f] \qquad (21.14)$$

This may be rearranged to obtain P_0:

$$P_0 = \frac{\bar{P}_1'}{1 + R_f + (\sigma_{jM}/\sigma_M^2)[R_M - R_f]} \qquad (21.15)$$

or

$$P_0 = \frac{\bar{P}_1'}{1 + R_f + (\lambda/\sigma_M)\sigma_{jM}} \qquad (21.16)$$

where λ was defined in Eq. (21.3) as the price of risk. Note that this corresponds to the risk-adjusted discount rate discussed in Chapter 18. The certainty equivalent formulation may be obtained from (21.16) by substituting[5] for σ_{jM} the equivalent $(1/P_0)\sigma_{P_1 R_M}$:

$$P_0 = \frac{\bar{P}_1' - (\lambda/\sigma_M)\sigma_{P_1 R_M}}{1 + R_f} \qquad (21.17)$$

THE CAPM AND COST OF CAPITAL

Chapter 4 stated that the cost of capital to the firm is the required rate of return. The cost of equity is the rate required by common shareholders, the cost of debt is

[5]See Copeland and Weston [2], p. 170.

Figure 21.5 The SML and capital investment.

the rate required by creditors, and so on. That being the case we can write k for $E[R_j]$, where k is the required rate of return. Then Eq. (21.6) becomes:

$$k_e = R_f + \beta_e[\overline{R}_M - R_f] \tag{21.18}$$

for the cost of equity capital, k_e, where β_e is the systematic risk of equity in the particular firm.

The weighted average cost of capital may be found as in Chapter 4 once the component costs have been obtained. Dropping the assumptions used to develop the CAPM, which meant that debt was debt and therefore risk free, how can the cost of debt be found? In principle the CAPM could be used, but how does one estimate beta for a firm's bonds, particularly when the firm has never defaulted? The cost of debt may be observed directly in the market for publicly traded bonds or estimated from market data on those that are. Company debt will always be required to yield more than government debt because the former is not risk free, whereas federal government debt is as close as we can come to approximating a risk-free security.

THE CAPM AND CAPITAL BUDGETING

One of the results yielded by the CAPM is that once we determine an asset's risk we will know the required rate of return it must yield. This being the case, if we can estimate the systematic risk of the capital investment proposal, we can apply the CAPM. Estimation of beta for a capital investment is a formidable task because we normally do not have a foundation of historical data on this or similar projects from which we might comfortably estimate the project's beta. Assuming we have obtained a beta, we could apply the risk-adjusted discount rate or the certainty equivalent method to find the net present value. Or, as illustrated in Figure 21.5, we may employ the security market line to determine whether or not individual capital investment projects should be undertaken.

When we evaluate a capital investment proposal that has the same risk as the firm as a whole, we can correctly use the firm's weighted average cost of capital. However, for projects whose risk is either greater or less than that of the firm, it is not appropriate to use the weighted average marginal cost of capital.

In Figure 21.5 proposal B has a higher expected return than the overall firm. Should the project be accepted? No. The return is greater and the risk is greater yet. In fact, because point B lies below the security market line, we can say that its risk is too great in relation to its expected return, or equivalently that its return is too low in relation to its risk. Proposal A has expected return less than the firm. But its risk is also less. In fact, because point A lies above the security market line, its return is greater than it need be for its level of risk or its risk less than it need be for the expected return. For projects having different systematic risk than the firm as a whole, the CAPM provides a rationale for accepting or rejecting them.

COMPARISON WITH PORTFOLIO APPROACHES

Two major theoretical approaches to evaluation of risky, interrelated projects are those of portfolio diversification along the lines pioneered by Markowitz (discussed in Chapter 19) and the approach implied by the CAPM.

The Markowitz approach requires that we solve a programming problem with a quadratic objective function. To do so we need the matrix of the variances and covariances of all assets that may be included in the portfolio. Then, once the quadratic programming problem has been solved, we must either solve again repeatedly until we have the efficient set or efficient frontier and then find a point of tangency with the investor's utility function or, alternatively, we must find the investor's coefficient of risk aversion at the outset, using this in the quadratic program to solve once for the optimum portfolio.

With the Markowitz portfolio approach we must do considerable computation after obtaining a burdensome amount of data. There may be serious questions about the accuracy of variance-covariance data and utility function estimates as well. Assuming that we have obtained accurate data and solved the quadratic programming problem, the result is a selection of proposals that may be unique to the utility function used or the coefficient of risk aversion. Different utility functions may be expected to yield different optimal portfolios.

The CAPM in contrast requires only that we know the security margin line and the expected return and the beta for any given investment. Since beta measures the systematic or nondiversifiable risk of an asset, other risk is assumed to be unimportant because (in theory at least) it can be eliminated by suitable diversification. In the case of the CAPM, the market determines, through the security margin line, what is an acceptable investment and what is not. In the Markowitz approach, the question of whether or not a particular project is acceptable is internal to the enterprise. It depends on the existing firm, the array of candidate projects, and a utility or investment function. The Markowitz approach assumes there are benefits to be gained through active diversification. The CAPM suggests, however, there is no advantage to diversification, although it implicitly requires that diversifiable risk is eliminated through appropriate portfolio construction.

SOME CRITICISMS OF THE CAPM

The question we need to be concerned with in a capital investment text is how appropriate a model or technique is to capital investments. The CAPM was developed, and its validity tested, for common stocks. Can it be transferred to capital-budgeting application without loss of validity?

There are some major differences between publicly traded securities and capital investments. Such securities are highly liquid, whereas capital investment projects may not have a secondary market other than for scrap. Securities approach the CAPM assumption of infinite divisibility much more closely than most capital investment proposals. There is usually little information available to the public about capital investment projects, much less a consensus about expected return and risk.

Commodity markets meet the conditions assumed by the CAPM much more closely than capital investments. Yet, in an empirical test of the CAPM, Holthausen and Hughes [9] concluded that the CAPM may not fit commodity markets as well as it does security markets. They also observed that returns on commodities do not seem closely related to the measures of nondiversifiable risk they employed (that is, the betas).

Rendleman [18] points out that although the CAPM provides a basis for valuing securities in a perfect and efficient capital market, there are problems in attempting to use it in capital budgeting. He examines the application of the CAPM under capital rationing, concluding that it is not appropriate "for a firm to use its own beta when computing the expected excess return of a project with risk characteristics identical to the firm itself." [6]

Myers and Turnbull [16] show that under certain circumstances a capital project's beta will be a function of the growth rate of the cash flows and the project life. They suggest it may not be possible to obtain betas that truly represent the systematic risk for the firm's cash flows.

Levy [10] was concerned with the use of the CAPM in public utility regulation. Although his remarks are addressed to utility company securities, they apply also, perhaps more strongly, to use of the CAPM for capital budgeting. His comments are:

1. If a public market for the utility's stock does not exist, the beta cannot be computed. . . .
2. Similarly, if a list of diversified companies were determined (on qualitative grounds) to be equivalent in risk to a particular non-traded utility, the average standard deviation of earnings of firms in the list could probably be used as an estimate of the standard deviation for the utility; but the same inference might not be appropriate regarding the beta. . . .
3. At least two studies . . . find that investors receive some incremental return for incurring diversifiable risk. . . .
4. Unless the independent variable in the regression equation is fully diversified to include bonds, real estate and other investments, the beta coefficient will not properly distinguish between diversifiable and non-diversifiable risk.

---

[6] Richard J. Rendleman, Jr., "Ranking Errors in CAPM Capital Budgeting Applications," *Financial Management*, Vol. 7, No. 4 (Winter 1978), p. 42.

5. Large disparities can exist in the beta coefficients for individual stocks when different computational methods are employed [such as time span]. . . .
6. Independent studies reveal marked instability of [calculated] betas over time. . . .
7. [Studies] indicate that returns on high beta stocks were lower than would be expected and returns on low beta stocks higher . . . the expected relationship between betas and individual stock returns prevailed *less than half the time.*
8. . . . tests will show, almost invariably, that the beta coefficients for individual stocks are not significantly different in a statistical sense from the general market beta of 1.00[7]

Fama [5], one of the major figures in the development and empirical testing of the CAPM, demonstrated that the future riskless rate, the market price of risk, or the elasticity of a capital project's expected cash flows with respect to the market return must be certain. Otherwise the CAPM cannot be properly employed. The only parameter that can be uncertain through time is that of the cash flows themselves.

CONCLUSION

The CAPM provides valuable insights into the valuation of securities in market equilibrium. Transfer of the model to capital-budgeting applications adds to the concerns raised about its applicability. Although on the surface the model would seem to simplify the process of selecting risky assets, it replaces one set of difficulties with others. The Markowitz portfolio approach requires the variance-covariance matrix and a utility function or risk-aversion coefficient. The CAPM requires expected return and beta for each investment. Estimation of the beta is not a trivial task and, once obtained, the beta may not be stable or statistically reliable.

To use the CAPM properly requires that only the cash flows be subject to risk. This is an assumption not likely to be approximated by most capital investment proposals. Furthermore, the CAPM replaces utility risk-aversion attitudes of owners or management, by external, market-determined value criteria. These do not reflect such matters as the risk of ruin to the firm and consequences to the owners and management.

QUESTIONS

1. How adequately do the CAPM assumptions match the realities of capital budgeting? Which assumptions deviate more widely from reality in the case of capital investments than they do for publicly traded securities?
2. One of the conclusions of the CAPM is that nonsystematic risk can be eliminated by diversification and therefore there is no reward for taking on investments with nonsystematic risk. And since systematic risk cannot be eliminated, those who take it on will be rewarded. Discuss in terms of large, indivisible capital investments; equilibrium; and the perfect market implication that profits are zero.

---

[7]Robert E. Levy, "Fair Return on Equity for Public Utilities," *Business Economics*, Vol. XIII, No. 4 (September 1978), pp. 49–50.

3. In the case of an acquisition of one firm by another the betas may sometimes be estimated. For capital investments it may be impossible to estimate objectively the betas. Discuss in terms of the articles by Rendleman [18] and Levy [10].
4. Assuming that all the problems with the security margin line and beta can be satisfactorily resolved, what advantage does the CAPM approach offer over the Markowitz approach?
5. Discuss the view that the CAPM imposes the market's composite opinion of the risk-return trade-off on the firm, whereas Markowitz portfolio diversification yields investment selections attuned to the risk-reward trade-offs of the owners or managers of the firm.
6. What are the similarities and differences between the capital margin line and the security margin line?
7. A small firm may not be able to diversify nonsystematic risk away if projects tend to be large and positively correlated. The CAPM suggests that projects whose risk-return coordinates place them above the SML are acceptable. Does this mean that such firms should ignore nonsystematic risk? Does it make a difference whether the firm is closely held or the shares widely held by the public and actively traded?
8. Review the commentary at the end of Chapter 18 on why simulation of single risky projects is used. Now that Chapters 19 and 21 have been covered, discuss this.
9. In equilibrium the return on the market portfolio must be greater than the riskless rate. Assume that the federal government raises the rates on all its securities in an effort to support its currency and suppress inflation and the rates become greater than corporate common stock. What are the implications of the CAPM? Can you suggest what the process may be by which equilibrium is again established?

PROBLEMS

22.1 (a) Calculate the security margin line for the following data:

$E[R]$	β	$E[R]$	β
2.0	2.2	2.5	3.5
1.5	1.3	2.6	3.4
2.0	2.5	3.4	4.4
2.9	3.0	1.6	1.0
1.9	2.9	1.1	0.5

What is the slope? The intercept?

(b) You missed some data in part (a); add it to the above data and recalculate the slope and the intercept.

$E[R]$	β	$E[R]$	β
1.1	2.9	0.3	1.4
2.3	3.1	0.2	2.2
3.8	4.0	2.7	3.3
0.9	2.1	1.6	3.1
0.8	2.8	1.2	2.3

(c) What do your results suggest about the adequacy of a security margin line calculated from only security prices and their beta estimates?

21.2 (a) Estimate the beta for the company whose data follow using all time periods. R_c is the return on the company shares, R_M on the market.

t	R_c	R_M	t	R_c	R_M	t	R_c	R_M
1	3.0	0.3	6	5.0	2.0	11	6.3	4.5
2	3.3	0.9	7	5.7	2.2	12	5.6	4.8
3	4.0	0.8	8	5.3	2.8	13	5.9	5.5
4	4.5	1.4	9	5.9	3.0	14	5.5	6.0
5	5.3	1.2	10	5.5	3.8	15	5.9	6.7

(b) Now estimate the beta first using only the last five observations, and then using the last ten. Compare with the result you got in part (a).

(c) Plot the data points on graph paper. What do you observe? Can you say conclusively what the beta of this firm is?

21.3 Project A has expected return of 20 percent and beta of 2.5; project B has expected return of 5 percent and beta of .4. The firm's beta is 1.3 and the equation of the security market line is $E[R] = .15 + .033\beta$. Should the firm accept either project? Discuss.

21.4 MPAC Mfg. Company has beta of 2.8 and sells for $24 a share. Expected return on MPAC shares is 15 percent and on short-term U.S. government securities is 12 percent. What will happen to the price of MPAC shares if, *ceteris paribus*, the covariance of its returns with the market falls 50 percent? Increases 100 percent?

21.5 In Chapter 4 CAPM formulation for the cost of equity capital was introduced:

$$k_e = R_F + \beta(R_M - R_F)$$

This is the return required on the firm's shares of common equity by the market, and relates risk and return. PACM Ltd. has beta of 1.6 and the riskless rate of return is 9 percent. What is the cost of equity if the market rate of return is 11 percent? If the market rate of return went up to 12 percent, what would the cost of equity be?

21.6 The beta of a portfolio is a linearly weighted average of the betas of the constituent assets. Assume for Problem 21.5 a market rate of return of 14 percent. The firm is considering acquisition of another firm one-fourth its size with beta of 2.3. What will be the effect on PACM Ltd.'s cost of equity?

Bibliography

1. Black, Fisher, "Capital Market Equilibrium with Restricted Borrowing," *Journal of Business,* Vol. 45 (July 1972), pp. 444–455.
2. Copeland, Thomas E., and Fred J. Weston, *Financial Theory and Corporate Policy* (Reading, Mass.: Addison-Wesley, 1979).
3. Fama, Eugene F., "Risk, Return, and Equilibrium: Some Clarifying Comments," *The Journal of Finance,* Vol. XXIII, No. 1 (March 1968), pp. 29–40.
4. ———, *Foundations of Finance* (New York: Basic Books, 1976).
5. ———, "Risk Adjusted Discount Rates and Capital Budgeting Under Uncertainty," *Journal of Financial Economics* (August 1977), pp. 1–24.
6. ———, and James D. MacBeth, "Risk, Return and Equilibrium: Empirical Test," *Journal of Political Economy,* Vol. 71 (May–June 1973), pp. 607–636.

7. Glassman, Gerald F., "Discounted Cash Flow versus the Capital Asset Pricing Model," *Public Utilities Fortnightly*, Vol. 102 (September 14, 1978), pp. 30–34.
8. Haley, Charles W., and Lawrence D. Schall, *The Theory of Financial Decisions*, 2nd ed. (New York: McGraw-Hill, 1979).
9. Holthausen, Duncan M., and John S. Hughes, "Commodity Returns and Capital Asset Pricing," *Financial Management*, Vol. 7, No. 2 (Summer 1978), pp. 37–44.
10. Levy, Robert E., "Fair Return on Equity for Public Utilities," *Business Economics*, Vol. XIII, No. 4 (September 1978), pp. 46–57.
11. Lintner, John, "Security Prices, Risk, and Maximal Gains from Diversification," *The Journal of Finance*, Vol. XX, No. 5 (December 1965), pp. 587–615.
12. ———, "The Aggregation of Investors' Diverse Judgments and Preferences in Purely Competitive Security Markets," *Journal of Financial and Quantitative Analysis*, Vol. IV, No. 6 (December 1969), pp. 347–400.
13. Miller, Merton, and Myron Scholes, "Rates of Return in Relation to Risk: A Re-Examination of Some Recent Findings," in M. C. Jensen, ed., *Studies in the Theory of Capital Markets* (New York: Praeger, 1972), pp. 47–78.
14. Modigliani, Franco, and Gerald Pogue, "An Introduction to Risk and Return," *Financial Analysts Journal* (March/April 1974), pp. 68–80 and (May/June 1974), pp. 69–85.
15. Mossin, Jan, "Equilibrium in a Capital Asset Market," *Econometrica*, Vol. 34 (October 1966), pp. 768–783.
16. Myers, Stewart C., and Stuart W. Turnbull, "Capital Budgeting and the Capital Asset Pricing Model: Good News and Bad News," *The Journal of Finance*, Vol. XXXII, No. 2 (May 1977), pp. 321–332.
17. Perrakis, Stylianas, "Capital Budgeting and Timing Uncertainty Within the CAPM," *Financial Management*, Vol. 8, No. 3 (Autumn 1979), pp. 32–40.
18. Rendleman, Richard J., Jr., "Ranking Errors in CAPM Capital Budgeting Applications," *Financial Management*, Vol. 7, No. 4 (Winter 1978), pp. 40–44.
19. Roll, Richard, "A Critique of the Asset Pricing Theory's Tests," *Journal of Financial Economics* (March 1977), pp. 129–176.
20. Sharpe, William F., "A Simplified Model for Portfolio Analysis," *Management Science*, Vol. IX, No. 1 (January 1963), pp. 277–293.
21. ———, "Capital Asset Prices: A Theory of Market Equilibrium Under Conditions of Risk," *The Journal of Finance*, Vol. XIX, No. 3 (September 1964).
22. Van Horne, James C., "An Application of the CAPM to Divisional Required Returns," *Financial Management*, Vol. 9, No. 1 (Spring 1980), pp. 14–19.

Part VI
CURRENT AND FUTURE CHALLENGES IN CAPITAL BUDGETING

Part VI

Chapter 22
Capital Investment in the 1980s

Out of the inflation of prices grew a speculating class; in the complete uncertainty as to the future, all business became a game of chance, and all businessmen, gamblers. . . .
Andrew Dickson White, Fiat Money Inflation in France, in the Eighteenth Century.

The issues affecting capital investment are complex in discussing the 1980s, and there is little public consensus about what ought to be done to control inflation, to produce energy alternatives to imported petroleum, or to solve any of the many other problems confronting us. This chapter deals with some material that by its nature is controversial. It is written in the hope that it will provide the reader with useful insights into the nature of problems confronting society in general and in particular those who must make capital investment decisions. The 1970s have provided a legacy for the following decade; the question is, what will be done with it?

INTRODUCTION

Since this is a book about capital investment at the microeconomic or firm level, it may seem inappropriate to some to undertake to discuss the causes and possible cures of problems exogenous to the individual enterprise. On the other hand, if individual firms are to make the best possible capital investment decisions, it is necessary to be aware of both developing and continuing external trends in order to incorporate them into the decision process. And if the environment has become unfavorable to capital investment, it is up to the business community to argue as persuasively for incentives (or removal of disincentives) as antibusiness advocates have argued for more and more onerous restrictions. Therefore, this chapter will not be constrained solely to discussion of microeconomic matters relating to capital investments, but will also examine related external factors and issues.

The productive private sector of the economy—companies and individuals who make investments in capital goods that will be used to produce other goods and services—may be either active or passive. It may be active in trying to make a hospitable environment, one in which capital investment is encouraged and allowed to earn profits, or it may passively accept an investment environment that has been determined by others who are willing to plead their cases persuasively in the public forums. In either case it is necessary that those making capital investment decisions understand underlying political-economic trends and incorporate this knowledge into their analytical processes. One might question whether the passive approach, in which investment is undertaken on the basis of trying to make the best of a possibly worsening environment, is desirable over the long term. However, individual firms face externalities that tend to move them into the passive mode: They could spend much money, time, and effort to gain more favorable treatment for investment, yet not benefit any more than similar firms that contribute nothing to their cause. Because of this, one may expect that whatever public advocacy might be it will come from industry or trade associations.

ENTERING THE 1980s

It is the 20th century's sickness that politicians practice economics. It was the 19th century's claim to glory that they did not.
Jason Alexander, *Philosophy for Investors* (San Francisco: Sitnalta Press)

A view becoming more widely shared as economic problems persisted at the close of the 1970s was that there existed

> ... conflict between politics and economics, wherein elected officials attempt to solve long-term problems with short-term solutions. These usually involve trying to increase consumption in the near term with the hopes that unemployment will fall. However, since little is done to encourage capital formation, the eventual result is an upward ratchet in inflation.... The markets perceive what Washington will not admit: there is no policy to increase long-term investment, lower inflation and cut the real tax burden. We appear to be drifting towards controls, regulations, more inflation and higher real taxes. Washington's response is more concern about the distribution of income than about its production.[1]

---

[1] Irwin L. Kellner, "Quarterly Business Conditions Analysis," *Business Report* (New York: Manufacturers Hanover Trust Company, Spring 1978), p. 1.

The size of the U.S. federal government continued to increase over the 1970s, both absolutely and relatively, as had its role in controlling private sector activity. The increased role of government can be measured in terms of number of employees, size of budgets, and annual output of pages of regulations and rulings from the multitude of departments, agencies, offices, and bureaus. But government failed to cure inflation or to provide assured energy.

Public policies that once seemed to work seem today to be much less effective in moving the economy in the desired direction. The doctrine of rational expectations[2] attributes the lessened impact of government economic policy to the greater sophistication of citizens in economic matters, and in increasing realism (some would say cynicism) about the ability of politicians and bureaucrats to do anything but make matters worse. Policy pronouncements no longer elicit the desired behavioral results from the public that they once did.

In the 1970s a great deal of attention focused on the economic and social problems associated with inflation, energy, environmental concerns, government interference in the private sector, and taxes. In mid-1979 the epithet "Uncertain Eighties" began to catch on to describe the decade ahead. Indeed, the 1970s themselves had been plagued with growing uncertainties, and little had been accomplished in terms of reducing them. And uncertainty beyond what is normal to business in a stable economy can affect investment adversely:

> A great many reasons might be offered for the lag in capital spending. What they all come down to, however, is that external circumstances have not supported an outlook for return on investment sufficient to justify, in the eyes of the businessmen involved, an aggressive commitment of investment funds. Long-term commitments, such as a major investment decision, unavoidably involve risk and uncertainty, but the greater the risk and uncertainty the greater the prospective return must be to justify the investment. In this regard, the very existence of inflation, because it compounds risks and uncertainties, has been a powerful deterrent to investment.[3]

That inflation clearly is a serious problem is widely accepted. But how might inflation be halted or reduced? An early prescription to stop inflation was offered by the Committee for Economic Development:

> We believe that long-term inflation can be prevented by action along three basic lines:
>
> 1. We must do everything possible to increase national productivity.
> 2. We must do everything necessary to keep demand from rising faster than production.
> 3. We must adopt and adhere to policies—primarily through the action of business and labor but, if necessary, through governmental action consistent with economic freedom—that keep prices and unit labor costs from rising, on the average, when demand is kept from outstripping production.

---

[2]Federal Reserve Bank of Minneapolis, Annual Report, 1977.
[3]Tilford Gaines, "Productivity, Prices and So Forth," *Economic Report* (New York: Manufacturers Hanover Trust, May 1978), p. 2.

Three lines of action are not only basic, individually, but they are also interrelated. Failure to carry any one of them can, and very likely will, vitiate the others, or make it impossible to carry out the others.[4]

This prescription was written in 1958. Inflation has become far worse than in the placid 1950s. And since the 1950s the problem has been complicated by monetary changes, energy, and a world that is economically and politically much different.

What are the major problems facing business in the "uncertain" 1980s? There are several. Inflation and uncertainty over energy supplies would have to be foremost on a list of problems. A complicating if not actually causative factor may stem from a tendency to make free enterprise the scapegoat for the mistakes or failures of government. And to the extent this is believed by the public, it aggravates an already demonstrably antibusiness public attitude—business enterprise has a public image problem—and contributes other problems. Government regulations on business have grown to the point where satisfying them has become an industry in itself for lawyers and accountants, and contributes not only to the cost of operating a business, but also to reducing the flexibility of domestic firms to meet foreign competition in overseas markets and in some cases even the home markets they once dominated (such as autos), or to provide innovative new products and services. If we accept the view that inflation is bad and that there is an inverse relationship between price inflation and productivity, then we should as a nation endeavor to increase productivity. And if we recognize that inflation of the money supply produces price inflation, we should demand that controls be placed on the creation of money.

The topics which follow all affect the environment in which capital investment decisions will be made in the 1980s. All are related in complex ways. It is not the purpose of this chapter to tie them neatly together by detailing all that is known about each one and its relationship to the others, but to present them so that the reader will have a basis for drawing his or her own conclusions.

INFLATION

Inflation has been a serious problem for over a decade not only because of its immediate effects, but also from the behavioral changes it tends to elicit. There is growing evidence that inflation has not only been undefeated, but it has also grown stronger (see Figure 22.1). There are indications that "normal" inflation is now considered to be roughly twice as high as it was in the 1950s and early 1960s. From the capital investment perspective, inflation makes the process of project evaluation more difficult. If the rate of price inflation were constant, it would not pose a particularly difficult analytical problem. However, changes in the rate of price inflation over time are more difficult to deal with. And imposition of selective price controls at some future date, possibly just as inflation is accelerating, can render otherwise accurate project evaluation worthless. Furthermore, "after-tax present

---

[4]Committee for Economic Development, *Report on Defense Against Inflation*, July 1958, p. 43.

The Purchasing Power of the Dollar

*Assuming an 8% Rise in Consumer Price Index, 1978 to 1979

Figure 22.1. Source: The Conference Board.

values are not neutral with respect to different rates of inflation, because depreciation charges are based on historical costs."[5] Nelson [19] has demonstrated that five propositions hold for the effect of inflation on business capital investment. Without going into the proofs, the propositions are:

> Proposition A. The optimal level of capital investment will depend in general on the rate of inflation. The amount invested will typically be smaller the higher the rate of inflation.
>
> Proposition B. The rate of inflation will influence the firm's choice of technologies of production through its choice of capital/labor ratio. Higher rates of inflation will typically be associated with lower capital/labor ratios.
>
> Proposition C. The net present value ranking of mutually exclusive investment projects will depend in general on the rate of inflation.
>
> Proposition D. Net present value rankings of mutually exclusive projects which differ with respect to durability will depend on the rate of inflation. Typically, rankings will change in favor of projects with lower durability at higher rates of inflation.
>
> Proposition E. Replacement policy will depend in general on the rate of inflation. The higher the rate of inflation the more likely will replacement be deferred to a future period.[6]

None of Nelson's propositions provides basis for good cheer, either to managers making investment decisions or to those concerned with the broad policy issues centering on how to increase the rate of new investment in the economy. Even without the tax effects cited by Nelson, price inflation increases the risks associated with capital investment.

Not all prices increase at the same rate. If the firm finds that its factor cost of labor or of capital is increasing at a faster pace than its product price can be

---

[5] Charles R. Nelson, "Inflation and Capital Budgeting," *The Journal of Finance*, Vol. XXXI, No. 3 (June 1975), p. 923.
[6] Ibid., pp. 923 and following.

increased (even without including depreciation tax effects), it may find decisions based on uniform price escalation to be incorrect. Imposing wage and price controls, even if equally effective in holding the increases to the same level, could still cause problems in capital intensive firms. The reason is that the cost of capital as a factor of production cannot be controlled as straightforwardly as other prices.

Let us consider again the capital asset pricing model's required return on equity capital:

$$k = R_f + \beta(\bar{R}_M - R_f) \tag{22.1}$$

If we treat the risk-free rate R_f as being the linear sum of a "pure" rate of interest and an inflation premium, we have:

$$R_f = R_p + i \tag{22.2}$$

Similarly, if the expected rate of return on the market portfolio may be considered a linear sum of the risk-free rate and a risk premium, ρ, we have:

$$\bar{R}_M = R_f + \rho = R_p + i + \rho \tag{22.3}$$

Now let us take the partial derivative of (22.1) with respect to the inflation premium:

$$\frac{\partial k}{\partial i} = \frac{\partial R_f}{\partial i} + \beta\left(\frac{\partial R_M}{\partial i}\right) - \beta\left(\frac{\partial R_f}{\partial i}\right)$$

Since (22.2) and (22.3) can be substituted, we obtain:

$$\frac{\partial k}{\partial i} = \frac{\partial R_p}{\partial i} + \frac{\partial i}{\partial i} + \beta\left\{\frac{\partial R_p}{\partial i} + \frac{\partial i}{\partial i} + \frac{\partial \rho}{\partial i}\right\} - \beta\left(\frac{\partial R_p}{\partial i} + \frac{\partial i}{\partial i}\right)$$

Assuming the pure rate of interest does not change with inflation, we obtain:

$$\frac{\partial k}{\partial i} = 1 + \beta\left(1 + \frac{\partial \rho}{\partial i}\right) - \beta$$

which simplifies to:

$$\frac{\partial k}{\partial i} = 1 + \beta\left(\frac{\partial \rho}{\partial i}\right) \tag{22.4}$$

According to Eq. (22.4) the change in the market's required rate of return on the firm's equity is a function of the firm's beta[7] and the rate of inflation. Thus we would expect the required return on equity to rise more rapidly for a high beta firm than for a low beta firm. The required rate of return on a zero beta portfolio would change by exactly the same amount as the change in inflation premium.

The conclusion that follows from Eq. (22.4) is that the firm's cost of equity capital will rise by more than the increase in the inflation rate. Although tax effects

---

[7] The beta has been treated as a constant. To have treated it as a variable would have raised many questions best treated in an investigation of the capital asset pricing model. Even if the beta were not constant over time, that is not necessarily the same as being a function of the inflation premium.

may be important, they are not the only effect on inflation, nor necessarily the most important. Yet we must recognize that inadequate depreciation allowances and illusory inventory "profits" aggravate inflation's effects as they influence tax changes.

At this juncture it is important to distinguish between *ex ante* and *ex post* inflation. *Ex ante* inflation is the *expected* inflation over some future span of time. *Ex post* inflation is the actual rate of inflation experienced over that same time span. Generally, the two rates will not be the same. Sometimes they will be close, other times (in particular when historically new high rates are established) they will be quite far apart. Small errors are not likely to be critical in capital budgeting, but large errors, particularly when the *ex post* rate is significantly higher than the *ex ante*, can be very troublesome. Such large errors may mean accepting projects that look profitable in prospect but later turn out unprofitable.

What can be done to cope with inflation when accurate forecasts of it cannot be reliably obtained? There is no general method, but several factors can help. It may be useful in the decision process, for instance, to evaluate projects at the beginning using high, low, and the most likely (mean or expected value) values for the discount rate and for cash flows. For proposals that are accepted, an annual review and abandonment analysis along the lines suggested in Chapter 15 can help to identify specific assets that should be held no longer.

The best public action with respect to inflation is to control it or stop it. If it cannot be stopped, at least by holding the rate within narrow limits, the economy could adjust to a new equilibrium. If the rate of inflation oscillates around an upward trend, the social and economic consequences are not only undesirable but harmful. Over the long run, when citizens no longer save, but buy (often on credit) because they believe that the rate of inflation is going to be greater than the cost of borrowing, the economy suffers. When savers learn that the rates they receive on savings accounts, time deposits, and bonds are less than the rate of inflation, they seek to put their money elsewhere. However, since the money they spend is not destroyed, it goes to others, who, in turn, will look to acquire things that will appreciate faster than the rate of inflation. As a consequence of growing behavior of this sort, prices increase still faster. And yet, over the 1970s the money supply increased sharply both domestically and offshore in the realm of "eurodollars." On top of the growth in money supply are the effects of monetary velocity-increasing changes in the domestic banking system such as NOW accounts and automatic funds transfers from savings to checking accounts.

The two charts in Table 22–1 contain compound annual rates of change for the U.S. money supply and for consumer prices. They are indicative of the relationship of money supply to prices.

Inflation affects international economic matters both through the destruction of currency value vis-à-vis any sounder currencies and commodities and through increased uncertainty. One view of the OPEC price increases in late 1973 is that they were a *result* of inflation, *not a primary cause*. This is not to say that the initial large price increases did not lead to further price inflation, but that inflation may have provided the initial impetus for a price increase. Since the U.S. dollar (until

Table 22-1.

MONEY SUPPLY—UNITED STATES COMPOUNDED ANNUAL RATES OF CHANGE[a]

Terminal Year	\	\	\	\	\	\	\	\	Initial Year	\	\	\	\	\	\	\	\	\	\	Billions of Dollars
	1959	1960	1961	1962	1963	1964	1965	1966	1967	1968	1969	1970	1971	1972	1973	1974	1975	1976	1977	
1960	−0.1																			143.5
1961	1.0	2.1																		146.5
1962	1.4	2.1	2.2																	149.7
1963	1.8	2.4	2.6	2.9																154.1
1964	2.2	2.8	3.0	3.5	4.0															160.3
1965	2.6	3.1	3.3	3.7	4.1	4.2														167.1
1966	2.9	3.4	3.6	4.0	4.3	4.5	4.7													174.9
1967	3.0	3.4	3.7	4.0	4.2	4.3	4.3	3.9												181.8
1968	3.4	3.9	4.2	4.5	4.8	5.0	5.2	5.5	7.2											194.8
1969	3.7	4.1	4.4	4.7	5.0	5.2	5.4	5.7	6.6	6.1										206.6
1970	3.7	4.1	4.3	4.6	4.8	5.0	5.1	5.2	5.7	4.9	3.8									214.5
1971	4.0	4.3	4.6	4.8	5.1	5.2	5.4	5.5	5.9	5.5	5.2	6.7								228.8
1972	4.2	4.6	4.8	5.0	5.3	5.4	5.6	5.8	6.1	5.9	5.8	6.9	7.1							245.0
1973	4.4	4.8	5.0	5.3	5.5	5.7	5.8	6.0	6.4	6.2	6.3	7.1	7.3	7.5						263.3
1974	4.5	4.8	5.0	5.3	5.5	5.6	5.8	5.9	6.2	6.1	6.1	6.7	6.7	6.5	5.5					277.7
1975	4.5	4.8	5.0	5.2	5.4	5.5	5.7	5.8	6.0	5.8	5.8	6.2	6.1	5.8	4.9	4.4				289.8
1976	4.5	4.8	5.0	5.2	5.4	5.5	5.6	5.7	5.9	5.8	5.7	6.0	5.9	5.6	5.0	4.8	5.3			305.1
1977	4.7	5.0	5.2	5.4	5.5	5.6	5.8	5.9	6.1	5.9	5.9	6.2	6.1	6.0	5.6	5.6	6.3	7.3		327.3
1978	4.8	5.1	5.3	5.5	5.7	5.8	5.9	6.0	6.2	6.1	6.1	6.4	6.4	6.3	6.0	6.2	6.8	7.5	7.8	352.8
	1959	1960	1961	1962	1963	1964	1965	1966	1967	1968	1969	1970	1971	1972	1973	1974	1975	1976	1977	

Initial Year

[a]Source: Board of Governors of the Federal Reserve System.

CONSUMER PRICES—UNITED STATES[b] COMPOUNDED ANNUAL RATES OF CHANGE

Terminal Year / Initial Year / 1967 = 100

Terminal Year	1959	1960	1961	1962	1963	1964	1965	1966	1967	1968	1969	1970	1971	1972	1973	1974	1975	1976	1977	1967=100
1960	1.6																			88.7
1961	1.3	1.0																		89.6
1962	1.2	1.1	1.1																	90.6
1963	1.2	1.1	1.2	1.2																91.7
1964	1.3	1.2	1.2	1.3	1.3															92.9
1965	1.3	1.3	1.3	1.4	1.5	1.7														94.5
1966	1.5	1.5	1.6	1.8	2.0	2.3	2.9													97.2
1967	1.7	1.7	1.8	2.0	2.2	2.5	2.9	2.9												100.0
1968	2.0	2.0	2.2	2.4	2.6	2.9	3.3	3.5	4.2											104.2
1969	2.3	2.4	2.6	2.8	3.0	3.4	3.8	4.1	4.8	5.4										109.8
1970	2.6	2.7	2.9	3.2	3.5	3.8	4.2	4.6	5.2	5.6	5.9									116.3
1971	2.8	2.9	3.1	3.3	3.6	3.9	4.2	4.5	4.9	5.2	5.1	4.3								121.3
1972	2.8	2.9	3.1	3.3	3.5	3.8	4.1	4.3	4.6	4.7	4.5	3.8	3.3							125.3
1973	3.1	3.2	3.4	3.6	3.8	4.1	4.4	4.6	4.9	5.0	4.9	4.6	4.8	6.2						133.1
1974	3.6	3.7	3.9	4.2	4.4	4.7	5.1	5.4	5.7	6.0	6.1	6.2	6.8	8.6	11.0					147.7
1975	3.9	4.1	4.3	4.5	4.8	5.1	5.5	5.8	6.2	6.4	6.6	6.7	7.4	8.8	10.1	9.1				161.2
1976	4.0	4.2	4.4	4.6	4.9	5.2	5.5	5.8	6.1	6.3	6.5	6.6	7.0	8.0	8.6	7.4	5.8			170.5
1977	4.1	4.3	4.5	4.7	5.0	5.3	5.6	5.8	6.1	6.4	6.5	6.6	6.9	7.7	8.1	7.1	6.1	6.5		181.5
1978	4.3	4.5	4.7	4.9	5.2	5.5	5.7	6.0	6.3	6.5	6.6	6.7	7.0	7.7	8.0	7.2	6.6	7.1	7.7	195.4
	1959	1960	1961	1962	1963	1964	1965	1966	1967	1968	1969	1970	1971	1972	1973	1974	1975	1976	1977	

Initial Year

[b]Source: Department of Labor, Bureau of Labor Statistics

1979) was the only means of payment for petroleum, and dollar reserves were the main store of wealth for the OPEC nations, it should not have been surprising that the members sought to be adequately compensated for what to some of them is their only significant economic resource, especially since they were trading one store of wealth for what was to have been another, but which turned out to be less than satisfactory. By not acting to promote energy alternatives in the 1970s or earlier, the United States itself made inevitable not only the increased purchase of United States farmland, apartment buildings, and securities by foreigners, but also made it vulnerable to external influences on its political affairs.

A case can be made that there is belief that the Phillips curve relationship (between inflation and unemployment) by those in control of government leads to their emphasis on controlling employment, and suggests that inflation will continue for quite some time. The causes of inflation are complex, but include monetary policy, taxes, transfer payments, productivity, and social and government attitudes toward, and regulation of, the private sector. All have an effect, although the precise nature of the interrelationships in the dynamics of inflation remains unknown.

PRODUCTIVITY

The economic theory of production is well developed and, aside from the empirical determination of relative compensations due to labor and capital, holds little controversy among knowledgeable persons. Production theory recognizes the interaction of land, labor, and capital—the factors of production. To some extent the factors are substitutable, although eventually the marginal rate of substitution declines. If we accept the premises that economic growth means increased output of goods and services, and goods and services are produced by combination of the factors of production, then if we want growth one of two things must happen. Either we increase the labor and capital available for production to move to a higher output level, or else we increase the productivity of labor and capital employed in production.

Increased productivity is a desirable objective, because more goods and services can be produced with the same factor combinations, which enables higher returns to labor and capital (without price increases on output), increased leisure, and enhanced ability to compete in foreign markets. It could also mean price reductions in the goods and services produced, or at least price stability.

In economic theory the returns to labor and capital are equal to their marginal value product to the firm. If one factor receives too much or too little, the productive system cannot be in long-term equilibrium and changes will be forthcoming. For instance, if the return to capital is less than it should be, there will be no new investment until the return rises to the degree necessary for attracting investors. This may mean a change in the relative factor intensity of the production process used.

Only recently has it begun to be fully recognized that government, although not a factor of production, nevertheless receives part of the value product of land, labor, and capital. If we think of government as a factor of production that produces

A LOSING RACE

ANNUAL RATES OF INCREASE
1967 to 1977

Country	Rate
Japan	6.8%
Denmark	6.6%
W. Germany	5.3%
Italy	5.3%
France	5.2%
Sweden	4.5%
Canada	3.5%
Britain	2.5%
U.S.	2.3%

U.S. industry is still the world's most efficient, but it has fallen behind in productivity growth.

Source: Bureau of Labor Statistics

Figure 22.2

fixed services to the firm regardless of the level of output, it becomes clear that the *real* value product is constant in such a case. However, the "wage" or return that must be paid to government increases over time with the higher proportions of taxes taken from workers and investors under "progressive" income taxes in an inflationary economy. With taxes rising faster than real income, the *real* tax bite taken from workers and investors increases. The irony of the situation is that government receives a return all out of proportion to what it is worth in the production process;[9] also the return to government increases at the expense of productive labor and capital when government fails to control inflation or actually contributes to it.

In the period 1967–1977 United States productivity growth was the lowest of the industrial nations as Figure 22.2 shows. The problem of productivity is a complex one. One facet of the productivity problem is that government appears to have demanded more of the private sector than productivity gains could have supported and tax revenues could pay for. The result is observed in price inflation that has lowered both the real wage and the real return on capital at the same time that government has grown, both absolutely and relatively in size and in control over the private sector.

In the 1970s business was increasingly made the scapegoat by politicians and bureaucrats. A great and continuing fuss was made over profits, to which the pejorative prefix "excess" was often associated. The public, ravaged as it was by unaccustomed inflation, was in a mood to believe the worst, especially since it appeared that workers and consumers were getting less than a fair share of business revenues.

[8] Merrill Shiels, Chris Harper, Lea Donosky, and Ronald Henkoff, "The Productivity Gap," *Newsweek* (May 22, 1978), p. 79.
[9] All the more so to the extent government interferes with efficient production.

Table 22-2. UNITED STATES INFLATION, CORPORATE PROFIT, AND TAX DATA

Year	Increase in Consumer Price Index	Effective Corporate Tax Rate	Corporate Profits as Percent of National Income
1968	4.7%	54%	12.0%
1969	6.1	60	10.6
1970	5.5	65	8.5
1971	3.4	62	9.0
1972	3.4	58	9.6
1973	8.8	64	9.0
1974	12.2	96	7.4
1975	7.0	73	8.2
1976	4.8	67	9.4
1977	6.8	66	9.2

Source: Bureau of Economic Analysis, U.S. Department of Commerce.

Seldom did facts get in the way of opinions, the business community being singularly inept at presenting the other side of the story, or perhaps feeling it was futile to try, or it was counterproductive, to engage in debate with an army of demagogues. The figures in Table 22–2, however, suggest that contrary to popular opinion, business profits were *not* high, but low and declining while real business taxes were simultaneously increasing.

The reason that profits declined while effective tax rates rose above the 48 percent marginal rate is that inflation has distorted inventory values and made insufficient the depreciation tax shield for replacing capital equipment. When the effects of depreciation are factored out, the real profit of business is seen to be less, whereas the real tax rate is much higher. Corporate profits have declined significantly since the 1960s; yet the general public has been influenced to believe that business in general is not only making "excessive" profits, but also that business "greed" is largely responsible for inflation. Yet, paradoxically, the public is not reminded that profits provide jobs, capital investment, competitiveness in foreign markets, pension money to retirement funds, and even much of the tax money that supports some of those who are attacking profit-oriented enterprise.

GOVERNMENT REGULATIONS

In the 1970s the proliferation of government regulations was perhaps the single greatest source of anger, frustration, and dismay to business in the private sector. Yet, despite growing concern about the adverse effects of government interference, there is little reason to be sanguine about the chances for a turn in the tide in the 1980s at the time of this writing. Nowhere has the burden of government regulation been more eloquently expressed than in the following reprinted article, first published by the National Federation of Independent Business (150 West 20th Avenue, San Mateo, Cal. 94403).

Murray L. Weidenbaum

THE FORGOTTEN CONSUMER:
Hidden Costs of Government Regulation

Of the many ways in which government can affect the rate of inflation, perhaps the least understood method is to require actions in the private sector which increase the cost of production and hence the prices of products and services sold to the public. Attention needs to be focused on these regulatory policy instruments because their use is becoming more widespread and neither the public nor government decision-makers realize their full inflationary effects.

At first blush, government imposition of socially desirable requirements on business through the regulatory process appears to be an inexpensive way of achieving national objectives. This practice apparently costs the government little and represents no significant direct burden on the taxpayer. But the public does not escape paying the cost. Every time, for example, the Environmental Protection Agency imposes a more costly (albeit less polluting) method of production on any firm the cost of the firm's product to the consumer will tend to rise. Similar effects flow from the other regulatory efforts, including those involving product safety, job health, and hiring and promotion policies. These higher prices, we should recognize, represent the "hidden tax" of regulation which is shifted from the taxpayer to the consumer.

It is not inevitable that every regulatory activity increase inflationary pressures. In those instances where regulation generates real benefits (such as a healthier and thus more productive work force) in excess of the costs it imposes, inflationary pressures should be reduced. What is at issue is not the worth of the objectives of these government agencies. Rather, *the point is that these forms of governmental intervention in the private sector involve heavy costs*. With some care and effort, the regulatory process can be revised so as to derive at lower costs many of the same benefits as are now achieved—if decision-makers begin to think in terms of least-cost solutions.

Impact of Government Regulation

Before we take on the task of investigating alternatives for reforming the regulatory process, it may be helpful to examine more closely the various economic effects of regulation, many of which affect the prices paid by consumers importantly but indirectly.

Regulation and Inflation

At times the impact of regulation on the price charged to the customer is direct and visible. For example, in the case of the passenger automobile the federal government has required the producers to incorporate a wide array of specified safety and environmental features. The Bureau of Labor Statistics each year costs out the effect on the price of the average car. Through 1977, the cumulative cost increase per vehicle of these mandated features come to over $500 (or $5 billion for all the vehicles sold in a year).

Government regulation increases the overhead cost of producing goods and services by imposing a rising burden of paperwork. There are over 4,400 different types of approved federal forms, excluding tax and banking forms. Individuals and business firms spend over 143 million man-hours a year filling them out. That is the equivalent of a small army. A few examples may convey a sharper impression of reality than the aggregate figures. A small, 5000 watt radio

Note: This report is adapted from Murray L. Weidenbaum, Government-Mandated Price Increases, American Enterprise Institute for Public Policy Research, Washington, D.C. 1975.

station in New Hampshire spent over $26 just to mail to the Federal Communications Commission its application for renewal of its license—and that was prior to the last postal rate increase. An Oregon company, operating three small television stations, reported that its license renewal application weighed 45 pounds.

The paperwork and ancillary requirements of federal agencies inevitably produce a "regulatory lag," a delay that can run into years and can be a costly drain on the time and budgets of private managers as well as public officials. The Federal Trade Commission averages nearly five years to complete a restraint-of-trade case. It took the Federal Power Commission 11 years to determine how to regulate the price of natural gas all the way back to the wellhead. The regulatory lag appears to be lengthening. Ten years ago, the director of planning of a west coast company obtained in 90 days what was then called zoning for a typical residential development. Currently, it takes the company two years to receive what is now called "entitlement to build" for one of its developments, following intensive work by a specialized group within its planning department aided by the public affairs staff. The preparation of environmental impact statements has become a major source of paperwork. The report for one off-shore oil field in the Santa Barbara Channel, for example, required nearly 1,300 pages and took two years to prepare.

Other aspects of government regulatory activities also can be costly. Several research efforts examining building regulations have documented repeated instances of increases in the price of housing as a result of local building codes. One study reported that overly stringent or outdated codes increase housing costs by somewhere between 5 and 10 percent of total unit costs.

Government inspectors are increasingly frequent, albeit unwelcomed, visitors to business premises. Milk plants experience an extraordinary variety of inspections. More than 20,000 state, county, local, and municipal milk jurisdictions exist in the United States. A USDA study reveals that milk plants are inspected about 24 times annually, even though the Public Health Service recommends only two a year. In one state, each milk plant averaged ninety-five inspections during a year. One milk plant, licensed by 250 local governments, three states and twenty other agencies, reported that it was inspected 47 times in one month.

Regulation and Innovation

Another hidden cost of government regulation is a reduced rate of introduction of new products. The longer it takes for a new product to be approved by a government agency—or the more costly the approval process—the less likely the new product will be created. In any event, innovation will be delayed. Regulation by the Interstate Commerce Commission delayed the introduction of unit trains by at least five years and delayed full use by the Southern Railroad of the "Big John" cars used to carry grain.

The 1962 amendments to the Food and Drug Act are delaying the introduction of effective drugs by about four years, as well as leading to higher prices for pharmaceutical products. As a result in large part of the more stringent drug regulations, the United States was the thirtieth country to approve the anti-cancer drug adriamycin, the fifty-first to approve the anti-tuberculosis drug rifampin, the sixty-fourth to approve the anti-allergenic drug cromolyn, and the one hundred sixth to approve the anti-bacterial drug co-trimoxazole.

Regulation and Capital Formation

Federal regulation also reduces the prospects for economic growth and productivity gain by levying a claim on a rising share of new capital formation. This effect of regulation is most evident in the environmental and safety areas. Business outlays for pollution control in 1975 were $3.8 billion higher than would have been the case in the absence of federal environmental requirements. Similarly, the cost to American industry of meeting the occupational health and safety regulations is about $3 billion a year. Thus these two programs alone account for 6 percent of total capital spending in the private sector of the American economy ($113 billion in 1975).

Capital formation is also adversely affected by the uncertainty about the future of regulations governing the introduction of new processes and products. An example is furnished in the report of a task force of the U.S. Energy Resources Council dealing with the possibility of developing a new synthetic fuel industry. In evaluating the impact of the Federal Water Pollution Control Act Amendments of 1972, the task force reported, "It would be next to impossible at this time to predict the impact of these requirements on synthetic fuels production."

In considering the National Environmental Policy Act of 1969, the task force stated that the major uncertainty was not whether a project would be allowed to proceed, but rather the length of time that it would be delayed pending the issuance of an environmental impact statement that would stand up in court. In assessing the overall impact of government regulatory activity on the establishment of a new energy industry, the task force concluded, "In summary, some of these requirements could easily hold up or permanently postpone any attempt to build and operate a synthetic fuels plant."

Regulation and Employment

Government regulation, albeit unintentionally, can have strongly adverse effects on employment. The minimum wage law, for example, has priced many teenagers out of labor markets. The 1966 increase in the statutory minimum wage reduced teenage employment in the United States in 1972 by 300,000 below what it otherwise would have been.

In construction labor—where unemployment rates are substantially above the national average—government regulation also acts to price some segments of the work force out of competitive labor markets. Under the Davis-Bacon legislation, the Secretary of Labor promulgates "prevailing" wages to be paid on federal and federally-supported construction projects. These federally mandated wage rates are often above those that actually prevail in the labor market where the work is to be done.

Regulation and Entrepreneurial Functions

One of the unmeasurable effects of government regulation is what it does to the basic entrepreneurial nature of the private enterprise system. To the extent that management's attention is diverted from traditional product development, production, and marketing concerns to meeting governmentally imposed social requirements, a significant bureaucratization of business activity results.

EXTENSION OF GOVERNMENT REGULATION OF BUSINESS, 1962-74

Year of Enactment	Name of Law	Purpose and Function
1962	Food and Drug Amendments	Requires pretesting of drugs for safety and effectiveness and labeling of drugs by generic names
1962	Air Pollution Control Act	Provides first modern ecology statute
1963	Equal Pay Act	Eliminates wage differentials based on sex
1964	Civil Rights Act	Creates Equal Employment Opportunity Commission (EEOC) to investigate charges of job discrimination
1965	Water Quality Act	Extends environmental concern to water

EXTENSION OF GOVERNMENT RECREATION OF BUSINESS, 1962–74

Year of Enactment	Name of Law	Purpose and Function
1965	Cigarette Labeling and Advertising Act	Requires labels on hazards of smoking
1966	Fair Packaging and Labeling Act	Requires producers to state what a package contains, how much it contains, and who made the product
1966	Child Protection Act	Bans sale of hazardous toys and articles
1966	Traffic Safety Act	Provides for a coordinated national safety program, including safety standards for motor vehicles
1966	Coal Mine Safety Amendments	Tightens controls on working controls
1967	Flammable Fabrics Act	Broadens federal authority to set safety standards for inflammable fabrics, including clothing and household products
1967	Wholesome Meat Act	Offers states federal assistance in establishing interstate inspection system and raises quality standards for imported meat
1967	Age Discrimination in Employment Act	Prohibits job discrimination against individuals aged 40 to 65
1968	Consumer Credit Protection Act (Truth-in-Lending)	Requires full disclosure of terms and conditions of finance charges in credit transactions
1968	Interstate Land Sales Full Disclosure Act	Provides safeguards against unscrupulous practices in interstate land sales
1968	Wholesome Poultry Products Act	Increases protection against impure poultry
1968	Radiation Control for Health and Safety Act	Provides for mandatory control standards and recall of faulty atomic products
1969	National Environmental Policy Act	Requires environmental impact statements for federal agencies and projects
1970	Public Health Smoking Act	Extends warning about the hazards of cigarette smoking
1970	Amendments to Federal Deposit Insurance Act	Prohibits issuance of unsolicited credit cards. Limits customer's liability in case of loss or theft to $50. Regulates credit bureaus and provides consumers access to files
1970	Securities Investor Protection Act	Provides greater protection for customers of brokers and dealers and members of national securities exchanges. Establishes a Securities Investor Protection Corporation, financed by fees on brokerage houses
1970	Poison Prevention Packaging Act	Authorizes standards for child-resistant packaging of hazardous substances
1970	Clean Air Amendments	Provides for setting air quality standards

EXTENSION OF GOVERNMENT RECREATION OF BUSINESS, 1962-74

Year of Enactment	Name of Law	Purpose and Function
1970	Occupational Safety and Health Act	Establishes safety and health standards that must be met by employers
1971	Lead-Based Paint Elimination Act	Provides assistance in developing and administering programs to eliminate lead-based paints
1971	Federal Boat Safety Act	Provides for a coordinated national boating safety program
1972	Consumer Product Safety Act	Establishes a commission to set safety standards for consumer products and bans products presenting undue risk of injury
1972	Federal Water Pollution Control Act	Declares an end to the discharge of pollutants into navigable waters by 1985 as a national goal
1972	Noise Pollution and Control Act	Regulates noise limits of products and transportation vehicles
1972	Equal Employment Opportunity Act	Gives EEOC the right to sue employers
1973	Emergency Petroleum Allocation Act	Establishes temporary control over petroleum
1973	Vocational Rehabilitation Act	Requires federal contractors to take affirmative action on hiring the handicapped
1973	Highway Speed Limit Reduction	Limits vehicles to speeds of 55 miles an hour
1973	Safe Drinking Water Act	Requires EPA to set national drinking water regulations
1974	Campaign Finance Amendments	Restricts amounts of political contributions
1974	Federal Energy Administration Act	Provides authority for mandatory energy conservation programs
1974	Employee Retirement Income Security Act	Sets new federal standards for employee pension programs

In employee pension fund management, for example, the recently enacted pension regulation has shifted much of the concern of fund managers from maximizing the return on the contributions to a more cautious approach of minimizing the likelihood that the managers will be criticized for their investment decisions. It thus becomes safer—although not necessarily more desirable for the employees covered—for the pension managers to keep more detailed records of their deliberations, to hire more outside experts (so that the responsibility can be diluted), and to avoid innovative investments.

In the occupational safety and health area, professional safety staffs are often diverted from their basic function of training workers in safer operating procedures to filling out forms, posting notices, and meeting other essentially bureaucratic requirements. The emphasis shifts to such trivia as raising and answering these types of questions: How big is a hole? When is a roof a floor? How frequently must spittoons be cleaned? Of greater concern no doubt is the detail of the regulations. OSHA directives, for example, contain very specific requirements for virtually every piece of equipment used in the production of steel. These requirements range from such major items as coke ovens all the way down to such minutiae as the ladders used in plants and the mandatory 42-inch height from the floor for portable fire extinguishers.

Recent statistics on occupational injuries and illnesses are hardly reassuring. The reported overall accident and illness rate did decline in the most recent period for which data are available, from 10.4 per 100 workers in 1974 to 9.1 in 1975. However, the number of workdays lost to injuries and illnesses per 100 workers actually rose, to 54.4 in 1975 from 53.1 in 1974. Apparently, on the average, the affected workers took more time off than in the previous year. This likely indicates that the injuries and illnesses that did occur in 1975 were typically more severe. Perhaps once again OSHA showed its instinct for the trivial, succeeding in reducing the number of minor accidents and illnesses.

The Impact on Small Business

Government regulation tends to hit smaller businesses disproportionately hard. Often the cost of meeting government requirements—such as filling out a specific form—is about the same for a small company with 10 employees as a large corporation with a staff of thousands. Not too surprisingly, it is the smaller business who often are forced out or hard pressed by the cumulative costs of government imposed burdens. For example, the 350 foundries that have closed down because they could not meet environmental, safety, and other federal mandates were mainly small companies. The thousands of firms that have been forced to terminate their pension plans because they could not afford the expensive federally-mandated overhead were generally small businesses.

Approaches to Regulatory Reform

A new way of looking at the effects of regulatory programs is needed. A parallel can be drawn to general economic policy-making, where important and at times conflicting objectives are recognized and attempts at reconciliation or trade-off are made (for example, as between reducing unemployment and curbing inflation). It is likewise necessary to reconcile the goals of specific government programs with national objectives.

Healthy working conditions, for example, are an important national objective, but not the *only* important national objective. And society has no stake in selecting the most costly and disruptive methods of achieving a higher degree of job safety. Similarly, we should relate environmental protection, product safety, and other regulatory efforts to costs to the consumer, availability of new products, and the employment of the work force. In part, this reconciliation needs to be made at the initial stages of the governmental process, when the Congress first considers a new regulatory program. Needless to add, Governmental officials must also be reminded that each addition of regulatory power reduces the extent of individual freedom and of private sector discretion.

Many of the proposals to reform government regulation involve the "sunset" mechanism—the compulsory periodic review by the Congress of each major regulatory program to determine whether it is worthwhile to continue it in the light of changing circumstances. A benefit/cost analysis would provide an objective mechanism to aid our legislators in making those important value judgments.

Benefit-Cost Analysis

One device for broadening the horizons of government policy-makers, administrators, and regulators is the economic impact statement. Policy-makers should be required to consider the costs (and other adverse effects) of their actions as well as the benefits—before they act.

In the fashion of the environmental impact statements (but hopefully without as much of the trivia), it would be helpful if the Congress enacted a statute requiring each regulatory agency to assess the impact of its proposed actions on the society as a whole, and particularly on the economy. Certainly the nation has no interest in choosing the most expensive or least efficient ways of achieving its environmental, safety or other social goals, and should not select them.

Much would depend on the "teeth" put into any required economic impact statement. Merely legislating the performance of some economic analysis by an unsympathetic regulator would serve little purpose beyond delaying the regulatory process and making it more costly. But limiting government regulation to those instances where the total benefits to society exceed the costs would be a major and desirable departure from current practice. Where the government agencies could not show that the costs they impose are less than the benefits, they would be forced to reevaluate their proposals and come back with more effective approaches—or be prevented from extending the scope of government power over the private sector.

Government regulation should be carried to the point where the incremental costs equal the incremental benefits, and no further. Overregulation—which can be defined as regulation for which the costs exceed the benefits—should be avoided. The approach suggested here would not eliminate government regulation, but it would streamline and likely reduce its scope and costs.

Changing Attitudes Toward Regulation

Basically, however, it is attitudes that need to be changed. Experience with the job safety program provides a cogent example. Although the government's safety rules have resulted in billions of dollars in public and private outlays, the basic goal of a safer work environment has not been achieved.

A more satisfying answer to improving the effectiveness of government regulation of private activities requires a basic change in the approach to regulation, and one not limited to the job safety program. Indeed, that program is used here merely as an illustration. If the objective of public policy is to reduce accidents, then public policy should focus directly on the reduction of accidents. Rather than emphasis being placed on issuing citations to employers who fail to fill forms out correctly or who do not post the required notices, it should be placed on the regulation of those employers with high and rising accident rates.

But the government should not be much concerned with the way a specific organization achieves a safer working environment. Some companies may find it more efficient to change work rules, others to buy new equipment, and still others to retrain workers. The making of this choice is precisely the kind of operational business decision-making that government should avoid, but that now dominates many regulatory programs.

Alternatives to Regulation

The promulgation by government of rules and regulations restricting or prescribing private activity of course is not the only means of accomplishing public objectives. Codes of behavior adhered to on a voluntary basis may often be effective. Trade associations on occasion have served such a socially useful function in upgrading the level of business performance.

In the case of the more traditional one-industry type of government regulation, a greater role should be given to the competitive process and to market forces. Unlike the newer forms of regulation which aim at regulating *all* industries and commercial activities with regard to a particular policy goal, such as clean air—the older systems of regulation are often mainly barriers to entry into a given industry, protecting existing firms from competition by potential new and small business. It is in this limited sense that deregulation is a viable option. The total elimination of regulations in the safety, ecology, and related areas does not appear to be a realistic possibility at the present time.

Indeed, any honest appraisal of government regulation must acknowledge that important and positive benefits have resulted from many of these activities—less pollution, fewer product hazards, reduced job discrimination, and other socially desirable goals of our society. But the "externalities" generated by federal regulation cannot justify government attempting to regulate every facet of private behavior.

The public needs to grasp the notion that government regulation is a potent and expensive medicine. It needs to be taken very carefully, in limited doses, and with full regard for all the adverse side effects—inflation, unemployment, loss of productivity, delay in getting new products, and loss of capital formation. We must avoid unwittingly overdosing the patient. Only when the public comes to understand how detrimental overregulation is to their own interests as consumers in the marketplace will we see a keener appreciation of this fact in the ranks of decision-makers in government.

FEDERAL EXPENDITURES FOR BUSINESS REGULATION
(FISCAL YEARS, $ MILLIONS)

Agency	1974	1975	1976
Agriculture	330	376	381
Health, Education, and Welfare	145	173	189
Interior	59	74	79
Justice	112	345	383
Labor	232	343	397
Transportation	178	212	234
Treasury	246	306	320
Civil Aeronautics Board	89	85	85
Commodity Futures Trading Commission	—	—	11
Consumer Product Safety Commission	19	43	37
Cost Accounting Standards Board	1	2	2
Council on Wage and Price Stability	—	1	2
Environmental Protection Agency	46	53	54
Equal Employment Opportunity Commission	42	54	60
Federal Communications Commission	38	49	50
Federal Energy Administration	33	127	208
Federal Maritime Commission	6	7	8
Federal Power Commission	27	37	36
Federal Trade Commission	32	41	45
International Trade Commission	7	9	10
Interstate Commerce Commission	38	47	50
National Labor Relations Board	55	63	70
National Transportation Safety Board	8	10	10
Nuclear Regulatory Commission	80	139	198
Occupational Safety and Health Review Commission	5	6	6
Renegotiation Board	5	5	5
Securities and Exchange Commission	35	45	49
Total	1868	2652	2979

Source: Budget of the U.S. Government for the Fiscal Year 1976.

Time magazine observed that:

> Perhaps what is more grating ultimately is the indispensability of lawyers in modern society: their skill at decoding laws written by Congressman-lawyers or their lawyer aids, at interpreting the regulations promulgated by bureaucrat-lawyers, at helping influence the decisions made by politician lawyers. The swashbuckling entrepreneur may not be a vanished species, but he is an endangered one; and in a complex, technological society he may not get very far without a secular priest, his lawyer, to minister to him. "I can't believe the change," says Atlanta Attorney Sidney O. Smith, recently retired from the federal bench. "Today a businessman cannot function without an attorney."[10]

The question that must be answered is, "Can society afford the continued and increasing burden of regulation?" If the answer is "no," then the next question is, "What can be done about it?" With the livelihoods of so many regulators, inspectors, and enforcers involved, and the resultant political repercussions of any attempt to change matters, the problem may become even worse before the trend of regulation turns. The turning point (if there is one) may come when the impact of regulations on the economy's ability to compete in foreign markets with less regulated foreign firms is realized.

From a capital investment perspective, the effects of government regulation are felt in their impact both on future costs and on future revenues. The prospect of ever greater regulation raises the uncertainty level with which the decision maker must cope. And the type of uncertainty introduced does not lend itself to statistical treatment. It is possible that business investment may turn more to favoring projects that promise to pay off over a short time horizon, over which there is intuitively reasonable assurance that no additional major regulatory constraint is likely. This suggests that, rather than turning away from the payback method of investment evaluation, firms may turn to it more than they have in the past.

CONTINGENCY PLANNING

We may define contingency planning in capital budgeting as programming into capital investment analysis a degree of flexibility, based on responses to probable future difficulties affecting the investment if it is undertaken. Determination of what the future problems are likely to be does not altogether lend itself to rigorous quantitative treatment. Rather, it involves a combination of economic and social insights and analysis, along with a sense of political sentiment, and an ability to combine myriad seemingly heterogeneous facts and perceptions into an intuitive appreciation of the likely course of events and probable future developments. Once these are identified we may question what effect each will likely have on the capital investment proposal, and what the reaction should be if it does become a reality. In the process of doing this it may be discovered that a small modification in the way a project is specified may make it more adaptable to future contingencies.

[10] "Those . . . Lawyers," *Time* (April 10, 1978), p. 42.

Contingency planning can be advantageous in normal times. If indeed the 1980s earn the title "decade of uncertainty," then contingency planning will prove indispensable. Those firms that insure their future abilities to adapt quickly to changing circumstances will perform better than those that do not. The difference in some instances will be between those that survive as viable enterprises and those that do not.

In 1979 Chrysler Corporation incurred devastating losses. Chrysler had not changed its production emphasis to smaller, more gasoline-efficient autos to the extent that Ford and General Motors had. Yet, although Chrysler could not sell the larger cars it had produced, its smaller models were in short supply, there was a severe shortage of railroad cars to haul grain shipments, and mass transit experts were pointing out that increased demand for public transit buses in the United States could not be met by domestic producers.

Did Chrysler use contingency planning in its capital investments? If it had, why did the firm not respond to changing demand by changing its production accordingly? Was Chrysler unable to make the required investments in new plant and equipment that could have provided the flexibility it needed? Was the company prevented from making such investments by having to spend instead on government-mandated changes in auto design and environmental protection equipment for its old facilities?

Chrysler is only one conspicuous example of a firm's viability being threatened by what would appear to be lack of contingency planning. Numerous other examples can be found. What of the petroleum refinery that is designed to produce the maximum ratio of gasoline to other distillates, should the auto industry move suddenly to production of diesel engines, perhaps by government order? And what of the processed meat companies if nitrates and nitrites are banned? What does a textile producer do who has invested in machinery that is designed to work only with fiber blends that are predominantly synthetic when oil prices suddenly increase to where cotton and wool are less costly? Producers of home heating units in 1979 found that orders for wood, coal, and multifuel models were numerous beyond their dreams, whereas their factories were generally designed to produce oil or gas models, with other models formerly a minor sales component.

Perhaps today Americans should turn to Europe for guidance in educating future managers, as Europe turned to the United States after World War II:

> "We lay a great deal of stress in our teaching on coping with uncertainty," says Uwe Kitzinger, INSEAD's [European Institute of Business Administration] dean.
>
> Many students have a business background before entering INSEAD. Others come from countries where uncertainties, such as political upheaval or state nationalization, are an accepted business hazard. The diversity of the MBA class has itself helped shape INSEAD's program says Dean Kitzinger.[11]

Abandonment analysis, which was discussed in Chapter 15, provides a step in the direction toward formal contingency planning in capital investment. More pow-

---

[11] Felix Kessler, "Manager's Journal: A European Challenge," *The Wall Street Journal* (December, 4, 1978).

erful tools are provided by decision tree analysis, which was discussed in Chapter 20, and by computer simulation. However, all these formal methods depend on the availability of quantitative data that may not be obtainable.

One thing should be clear about contingency planning: In the 1980s it must be done, at least for the larger investment projects. How it should be done is another matter. This author believes that after the usual "hard" data are gathered and processed, acceptable major projects should be reviewed by a team (the author hesitates to use the word "committee") whose members are diverse in terms of background and specialization. The purpose of the review is to ask "what if . . . ?" questions about the project concerning reasonably possible future contingencies to (in a sense) play devil's advocate. An effective team ought to include both technical persons and those oriented toward the humanities and social sciences. If possible, they should be persons who have one another's mutual respect in order to avoid unproductive bickering. The team would bring its list of contingencies back to the decision makers, who then would review the project in their light and make whatever modifications were necessary, or even reject the project on their basis.

CONCLUSION

To the extent there is agreement that uncertainty fosters shorter planning horizons, we may expect the private sector to undertake fewer and fewer investments that, whatever their merits, fail to pay off quickly but have deferred benefits. The result will be a decline in the stock of capital, whereas the labor force continues to expand with population growth. The inevitable consequence (given the level of technology that prevails) is for output of goods and services to decline, particularly in per capita terms, as population continues to grow. Any general distrust of market forces is likely to be augmented by such a course of events. Those who see their political fortunes advanced by it will almost certainly accelerate their attacks on private enterprise and the market economy, and further unfavorable legislation is likely to result, thus replacing market judgment with bureaucratic mandate. Those who recognize the inferiority of administrative allocation of resources in comparison to the efficiency of the marketplace may be able to reverse the move to still greater government control, if they have the will to do so. Their record in the 1970s is not much to inspire hope. However, as more and more individuals have begun to feel personally the impact of the trend to more government, politicians have moved their rhetoric in order to be associated with causes directed to less government—including some who were responsible for it in the first instance. The decade of the 1980s may be decisive in determining whether the trend away from a relative free market economy toward collectivist aspirations will continue, or whether the trend will be broken.

At the level of the individual enterprise, over the short run at least, the economic environment and the disturbances to it must be taken as given, as exogenous. Over the longer term, however, it may be possible to make changes in the environment. One type of desirable change would be to minimize policy "surprises." Another type of change would be to carry the role of government still further, to try to eliminate uncertainty with government planning that would attempt to force events and institutions to conform to the plan, with less freedom of action for all. There is precedent for this in the centrally planned Marxist economies.

The rationale and effectiveness of the theory and application of capital investment analysis, and the decisions it yields, are compromised to the extent forecasts are rendered useless by random shocks. Capital investment analysis of risky, interrelated projects may be more sensitive to sudden changes in the project relationships than has been generally realized.

In this book a distinction was made between risk and uncertainty. With risk, the probability distributions of relevant variables are known or can be estimated with useful precision. Exact outcomes cannot be predicted, but rational decisions may be based on statistical evidence. With uncertainty, the governing probability distributions are unknown and cannot be estimated. In a state of economic equilibrium it may be reasonable to expect risk to prevail; in times of social and economic change, uncertainty. Minimization of adverse results may be the major concern in an uncertain environment, and to the extent this can be done by minimal time exposure we may expect the payback criterion to weigh more and more heavily in the capital expenditure decision. The environment may reward use of a capital investment measure that in more settled times is inferior to others.

We shall have to wait for the 1990s to see what happened in the 1980s. We may hope that by recognizing what some of the problems are at the outset that in ten years some solutions will be found that will make the 1990s a decade in which there can again be real growth, prosperity, freedom, and optimism for a better future.

Bibliography

1. "America Catches the British Disease," *World Business Weekly*, Vol. 3, No. 14 (April 14, 1980), pp. 5–6.
2. Andreski, Stanislav, *Social Sciences as Sorcery* (New York: St. Martins, 1972).
3. Bennett, James, T., and Manuel H. Johnson, "Paperwork and Bureaucracy," *Economic Inquiry*, Vol. XVII, No. 3, (July 1979), pp. 435–451.
4. Committee for Economic Development, *Report on Defense Against Inflation*, A Statement on National Policy by the Research and Policy Committee of the Committee for Economic Development, New York, 1958.
5. ————, *Fighting Inflation and Promoting Growth*, A Statement by the Research and Policy Committee of the Committee for Economic Development, New York, 1976.
6. Federal Reserve Bank of Minneapolis, *Annual Report 1977: Rational Expectations—Fresh Ideas That Challenge Some Established Views of Policy Making*, Minneapolis, Minnesota, 1978.
7. Federal Reserve Bank of Minneapolis, *Annual Report 1978: Eliminating Policy Surprises: An Inexpensive Way to Beat Inflation*, Minneapolis, Minnesota, 1979.
8. Freidenfelds, John, and Michael Kennedy, "Price Inflation and Long-Term Present-Worth Studies," *The Engineering Economist*, Vol. 24, No. 3 (Spring 1978), pp. 143–160.
9. Friedman, Milton, "What Belongs to Whom?," *Newsweek*, (March 13, 1978), p. 71.
10. Gaines, Tilford, "Productivity, Prices and So Forth," *Economic Report* (New York: Manufacturers Hanover Trust, May 1978).

11. Hamada, Robert S., "Financial Theory and Taxation in an Inflationary World: Some Public Policy Issues," *The Journal of Finance*, Vol. XXXIV (May 1979), pp. 347–370.
12. Howlett, Gareth, "Socialism," *The Economist*, Vol. 266, No. 7021, March 25, 1978, p. 4.
13. Juster, Thomas, and George Katona, "The Psychology of Inflation," *Economic Outlook USA*, Vol. 6, No. 1 (Winter 1978–1979), pp. 16–19.
14. Kellner, Irwin L., "Quarterly Business Conditions Analysis," (New York: Manufacturers Hanover Trust, Spring 1978).
15. Kessler, Felix, "Managers Journal: A European Challenge," *The Wall Street Journal* (December 4, 1978).
16. Lintner, John, "Inflation and Security Returns," *The Journal of Finance*, Vol. XXX, No. 2 (May 1975), pp. 259–280.
17. "Losing the Lead? Many Americans Fear the Economy's Ability to Compete Is Waning," *The Wall Street Journal* (April 17, 1978), p. 14.
18. Malkiel, Burton G., "The Capital Formation Problem in the United States," *The Journal of Finance*, Vol. XXXIV, No. 2 (May 1979), pp. 291–306.
19. Nelson, Charles R., "Inflation and Capital Budgeting," *The Journal of Finance*, Vol. XXXI, No. 3 (June 1976), pp. 923–931.
20. Parkinson, C. Northcote, *The Evolution of Political Thought* (New York: Viking, 1958).
21. Pyun, C. S., "A Note on Capital Asset Pricing Model Under Uncertain Inflation," *Journal of Financial and Quantitative Analysis*, Vol. XV, No. 2 (June 1980), pp. 425–434.
22. "Review and Outlook: The Economy in the 1980's," *The Wall Street Journal*, Vol. 15 (August 1979), p. 14.
23. "Review and Outlook: Truth in Taxation," *The Wall Street Journal*, Vol. 23 (August 1979), p. 20.
24. "Shell's 'Multiple Scenario Planning'," *World Business Weekly*, Vol. 3, No. 13 (April 7, 1980), pp. 14–15.
25. "Those . . . Lawyers," *Time* (April 10, 1978), p. 42.
26. Van Horne, James C., "A Note on Biases in Capital Budgeting Introduced by Inflation," *Journal of Financial And Quantitative Analysis*, Vol. VI, No. 1 (January 1971).
27. Weidenbaum, Murray L., "The Forgotten Consumer: Hidden Costs of Government Regulation," *Public Policy Discussion Series* (Washington: National Federation of Independent Business), p. 1.

Appendix A-1

Formulas for Interest and Discount

For:
- P = Principal or Present Value
- F = Future Value
- R = Annuity Periodic Receipt or Payment
- i = Annual Rate of Interest (in decimal)
- N = Number of Annual Periods

Table A-1. Single Payment Compound Amount Factor. To find F for a given P, $F = P(1 + i)^N$

Table A-2. Single Payment Present Worth Factor. To find P for a given F, $P = F(1 + i)^{-N}$

° Ordinary† Annuity Sinking Fund Factor. To find R for a given F, $R = F[i/((1 + i)^N - 1)]$

° Ordinary† Annuity Capital Recovery Factor. To find R for a given P, $R = P[i/(1 - (1 + i)^{-N})]$

Table A-3. Ordinary† Annuity Compound Amount Factor. To find F for a given R received at the end of each period, $F = R\left\{\dfrac{(1 + i)^N - 1}{i}\right\}$

Table A-4. Ordinary† Annuity Present Worth Factor. To find P for a given R received at the end of each period $F = R\left\{\dfrac{1 - (1 + i)^{-N}}{i}\right\}$

° To convert a *nominal* annual rate j, compounded M times per year, to its *effective* annual counterpart, i, use the relationship, $(1 + i) = (1 + j/M)^M$

° At *continuous* interest rate i, $F = Pe^{iN}$, where e is the base of natural logarithms, 2.71828.

° These factors are not tabulated.

† Ordinary annuities normally apply to capital investment problems. With them the periodic payments, R, occur at the end of each period. With "annuities due" they would occur at the beginning.

Table A-1. Single Payment Compound Amount Factor. To find F for a given P. $F = P(1 + i)^N$

$i\%$ / N	1	2	3	4	5	6	7	8	9	10
1	1.010000	1.020000	1.030000	1.040000	1.050000	1.060000	1.070000	1.080000	1.090000	1.100000
2	1.020100	1.040400	1.060900	1.081600	1.102500	1.123600	1.144900	1.166400	1.188100	1.210000
3	1.030301	1.061208	1.092727	1.124864	1.157625	1.191016	1.225043	1.259712	1.295029	1.331000
4	1.040604	1.082432	1.125509	1.169859	1.215506	1.262477	1.310796	1.360489	1.411582	1.464100
5	1.051010	1.104081	1.159274	1.216653	1.276282	1.338226	1.402552	1.469328	1.538624	1.610510
6	1.061520	1.126162	1.194052	1.265319	1.340096	1.418519	1.500730	1.586874	1.677100	1.771561
7	1.072135	1.148686	1.229874	1.315932	1.407100	1.503630	1.605781	1.713824	1.828039	1.948717
8	1.082857	1.171659	1.266770	1.368569	1.477455	1.593848	1.718186	1.850930	1.992563	2.143589
9	1.093685	1.195093	1.304773	1.423312	1.551328	1.689479	1.838459	1.999005	2.171893	2.357948
10	1.104622	1.218994	1.343916	1.480244	1.628895	1.790848	1.967151	2.158925	2.367364	2.593742
11	1.115668	1.243374	1.384234	1.539454	1.710339	1.898299	2.104852	2.331639	2.580426	2.853117
12	1.126825	1.268242	1.425761	1.601032	1.795856	2.012196	2.252192	2.518170	2.812665	3.138428
13	1.138093	1.293607	1.468534	1.665074	1.885649	2.132928	2.409845	2.719624	3.065805	3.452271
14	1.149474	1.319479	1.512590	1.731676	1.979932	2.260904	2.578534	2.937194	3.341727	3.797498
15	1.160969	1.345868	1.557967	1.800944	2.078928	2.396558	2.759032	3.172169	3.642482	4.177248
16	1.172579	1.372786	1.604706	1.872981	2.182875	2.540352	2.952164	3.425943	3.970306	4.594973
17	1.184304	1.400241	1.652848	1.947900	2.292018	2.692773	3.158815	3.700018	4.327633	5.054470
18	1.196147	1.428246	1.702433	2.025817	2.406619	2.854339	3.379932	3.996019	4.717120	5.559917
19	1.208109	1.456811	1.753506	2.106849	2.526950	3.025600	3.616528	4.315701	5.141661	6.115909
20	1.220190	1.485947	1.806111	2.191123	2.653298	3.207135	3.869684	4.660957	5.604411	6.727500
21	1.232392	1.515666	1.860295	2.278768	2.785963	3.399564	4.140562	5.033834	6.108808	7.400250
22	1.244716	1.545980	1.916103	2.369919	2.925261	3.603537	4.430402	5.436540	6.658600	8.140275
23	1.257163	1.576899	1.973587	2.464716	3.071524	3.819750	4.740530	5.871464	7.257874	8.954302
24	1.269735	1.608437	2.032794	2.563304	3.225100	4.048935	5.072367	6.341181	7.911083	9.849733
25	1.282432	1.640606	2.093778	2.665836	3.386355	4.291871	5.427433	6.848475	8.623081	10.834706
26	1.295256	1.673418	2.156591	2.772470	3.555673	4.549383	5.807353	7.396353	9.399158	11.918177
27	1.308209	1.706886	2.221289	2.883369	3.733456	4.822346	6.213868	7.988061	10.245082	13.109994
28	1.321291	1.741024	2.287928	2.998703	3.920129	5.111687	6.648838	8.627106	11.167140	14.420994
29	1.334504	1.775845	2.355566	3.118651	4.116136	5.418388	7.114257	9.317275	12.172182	15.863093
30	1.347849	1.811362	2.427262	3.243398	4.321942	5.743491	7.612255	10.062657	13.267678	17.449402
31	1.361327	1.847589	2.500080	3.373133	4.538039	6.088101	8.145113	10.867669	14.461770	19.194342
32	1.374941	1.884541	2.575083	3.508059	4.764941	6.453387	8.715271	11.737083	15.763209	21.113777
33	1.388690	1.922231	2.652335	3.648381	5.003189	6.840590	9.325340	12.676050	17.182028	23.225154
34	1.402577	1.960676	2.731905	3.794316	5.253348	7.251025	9.978114	13.690134	18.728411	25.547670
35	1.416603	1.999890	2.813862	3.946089	5.516015	7.686087	10.676581	14.785344	20.413968	28.102437
36	1.430769	2.039887	2.898278	4.103933	5.791816	8.147252	11.423942	15.968172	22.251225	30.912681
37	1.445076	2.080685	2.985227	4.268090	6.081407	8.636087	12.223618	17.245626	24.253835	34.003949
38	1.459527	2.122299	3.074783	4.438813	6.385477	9.154252	13.079271	18.625276	26.436680	37.404343
39	1.474123	2.164745	3.167027	4.616366	6.704751	9.703507	13.994820	20.115298	28.815982	41.144778
40	1.488864	2.208040	3.262038	4.801021	7.039989	10.285718	14.974458	21.724521	31.409420	45.259256

(Continued)

Table A-1. Single Payment Compound Amount Factor. To find F for a given P. $F = P(1 + i)^N$

$i\%$ N	1	2	3	4	5	6	7	8	9	10
41	1.503752	2.252200	3.359899	4.993061	7.391988	10.902861	16.022670	23.462483	34.236268	49.785181
42	1.518790	2.297244	3.460696	5.192784	7.761588	11.557033	17.144257	25.339482	37.317532	54.763699
43	1.533978	2.343189	3.564517	5.400495	8.149667	12.250455	18.344355	27.366640	40.676110	60.240069
44	1.549318	2.390053	3.671452	5.616515	8.557150	12.985482	19.628460	29.555972	44.336960	66.264076
45	1.564811	2.437854	3.781596	5.841176	8.985008	13.764611	21.002452	31.920449	48.327286	72.890484
46	1.580459	2.486611	3.895044	6.074823	9.434258	14.590487	22.472623	34.474085	52.676742	80.179532
47	1.596263	2.536344	4.011895	6.317816	9.905971	15.465917	24.045707	37.232012	57.417649	88.197485
48	1.612226	2.587070	4.132252	6.570320	10.401270	16.393872	25.728907	40.210573	62.585237	97.017234
49	1.628348	2.638812	4.256219	6.833349	10.921333	17.377504	27.529930	43.427419	68.217908	106.718957
50	1.644632	2.691588	4.383906	7.106683	11.467400	18.420154	29.457025	46.901613	74.357520	117.390853
51	1.661078	2.745420	4.515423	7.390951	12.040770	19.525364	31.519017	50.653742	81.049697	129.129938
52	1.677689	2.800328	4.650886	7.686589	12.642808	20.696885	33.725348	54.706041	88.344170	142.042932
53	1.694466	2.856335	4.790412	7.994052	13.274949	21.938698	36.086122	59.082524	96.295145	156.247225
54	1.711410	2.913461	4.934125	8.313814	13.938696	23.255020	38.612151	63.809106	104.961708	171.871948
55	1.728525	2.971731	5.082149	8.646367	14.635631	24.650322	41.315001	68.913856	114.408262	189.059142
56	1.745810	3.031165	5.234613	8.992222	15.367412	26.129341	44.207052	74.426965	124.705005	207.965057
57	1.763268	3.091789	5.391651	9.351910	16.135783	27.697101	47.301545	80.381122	135.928456	228.761562
58	1.780901	3.153624	5.553401	9.725987	16.942572	29.358927	50.612653	86.811612	148.162017	251.637719
59	1.798710	3.216697	5.720003	10.115026	17.789701	31.120463	54.155539	93.756540	161.496598	276.801490
60	1.816697	3.281031	5.891603	10.519627	18.679186	32.987691	57.946427	101.257064	176.031292	304.481640
61	1.834864	3.346651	6.068351	10.940413	19.613145	34.966952	62.002677	109.357629	191.874108	334.929803
62	1.853212	3.413584	6.250402	11.378029	20.593802	37.064969	66.342864	118.106239	209.142778	368.422784
63	1.871744	3.481856	6.437914	11.833150	21.623493	39.288600	70.986865	127.554738	227.965628	405.265062
64	1.890462	3.551493	6.631051	12.306476	22.704667	41.646200	75.955945	137.759117	248.482535	445.791568
65	1.909366	3.622523	6.829983	12.798735	23.839901	44.144972	81.272861	148.779847	270.845963	490.370725
66	1.928460	3.694974	7.034882	13.310685	25.031896	46.793670	86.961962	160.682234	295.222099	539.407798
67	1.947745	3.768873	7.245929	13.843112	26.283490	49.601290	93.049299	173.536813	321.792088	593.348578
68	1.967222	3.844251	7.463307	14.396836	27.597665	52.577368	99.562750	187.419758	350.753376	652.683435
69	1.986894	3.921136	7.687206	14.972710	28.977548	55.732010	106.532142	202.413339	382.321180	717.951779
70	2.006763	3.999558	7.917822	15.571618	30.426426	59.075930	113.989392	218.606406	416.730086	789.746957
71	2.026831	4.079549	8.155357	16.194483	31.947747	62.620486	121.968650	236.094918	454.235794	868.721652
72	2.047099	4.161140	8.400017	16.842263	33.545134	66.377715	130.506455	254.982512	495.117015	955.593818
73	2.067570	4.244363	8.652018	17.515953	35.222391	70.360378	139.641907	275.381113	539.677547	********
74	2.088246	4.329250	8.911578	18.216591	36.983510	74.582001	149.416840	297.411602	588.248526	********
75	2.109128	4.415835	9.178926	18.945255	38.832686	79.056921	159.876019	321.204530	641.190893	********
76	2.130220	4.504152	9.454293	19.703065	40.774320	83.800336	171.067341	346.900892	698.898074	********
77	2.151522	4.594235	9.737922	20.491187	42.813036	88.828356	183.042055	374.652964	761.798900	********
78	2.173037	4.686120	10.030060	21.310835	44.953688	94.158058	195.854998	404.625201	830.360801	********
79	2.194768	4.779842	10.330962	22.163268	47.201372	99.807541	209.564848	436.995217	905.093274	********
80	2.216715	4.875439	10.640891	23.049799	49.561441	105.795993	224.234388	471.954834	986.551668	********

(Continued)

Table A-1. Single Payment Compound Amount Factor. To find F for a given P. $F = P(1 + i)^N$

$i\%$ / N	1	2	3	4	5	6	7	8	9	10
81	2.238882	4.972948	10.960117	23.971791	52.039513	112.143753	239.930795	509.711221	**********	**********
82	2.261271	5.072407	11.288921	24.930663	54.641489	118.872378	256.725950	550.488119	**********	**********
83	2.283884	5.173855	11.627588	25.927889	57.373563	126.004721	274.696767	594.527168	**********	**********
84	2.306723	5.277332	11.976416	26.965005	60.242241	133.565004	293.925541	642.089342	**********	**********
85	2.329790	5.382879	12.335709	28.043605	63.254353	141.578904	314.500328	693.456489	**********	**********
86	2.353088	5.490536	12.705780	29.165349	66.417071	150.073639	336.515351	748.933008	**********	**********
87	2.376619	5.600347	13.086953	30.331963	69.737925	159.078057	360.071426	808.847649	**********	**********
88	2.400385	5.712354	13.479562	31.545242	73.224821	168.622741	385.276426	873.555461	**********	**********
89	2.424389	5.826601	13.883949	32.807051	76.886062	178.740105	412.245776	943.439897	**********	**********
90	2.448633	5.943133	14.300467	34.119333	80.730365	189.464511	441.102980	**********	**********	**********
91	2.473119	6.061996	14.729481	35.484107	84.766883	200.832382	471.980188	**********	**********	**********
92	2.497850	6.183236	15.171366	36.903471	89.005227	212.882325	505.018802	**********	**********	**********
93	2.522829	6.306900	15.626507	38.379610	93.455489	225.655264	540.370118	**********	**********	**********
94	2.548057	6.433038	16.095302	39.914794	98.128263	239.194580	578.196026	**********	**********	**********
95	2.573538	6.561699	16.578161	41.511386	103.034676	253.546255	618.669748	**********	**********	**********
96	2.599273	6.692933	17.075506	43.171841	108.186410	268.759030	661.976630	**********	**********	**********
97	2.625266	6.826792	17.587771	44.898715	113.595731	284.884572	708.314994	**********	**********	**********
98	2.651518	6.963328	18.115404	46.694664	119.275517	301.977646	757.897044	**********	**********	**********
99	2.678033	7.102594	18.658866	48.562450	125.239293	320.096305	810.949837	**********	**********	**********
100	2.704814	7.244646	19.218632	50.504948	131.501258	339.302084	867.716326	**********	**********	**********
101	2.731862	7.389539	19.795191	52.525146	138.076321	359.660209	928.456468	**********	**********	**********
102	2.759181	7.537330	20.389047	54.626152	144.980137	381.239821	993.448421	**********	**********	**********
103	2.786772	7.688076	21.000718	56.811198	152.229144	404.114210	**********	**********	**********	**********
104	2.814640	7.841838	21.630740	59.083646	159.840601	428.361063	**********	**********	**********	**********
105	2.842787	7.998675	22.279662	61.446992	167.832631	454.062727	**********	**********	**********	**********
106	2.871214	8.158648	22.948052	63.904871	176.224262	481.306490	**********	**********	**********	**********
107	2.899927	8.321821	23.636493	66.461066	185.035475	510.184880	**********	**********	**********	**********
108	2.928926	8.488258	24.345588	69.119509	194.287249	540.795972	**********	**********	**********	**********
109	2.958215	8.658023	25.075956	71.884289	204.001612	573.243731	**********	**********	**********	**********
110	2.987797	8.831183	25.828234	74.759661	214.201692	607.638355	**********	**********	**********	**********
111	3.017675	9.007807	26.603081	77.750047	224.911777	644.096656	**********	**********	**********	**********
112	3.047852	9.187963	27.401174	80.860049	236.157366	683.742455	**********	**********	**********	**********
113	3.078330	9.371722	28.223209	84.094451	247.965234	723.707003	**********	**********	**********	**********
114	3.109114	9.559157	29.069905	87.458229	260.363496	767.129423	**********	**********	**********	**********
115	3.140205	9.750340	29.942002	90.956558	273.381671	813.157188	**********	**********	**********	**********
116	3.171607	9.945347	30.840262	94.594821	287.050754	861.946619	**********	**********	**********	**********
117	3.203323	10.144254	31.765470	98.378614	301.403292	913.663417	**********	**********	**********	**********
118	3.235356	10.347139	32.718434	102.313758	316.473456	968.483222	**********	**********	**********	**********
119	3.267710	10.554081	33.699988	106.406268	332.297129	**********	**********	**********	**********	**********
120	3.300387	10.765163	34.710987	110.662561	348.911986	**********	**********	**********	**********	**********

(Continued)

Table A-1. Single Payment Compound Amount Factor. To find F for a given P. $F = P(1 + i)^N$

$i\%$ / N	11	12	13	14	15	16	17	18	19	20
1	1.110000	1.120000	1.130000	1.140000	1.150000	1.160000	1.170000	1.180000	1.190000	1.200000
2	1.232100	1.254400	1.276900	1.299600	1.322500	1.345600	1.368900	1.392400	1.416100	1.440000
3	1.367631	1.404928	1.442897	1.481544	1.520875	1.560896	1.601613	1.643032	1.685159	1.728000
4	1.518070	1.573519	1.630474	1.688960	1.749006	1.810639	1.873887	1.938778	2.005339	2.073600
5	1.685058	1.762342	1.842435	1.925415	2.011357	2.100342	2.192448	2.287758	2.386354	2.488320
6	1.870415	1.973823	2.081952	2.194973	2.313061	2.436396	2.565164	2.699554	2.839761	2.985984
7	2.076160	2.210681	2.352605	2.502269	2.660020	2.826220	3.001242	3.185474	3.379315	3.583181
8	2.304538	2.475963	2.658444	2.852586	3.059023	3.278415	3.511453	3.758859	4.021385	4.299817
9	2.558037	2.773079	3.004042	3.251949	3.517876	3.802963	4.108400	4.435454	4.785449	5.159780
10	2.839421	3.105848	3.394567	3.707221	4.045558	4.411435	4.806828	5.233836	5.694684	6.191736
11	3.151757	3.478550	3.835861	4.226232	4.652391	5.117265	5.623989	6.175926	6.776674	7.430084
12	3.498451	3.895976	4.334523	4.817905	5.350250	5.936067	6.580067	7.287593	8.064242	8.916100
13	3.883280	4.363493	4.898011	5.492411	6.152788	6.885791	7.698679	8.599359	9.596448	10.699321
14	4.310441	4.887112	5.534753	6.261349	7.075706	7.987518	9.007454	10.147244	11.419773	12.839185
15	4.784589	5.473566	6.254270	7.137938	8.137062	9.265521	10.538721	11.973748	13.589530	15.407022
16	5.310894	6.130394	7.067326	8.137249	9.357621	10.748004	12.330304	14.129023	16.171540	18.488426
17	5.895093	6.866041	7.986078	9.276464	10.761264	12.467685	14.426456	16.672247	19.244133	22.186111
18	6.543553	7.689966	9.024268	10.575169	12.375264	14.462514	16.878953	19.673251	22.900518	26.623333
19	7.263344	8.612762	10.197423	12.055693	14.231772	16.776517	19.748375	23.214436	27.251616	31.948000
20	8.062312	9.646293	11.523088	13.743490	16.366537	19.460759	23.105599	27.393035	32.429423	38.337600
21	8.949166	10.803848	13.021089	15.667578	18.821518	22.574481	27.033551	32.323781	38.591014	46.005120
22	9.933574	12.100310	14.713831	17.861039	21.644746	26.186398	31.629255	38.142061	45.923307	55.206144
23	11.026267	13.552347	16.626629	20.361585	24.891458	30.376222	37.006228	45.007632	54.648735	66.247373
24	12.239157	15.178629	18.788091	23.212207	28.625176	35.236417	43.297287	53.109006	65.031994	79.496847
25	13.585464	17.000064	21.230542	26.461916	32.918953	40.874244	50.657826	62.668627	77.388073	95.396217
26	15.079865	19.040072	23.990513	30.166584	37.856796	47.414123	59.269656	73.948980	92.091807	114.475460
27	16.738650	21.324881	27.109279	34.389906	43.535315	55.000382	69.345497	87.259797	109.589251	137.370552
28	18.579901	23.883866	30.633486	39.204493	50.065612	63.800404	81.134232	102.966760	130.411208	164.844662
29	20.623691	26.749930	34.615839	44.693122	57.575454	74.008515	94.927051	121.500541	155.189338	197.813595
30	22.892297	29.959922	39.115898	50.950159	66.211772	85.849877	111.064650	143.370638	184.675312	237.376314
31	25.410449	33.555113	44.200965	58.083181	76.143538	99.585857	129.945641	169.177353	219.763621	284.851577
32	28.205599	37.581726	49.947090	66.214826	87.565068	115.519594	152.036399	199.629277	261.518710	341.821892
33	31.308214	42.091533	56.440212	75.484902	100.699829	134.002729	177.882587	235.562547	311.207264	410.186270
34	34.752118	47.142512	63.777439	86.052788	115.804803	155.443166	208.122627	277.963805	370.336645	492.223524
35	38.574851	52.799620	72.068506	98.100178	133.175523	180.314073	243.503474	327.997290	440.700607	590.668229
36	42.818085	59.135574	81.437412	111.834203	153.151852	209.164324	284.899064	387.036802	524.433722	708.801875
37	47.528074	66.231843	92.024276	127.490992	176.124630	242.630616	333.331905	456.703427	624.076130	850.562250
38	52.756162	74.179664	103.987432	145.339731	202.543324	281.451515	389.998329	538.910044	742.650594	**********
39	58.559340	83.081224	117.505798	165.687293	232.924823	326.483757	456.298045	635.913852	883.754207	**********
40	65.000867	93.050970	132.781552	188.883514	267.863546	378.721158	533.868713	750.378345	**********	**********

(Continued)

354

Table A-1. Single Payment Compound Amount Factor. To find F for a given P. $F = P(1 + i)^N$

$i\%$ / N	11	12	13	14	15	16	17	18	19	20
41	72.150963	104.217087	150.043153	215.327206	308.043078	439.316544	624.626394	885.446447	********	********
42	80.087569	116.723137	169.548763	245.473015	354.249540	509.607191	730.812881	********	********	********
43	88.897201	130.729914	191.590103	279.839237	407.386971	591.144341	855.051071	********	********	********
44	98.675893	146.417503	216.496816	319.016730	468.495017	685.727436	********	********	********	********
45	109.530242	163.987604	244.641402	363.679072	538.769269	795.443826	********	********	********	********
46	121.578568	183.666116	276.444784	414.594142	619.584659	922.714838	********	********	********	********
47	134.952211	205.706050	312.382606	472.637322	712.522358	********	********	********	********	********
48	149.796954	230.390776	352.992345	538.806547	819.400712	********	********	********	********	********
49	166.274619	258.037669	398.881350	614.239464	942.310819	********	********	********	********	********
50	184.564827	289.002190	450.735925	700.232988	********	********	********	********	********	********
51	204.866958	323.682453	509.331595	798.265607	********	********	********	********	********	********
52	227.402323	362.524347	575.544703	910.022792	********	********	********	********	********	********
53	252.416579	406.027269	650.365514	********	********	********	********	********	********	********
54	280.182402	454.750541	734.913031	********	********	********	********	********	********	********
55	311.002466	509.320606	830.451725	********	********	********	********	********	********	********
56	345.212738	570.439078	938.410449	********	********	********	********	********	********	********
57	383.186139	638.891768	********	********	********	********	********	********	********	********
58	425.336614	715.558780	********	********	********	********	********	********	********	********
59	472.123642	801.425833	********	********	********	********	********	********	********	********
60	524.057242	897.596933	********	********	********	********	********	********	********	********
61	581.703539	********	********	********	********	********	********	********	********	********
62	645.690928	********	********	********	********	********	********	********	********	********
63	716.716930	********	********	********	********	********	********	********	********	********
64	795.555793	********	********	********	********	********	********	********	********	********
65	883.066930	********	********	********	********	********	********	********	********	********
66	980.204292	********	********	********	********	********	********	********	********	********
67	********	********	********	********	********	********	********	********	********	********
68	********	********	********	********	********	********	********	********	********	********
69	********	********	********	********	********	********	********	********	********	********
70	********	********	********	********	********	********	********	********	********	********
71	********	********	********	********	********	********	********	********	********	********
72	********	********	********	********	********	********	********	********	********	********
73	********	********	********	********	********	********	********	********	********	********
74	********	********	********	********	********	********	********	********	********	********
75	********	********	********	********	********	********	********	********	********	********
76	********	********	********	********	********	********	********	********	********	********
77	********	********	********	********	********	********	********	********	********	********
78	********	********	********	********	********	********	********	********	********	********
79	********	********	********	********	********	********	********	********	********	********
80	********	********	********	********	********	********	********	********	********	********

(Continued)

Table A-1. Single Payment Compound Amount Factor. To find F for a given P. $F = P(1 + i)^N$

$i\%$ / N	21	22	23	24	25	26	27	28	29	30
1	1.210000	1.220000	1.230000	1.240000	1.250000	1.260000	1.270000	1.280000	1.290000	1.300000
2	1.464100	1.488400	1.512900	1.537600	1.562500	1.587600	1.612900	1.638400	1.664100	1.690000
3	1.771561	1.815848	1.860867	1.906624	1.953125	2.000376	2.048383	2.097152	2.146689	2.197000
4	2.143589	2.215335	2.288866	2.364514	2.441406	2.520474	2.601446	2.684355	2.769229	2.856100
5	2.593742	2.702708	2.815306	2.931625	3.051758	3.175797	3.303837	3.435974	3.572305	3.712930
6	3.138428	3.297304	3.462826	3.635215	3.814697	4.001504	4.195873	4.398047	4.608274	4.826809
7	3.797498	4.022711	4.259276	4.507667	4.768372	5.041895	5.328759	5.629500	5.944673	6.274852
8	4.594973	4.907707	5.238909	5.589507	5.960464	6.352788	6.767523	7.205759	7.668628	8.157307
9	5.559917	5.987403	6.443859	6.930988	7.450581	8.004513	8.594755	9.223372	9.892530	10.604499
10	6.727500	7.304631	7.925946	8.594426	9.313226	10.085686	10.915339	11.805916	12.761364	13.785849
11	8.140275	8.911650	9.748914	10.657088	11.641532	12.707965	13.862649	15.111573	16.462160	17.921604
12	9.849733	10.872213	11.991164	13.214789	14.551915	16.012035	17.605350	19.342813	21.236186	23.298085
13	11.918177	13.264060	14.749132	16.386338	18.189894	20.175165	22.358801	24.758801	27.394680	30.287511
14	14.420994	16.182202	18.141432	20.319059	22.737368	25.420707	28.395668	31.691265	35.339137	39.373764
15	17.449402	19.742287	22.313961	25.195633	28.421709	32.030091	36.062499	40.564819	45.587487	51.185893
16	21.113777	24.085590	27.446172	31.242585	35.527137	40.357915	45.799373	51.922969	58.807859	66.541661
17	25.547670	29.384420	33.758792	38.740806	44.408921	50.850973	58.165204	66.461400	75.862137	86.504159
18	30.912681	35.846992	41.523314	48.038599	55.511151	64.072226	73.869809	85.070592	97.862157	112.455407
19	37.404343	43.735771	51.073676	59.567863	69.388939	80.731005	93.814658	108.890357	126.242183	146.192029
20	45.259256	53.357640	62.820622	73.864150	86.736174	101.721066	119.144615	139.379657	162.852416	190.049638
21	54.763699	65.096321	77.269364	91.591546	108.420217	128.168543	151.313661	178.405962	210.079617	247.064529
22	66.264076	79.417512	95.041318	113.573517	135.525272	161.492364	192.168350	228.359631	271.002705	321.183888
23	80.179532	96.889364	116.900822	140.831161	169.406589	203.480379	244.053804	292.300327	349.593490	417.539054
24	97.017234	118.205024	143.788010	174.630639	211.758237	256.385277	309.948332	374.144419	450.975602	542.800770
25	117.390853	144.210130	176.859253	216.541993	264.697796	323.045450	393.634381	478.904857	581.758527	705.641001
26	142.042932	175.936358	217.536881	268.512071	330.872245	407.037266	499.915664	612.998216	750.468500	917.333302
27	171.871948	214.642357	267.570364	332.954968	413.590306	512.866956	634.892893	784.637717	968.104365	**********
28	207.965057	261.863675	329.111547	412.864160	516.987883	646.212364	806.313974	**********	**********	**********
29	251.637719	319.473684	404.807203	511.951559	646.234854	814.227579	**********	**********	**********	**********
30	304.481640	389.757894	497.912860	634.819933	807.793567	**********	**********	**********	**********	**********
31	368.422784	475.504631	612.432818	787.176717	**********	**********	**********	**********	**********	**********
32	445.791568	580.115660	753.292366	976.099129	**********	**********	**********	**********	**********	**********
33	539.407798	707.741093	926.549610	**********	**********	**********	**********	**********	**********	**********
34	652.683435	863.444133	**********	**********	**********	**********	**********	**********	**********	**********
35	789.746957	**********	**********	**********	**********	**********	**********	**********	**********	**********
36	955.593818	**********	**********	**********	**********	**********	**********	**********	**********	**********
37	**********	**********	**********	**********	**********	**********	**********	**********	**********	**********
38	**********	**********	**********	**********	**********	**********	**********	**********	**********	**********
39	**********	**********	**********	**********	**********	**********	**********	**********	**********	**********
40	**********	**********	**********	**********	**********	**********	**********	**********	**********	**********

(Continued)

Table A-1. Single Payment Compound Amount Factor. To find F for a given P. $F = P(1 + i)^N$

$i\%$ / N	31	32	33	34	35	36	37	38	39	40
1	1.310000	1.320000	1.330000	1.340000	1.350000	1.360000	1.370000	1.380000	1.390000	1.400000
2	1.716100	1.742400	1.768900	1.795600	1.822500	1.849600	1.876900	1.904400	1.932100	1.960000
3	2.248091	2.299968	2.352637	2.406104	2.460375	2.515556	2.571353	2.628072	2.685619	2.744000
4	2.944999	3.035958	3.129007	3.224179	3.321506	3.421020	3.522754	3.626739	3.733010	3.841600
5	3.857949	4.007464	4.161580	4.320400	4.484033	4.652587	4.826172	5.004900	5.188884	5.378240
6	5.053913	5.289853	5.534901	5.789336	6.053445	6.327519	6.611856	6.906762	7.212549	7.529536
7	6.620626	6.982606	7.361418	7.757711	8.172151	8.605426	9.058243	9.531332	10.025444	10.541350
8	8.673020	9.217040	9.790686	10.395333	11.032404	11.703379	12.409793	13.153238	13.935367	14.757891
9	11.361657	12.166492	13.021613	13.929746	14.893745	15.916595	17.001416	18.151469	19.370160	20.661047
10	14.883770	16.059770	17.318745	18.665859	20.106556	21.646570	23.291940	25.049027	26.924522	28.925465
11	19.497739	21.198896	23.033930	25.012251	27.143850	29.433335	31.909958	34.567658	37.425086	40.495652
12	25.542038	27.982543	30.635127	33.516417	36.644198	40.037495	43.716643	47.703367	52.020869	56.693912
13	33.460070	36.936956	40.744720	44.911998	49.469667	54.450994	59.891801	65.830647	72.309008	79.371477
14	43.832692	48.756782	54.190477	60.182078	66.784051	74.053351	82.051767	90.846293	100.509521	111.120068
15	57.420826	64.358953	72.073334	80.643984	90.158469	100.712558	112.410921	125.367884	139.708234	155.568096
16	75.221282	84.953818	95.857535	108.062939	121.713933	136.969078	154.002962	173.007680	194.194446	217.795334
17	98.539879	112.139039	127.490521	144.804338	164.313809	186.277947	210.984058	238.750598	269.930279	304.913467
18	129.087242	148.023532	169.562393	194.037813	221.823643	253.338008	289.048160	329.475826	375.203088	426.878854
19	169.104287	195.391062	225.517983	260.010669	299.461918	344.539690	395.995979	454.676640	521.532293	597.630396
20	221.526616	257.916202	299.938917	348.414297	404.273589	468.573979	542.514491	627.453763	724.929887	836.682554
21	290.199867	340.449386	398.918760	466.875157	545.769345	637.260611	743.244853	865.886193	********	********
22	380.161826	449.393190	530.561951	625.612711	736.788616	866.674431	********	********	********	********
23	498.011931	593.199010	705.647394	838.321033	994.664631	********	********	********	********	********
24	652.395709	783.022694	936.511035	********	********	********	********	********	********	********
25	854.638378	********	********	********	********	********	********	********	********	********
26	********	********	********	********	********	********	********	********	********	********
27	********	********	********	********	********	********	********	********	********	********
28	********	********	********	********	********	********	********	********	********	********
29	********	********	********	********	********	********	********	********	********	********
30	********	********	********	********	********	********	********	********	********	********
31	********	********	********	********	********	********	********	********	********	********
32	********	********	********	********	********	********	********	********	********	********
33	********	********	********	********	********	********	********	********	********	********
34	********	********	********	********	********	********	********	********	********	********
35	********	********	********	********	********	********	********	********	********	********
36	********	********	********	********	********	********	********	********	********	********
37	********	********	********	********	********	********	********	********	********	********
38	********	********	********	********	********	********	********	********	********	********
39	********	********	********	********	********	********	********	********	********	********
40	********	********	********	********	********	********	********	********	********	********

(Continued)

Table A-1. Single Payment Compound Amount Factor. To find F for a given P. $F = P(1 + i)^N$

$i\%$ / N	41	42	43	44	45	46	47	48	49	50
1	1.410000	1.420000	1.430000	1.440000	1.450000	1.460000	1.470000	1.480000	1.490000	1.500000
2	1.988100	2.016400	2.044900	2.073600	2.102500	2.131600	2.160900	2.190400	2.220100	2.250000
3	2.803221	2.863288	2.924207	2.985984	3.048625	3.112136	3.176523	3.241792	3.307949	3.375000
4	3.952542	4.065869	4.181616	4.299817	4.420506	4.543719	4.669489	4.797852	4.928844	5.062500
5	5.573084	5.773534	5.979711	6.191736	6.409734	6.633829	6.864149	7.100821	7.343978	7.593750
6	7.858048	8.198418	8.550987	8.916100	9.294114	9.685390	10.090298	10.509215	10.942527	11.390625
7	11.079848	11.641754	12.227911	12.839185	13.476466	14.140670	14.832739	15.553639	16.304365	17.085938
8	15.622585	16.531290	17.485912	18.488426	19.540876	20.645378	21.804126	23.019385	24.293503	25.628906
9	22.027845	23.474432	25.004855	26.623333	28.334269	30.142252	32.052065	34.068690	36.197320	38.443359
10	31.059262	33.333694	35.756942	38.337600	41.084691	44.007688	47.116535	50.421662	53.934007	57.665039
11	43.793559	47.333845	51.132428	55.206144	59.572802	64.251225	69.261307	74.624059	80.361670	86.497559
12	61.748918	67.214061	73.119371	79.496847	86.380562	93.806789	101.814121	110.443608	119.738888	129.746338
13	87.065974	95.443966	104.560701	114.475460	125.251815	136.957912	149.666758	163.456539	178.410943	194.619507
14	122.763024	135.530432	149.521803	164.844662	181.615132	199.958551	220.010134	241.915678	265.832305	291.929260
15	173.095864	192.453213	213.816178	237.376314	263.341942	291.939484	323.414898	358.035204	396.090135	437.893890
16	244.065168	273.283562	305.757134	341.821892	381.845816	426.231647	475.419900	529.892102	590.174301	656.840836
17	344.131886	388.062658	437.232702	492.223524	553.676433	622.298205	698.867252	784.240311	879.359709	985.261253
18	485.225960	551.048975	625.242764	708.801875	802.830827	908.555379	********	********	********	********
19	684.168603	782.489544	894.097153	********	********	********	********	********	********	********
20	964.677731	********	********	********	********	********	********	********	********	********
21	********	********	********	********	********	********	********	********	********	********
22	********	********	********	********	********	********	********	********	********	********
23	********	********	********	********	********	********	********	********	********	********
24	********	********	********	********	********	********	********	********	********	********
25	********	********	********	********	********	********	********	********	********	********
26	********	********	********	********	********	********	********	********	********	********
27	********	********	********	********	********	********	********	********	********	********
28	********	********	********	********	********	********	********	********	********	********
29	********	********	********	********	********	********	********	********	********	********
30	********	********	********	********	********	********	********	********	********	********
31	********	********	********	********	********	********	********	********	********	********
32	********	********	********	********	********	********	********	********	********	********
33	********	********	********	********	********	********	********	********	********	********
34	********	********	********	********	********	********	********	********	********	********
35	********	********	********	********	********	********	********	********	********	********
36	********	********	********	********	********	********	********	********	********	********
37	********	********	********	********	********	********	********	********	********	********
38	********	********	********	********	********	********	********	********	********	********
39	********	********	********	********	********	********	********	********	********	********
40	********	********	********	********	********	********	********	********	********	********

(Continued)

Table A-1. Single Payment Compound Amount Factor. To find F for a given P. $F = P(1 + i)^N$

$i\%$ / N	51	52	53	54	55	56	57	58	59	60
1	1.510000	1.520000	1.530000	1.540000	1.550000	1.560000	1.570000	1.580000	1.590000	1.600000
2	2.280100	2.310400	2.340900	2.371600	2.402500	2.433600	2.464900	2.496400	2.528100	2.560000
3	3.442951	3.511808	3.581577	3.652264	3.723875	3.796416	3.869893	3.944312	4.019679	4.096000
4	5.198856	5.337948	5.479813	5.624487	5.772006	5.922409	6.075732	6.232013	6.391290	6.553600
5	7.850273	8.113681	8.384114	8.661709	8.946610	9.238958	9.538899	9.846580	10.162150	10.485760
6	11.853912	12.332795	12.827694	13.339032	13.867245	14.412774	14.976072	15.557597	16.157819	16.777216
7	17.899406	18.745849	19.626372	20.542110	21.494230	22.483928	23.512433	24.581004	25.690933	26.843546
8	27.028104	28.493691	30.028348	31.634849	33.316056	35.074928	36.914519	38.837986	40.848583	42.949673
9	40.812437	43.310410	45.943373	48.717668	51.639887	54.716888	57.955796	61.364017	64.949247	68.719477
10	61.626780	65.831823	70.293361	75.025208	80.041825	85.358345	90.990599	96.955147	103.269302	109.951163
11	93.056437	100.064370	107.548842	115.538820	124.064829	133.159017	142.855240	153.189132	164.198191	175.921860
12	140.515220	152.097843	164.549728	177.929783	192.300484	207.728067	224.282728	242.038829	261.075123	281.474977
13	212.177982	231.188721	251.761084	274.011866	298.065751	324.055785	352.123882	382.421350	415.109446	450.359963
14	320.388753	351.406857	385.194459	421.978274	462.001914	505.527024	552.834495	604.225733	660.024019	720.575940
15	483.787017	534.138422	589.347523	649.846542	716.102966	788.622158	867.950157	954.676658	********	********
16	730.518396	811.890402	901.701710	********	********	********	********	********	********	********
17	********	********	********	********	********	********	********	********	********	********
18	********	********	********	********	********	********	********	********	********	********
19	********	********	********	********	********	********	********	********	********	********
20	********	********	********	********	********	********	********	********	********	********
21	********	********	********	********	********	********	********	********	********	********
22	********	********	********	********	********	********	********	********	********	********
23	********	********	********	********	********	********	********	********	********	********
24	********	********	********	********	********	********	********	********	********	********
25	********	********	********	********	********	********	********	********	********	********
26	********	********	********	********	********	********	********	********	********	********
27	********	********	********	********	********	********	********	********	********	********
28	********	********	********	********	********	********	********	********	********	********
29	********	********	********	********	********	********	********	********	********	********
30	********	********	********	********	********	********	********	********	********	********
31	********	********	********	********	********	********	********	********	********	********
32	********	********	********	********	********	********	********	********	********	********
33	********	********	********	********	********	********	********	********	********	********
34	********	********	********	********	********	********	********	********	********	********
35	********	********	********	********	********	********	********	********	********	********
36	********	********	********	********	********	********	********	********	********	********
37	********	********	********	********	********	********	********	********	********	********
38	********	********	********	********	********	********	********	********	********	********
39	********	********	********	********	********	********	********	********	********	********
40	********	********	********	********	********	********	********	********	********	********

Table A–2. Single Payment Present Worth Factor. To find P for a given F. $P = F(1 + i)^{-N}$

N \ i%	1	2	3	4	5	6	7	8	9	10
1	.990099	.980392	.970874	.961538	.952381	.943396	.934579	.925926	.917431	.909091
2	.980296	.961169	.942596	.924556	.907029	.889996	.873439	.857339	.841680	.826446
3	.970590	.942322	.915142	.888996	.863838	.839619	.816298	.793832	.772183	.751315
4	.960980	.923845	.888487	.854804	.822702	.792094	.762895	.735030	.708425	.683013
5	.951466	.905731	.862609	.821927	.783526	.747258	.712986	.680583	.649931	.620921
6	.942045	.887971	.837484	.790315	.746215	.704961	.666342	.630170	.596267	.564474
7	.932718	.870560	.813092	.759918	.710681	.665057	.622750	.583490	.547034	.513158
8	.923483	.853490	.789409	.730690	.676839	.627412	.582009	.540269	.501866	.466507
9	.914340	.836755	.766417	.702587	.644609	.591898	.543934	.500249	.460428	.424098
10	.905287	.820348	.744094	.675564	.613913	.558395	.508349	.463193	.422411	.385543
11	.896324	.804263	.722421	.649581	.584679	.526788	.475093	.428883	.387533	.350494
12	.887449	.788493	.701380	.624597	.556837	.496969	.444012	.397114	.355535	.318631
13	.878663	.773033	.680951	.600574	.530321	.468839	.414964	.367698	.326179	.289664
14	.869963	.757875	.661118	.577475	.505068	.442301	.387817	.340461	.299246	.263331
15	.861349	.743015	.641862	.555265	.481017	.417265	.362446	.315242	.274538	.239392
16	.852821	.728446	.623167	.533908	.458112	.393646	.338735	.291890	.251870	.217629
17	.844377	.714163	.605016	.513373	.436297	.371364	.316574	.270269	.231073	.197845
18	.836017	.700159	.587395	.493628	.415521	.350344	.295864	.250249	.211994	.179859
19	.827740	.686431	.570286	.474642	.395734	.330513	.276508	.231712	.194490	.163508
20	.819544	.672971	.553676	.456387	.376889	.311805	.258419	.214548	.178431	.148644
21	.811430	.659776	.537549	.438834	.358942	.294155	.241513	.198656	.163698	.135131
22	.803396	.646839	.521893	.421955	.341850	.277505	.225713	.183941	.150182	.122846
23	.795442	.634156	.506692	.405726	.325571	.261797	.210947	.170315	.137781	.111678
24	.787566	.621721	.491934	.390121	.310068	.246979	.197147	.157699	.126405	.101526
25	.779768	.609531	.477606	.375117	.295303	.232999	.184249	.146018	.115968	.092296
26	.772048	.597579	.463695	.360689	.281241	.219810	.172195	.135202	.106393	.083905
27	.764404	.585862	.450189	.346817	.267848	.207368	.160930	.125187	.097608	.076278
28	.756836	.574375	.437077	.333477	.255094	.195630	.150402	.115914	.089548	.069343
29	.749342	.563112	.424346	.320651	.242946	.184557	.140563	.107328	.082155	.063039
30	.741923	.552071	.411987	.308319	.231377	.174110	.131367	.099377	.075371	.057309
31	.734577	.541246	.399987	.296460	.220359	.164255	.122773	.092016	.069148	.052099
32	.727304	.530633	.388337	.285058	.209866	.154957	.114741	.085200	.063438	.047362
33	.720103	.520229	.377026	.274094	.199873	.146186	.107235	.078889	.058200	.043057
34	.712973	.510028	.366045	.263552	.190355	.137912	.100219	.073045	.053395	.039143
35	.705914	.500028	.355383	.253415	.181290	.130105	.093663	.067635	.048986	.035584
36	.698925	.490223	.345032	.243669	.172657	.122741	.087535	.062625	.044941	.032349
37	.692005	.480611	.334983	.234297	.164436	.115793	.081868	.057986	.041231	.029408
38	.685153	.471187	.325226	.225297	.156605	.109239	.076457	.053690	.037826	.026735
39	.678370	.461948	.315754	.216621	.149148	.103056	.071455	.049713	.034703	.024304
40	.671653	.452890	.306557	.208289	.142046	.097222	.066780	.046031	.031838	.022095

(Continued)

Table A–2. Single Payment Present Worth Factor. To find P for a given F. $P = F(1 + i)^{-N}$

i% N	1	2	3	4	5	6	7	8	9	10
41	.665003	.444010	.297628	.200278	.135282	.091719	.062412	.042621	.029209	.020086
42	.658419	.435304	.288959	.192575	.128840	.086527	.058329	.039464	.026797	.018260
43	.651900	.426769	.280543	.185168	.122704	.081630	.054513	.036545	.024584	.016600
44	.645445	.418401	.272372	.178046	.116861	.077009	.050946	.033834	.022555	.015091
45	.639055	.410197	.264439	.171198	.111297	.072650	.047613	.031328	.020692	.013719
46	.632728	.402154	.256737	.164614	.105997	.068538	.044499	.029007	.018984	.012472
47	.626463	.394268	.249259	.158283	.100949	.064658	.041587	.026859	.017416	.011338
48	.620260	.386538	.241999	.152195	.096142	.060998	.038867	.024869	.015978	.010307
49	.614119	.378958	.234950	.146341	.091564	.057546	.036324	.023027	.014659	.009370
50	.608039	.371528	.228107	.140713	.087204	.054288	.033948	.021321	.013449	.008519
51	.602019	.364243	.221463	.135301	.083051	.051215	.031727	.019742	.012338	.007744
52	.596058	.357101	.215013	.130097	.079096	.048316	.029651	.018280	.011319	.007040
53	.590156	.350099	.208750	.125093	.075330	.045582	.027711	.016925	.010385	.006400
54	.584313	.343234	.202670	.120282	.071743	.043001	.025899	.015672	.009527	.005818
55	.578528	.336504	.196767	.115656	.068326	.040567	.024204	.014511	.008741	.005289
56	.572800	.329906	.191036	.111207	.065073	.038271	.022621	.013436	.008019	.004809
57	.567129	.323437	.185472	.106930	.061974	.036105	.021141	.012441	.007357	.004371
58	.561514	.317095	.180070	.102817	.059023	.034061	.019758	.011519	.006749	.003974
59	.555954	.310878	.174825	.098863	.056212	.032133	.018465	.010666	.006192	.003613
60	.550450	.304782	.169733	.095060	.053536	.030314	.017257	.009876	.005681	.003284
61	.545000	.298806	.164789	.091404	.050986	.028598	.016128	.009144	.005212	.002986
62	.539604	.292947	.159990	.087889	.048558	.026980	.015073	.008467	.004781	.002714
63	.534261	.287203	.155330	.084508	.046246	.025453	.014087	.007840	.004387	.002468
64	.528971	.281572	.150806	.081258	.044044	.024012	.013166	.007259	.004024	.002243
65	.523734	.276051	.146413	.078133	.041946	.022653	.012304	.006721	.003692	.002039
66	.518548	.270638	.142149	.075128	.039949	.021370	.011499	.006223	.003387	.001854
67	.513414	.265331	.138000	.072238	.038047	.020161	.010747	.005762	.003108	.001685
68	.508331	.260129	.133989	.069460	.036235	.019020	.010044	.005336	.002851	.001532
69	.503298	.255028	.130086	.066788	.034509	.017943	.009387	.004940	.002616	.001393
70	.498315	.250028	.126297	.064219	.032866	.016927	.008773	.004574	.002400	.001266
71	.493381	.245125	.122619	.061749	.031301	.015969	.008199	.004236	.002201	.001151
72	.488496	.240319	.119047	.059374	.029811	.015065	.007662	.003922	.002020	.001046
73	.483659	.235607	.115580	.057091	.028391	.014213	.007161	.003631	.001853	.000951
74	.478871	.230987	.112214	.054895	.027039	.013408	.006693	.003362	.001700	.000865
75	.474129	.226458	.108945	.052784	.025752	.012649	.006255	.003113	.001560	.000786
76	.469435	.222017	.105772	.050754	.024525	.011933	.005846	.002883	.001431	.000715
77	.464787	.217664	.102691	.048801	.023357	.011258	.005463	.002669	.001313	.000650
78	.460185	.213396	.099700	.046924	.022245	.010620	.005106	.002471	.001204	.000591
79	.455629	.209212	.096796	.045120	.021186	.010019	.004772	.002288	.001105	.000537
80	.451118	.205110	.093977	.043384	.020177	.009452	.004460	.002119	.001014	.000488

(Continued)

Table A-2. Single Payment Present Worth Factor. To find P for a given F. $P = F(1+i)^{-N}$

$i\%$ / N	1	2	3	4	5	6	7	8	9	10
81	.446651	.201088	.091240	.041716	.019216	.008917	.004168	.001962	.000930	.000444
82	.442229	.197145	.088582	.041111	.018301	.008412	.003895	.001817	.000853	.000403
83	.437851	.193279	.086002	.038569	.017430	.007936	.003640	.001682	.000783	.000367
84	.433515	.189490	.083497	.037085	.016600	.007487	.003402	.001557	.000718	.000333
85	.429223	.185774	.081065	.035659	.015809	.007063	.003180	.001442	.000659	.000303
86	.424974	.182132	.078704	.034287	.015056	.006663	.002972	.001335	.000604	.000276
87	.420766	.178560	.076412	.032969	.014339	.006286	.002777	.001236	.000554	.000251
88	.416600	.175059	.074186	.031701	.013657	.005930	.002596	.001145	.000509	.000228
89	.412475	.171627	.072026	.030481	.013006	.005595	.002426	.001060	.000467	.000207
90	.408391	.168261	.069928	.029309	.012387	.005278	.002267	.000981	.000428	.000188
91	.404348	.164962	.067891	.028182	.011797	.004979	.002119	.000909	.000393	.000171
92	.400344	.161728	.065914	.027098	.011235	.004697	.001980	.000841	.000360	.000156
93	.396380	.158556	.063994	.026056	.010700	.004432	.001851	.000779	.000331	.000141
94	.392456	.155448	.062130	.025053	.010191	.004181	.001730	.000721	.000303	.000129
95	.388570	.152400	.060320	.024090	.009705	.003944	.001616	.000668	.000278	.000117
96	.384723	.149411	.058563	.023163	.009243	.003721	.001511	.000618	.000255	.000106
97	.380914	.146482	.056858	.022272	.008803	.003510	.001412	.000573	.000234	.000097
98	.377142	.143609	.055202	.021416	.008384	.003312	.001319	.000530	.000215	.000088
99	.373408	.140794	.053594	.020592	.007985	.003124	.001233	.000491	.000197	.000080
100	.369711	.138033	.052033	.019800	.007604	.002947	.001152	.000455	.000181	.000073
101	.366051	.135326	.050517	.019039	.007242	.002780	.001077	.000421	.000166	.000066
102	.362426	.132673	.049046	.018306	.006897	.002623	.001007	.000390	.000152	.000060
103	.358838	.130072	.047617	.017602	.006569	.002475	.000941	.000361	.000140	.000055
104	.355285	.127521	.046231	.016925	.006256	.002334	.000879	.000334	.000128	.000050
105	.351768	.125021	.044884	.016274	.005958	.002202	.000822	.000309	.000118	.000045
106	.348285	.122569	.043577	.015648	.005675	.002078	.000768	.000286	.000108	.000041
107	.344836	.120166	.042307	.015046	.005404	.001960	.000718	.000265	.000099	.000037
108	.341422	.117810	.041075	.014468	.005147	.001849	.000671	.000245	.000091	.000034
109	.338042	.115500	.039879	.013911	.004902	.001744	.000627	.000227	.000083	.000031
110	.334695	.113235	.038717	.013376	.004668	.001646	.000586	.000211	.000076	.000028
111	.331381	.111015	.037590	.012862	.004446	.001553	.000548	.000195	.000070	.000025
112	.328100	.108838	.036495	.012367	.004234	.001465	.000512	.000181	.000064	.000023
113	.324851	.106704	.035432	.011891	.004033	.001382	.000478	.000167	.000059	.000021
114	.321635	.104612	.034400	.011434	.003841	.001304	.000447	.000155	.000054	.000019
115	.318451	.102561	.033398	.010994	.003658	.001230	.000418	.000143	.000050	.000017
116	.315298	.100550	.032425	.010571	.003484	.001160	.000390	.000133	.000046	.000016
117	.312176	.098578	.031481	.010165	.003318	.001094	.000365	.000123	.000042	.000014
118	.309085	.096645	.030564	.009774	.003160	.001033	.000341	.000114	.000038	.000013
119	.306025	.094750	.029674	.009398	.003009	.000974	.000319	.000105	.000035	.000012
120	.302995	.092892	.028809	.009036	.002866	.000919	.000298	.000098	.000032	.000011

(Continued)

Table A-2. Single Payment Present Worth Factor. To find P for a given F. $P = F(1 + i)^{-N}$

$i\%$ N	11	12	13	14	15	16	17	18	19	20
1	.900901	.892857	.884956	.877193	.869565	.862069	.854701	.847458	.840336	.833333
2	.811622	.797194	.783147	.769468	.756144	.743163	.730514	.718184	.706165	.694444
3	.731191	.711780	.693050	.674972	.657516	.640658	.624371	.608631	.593416	.578704
4	.658731	.635518	.613319	.592080	.571753	.552291	.533650	.515789	.498669	.482253
5	.593451	.567427	.542760	.519369	.497177	.476113	.456111	.437109	.419049	.401878
6	.534641	.506631	.480319	.455587	.432328	.410442	.389839	.370432	.352142	.334898
7	.481658	.452349	.425061	.399637	.375937	.353830	.333195	.313925	.295918	.279082
8	.433926	.403883	.376160	.350559	.326902	.305025	.284782	.266038	.248671	.232568
9	.390925	.360610	.332885	.307508	.284262	.262953	.243404	.225456	.208967	.193807
10	.352184	.321973	.294588	.269744	.247185	.226684	.208037	.191064	.175602	.161506
11	.317283	.287476	.260698	.236617	.214943	.195417	.177810	.161919	.147565	.134588
12	.285841	.256675	.230706	.207559	.186907	.168463	.151974	.137220	.124004	.112157
13	.257514	.229174	.204165	.182803	.162528	.145227	.129892	.116288	.104205	.093464
14	.231995	.204620	.180677	.159710	.141329	.125195	.111019	.098549	.087567	.077887
15	.209004	.182696	.159891	.140096	.122894	.107927	.094888	.083516	.073586	.064905
16	.188292	.163122	.141496	.122892	.106865	.093041	.081101	.070776	.061837	.054088
17	.169633	.145644	.125218	.107800	.092926	.080207	.069317	.059980	.051964	.045073
18	.152822	.130040	.110812	.094561	.080805	.069144	.059245	.050830	.043667	.037561
19	.137678	.116107	.098064	.082948	.070265	.059607	.050637	.043077	.036695	.031301
20	.124034	.103667	.086782	.072762	.061100	.051385	.043280	.036506	.030836	.026084
21	.111742	.092560	.076798	.063826	.053131	.044298	.036991	.030937	.025913	.021737
22	.100669	.082643	.067963	.055988	.046201	.038188	.031616	.026218	.021775	.018114
23	.090693	.073788	.060144	.049112	.040174	.032920	.027022	.022218	.018299	.015095
24	.081705	.065882	.053225	.043081	.034934	.028380	.023096	.018829	.015377	.012579
25	.073608	.058823	.047102	.037790	.030378	.024465	.019740	.015957	.012922	.010483
26	.066314	.052521	.041683	.033149	.026415	.021091	.016872	.013523	.010859	.008735
27	.059742	.046894	.036888	.029078	.022970	.018182	.014421	.011460	.009125	.007280
28	.053822	.041869	.032644	.025507	.019974	.015674	.012325	.009712	.007668	.006066
29	.048488	.037383	.028889	.022375	.017369	.013512	.010534	.008230	.006444	.005055
30	.043683	.033378	.025565	.019627	.015103	.011648	.009004	.006975	.005415	.004213
31	.039354	.029802	.022624	.017217	.013133	.010042	.007696	.005911	.004550	.003511
32	.035454	.026609	.020021	.015102	.011420	.008657	.006577	.005009	.003824	.002926
33	.031940	.023758	.017718	.013248	.009931	.007463	.005622	.004245	.003213	.002438
34	.028775	.021212	.015680	.011621	.008635	.006433	.004805	.003598	.002700	.002032
35	.025924	.018940	.013876	.010194	.007509	.005546	.004107	.003049	.002269	.001693
36	.023355	.016910	.012279	.008942	.006529	.004781	.003510	.002584	.001907	.001411
37	.021040	.015098	.010867	.007844	.005678	.004121	.003000	.002190	.001602	.001175
38	.018955	.013481	.009617	.006880	.004937	.003553	.002564	.001856	.001347	.000980
39	.017077	.012036	.008510	.006035	.004293	.003063	.002192	.001573	.001132	.000816
40	.015384	.010747	.007531	.005294	.003733	.002640	.001873	.001333	.000951	.000680

(Continued)

Table A-2. Single Payment Present Worth Factor. To find P for a given F. $P = F(1 + i)^{-N}$

$i\%$ / N	11	12	13	14	15	16	17	18	19	20
41	.013860	.009995	.006665	.004644	.003246	.002276	.001601	.001129	.000799	.000567
42	.012486	.008567	.005898	.004074	.002823	.001962	.001368	.000957	.000671	.000472
43	.011249	.007649	.005219	.003573	.002455	.001692	.001170	.000811	.000564	.000394
44	.010134	.006830	.004619	.003135	.002134	.001458	.001000	.000687	.000474	.000328
45	.009130	.006098	.004088	.002750	.001856	.001257	.000854	.000583	.000398	.000273
46	.008225	.005445	.003617	.002412	.001614	.001084	.000730	.000494	.000335	.000228
47	.007410	.004861	.003201	.002116	.001403	.000934	.000624	.000418	.000281	.000190
48	.006676	.004340	.002833	.001856	.001220	.000805	.000533	.000355	.000236	.000158
49	.006014	.003875	.002507	.001628	.001061	.000694	.000456	.000300	.000199	.000132
50	.005418	.003460	.002219	.001428	.000923	.000599	.000390	.000255	.000167	.000110
51	.004881	.003089	.001963	.001253	.000802	.000516	.000333	.000216	.000140	.000092
52	.004397	.002758	.001737	.001099	.000698	.000445	.000285	.000183	.000118	.000076
53	.003962	.002463	.001538	.000964	.000607	.000383	.000243	.000155	.000099	.000064
54	.003569	.002199	.001361	.000846	.000528	.000331	.000208	.000131	.000083	.000053
55	.003215	.001963	.001204	.000742	.000459	.000285	.000178	.000111	.000070	.000044
56	.002897	.001753	.001066	.000651	.000399	.000246	.000152	.000094	.000059	.000037
57	.002610	.001565	.000943	.000571	.000347	.000212	.000130	.000080	.000049	.000031
58	.002351	.001398	.000835	.000501	.000302	.000183	.000111	.000068	.000042	.000026
59	.002118	.001248	.000739	.000439	.000262	.000157	.000095	.000057	.000035	.000021
60	.001908	.001114	.000654	.000385	.000228	.000136	.000081	.000049	.000029	.000018
61	.001719	.000995	.000578	.000338	.000198	.000117	.000069	.000041	.000025	.000015
62	.001549	.000888	.000512	.000296	.000172	.000101	.000059	.000035	.000021	.000012
63	.001395	.000793	.000453	.000260	.000150	.000087	.000051	.000030	.000017	.000010
64	.001257	.000708	.000401	.000228	.000130	.000075	.000043	.000025	.000015	.000009
65	.001132	.000632	.000355	.000200	.000113	.000065	.000037	.000021	.000012	.000007
66	.001020	.000564	.000314	.000176	.000099	.000056	.000032	.000018	.000010	.000006
67	.000919	.000504	.000278	.000154	.000086	.000048	.000027	.000015	.000009	.000005
68	.000828	.000450	.000246	.000135	.000075	.000041	.000023	.000013	.000007	.000004
69	.000746	.000402	.000218	.000118	.000065	.000036	.000020	.000011	.000006	.000003
70	.000672	.000359	.000193	.000104	.000056	.000031	.000017	.000009	.000005	.000003
71	.000605	.000320	.000170	.000091	.000049	.000027	.000014	.000008	.000004	.000002
72	.000545	.000286	.000151	.000080	.000043	.000023	.000012	.000007	.000004	.000002
73	.000491	.000255	.000133	.000070	.000037	.000020	.000011	.000006	.000003	.000002
74	.000443	.000228	.000118	.000062	.000032	.000017	.000009	.000005	.000003	.000001
75	.000399	.000204	.000105	.000054	.000028	.000015	.000008	.000004	.000002	.000001
76	.000359	.000182	.000092	.000047	.000024	.000013	.000007	.000003	.000002	.000001
77	.000324	.000162	.000082	.000042	.000021	.000011	.000005	.000003	.000002	.000001
78	.000292	.000145	.000072	.000036	.000018	.000009	.000005	.000002	.000001	.000001
79	.000263	.000129	.000064	.000032	.000016	.000008	.000004	.000002	.000001	.000001
80	.000237	.000115	.000057	.000028	.000014	.000007	.000004	.000002	.000001	.000000

(Continued)

Table A–2. Single Payment Present Worth Factor. To find P for a given F. $P = F(1 + i)^{-N}$

i% / N	21	22	23	24	25	26	27	28	29	30
1	.826446	.819672	.813008	.806452	.800000	.793651	.787402	.781250	.775194	.769231
2	.683013	.671862	.660982	.650364	.640000	.629882	.620001	.610352	.600925	.591716
3	.564474	.550707	.537384	.524487	.512000	.499906	.488190	.476837	.465834	.455166
4	.466507	.451399	.436897	.422974	.409600	.396751	.384402	.372529	.361111	.350128
5	.385543	.369999	.355201	.341108	.327680	.314882	.302678	.291038	.279931	.269329
6	.318631	.303278	.288781	.275087	.262144	.249906	.238329	.227374	.217001	.207176
7	.263331	.248589	.234782	.221844	.209715	.198338	.187661	.177636	.168218	.159366
8	.217629	.203761	.190879	.178907	.167772	.157411	.147765	.138778	.130401	.122589
9	.179859	.167017	.155187	.144280	.134218	.124930	.116350	.108420	.101086	.094300
10	.148644	.136899	.126168	.116354	.107374	.099150	.091614	.084703	.078362	.072538
11	.122846	.112213	.102576	.093834	.085899	.078691	.072137	.066174	.060745	.055799
12	.101526	.091978	.083395	.075673	.068719	.062453	.056801	.051699	.047089	.042922
13	.083905	.075391	.067801	.061026	.054976	.049566	.044725	.040390	.036503	.033017
14	.069343	.061796	.055122	.049215	.043980	.039338	.035217	.031554	.028297	.025398
15	.057309	.050653	.044815	.039689	.035184	.031221	.027730	.024652	.021936	.019537
16	.047362	.041519	.036435	.032008	.028147	.024778	.021834	.019259	.017005	.015028
17	.039143	.034032	.029622	.025813	.022518	.019665	.017192	.015046	.013182	.011560
18	.032349	.027895	.024083	.020817	.018014	.015607	.013537	.011755	.010218	.008892
19	.026735	.022865	.019580	.016788	.014412	.012387	.010659	.009184	.007921	.006840
20	.022095	.018741	.015918	.013538	.011529	.009831	.008393	.007175	.006393	.005262
21	.018260	.015362	.012942	.010918	.009223	.007802	.006609	.005605	.004760	.004048
22	.015091	.012592	.010522	.008805	.007379	.006192	.005204	.004379	.003690	.003113
23	.012472	.010321	.008554	.007101	.005903	.004914	.004097	.003421	.002860	.002395
24	.010307	.008460	.006955	.005726	.004722	.003900	.003226	.002673	.002217	.001842
25	.008519	.006934	.005654	.004618	.003778	.003096	.002540	.002088	.001719	.001417
26	.007040	.005684	.004597	.003724	.003022	.002457	.002000	.001631	.001333	.001090
27	.005818	.004659	.003737	.003003	.002418	.001950	.001575	.001274	.001033	.000839
28	.004839	.003819	.003038	.002422	.001934	.001547	.001240	.000996	.000801	.000645
29	.003974	.003130	.002470	.001953	.001547	.001238	.000977	.000778	.000621	.000496
30	.003284	.002566	.002008	.001575	.001238	.000975	.000769	.000608	.000481	.000382
31	.002714	.002103	.001633	.001270	.000990	.000774	.000605	.000475	.000373	.000294
32	.002243	.001724	.001328	.001024	.000792	.000614	.000477	.000371	.000289	.000226
33	.001854	.001413	.001079	.000826	.000634	.000487	.000375	.000290	.000224	.000174
34	.001532	.001158	.000877	.000666	.000507	.000387	.000296	.000226	.000174	.000134
35	.001266	.000949	.000713	.000537	.000406	.000307	.000233	.000177	.000135	.000103
36	.001046	.000778	.000580	.000433	.000325	.000244	.000183	.000138	.000104	.000079
37	.000865	.000638	.000472	.000349	.000260	.000193	.000144	.000108	.000081	.000061
38	.000715	.000523	.000383	.000282	.000208	.000153	.000114	.000084	.000063	.000047
39	.000591	.000429	.000312	.000227	.000166	.000122	.000089	.000066	.000049	.000036
40	.000488	.000351	.000253	.000183	.000133	.000097	.000070	.000051	.000038	.000028

(Continued)

Table A–2. Single Payment Present Worth Factor. To find P for a given F. $P = F(1 + i)^{-N}$

$i\%$ / N	31	32	33	34	35	36	37	38	39	40
1	.763359	.757576	.751880	.746269	.740741	.735294	.729927	.724638	.719424	.714286
2	.582717	.573921	.565323	.556917	.548697	.540657	.532793	.525100	.517572	.510204
3	.444822	.434789	.425055	.415610	.406442	.397542	.388900	.380507	.372354	.364431
4	.339540	.329385	.319590	.310156	.301068	.292310	.283869	.275730	.267880	.260308
5	.259205	.249534	.240293	.231460	.223014	.214934	.207204	.199804	.192720	.185934
6	.197866	.189041	.180672	.172731	.165195	.158040	.151243	.144786	.138647	.132810
7	.151043	.143213	.135843	.128904	.122367	.116206	.110397	.104917	.099746	.094865
8	.115300	.108495	.102138	.096197	.090642	.085445	.080582	.076027	.071760	.067760
9	.088015	.082193	.076795	.071789	.067142	.062828	.058819	.055092	.051626	.048400
10	.067187	.062267	.057741	.053574	.049735	.046197	.042933	.039922	.037141	.034572
11	.051288	.047172	.043414	.039980	.036841	.033968	.031338	.028929	.026720	.024694
12	.039151	.035737	.032642	.029836	.027289	.024977	.022875	.020963	.019223	.017639
13	.029886	.027073	.024543	.022266	.020214	.018365	.016697	.015190	.013830	.012599
14	.022814	.020510	.018453	.016616	.014974	.013504	.012187	.011008	.009949	.008999
15	.017415	.015538	.013875	.012400	.011092	.009929	.008896	.007977	.007158	.006428
16	.013294	.011771	.010432	.009254	.008216	.007301	.006493	.005780	.005149	.004591
17	.010148	.008918	.007844	.006906	.006086	.005368	.004740	.004188	.003705	.003280
18	.007747	.006756	.005898	.005154	.004508	.003947	.003460	.003035	.002665	.002343
19	.005914	.005118	.004434	.003856	.003339	.002902	.002525	.002199	.001917	.001673
20	.004514	.003877	.003334	.002870	.002474	.002134	.001843	.001594	.001379	.001195
21	.003446	.002937	.002507	.002142	.001832	.001569	.001345	.001155	.000992	.000854
22	.002630	.002225	.001885	.001598	.001357	.001154	.000982	.000837	.000714	.000610
23	.002008	.001686	.001417	.001193	.001005	.000848	.000717	.000606	.000514	.000436
24	.001533	.001277	.001066	.000890	.000745	.000624	.000523	.000439	.000370	.000311
25	.001170	.000968	.000801	.000664	.000552	.000459	.000382	.000318	.000266	.000222
26	.000893	.000733	.000602	.000496	.000409	.000337	.000279	.000231	.000191	.000159
27	.000682	.000555	.000453	.000370	.000303	.000248	.000203	.000167	.000138	.000113
28	.000520	.000421	.000341	.000276	.000224	.000182	.000149	.000121	.000099	.000081
29	.000397	.000319	.000256	.000206	.000166	.000134	.000108	.000088	.000071	.000058
30	.000303	.000241	.000193	.000154	.000123	.000099	.000079	.000064	.000051	.000041
31	.000232	.000183	.000145	.000115	.000091	.000072	.000058	.000046	.000037	.000030
32	.000177	.000139	.000109	.000086	.000068	.000053	.000042	.000033	.000027	.000021
33	.000135	.000105	.000082	.000064	.000050	.000039	.000031	.000024	.000019	.000015
34	.000103	.000080	.000062	.000048	.000037	.000029	.000022	.000018	.000014	.000011
35	.000079	.000060	.000046	.000036	.000027	.000021	.000016	.000013	.000010	.000008
36	.000060	.000046	.000035	.000027	.000020	.000016	.000012	.000009	.000007	.000005
37	.000046	.000035	.000026	.000020	.000015	.000011	.000009	.000007	.000005	.000004
38	.000035	.000026	.000020	.000015	.000011	.000008	.000006	.000005	.000004	.000003
39	.000027	.000020	.000015	.000011	.000008	.000006	.000005	.000004	.000003	.000002
40	.000020	.000015	.000011	.000008	.000006	.000005	.000003	.000003	.000002	.000001

(Continued)

Table A-2. Single Payment Present Worth Factor. To find P for a given F. $P = F(1 + i)^{-N}$

$i\%$ / N	41	42	43	44	45	46	47	48	49	50
1	.709220	.704225	.699301	.694444	.689655	.684932	.680272	.675676	.671141	.666667
2	.502993	.495933	.489021	.482253	.475624	.469131	.462770	.456538	.450430	.444444
3	.356732	.349249	.341973	.334898	.328017	.321323	.314810	.308471	.302302	.296296
4	.253000	.245950	.239142	.232568	.226218	.220084	.214156	.208427	.202887	.197531
5	.179434	.173204	.167232	.161506	.156013	.150743	.145684	.140829	.136166	.131687
6	.127258	.121975	.116946	.112157	.107595	.103248	.099105	.095155	.091387	.087791
7	.090254	.085898	.081781	.077887	.074201	.070718	.067418	.064294	.061333	.058528
8	.064010	.060491	.057189	.054088	.051175	.048437	.045863	.043442	.041163	.039018
9	.045397	.042600	.039992	.037561	.035293	.033176	.031199	.029352	.027626	.026012
10	.032197	.030000	.027967	.026084	.024340	.022723	.021224	.019833	.018541	.017342
11	.022834	.021127	.019557	.018114	.016786	.015564	.014438	.013401	.012444	.011561
12	.016195	.014878	.013676	.012579	.011577	.010660	.009822	.009054	.008352	.007707
13	.011486	.010477	.009564	.008735	.007984	.007302	.006682	.006118	.005605	.005138
14	.008146	.007378	.006688	.006066	.005506	.005001	.004545	.004134	.003762	.003425
15	.005777	.005196	.004677	.004213	.003797	.003425	.003092	.002793	.002525	.002284
16	.004097	.003659	.003271	.002926	.002619	.002346	.002103	.001887	.001694	.001522
17	.002906	.002577	.002287	.002032	.001806	.001607	.001431	.001275	.001137	.001015
18	.002061	.001815	.001599	.001411	.001246	.001101	.000973	.000862	.000763	.000677
19	.001462	.001278	.001118	.000980	.000860	.000754	.000662	.000582	.000512	.000451
20	.001037	.000900	.000782	.000680	.000592	.000516	.000450	.000393	.000344	.000301
21	.000735	.000634	.000547	.000472	.000409	.000354	.000306	.000266	.000231	.000200
22	.000521	.000446	.000382	.000328	.000282	.000242	.000208	.000180	.000155	.000134
23	.000370	.000314	.000267	.000228	.000194	.000166	.000142	.000121	.000104	.000089
24	.000262	.000221	.000187	.000158	.000134	.000114	.000096	.000082	.000070	.000059
25	.000186	.000156	.000131	.000110	.000092	.000078	.000066	.000055	.000047	.000040
26	.000132	.000110	.000091	.000076	.000064	.000053	.000045	.000037	.000031	.000026
27	.000094	.000077	.000064	.000053	.000044	.000037	.000030	.000025	.000021	.000018
28	.000066	.000054	.000045	.000037	.000030	.000025	.000021	.000017	.000014	.000012
29	.000047	.000038	.000031	.000026	.000021	.000017	.000014	.000012	.000009	.000008
30	.000033	.000027	.000022	.000018	.000014	.000012	.000010	.000008	.000006	.000005
31	.000024	.000019	.000015	.000012	.000010	.000008	.000007	.000005	.000004	.000003
32	.000017	.000013	.000011	.000009	.000007	.000006	.000004	.000004	.000003	.000002
33	.000012	.000009	.000007	.000006	.000005	.000004	.000003	.000002	.000002	.000002
34	.000008	.000007	.000005	.000004	.000003	.000003	.000002	.000001	.000001	.000001
35	.000006	.000005	.000004	.000003	.000002	.000002	.000001	.000001	.000001	.000001
36	.000004	.000003	.000003	.000002	.000002	.000001	.000001	.000001	.000001	.000000
37	.000003	.000002	.000002	.000002	.000001	.000001	.000001	.000001	.000000	.000000
38	.000002	.000002	.000001	.000001	.000001	.000001	.000000	.000000	.000000	.000000
39	.000002	.000001	.000001	.000001	.000001	.000000	.000000	.000000	.000000	.000000
40	.000001	.000001	.000001	.000000	.000000	.000000	.000000	.000000	.000000	.000000

(Continued)

Table A-2. Single Payment Present Worth Factor. To find P for a given F. $P = F(1 + i)^{-N}$

$i\%$ / N	51	52	53	54	55	56	57	58	59	60
1	.662252	.657895	.653595	.649351	.645161	.641026	.636943	.632911	.628931	.625000
2	.438577	.432825	.427186	.421656	.416233	.410914	.405696	.400577	.395554	.390625
3	.290449	.284754	.279207	.273803	.268537	.263406	.258405	.253530	.248776	.244141
4	.192350	.187338	.182488	.177794	.173250	.168850	.164589	.160462	.156463	.152588
5	.127384	.123249	.119273	.115451	.111774	.108237	.104834	.101558	.098404	.095367
6	.084360	.081085	.077956	.074968	.072112	.069383	.066773	.064277	.061890	.059605
7	.055868	.053345	.050952	.048680	.046524	.044476	.042531	.040682	.038924	.037253
8	.036999	.035095	.033302	.031611	.030016	.028510	.027090	.025748	.024481	.023283
9	.024502	.023089	.021766	.020526	.019365	.018276	.017255	.016296	.015397	.014552
10	.016227	.015190	.014226	.013329	.012493	.011715	.010990	.010314	.009683	.009095
11	.010746	.009994	.009298	.008655	.008060	.007510	.007000	.006528	.006090	.005684
12	.007117	.006575	.006077	.005620	.005200	.004814	.004459	.004132	.003830	.003553
13	.004713	.004325	.003972	.003649	.003355	.003086	.002840	.002615	.002409	.002220
14	.003121	.002846	.002596	.002370	.002164	.001978	.001809	.001655	.001515	.001388
15	.002067	.001872	.001697	.001539	.001396	.001268	.001152	.001047	.000953	.000867
16	.001369	.001232	.001109	.000999	.000901	.000813	.000734	.000663	.000599	.000542
17	.000907	.000810	.000725	.000649	.000581	.000521	.000467	.000420	.000377	.000339
18	.000600	.000533	.000474	.000421	.000375	.000334	.000298	.000266	.000237	.000212
19	.000398	.000351	.000310	.000274	.000242	.000214	.000190	.000168	.000149	.000132
20	.000263	.000231	.000202	.000178	.000156	.000137	.000121	.000106	.000094	.000083
21	.000174	.000152	.000132	.000115	.000101	.000088	.000077	.000067	.000059	.000052
22	.000115	.000100	.000086	.000075	.000065	.000056	.000049	.000043	.000037	.000032
23	.000076	.000066	.000057	.000049	.000042	.000036	.000031	.000027	.000023	.000020
24	.000051	.000043	.000037	.000032	.000027	.000023	.000020	.000017	.000015	.000013
25	.000034	.000028	.000024	.000021	.000017	.000015	.000013	.000011	.000009	.000008
26	.000022	.000019	.000016	.000013	.000011	.000010	.000008	.000007	.000006	.000005
27	.000015	.000012	.000010	.000009	.000007	.000006	.000005	.000004	.000004	.000003
28	.000010	.000008	.000007	.000006	.000005	.000004	.000003	.000003	.000002	.000002
29	.000006	.000005	.000004	.000004	.000003	.000003	.000002	.000002	.000001	.000001
30	.000004	.000004	.000003	.000002	.000002	.000002	.000001	.000001	.000001	.000001
31	.000003	.000002	.000002	.000002	.000001	.000001	.000001	.000001	.000001	.000001
32	.000002	.000002	.000001	.000001	.000001	.000001	.000000	.000000	.000000	.000000
33	.000001	.000001	.000001	.000001	.000000	.000000	.000000	.000000	.000000	.000000
34	.000001	.000001	.000000	.000000	.000000	.000000	.000000	.000000	.000000	.000000
35	.000001	.000000	.000000	.000000	.000000	.000000	.000000	.000000	.000000	.000000
36	.000000	.000000	.000000	.000000	.000000	.000000	.000000	.000000	.000000	.000000
37	.000000	.000000	.000000	.000000	.000000	.000000	.000000	.000000	.000000	.000000
38	.000000	.000000	.000000	.000000	.000000	.000000	.000000	.000000	.000000	.000000
39	.000000	.000000	.000000	.000000	.000000	.000000	.000000	.000000	.000000	.000000
40	.000000	.000000	.000000	.000000	.000000	.000000	.000000	.000000	.000000	.000000

Table A-3. Ordinary Annuity Compound Amount Factor. To find F for a given R received at the end of each period. $F = R \dfrac{(1+i)^N - 1}{i}$

N \ i%	1	2	3	4	5	6	7	8	9	10
1	1.000000	1.000000	1.000000	1.000000	1.000000	1.000000	1.000000	1.000000	1.000000	1.000000
2	2.010000	2.020000	2.030000	2.040000	2.050000	2.060000	2.070000	2.080000	2.090000	2.100000
3	3.030100	3.060400	3.090900	3.121600	3.152500	3.183600	3.214900	3.246400	3.278100	3.310000
4	4.060401	4.121608	4.183627	4.246464	4.310125	4.374616	4.439943	4.506112	4.573129	4.641000
5	5.101005	5.204040	5.309136	5.416323	5.525631	5.637093	5.750739	5.866601	5.984711	6.105100
6	6.152015	6.308121	6.468410	6.632975	6.801913	6.975319	7.153291	7.335929	7.523335	7.715610
7	7.213535	7.434283	7.662462	7.898294	8.142008	8.393838	8.654021	8.922803	9.200435	9.487171
8	8.285671	8.582969	8.892336	9.214226	9.549109	9.897464	10.259803	10.636628	11.028474	11.435888
9	9.368527	9.754628	10.159106	10.582795	11.026564	11.491316	11.977989	12.487558	13.021036	13.579477
10	10.462213	10.949721	11.463879	12.006107	12.577893	13.180795	13.816448	14.486562	15.192930	15.937425
11	11.566835	12.168715	12.807796	13.486351	14.206787	14.971643	15.783599	16.645487	17.560293	18.531167
12	12.682503	13.412090	14.192030	15.025805	15.917127	16.869941	17.888451	18.977126	20.140720	21.384284
13	13.809328	14.680332	15.617790	16.626838	17.712983	18.882138	20.140643	21.495297	22.953385	24.522712
14	14.947421	15.973938	17.086324	18.291911	19.598632	21.015066	22.550488	24.214920	26.019189	27.974983
15	16.096896	17.293417	18.598914	20.023588	21.578564	23.275970	25.129022	27.152114	29.360916	31.772482
16	17.257864	18.639285	20.156881	21.824531	23.657492	25.672528	27.888054	30.324283	33.003399	35.949730
17	18.430443	20.012071	21.761588	23.697512	25.840366	28.212880	30.840217	33.750226	36.973705	40.544703
18	19.614748	21.412312	23.414435	25.645413	28.132385	30.905653	33.999033	37.450244	41.301338	45.599173
19	20.810895	22.840559	25.116868	27.671229	30.539004	33.759992	37.378965	41.446263	46.018458	51.159090
20	22.019004	24.297370	26.870374	29.778079	33.065954	36.785591	40.995492	45.761964	51.160120	57.274999
21	23.239194	25.783317	28.676486	31.969202	35.719252	39.992727	44.865177	50.422921	56.764530	64.002499
22	24.471586	27.298984	30.536780	34.247970	38.505214	43.392290	49.005739	55.456755	62.873338	71.402749
23	25.716302	28.844963	32.452884	36.617889	41.430475	46.995828	53.436141	60.893296	69.531939	79.543024
24	26.973465	30.421862	34.426470	39.082604	44.501999	50.815577	58.176671	66.764759	76.789813	88.497327
25	28.243200	32.030300	36.459264	41.645908	47.727099	54.864512	63.249038	73.105940	84.700896	98.347059
26	29.525631	33.670906	38.553042	44.311745	51.113454	59.156383	68.676470	79.954415	93.323977	109.181765
27	30.820888	35.344324	40.709634	47.084214	54.669126	63.705766	74.483823	87.350768	102.723135	121.099942
28	32.129097	37.051210	42.930923	49.967583	58.402583	68.528112	80.697691	95.338830	112.968217	134.209936
29	33.450388	38.792235	45.218850	52.966286	62.322712	73.639798	87.346529	103.965936	124.135356	148.630930
30	34.784892	40.568079	47.575416	56.084938	66.438848	79.058186	94.460786	113.283211	136.307539	164.494023
31	36.132740	42.379441	50.002678	59.328335	70.760790	84.801677	102.073041	123.345868	149.575217	181.943425
32	37.494068	44.227030	52.502759	62.701841	75.298829	90.889778	110.218154	134.213537	164.036987	201.137767
33	38.869009	46.111570	55.077841	66.209527	80.063771	97.343165	118.933425	145.950620	179.800315	222.251544
34	40.257699	48.033802	57.730177	69.857909	85.066959	104.183755	128.258765	158.626670	196.982344	245.476699
35	41.660276	49.994478	60.462082	73.652225	90.320307	111.434780	138.236878	172.316804	215.710755	271.024368
36	43.076878	51.994367	63.275944	77.598314	95.836323	119.120867	148.913460	187.102148	236.124723	299.126805
37	44.507647	54.034255	66.174223	81.702246	101.628139	127.268119	160.337402	203.070320	258.375948	330.039486
38	45.952724	56.114940	69.159449	85.970336	107.709546	135.904206	172.561020	220.315465	282.629783	364.043434
39	47.412251	58.237238	72.234233	90.409150	114.095023	145.058458	185.640292	238.941221	309.066463	401.447778
40	48.886373	60.401983	75.401260	95.025516	120.799774	154.761966	199.635112	259.056519	337.882445	442.592556

(Continued)

Table A-3. Ordinary Annuity Compound Amount Factor. To find F for a given R received at the end of each period. $F = R\dfrac{(1+i)^N - 1}{i}$

$i\%$ / N	1	2	3	4	5	6	7	8	9	10
41	50.375237	62.610023	78.663298	99.826536	127.839763	165.047684	214.609570	280.781040	369.291865	487.851811
42	51.878989	64.862223	82.023196	104.819598	135.231751	175.950545	230.632240	304.243523	403.528133	537.636992
43	53.397779	67.159468	85.483982	110.012382	142.993339	187.507577	247.776496	329.583005	440.845665	592.400692
44	54.931757	69.502657	89.048409	115.412877	151.143006	199.758032	266.120851	356.949646	481.521775	652.640761
45	56.481075	71.892710	92.719861	121.023392	159.700156	212.743514	285.749311	386.505617	525.858734	718.904837
46	58.045885	74.330564	96.501457	126.870568	168.685164	226.508125	306.751763	418.426067	574.186021	791.795321
47	59.626344	76.817176	100.396501	132.945390	178.119422	241.098612	329.224386	452.900152	626.862762	871.974853
48	61.222608	79.353519	104.408396	139.263206	188.025393	256.564529	353.270093	490.132164	684.280411	960.172338
49	62.834834	81.940590	108.540648	145.833734	198.426663	272.958401	378.999000	530.342737	746.865648	**********
50	64.463182	84.579401	112.796867	152.667084	209.347996	290.335905	406.528929	573.770156	815.083556	**********
51	66.107814	87.270989	117.180773	159.773767	220.815396	308.756059	435.985955	620.671769	889.441076	**********
52	67.768892	90.016409	121.696197	167.164718	232.856165	328.281422	467.504971	671.325510	970.490773	**********
53	69.446581	92.816737	126.347082	174.851306	245.499874	348.978308	501.230319	726.031551	**********	**********
54	71.141047	95.673072	131.137495	182.845359	258.773922	370.917006	537.316442	785.114075	**********	**********
55	72.852457	98.586534	136.071620	191.159173	272.712618	394.172027	575.928593	848.923201	**********	**********
56	74.580982	101.558264	141.153768	199.805540	287.348249	418.822348	617.243594	917.837058	**********	**********
57	76.326792	104.589430	146.388381	208.797762	302.715662	444.951689	661.450646	992.264022	**********	**********
58	78.090060	107.681218	151.780033	218.149672	318.851445	472.648790	708.752191	**********	**********	**********
59	79.870960	110.834843	157.333434	227.875659	335.794017	502.007718	759.364844	**********	**********	**********
60	81.669670	114.051539	163.053437	237.990685	353.583718	533.128181	813.520383	**********	**********	**********
61	83.486367	117.332570	168.945040	248.510313	372.262904	566.115872	871.466810	**********	**********	**********
62	85.321230	120.679222	175.013391	259.450725	391.876049	601.082824	933.469487	**********	**********	**********
63	87.174443	124.092806	181.263793	270.828754	412.469851	638.147793	999.812351	**********	**********	**********
64	89.046187	127.574662	187.701707	282.661900	434.093344	677.436661	**********	**********	**********	**********
65	90.936649	131.126155	194.332758	294.968380	456.798011	719.082861	**********	**********	**********	**********
66	92.846015	134.748679	201.162741	307.767116	480.637912	763.227832	**********	**********	**********	**********
67	94.774475	138.443652	208.197623	321.077800	505.669807	810.021502	**********	**********	**********	**********
68	96.722220	142.212525	215.443551	334.920912	531.953298	859.622792	**********	**********	**********	**********
69	98.689442	146.056776	222.906858	349.317749	559.550963	912.200160	**********	**********	**********	**********
70	100.676337	149.977911	230.594064	364.290459	588.528511	967.932170	**********	**********	**********	**********
71	102.683100	153.977469	238.511886	379.862077	618.954936	**********	**********	**********	**********	**********
72	104.709931	158.057019	246.667242	396.056560	650.902683	**********	**********	**********	**********	**********
73	106.757031	162.218159	255.067259	412.898823	684.447817	**********	**********	**********	**********	**********
74	108.824601	166.462522	263.719277	430.414776	719.670208	**********	**********	**********	**********	**********
75	110.912847	170.791773	272.630856	449.631367	756.653718	**********	**********	**********	**********	**********
76	113.021975	175.207608	281.809781	467.576621	795.486404	**********	**********	**********	**********	**********
77	115.152195	179.711760	291.264075	487.279686	836.260725	**********	**********	**********	**********	**********
78	117.303717	184.305996	301.001997	507.770873	879.073761	**********	**********	**********	**********	**********
79	119.476754	188.992115	311.032057	529.081708	924.027449	**********	**********	**********	**********	**********
80	121.671522	193.771958	321.363019	551.244977	971.228821	**********	**********	**********	**********	**********

(Continued)

Table A–3. Ordinary Annuity Compound Amount Factor. To find F for a given R received at the end of each period. $F = R \dfrac{(1+i)^N - 1}{i}$

$i\%$ / N	1	2	3	4	5	6	7	8	9	10
81	123.888237	198.647397	332.003909	574.294776	**********	**********	**********	**********	**********	**********
82	126.127119	203.620345	342.964026	598.266567	**********	**********	**********	**********	**********	**********
83	128.388390	208.692752	354.252947	623.197230	**********	**********	**********	**********	**********	**********
84	130.672274	213.866607	365.880536	649.125119	**********	**********	**********	**********	**********	**********
85	132.978997	219.143939	377.856952	676.090123	**********	**********	**********	**********	**********	**********
86	135.308787	224.526818	390.192660	704.133728	**********	**********	**********	**********	**********	**********
87	137.661875	230.017354	402.898440	733.299078	**********	**********	**********	**********	**********	**********
88	140.038494	235.617701	415.985393	763.631041	**********	**********	**********	**********	**********	**********
89	142.438879	241.330055	429.464955	795.176282	**********	**********	**********	**********	**********	**********
90	144.863267	247.156656	443.348904	827.983334	**********	**********	**********	**********	**********	**********
91	147.311900	253.099789	457.649371	862.102667	**********	**********	**********	**********	**********	**********
92	149.785019	259.161785	472.378852	897.586774	**********	**********	**********	**********	**********	**********
93	152.282869	265.345021	487.550217	934.490245	**********	**********	**********	**********	**********	**********
94	154.805698	271.651921	503.176724	972.869854	**********	**********	**********	**********	**********	**********
95	157.353755	278.084960	519.272026	**********	**********	**********	**********	**********	**********	**********
96	159.927293	284.646659	535.850186	**********	**********	**********	**********	**********	**********	**********
97	162.526565	291.339592	552.925692	**********	**********	**********	**********	**********	**********	**********
98	165.151831	298.166384	570.513463	**********	**********	**********	**********	**********	**********	**********
99	167.803349	305.129712	588.628867	**********	**********	**********	**********	**********	**********	**********
100	170.481383	312.232306	607.287733	**********	**********	**********	**********	**********	**********	**********
101	173.186197	319.476952	626.506365	**********	**********	**********	**********	**********	**********	**********
102	175.918059	326.866491	646.301556	**********	**********	**********	**********	**********	**********	**********
103	178.677239	334.403821	666.690602	**********	**********	**********	**********	**********	**********	**********
104	181.464012	342.091897	687.691320	**********	**********	**********	**********	**********	**********	**********
105	184.278652	349.933735	709.322060	**********	**********	**********	**********	**********	**********	**********
106	187.121438	357.932410	731.601722	**********	**********	**********	**********	**********	**********	**********
107	189.992653	366.091058	754.549773	**********	**********	**********	**********	**********	**********	**********
108	192.892579	374.412879	778.186267	**********	**********	**********	**********	**********	**********	**********
109	195.821505	382.901137	802.531855	**********	**********	**********	**********	**********	**********	**********
110	198.779720	391.559160	827.607810	**********	**********	**********	**********	**********	**********	**********
111	201.767517	400.390343	853.436045	**********	**********	**********	**********	**********	**********	**********
112	204.785192	409.398150	880.039126	**********	**********	**********	**********	**********	**********	**********
113	207.833044	418.586113	907.440300	**********	**********	**********	**********	**********	**********	**********
114	210.911375	427.957835	935.663509	**********	**********	**********	**********	**********	**********	**********
115	214.020489	437.516992	964.733414	**********	**********	**********	**********	**********	**********	**********
116	217.160693	447.267331	994.675416	**********	**********	**********	**********	**********	**********	**********
117	220.332300	457.212678	**********	**********	**********	**********	**********	**********	**********	**********
118	223.535623	467.356932	**********	**********	**********	**********	**********	**********	**********	**********
119	226.770980	477.704070	**********	**********	**********	**********	**********	**********	**********	**********
120	230.038689	488.258152	**********	**********	**********	**********	**********	**********	**********	**********

(Continued)

Table A-3. Ordinary Annuity Compound Amount Factor. To find F for a given R received at the end of each period. $F = R \dfrac{(1+i)^N - 1}{i}$

$i\%$ \ N	11	12	13	14	15	16	17	18	19	20
1	1.000000	1.000000	1.000000	1.000000	1.000000	1.000000	1.000000	1.000000	1.000000	1.000000
2	2.110000	2.120000	2.130000	2.140000	2.150000	2.160000	2.170000	2.180000	2.190000	2.200000
3	3.342100	3.374400	3.406900	3.439600	3.472500	3.505600	3.538900	3.572400	3.606100	3.640000
4	4.709731	4.779328	4.849797	4.921144	4.993375	5.066496	5.140513	5.215432	5.291259	5.368000
5	6.227801	6.352847	6.480271	6.610104	6.742381	6.877135	7.014400	7.154210	7.296598	7.441600
6	7.912860	8.115189	8.322706	8.535519	8.753738	8.977477	9.206848	9.441968	9.682952	9.929920
7	9.783274	10.089012	10.404658	10.730491	11.066799	11.413873	11.772012	12.141522	12.522713	12.915904
8	11.859434	12.299693	12.757263	13.232760	13.726819	14.240093	14.773255	15.326996	15.902028	16.499085
9	14.163972	14.775656	15.415707	16.085347	16.785842	17.518508	18.284708	19.085855	19.923413	20.798902
10	16.722009	17.548735	18.419749	19.337295	20.303718	21.321469	22.393108	23.521309	24.708862	25.958682
11	19.561430	20.654583	21.814317	23.044516	24.349276	25.732904	27.199937	28.755144	30.403546	32.150419
12	22.713187	24.133133	25.650178	27.270749	29.001667	30.850169	32.823926	34.931070	37.180220	39.580502
13	26.211638	28.029109	29.984701	32.088654	34.351917	36.786196	39.403993	42.218663	45.244461	48.496603
14	30.094918	32.392602	34.882712	37.581065	40.504705	43.671987	47.102672	50.818022	54.840909	59.195923
15	34.405359	37.279715	40.417464	43.842414	47.580411	51.659505	56.110126	60.965266	66.260682	72.035108
16	39.189948	42.753280	46.671735	50.980352	55.717472	60.925026	66.648848	72.939014	79.850211	87.442129
17	44.500843	48.883674	53.739060	59.117601	65.075093	71.673030	78.979152	87.068036	96.021751	105.930555
18	50.395936	55.749715	61.725138	68.394066	75.836357	84.140715	93.405608	103.740283	115.265884	128.116666
19	56.939488	63.439681	70.749406	78.969235	88.211811	98.603230	110.284561	123.413534	138.166402	154.740000
20	64.202832	72.052442	80.946829	91.024928	102.443583	115.379747	130.032936	146.627970	165.418018	186.688000
21	72.265144	81.698736	92.469917	104.768418	118.810120	134.840506	153.138535	174.021005	197.847442	225.025600
22	81.214309	92.502584	105.491006	120.435996	137.631635	157.414987	180.172086	206.344785	236.438456	271.030719
23	91.147884	104.602894	120.204837	138.297035	159.276384	183.601385	211.801341	244.486847	282.361762	326.236863
24	102.174151	118.155241	136.831465	158.658620	184.167841	213.977607	248.807569	289.494479	337.010497	392.484236
25	114.413307	133.333870	155.619556	181.870827	212.793017	249.214024	292.104856	342.603486	402.042491	471.981083
26	127.998771	150.333934	176.850098	208.332743	245.711970	290.088267	342.762681	405.272113	479.430565	567.377300
27	143.078636	169.374007	200.840611	234.499327	283.568766	337.502390	402.032337	479.221093	571.522372	681.852760
28	159.817286	190.698987	227.949880	272.889233	327.104080	392.502773	471.377835	566.480890	681.111623	819.223312
29	178.397187	214.582754	258.583376	312.093725	377.169693	456.303216	552.512066	669.447450	811.522831	984.067974
30	199.020878	241.332684	293.199215	356.786847	434.745146	530.311731	647.439118	790.947991	966.712169	**********
31	221.913174	271.292606	332.315113	407.737006	500.956918	616.161608	758.503768	934.318630	**********	**********
32	247.323624	304.847719	376.516078	465.820186	577.100456	715.747465	888.449408	**********	**********	**********
33	275.529222	342.429446	426.463168	532.035012	664.665524	831.267059	**********	**********	**********	**********
34	306.837437	384.520979	482.903380	607.519914	765.365353	965.269789	**********	**********	**********	**********
35	341.589555	431.663496	546.680819	693.572702	881.170156	**********	**********	**********	**********	**********
36	380.164406	484.463116	618.749325	791.672881	**********	**********	**********	**********	**********	**********
37	422.982490	543.598690	700.186738	903.507084	**********	**********	**********	**********	**********	**********
38	470.510564	609.830633	792.211014	**********	**********	**********	**********	**********	**********	**********
39	523.266726	684.010197	896.198445	**********	**********	**********	**********	**********	**********	**********
40	581.826066	767.091420	**********	**********	**********	**********	**********	**********	**********	**********

(Continued)

Table A-3. Ordinary Annuity Compound Amount Factor. To find F for a given R received at the end of each period. $F = R\dfrac{(1+i)^N - 1}{i}$

$i\%$ / N	21	22	23	24	25	26	27	28	29	30
1	1.000000	1.000000	1.000000	1.000000	1.000000	1.000000	1.000000	1.000000	1.000000	1.000000
2	2.210000	2.220000	2.230000	2.240000	2.250000	2.260000	2.270000	2.280000	2.290000	2.300000
3	3.674100	3.708400	3.742900	3.777600	3.812500	3.847600	3.882900	3.918400	3.954100	3.990000
4	5.445661	5.524248	5.603767	5.684224	5.765625	5.847976	5.931283	6.015552	6.100789	6.187000
5	7.589250	7.739583	7.892633	8.048438	8.207031	8.368450	8.532729	8.699907	8.870018	9.043100
6	10.182992	10.442291	10.707939	10.980063	11.258789	11.544247	11.836566	12.135880	12.442323	12.756030
7	13.321421	13.739595	14.170765	14.615278	15.073486	15.545751	16.032439	16.533927	17.050597	17.582839
8	17.118919	17.762306	18.430041	19.122945	19.841858	20.587646	21.361198	22.163426	22.995270	23.857691
9	21.713892	22.670013	23.668950	24.712451	25.802322	26.940434	28.128721	29.369186	30.663898	32.014998
10	27.273809	28.657416	30.112809	31.643440	33.252903	34.944947	36.723476	38.592558	40.556428	42.619497
11	34.001309	35.962047	38.038755	40.237865	42.566129	45.030633	47.638815	50.398474	53.317792	56.405346
12	42.141584	44.873697	47.787669	50.894953	54.207661	57.738598	61.501295	65.510047	69.779952	74.326950
13	51.991317	55.745911	59.778833	64.109741	68.759576	73.750633	79.106644	84.852860	91.016138	97.625036
14	63.909493	69.010011	74.527964	80.496079	86.949470	93.925798	101.465438	109.611661	118.410819	127.912546
15	78.330487	85.192213	92.669396	100.815138	109.686838	119.346505	129.861106	141.302926	153.749956	167.286310
16	95.779889	104.934500	114.983357	126.010772	138.108547	151.376596	165.923605	181.867745	199.337443	218.472203
17	116.893666	129.020090	142.429529	157.253357	173.635684	191.734511	211.722978	233.790714	258.145302	285.013864
18	142.441336	158.404510	176.188221	195.994162	218.044605	242.585484	269.888182	300.252113	334.007439	371.518023
19	173.354016	194.253563	217.711635	244.032761	273.555756	306.657710	343.757991	385.322705	431.869596	483.973430
20	210.758360	237.989273	268.785311	303.600624	342.944695	387.388715	437.572649	494.213062	558.111779	630.165459
21	256.017615	291.346913	331.605932	377.464774	429.680869	489.109781	556.717264	633.592720	720.964195	820.215097
22	310.781315	356.443234	408.875297	469.056320	538.101086	617.278324	708.030926	811.998682	931.043812	********
23	377.045391	435.860746	503.916615	582.629836	673.626358	778.770688	900.199276	********	********	********
24	457.224923	532.750110	620.817437	723.460997	843.032947	982.251067	********	********	********	********
25	554.242157	650.955134	764.605447	898.091636	********	********	********	********	********	********
26	671.633009	795.165264	941.464700	********	********	********	********	********	********	********
27	813.675941	971.101622	********	********	********	********	********	********	********	********
28	985.547889	********	********	********	********	********	********	********	********	********
29	********	********	********	********	********	********	********	********	********	********
30	********	********	********	********	********	********	********	********	********	********
31	********	********	********	********	********	********	********	********	********	********
32	********	********	********	********	********	********	********	********	********	********
33	********	********	********	********	********	********	********	********	********	********
34	********	********	********	********	********	********	********	********	********	********
35	********	********	********	********	********	********	********	********	********	********
36	********	********	********	********	********	********	********	********	********	********
37	********	********	********	********	********	********	********	********	********	********
38	********	********	********	********	********	********	********	********	********	********
39	********	********	********	********	********	********	********	********	********	********
40	********	********	********	********	********	********	********	********	********	********

(Continued)

Table A-3. Ordinary Annuity Compound Amount Factor. To find F for a given R received at the end of each period. $F = R \dfrac{(1+i)^N - 1}{i}$

$i\%$ / N	31	32	33	34	35	36	37	38	39	40
1	1.000000	1.000000	1.000000	1.000000	1.000000	1.000000	1.000000	1.000000	1.000000	1.000000
2	2.310000	2.320000	2.330000	2.340000	2.350000	2.360000	2.370000	2.380000	2.390000	2.400000
3	4.026100	4.062400	4.098900	4.135600	4.172500	4.209600	4.246900	4.284400	4.322100	4.360000
4	6.274191	6.362368	6.451537	6.541704	6.632875	6.725056	6.818253	6.912472	7.007719	7.104000
5	9.219190	9.398326	9.580544	9.765883	9.954381	10.146076	10.341007	10.539211	10.740729	10.945600
6	13.077139	13.405790	13.742124	14.086284	14.438415	14.798664	15.167179	15.544112	15.929614	16.323840
7	18.131052	18.695643	19.277025	19.875620	20.491860	21.126182	21.779035	22.450874	23.142163	23.853376
8	24.751679	25.678249	26.638443	27.633331	28.664011	29.731608	30.837278	31.982206	33.167607	34.394726
9	33.424699	34.895288	36.429129	38.028664	39.696415	41.434987	43.247071	45.135445	47.102974	49.152617
10	44.786356	47.061780	49.450741	51.958409	54.590160	57.351582	60.248488	63.286914	66.473133	69.813664
11	59.670126	63.121550	66.769486	70.624268	74.696715	78.998152	83.540428	88.335941	93.397655	98.739129
12	79.167865	84.320446	89.803417	95.636566	101.840566	108.437487	115.450387	122.903598	130.822741	139.234781
13	104.709903	112.302988	120.438544	129.152936	138.484764	148.474982	159.167030	170.606966	182.843610	195.928693
14	138.169973	149.239945	161.183264	174.064934	187.954431	202.925976	219.058831	236.437613	255.152618	275.300171
15	182.002664	197.996727	215.373740	234.247012	254.738482	276.973327	301.110598	327.283905	355.662139	386.420239
16	239.423490	262.355680	287.447075	314.890996	344.896951	377.691885	413.521520	452.651790	495.370373	541.988334
17	314.644772	347.309497	383.304610	422.953935	466.610884	514.660963	567.524482	625.659470	689.564819	759.783668
18	413.184651	459.448536	510.795131	567.758273	630.924694	700.938810	778.508540	864.410068	959.495099	********
19	542.271893	607.472068	630.357524	761.796086	852.748336	954.276918	********	********	********	********
20	711.376180	802.863130	905.875507	********	********	********	********	********	********	********
21	932.902796	********	********	********	********	********	********	********	********	********
22	********	********	********	********	********	********	********	********	********	********
23	********	********	********	********	********	********	********	********	********	********
24	********	********	********	********	********	********	********	********	********	********
25	********	********	********	********	********	********	********	********	********	********
26	********	********	********	********	********	********	********	********	********	********
27	********	********	********	********	********	********	********	********	********	********
28	********	********	********	********	********	********	********	********	********	********
29	********	********	********	********	********	********	********	********	********	********
30	********	********	********	********	********	********	********	********	********	********
31	********	********	********	********	********	********	********	********	********	********
32	********	********	********	********	********	********	********	********	********	********
33	********	********	********	********	********	********	********	********	********	********
34	********	********	********	********	********	********	********	********	********	********
35	********	********	********	********	********	********	********	********	********	********
36	********	********	********	********	********	********	********	********	********	********
37	********	********	********	********	********	********	********	********	********	********
38	********	********	********	********	********	********	********	********	********	********
39	********	********	********	********	********	********	********	********	********	********
40	********	********	********	********	********	********	********	********	********	********

(Continued)

Table A-3. Ordinary Annuity Compound Amount Factor. To find F for a given R received at the end of each period. $F = R\dfrac{(1+i)^N - 1}{i}$

$i\%$ / N	41	42	43	44	45	46	47	48	49	50
1	1.000000	1.000000	1.000000	1.000000	1.000000	1.000000	1.000000	1.000000	1.000000	1.000000
2	2.410000	2.420000	2.430000	2.440000	2.450000	2.460000	2.470000	2.480000	2.490000	2.500000
3	4.398100	4.436400	4.474900	4.513600	4.552500	4.591600	4.630900	4.670400	4.710100	4.750000
4	7.201321	7.299688	7.399107	7.499584	7.601125	7.703736	7.807423	7.912192	8.018049	8.125000
5	11.153863	11.365557	11.580723	11.799401	12.021631	12.247455	12.476912	12.710044	12.946893	13.187500
6	16.726946	17.139091	17.560434	17.991137	18.431365	18.881284	19.341060	19.810865	20.290871	20.781250
7	24.584994	25.337509	26.111420	26.907238	27.725480	28.566674	29.431359	30.320081	31.233397	32.171875
8	35.664842	36.979263	38.339331	39.746422	41.201946	42.707344	44.264097	45.873719	47.537762	49.257813
9	51.287427	53.510553	55.825244	58.234848	60.742821	63.352723	66.068223	68.893105	71.831265	74.886719
10	73.315272	76.984986	80.830099	84.858182	89.077091	93.494975	98.120288	102.961795	108.028585	113.330078
11	104.374534	110.318680	116.587041	123.195782	130.161781	137.502663	145.236823	153.383457	161.962592	170.995117
12	148.168093	157.652525	167.719469	178.401925	189.734583	201.753889	214.498130	228.007516	242.324261	257.492676
13	209.917011	224.866586	240.838840	257.898773	276.115145	295.560677	316.312251	338.451124	362.063150	387.239014
14	296.982985	320.310551	345.399541	372.374233	401.366961	432.518589	465.979010	501.907663	540.474093	581.858521
15	419.746009	455.840983	494.921344	537.218895	582.982093	632.477140	685.989144	743.823342	806.306398	873.787781
16	592.841872	648.294196	708.737522	774.595209	846.324035	924.416625	********	********	********	********
17	836.907040	921.577758	********	********	********	********	********	********	********	********
18	********	********	********	********	********	********	********	********	********	********
19	********	********	********	********	********	********	********	********	********	********
20	********	********	********	********	********	********	********	********	********	********
21	********	********	********	********	********	********	********	********	********	********
22	********	********	********	********	********	********	********	********	********	********
23	********	********	********	********	********	********	********	********	********	********
24	********	********	********	********	********	********	********	********	********	********
25	********	********	********	********	********	********	********	********	********	********
26	********	********	********	********	********	********	********	********	********	********
27	********	********	********	********	********	********	********	********	********	********
28	********	********	********	********	********	********	********	********	********	********
29	********	********	********	********	********	********	********	********	********	********
30	********	********	********	********	********	********	********	********	********	********
31	********	********	********	********	********	********	********	********	********	********
32	********	********	********	********	********	********	********	********	********	********
33	********	********	********	********	********	********	********	********	********	********
34	********	********	********	********	********	********	********	********	********	********
35	********	********	********	********	********	********	********	********	********	********
36	********	********	********	********	********	********	********	********	********	********
37	********	********	********	********	********	********	********	********	********	********
38	********	********	********	********	********	********	********	********	********	********
39	********	********	********	********	********	********	********	********	********	********
40	********	********	********	********	********	********	********	********	********	********

(Continued)

Table A-3. Ordinary Annuity Compound Amount Factor. To find F for a given R received at the end of each period. $F = R\dfrac{(1+i)^N - 1}{i}$

$i\%$ N	51	52	53	54	55	56	57	58	59	60
1	1.000000	1.000000	1.000000	1.000000	1.000000	1.000000	1.000000	1.000000	1.000000	1.000000
2	2.510000	2.520000	2.530000	2.540000	2.550000	2.560000	2.570000	2.580000	2.590000	2.600000
3	4.790100	4.830400	4.870900	4.911600	4.952500	4.993600	5.034900	5.076400	5.118100	5.160000
4	8.233051	8.342208	8.452477	8.563864	8.676375	8.790016	8.904793	9.020712	9.137779	9.256000
5	13.431907	13.680156	13.932290	14.188351	14.448381	14.712425	14.980525	15.252725	15.529069	15.809600
6	21.282180	21.793837	22.316403	22.850060	23.394991	23.951383	24.519424	25.099305	25.691219	26.295360
7	33.136091	34.126633	35.144097	36.189092	37.262236	38.364157	39.495496	40.656903	41.849038	43.072576
8	51.035498	52.872482	54.770469	56.731202	58.756466	60.848086	63.007929	65.237906	67.539971	69.916122
9	78.063601	81.366172	84.798817	88.366051	92.072522	95.923013	99.922448	104.075892	108.388554	112.865795
10	118.876038	124.676582	130.742190	137.083719	143.712409	150.639901	157.878244	165.439900	173.337801	181.585271
11	180.502818	190.508405	201.035551	212.108927	223.754234	235.998245	248.868843	262.395056	276.607103	291.536434
12	273.559255	290.572775	308.584393	327.647747	347.819062	369.157263	391.724083	415.584188	440.805294	467.458295
13	414.074475	442.670618	473.134122	505.577530	540.119547	576.885330	616.006811	657.623017	701.880417	748.933271
14	626.252457	673.859340	724.895206	779.589397	838.185297	900.941115	968.130693	********	********	********
15	946.641210	********	********	********	********	********	********	********	********	********
16	********	********	********	********	********	********	********	********	********	********
17	********	********	********	********	********	********	********	********	********	********
18	********	********	********	********	********	********	********	********	********	********
19	********	********	********	********	********	********	********	********	********	********
20	********	********	********	********	********	********	********	********	********	********
21	********	********	********	********	********	********	********	********	********	********
22	********	********	********	********	********	********	********	********	********	********
23	********	********	********	********	********	********	********	********	********	********
24	********	********	********	********	********	********	********	********	********	********
25	********	********	********	********	********	********	********	********	********	********
26	********	********	********	********	********	********	********	********	********	********
27	********	********	********	********	********	********	********	********	********	********
28	********	********	********	********	********	********	********	********	********	********
29	********	********	********	********	********	********	********	********	********	********
30	********	********	********	********	********	********	********	********	********	********
31	********	********	********	********	********	********	********	********	********	********
32	********	********	********	********	********	********	********	********	********	********
33	********	********	********	********	********	********	********	********	********	********
34	********	********	********	********	********	********	********	********	********	********
35	********	********	********	********	********	********	********	********	********	********
36	********	********	********	********	********	********	********	********	********	********
37	********	********	********	********	********	********	********	********	********	********
38	********	********	********	********	********	********	********	********	********	********
39	********	********	********	********	********	********	********	********	********	********
40	********	********	********	********	********	********	********	********	********	********

Table A-4. Ordinary Annuity Present Worth Factor. To find P for a given R received at the end of each period. $P = R \dfrac{1 - (1+i)^{-N}}{i}$

i% / N	1	2	3	4	5	6	7	8	9	10
1	.990099	.980392	.970874	.961538	.952381	.943396	.934579	.925926	.917431	.909091
2	1.970395	1.941561	1.913470	1.886095	1.859410	1.833393	1.808018	1.783265	1.759111	1.735537
3	2.940985	2.883883	2.828611	2.775091	2.723248	2.673012	2.624316	2.577097	2.531295	2.486852
4	3.901966	3.807729	3.717098	3.629895	3.545951	3.465106	3.387211	3.312127	3.239720	3.169865
5	4.853431	4.713460	4.579707	4.451822	4.329477	4.212364	4.100197	3.992710	3.889651	3.790787
6	5.795476	5.601431	5.417191	5.242137	5.075692	4.917324	4.766540	4.622880	4.485919	4.355261
7	6.728195	6.471991	6.230283	6.002055	5.786373	5.582381	5.389289	5.206370	5.032953	4.868419
8	7.651678	7.325481	7.019692	6.732745	6.463213	6.209794	5.971299	5.746639	5.534819	5.334926
9	8.566018	8.162237	7.786109	7.435332	7.107822	6.801692	6.515232	6.246888	5.995247	5.759024
10	9.471305	8.982585	8.530203	8.110896	7.721735	7.360087	7.023582	6.710081	6.417658	6.144567
11	10.367628	9.786848	9.252624	8.760477	8.306414	7.886875	7.498674	7.138964	6.805191	6.495061
12	11.255077	10.575341	9.954004	9.385074	8.863252	8.383844	7.942686	7.536078	7.160725	6.813692
13	12.133740	11.348374	10.634955	9.985648	9.393573	8.852683	8.357651	7.903776	7.486904	7.103356
14	13.003703	12.106249	11.296073	10.563123	9.898641	9.294984	8.745468	8.244237	7.786150	7.366687
15	13.865053	12.849264	11.937935	11.118387	10.379658	9.712249	9.107914	8.559479	8.060688	7.606080
16	14.717874	13.577709	12.561102	11.652296	10.837770	10.105895	9.446649	8.851369	8.312558	7.823709
17	15.562251	14.291872	13.166118	12.165669	11.274066	10.477260	9.763223	9.121638	8.543631	8.021553
18	16.398269	14.992031	13.753513	12.659297	11.689587	10.827603	10.059087	9.371887	8.755625	8.201412
19	17.226008	15.678462	14.323799	13.133939	12.085321	11.158116	10.335595	9.603599	8.950115	8.364920
20	18.045553	16.351433	14.877475	13.590326	12.462210	11.469921	10.594014	9.818147	9.128546	8.513564
21	18.856983	17.011209	15.415024	14.029160	12.821153	11.764077	10.835527	10.016803	9.292244	8.648694
22	19.660379	17.658048	15.936917	14.451115	13.163003	12.041582	11.061240	10.200744	9.442425	8.771540
23	20.455821	18.292204	16.443608	14.856842	13.488574	12.303379	11.272187	10.371059	9.580207	8.883218
24	21.243387	18.913926	16.935542	15.246963	13.798642	12.550358	11.469334	10.528758	9.706612	8.984744
25	22.023156	19.523456	17.413148	15.622080	14.093945	12.783356	11.653583	10.674776	9.822580	9.077040
26	22.795204	20.121036	17.876842	15.982769	14.375185	13.003166	11.825779	10.809978	9.928972	9.160945
27	23.559608	20.706898	18.327031	16.329586	14.643034	13.210534	11.986709	10.935165	10.026580	9.237223
28	24.316443	21.281272	18.764108	16.663063	14.898127	13.406164	12.137111	11.051078	10.116280	9.306567
29	25.065785	21.844385	19.188455	16.983715	15.141074	13.590721	12.277674	11.158406	10.198283	9.369606
30	25.807708	22.396456	19.600441	17.292033	15.372451	13.764831	12.409041	11.257783	10.273654	9.426914
31	26.542285	22.937702	20.000428	17.588494	15.592811	13.929086	12.531814	11.349799	10.342802	9.479013
32	27.269589	23.468335	20.388766	17.873551	15.802677	14.084043	12.646555	11.434999	10.406240	9.526376
33	27.989693	23.988564	20.765792	18.147646	16.002549	14.230230	12.753790	11.513888	10.464441	9.569432
34	28.702666	24.498592	21.131837	18.411198	16.192904	14.368141	12.853909	11.586939	10.517835	9.608575
35	29.408580	24.998619	21.487220	18.664613	16.374194	14.498246	12.947672	11.654568	10.566821	9.644159
36	30.107505	25.488842	21.832252	18.908282	16.546852	14.620987	13.035208	11.717193	10.611763	9.676508
37	30.799510	25.969453	22.167235	19.142579	16.711287	14.736780	13.117017	11.775179	10.652993	9.705917
38	31.484663	26.440641	22.492462	19.367864	16.867893	14.846019	13.193473	11.828869	10.690820	9.732651
39	32.163033	26.902589	22.808215	19.584485	17.017041	14.949075	13.264928	11.878582	10.725523	9.756956
40	32.834686	27.355479	23.114772	19.792774	17.159086	15.046297	13.331709	11.924613	10.757360	9.779051

(Continued)

Table A–4. Ordinary Annuity Present Worth Factor. To find P for a given R received at the end of each period. $P = R \dfrac{1-(1+i)^{-N}}{i}$

$i\%$ / N	1	2	3	4	5	6	7	8	9	10
41	33.499689	27.799489	23.412400	19.993052	17.294368	15.138016	13.394120	11.967235	10.786569	9.799137
42	34.158108	28.234794	23.701359	20.185627	17.423208	15.224543	13.452449	12.006699	10.813366	9.817397
43	34.810008	28.661562	23.981902	20.370795	17.545912	15.306173	13.506962	12.043240	10.837950	9.833998
44	35.455454	29.079963	24.254274	20.548841	17.662773	15.383182	13.557908	12.077074	10.860505	9.849089
45	36.094508	29.490160	24.518713	20.720040	17.774070	15.455832	13.605522	12.108402	10.881197	9.862808
46	36.727236	29.892314	24.775449	20.884654	17.880066	15.524370	13.650020	12.137409	10.900181	9.875280
47	37.353699	30.286582	25.024708	21.042936	17.981016	15.589028	13.691608	12.164267	10.917597	9.886618
48	37.973959	30.673120	25.266707	21.195131	18.077158	15.650027	13.730474	12.189136	10.933575	9.896296
49	38.588079	31.052078	25.501657	21.341472	18.168722	15.707572	13.766799	12.212163	10.948234	9.906296
50	39.196118	31.423606	25.729764	21.482185	18.255925	15.761861	13.800746	12.233485	10.961683	9.914814
51	39.798136	31.787849	25.951227	21.617485	18.338977	15.813076	13.832473	12.253227	10.974021	9.922559
52	40.394194	32.144950	26.166240	21.747582	18.418073	15.861393	13.862124	12.271506	10.985340	9.929599
53	40.984351	32.495049	26.374990	21.872675	18.493403	15.906974	13.889836	12.288432	10.995725	9.935999
54	41.568664	32.838283	26.577660	21.992957	18.565146	15.949976	13.915735	12.304103	11.005252	9.941817
55	42.147192	33.174788	26.774428	22.108612	18.633472	15.990543	13.939939	12.318614	11.013993	9.947106
56	42.719992	33.504694	26.965464	22.219819	18.698545	16.028814	13.962560	12.332050	11.022012	9.951915
57	43.287121	33.828131	27.150936	22.326749	18.760519	16.064919	13.983701	12.344491	11.029369	9.956286
58	43.848635	34.145226	27.331005	22.429567	18.819542	16.098980	14.003458	12.356010	11.036118	9.960260
59	44.404589	34.456104	27.505831	22.528430	18.875754	16.131113	14.021924	12.366676	11.042310	9.963873
60	44.955038	34.760887	27.675564	22.623490	18.929290	16.161428	14.039181	12.376552	11.047991	9.967157
61	45.500038	35.059693	27.840353	22.714894	18.980276	16.190026	14.055309	12.385696	11.053203	9.970143
62	46.039642	35.352640	28.000343	22.802783	19.028834	16.217006	14.070383	12.394163	11.057984	9.972857
63	46.573903	35.639843	28.155673	22.887291	19.075080	16.242458	14.084470	12.402003	11.062371	9.975325
64	47.102874	35.921415	28.306478	22.968549	19.119124	16.266470	14.097635	12.409262	11.066395	9.977568
65	47.626608	36.197466	28.452892	23.046682	19.161070	16.289123	14.109940	12.415983	11.070087	9.979607
66	48.145156	36.468103	28.595040	23.121019	19.201019	16.310493	14.121439	12.422207	11.073475	9.981461
67	48.658571	36.733435	28.733049	23.194048	19.239066	16.330654	14.132186	12.427969	11.076582	9.983147
68	49.166901	36.993564	28.867038	23.263507	19.275301	16.349673	14.142230	12.433305	11.079433	9.984679
69	49.670199	37.248592	28.997124	23.330296	19.309810	16.367617	14.151617	12.438245	11.082049	9.986071
70	50.168514	37.498619	29.123421	23.394515	19.342677	16.384544	14.160389	12.442820	11.084449	9.987338
71	50.661895	37.743744	29.246040	23.456264	19.373978	16.400513	14.168588	12.447055	11.086650	9.988489
72	51.150391	37.984063	29.365088	23.515639	19.403788	16.415578	14.176251	12.450977	11.088670	9.989535
73	51.634051	38.219670	29.480667	23.572730	19.432179	16.429791	14.183412	12.454608	11.090523	9.990487
74	52.112922	38.450657	29.592881	23.627625	19.459218	16.443219	14.190104	12.457971	11.092223	9.991351
75	52.587051	38.677114	29.701826	23.680408	19.484970	16.455848	14.196359	12.461084	11.093782	9.992138
76	53.056486	38.899132	29.807598	23.731162	19.509495	16.467781	14.202205	12.463967	11.095213	9.992852
77	53.521274	39.116796	29.910290	23.779963	19.533853	16.479039	14.207668	12.466636	11.096526	9.993502
78	53.981459	39.330192	30.009990	23.826888	19.555098	16.489659	14.212774	12.469107	11.097730	9.994093
79	54.437088	39.539404	30.106736	23.872008	19.576284	16.499679	14.217546	12.471396	11.098835	9.994630
80	54.888206	39.744511	30.200763	23.915392	19.596460	16.509131	14.222005	12.473514	11.099849	9.995118

(Continued)

Table A-4. Ordinary Annuity Present Worth Factor. To find P for a given R received at the end of each period. $P = R\dfrac{1-(1+i)^{-N}}{i}$

N \ i%	1	2	3	4	5	6	7	8	9	10
81	55.334858	39.945602	30.292003	23.957108	19.615677	16.518048	14.226173	12.475476	11.100778	9.995562
82	55.777087	40.142747	30.380586	23.997219	19.633978	16.526460	14.230069	12.477293	11.101632	9.995965
83	56.214937	40.336026	30.466588	24.035787	19.651407	16.534396	14.233709	12.478975	11.102414	9.996332
84	56.648453	40.525516	30.550086	24.072872	19.668007	16.541883	14.237111	12.480532	11.103132	9.996666
85	57.077676	40.711290	30.631151	24.108531	19.683816	16.548947	14.240291	12.481974	11.103791	9.996969
86	57.502650	40.893422	30.709855	24.142818	19.698873	16.555610	14.243262	12.483310	11.104396	9.997244
87	57.923415	41.071982	30.786267	24.175787	19.713212	16.561896	14.246040	12.484546	11.104950	9.997495
88	58.340015	41.247041	30.860454	24.207487	19.726869	16.567827	14.248635	12.485691	11.105459	9.997723
89	58.752490	41.418668	30.932472	24.237969	19.739877	16.573421	14.251061	12.486751	11.105926	9.997930
90	59.160881	41.586929	31.002407	24.267278	19.752262	16.578699	14.253328	12.487732	11.106354	9.998118
91	59.565229	41.751891	31.070298	24.295459	19.764059	16.583679	14.255447	12.488641	11.106746	9.998289
92	59.965573	41.913619	31.136212	24.322557	19.775294	16.588376	14.257427	12.489482	11.107107	9.998444
93	60.361954	42.072175	31.200206	24.348612	19.785994	16.592808	14.259277	12.490261	11.107437	9.998586
94	60.754410	42.227623	31.262336	24.373666	19.796185	16.596988	14.261007	12.490983	11.107741	9.998714
95	61.142980	42.380023	31.322656	24.397756	19.805891	16.600932	14.262623	12.491651	11.108019	9.998831
96	61.527703	42.529434	31.381219	24.420919	19.815134	16.604653	14.264134	12.492269	11.108274	9.998938
97	61.908617	42.675916	31.438077	24.443191	19.823937	16.608163	14.265546	12.492842	11.108509	9.999034
98	62.285759	42.819525	31.493279	24.464607	19.832321	16.611475	14.266865	12.493372	11.108724	9.999122
99	62.659168	42.960319	31.546872	24.485199	19.840306	16.614599	14.268098	12.493863	11.108921	9.999202
100	63.028879	43.098352	31.598905	24.504999	19.847910	16.617546	14.269251	12.494318	11.109102	9.999274
101	63.394929	43.233678	31.649423	24.524037	19.855153	16.620327	14.270328	12.494738	11.109267	9.999340
102	63.757356	43.366351	31.698469	24.542344	19.862050	16.622950	14.271334	12.495128	11.109420	9.999400
103	64.116194	43.496423	31.746086	24.559946	19.868619	16.625424	14.272275	12.495489	11.109559	9.999455
104	64.471479	43.623944	31.792317	24.576871	19.874875	16.627759	14.273154	12.495823	11.109687	9.999504
105	64.823247	43.748964	31.837201	24.593145	19.880834	16.629961	14.273976	12.496133	11.109805	9.999549
106	65.171531	43.871534	31.880777	24.608794	19.886508	16.632039	14.274744	12.496419	11.109913	9.999590
107	65.516368	43.991700	31.923085	24.623840	19.891913	16.633999	14.275462	12.496684	11.110012	9.999628
108	65.857790	44.109510	31.964150	24.638308	19.897060	16.635848	14.276132	12.496930	11.110103	9.999661
109	66.195832	44.225009	32.004039	24.652219	19.901962	16.637592	14.276759	12.497157	11.110186	9.999692
110	66.530526	44.338245	32.042756	24.665595	19.906630	16.639238	14.277345	12.497368	11.110262	9.999720
111	66.861907	44.449259	32.080346	24.678457	19.911076	16.640791	14.277893	12.497563	11.110332	9.999746
112	67.190007	44.558097	32.116840	24.690824	19.915311	16.642255	14.278404	12.497743	11.110397	9.999769
113	67.514859	44.664801	32.152272	24.702715	19.919344	16.643637	14.278882	12.497911	11.110456	9.999790
114	67.836494	44.769413	32.186672	24.714149	19.923184	16.644941	14.279329	12.498065	11.110510	9.999809
115	68.154944	44.871974	32.220070	24.725144	19.926842	16.646170	14.279747	12.498209	11.110559	9.999826
116	68.470242	44.972523	32.252495	24.735715	19.930326	16.647331	14.280138	12.498341	11.110605	9.999842
117	68.782418	45.071101	32.283976	24.745880	19.933644	16.648425	14.280502	12.498464	11.110647	9.999856
118	69.091503	45.167746	32.314540	24.755654	19.936804	16.649458	14.280843	12.498578	11.110685	9.999869
119	69.397527	45.262496	32.344213	24.765052	19.939813	16.650432	14.281162	12.498683	11.110720	9.999881
120	69.700522	45.355389	32.373023	24.774088	19.942679	16.651351	14.281460	12.498781	11.110753	9.999892

(Continued)

Table A-4. Ordinary Annuity Present Worth Factor. To find P for a given R received at the end of each period. $P = R \dfrac{1 - (1+i)^{-N}}{i}$

$i\%$ / N	11	12	13	14	15	16	17	18	19	20
1	.900901	.892857	.884956	.877193	.869565	.862069	.854701	.847458	.840336	.833333
2	1.712523	1.690051	1.668102	1.646661	1.625709	1.605232	1.585214	1.565642	1.546501	1.527778
3	2.443715	2.401831	2.361153	2.321632	2.283225	2.245890	2.209585	2.174273	2.139917	2.106481
4	3.102446	3.037349	2.974471	2.913712	2.854978	2.798181	2.743235	2.690062	2.638586	2.588735
5	3.695897	3.604776	3.517231	3.433081	3.352155	3.274294	3.199346	3.127171	3.057635	2.990612
6	4.230538	4.111407	3.997550	3.888668	3.784483	3.684736	3.589185	3.497603	3.409777	3.325510
7	4.712196	4.563757	4.422610	4.288305	4.160420	4.038565	3.922380	3.811528	3.705695	3.604592
8	5.146123	4.967640	4.798770	4.638864	4.487483	4.343591	4.207163	4.077566	3.954366	3.837160
9	5.537048	5.328250	5.131655	4.946372	4.771584	4.606544	4.450566	4.303023	4.163332	4.030967
10	5.889232	5.650223	5.426243	5.216116	5.018769	4.833227	4.658604	4.494086	4.338935	4.192472
11	6.206515	5.937699	5.686941	5.452733	5.233712	5.028644	4.836413	4.656005	4.486500	4.327060
12	6.492356	6.194374	5.917647	5.660292	5.420619	5.197107	4.988387	4.793225	4.610504	4.439217
13	6.749870	6.423548	6.121812	5.842362	5.583147	5.342334	5.118280	4.909513	4.714709	4.532681
14	6.981865	6.628168	6.302488	6.002072	5.724476	5.467529	5.229299	5.008062	4.802277	4.610567
15	7.190870	6.810864	6.462379	6.142168	5.847370	5.575456	5.324187	5.091578	4.875863	4.675473
16	7.379162	6.973986	6.603875	6.265060	5.954243	5.668497	5.405288	5.162354	4.937700	4.729561
17	7.548794	7.119630	6.729093	6.372859	6.047161	5.748704	5.474605	5.222334	4.989664	4.774634
18	7.701617	7.249670	6.839905	6.467420	6.127966	5.817848	5.533851	5.273164	5.033331	4.812195
19	7.839294	7.365777	6.937969	6.550369	6.198231	5.877455	5.584488	5.316241	5.070026	4.843496
20	7.963328	7.469444	7.024752	6.623131	6.259331	5.928841	5.627767	5.352746	5.100862	4.869580
21	8.075070	7.562003	7.101550	6.686957	6.312462	5.973139	5.664758	5.383683	5.126775	4.891316
22	8.175739	7.644646	7.169513	6.742944	6.358663	6.011326	5.696375	5.409901	5.148550	4.909430
23	8.266432	7.718434	7.229658	6.792056	6.398837	6.044247	5.723397	5.432120	5.166849	4.924525
24	8.348137	7.784316	7.282883	6.835137	6.433771	6.072627	5.746493	5.450949	5.182226	4.937104
25	8.421745	7.843139	7.329985	6.872927	6.464149	6.097092	5.766234	5.466906	5.195148	4.947587
26	8.488058	7.895660	7.371668	6.906077	6.490564	6.118182	5.783106	5.480429	5.206007	4.956323
27	8.547800	7.942554	7.408556	6.935154	6.513534	6.136364	5.797526	5.491889	5.215132	4.963602
28	8.601622	7.984423	7.441200	6.960662	6.533508	6.152038	5.809851	5.501601	5.222800	4.969668
29	8.650110	8.021806	7.470088	6.983037	6.550877	6.165550	5.820386	5.509831	5.229243	4.974724
30	8.693793	8.055184	7.495653	7.002664	6.565980	6.177198	5.829390	5.516806	5.234658	4.978936
31	8.733146	8.084986	7.518277	7.019881	6.579113	6.187240	5.837085	5.522717	5.239209	4.982447
32	8.768600	8.111594	7.538299	7.034983	6.590533	6.195897	5.843663	5.527726	5.243033	4.985372
33	8.800541	8.135352	7.556016	7.048231	6.600463	6.203359	5.849284	5.531971	5.246246	4.987810
34	8.829316	8.156564	7.571696	7.059862	6.609093	6.209792	5.854089	5.535569	5.248946	4.989842
35	8.855240	8.175504	7.585572	7.070045	6.616607	6.215338	5.858196	5.538618	5.251215	4.991535
36	8.878594	8.192414	7.597851	7.078987	6.623137	6.220119	5.861706	5.541201	5.253122	4.992946
37	8.899635	8.207513	7.608718	7.086831	6.628815	6.224241	5.864706	5.543391	5.254724	4.994122
38	8.918590	8.220993	7.618334	7.093711	6.633752	6.227794	5.867270	5.545247	5.256071	4.995101
39	8.935666	8.233030	7.626844	7.099747	6.638045	6.230857	5.869461	5.546819	5.257202	4.995918
40	8.951051	8.243777	7.634376	7.105041	6.641778	6.233497	5.871335	5.548152	5.258153	4.996598

(Continued)

Table A-4. Ordinary Annuity Present Worth Factor. To find P for a given R received at the end of each period. $P = R\dfrac{1-(1+i)^{-N}}{i}$

$i\%$ / N	11	12	13	14	15	16	17	18	19	20
41	8.964911	8.253372	7.641040	7.109685	6.645025	6.235773	5.872936	5.549281	5.258952	4.997165
42	8.977397	8.261939	7.646938	7.113759	6.647848	6.237736	5.874304	5.550238	5.259624	4.997638
43	8.988646	8.269589	7.652158	7.117332	6.650302	6.239427	5.875473	5.551049	5.260188	4.998031
44	8.998780	8.276418	7.656777	7.120467	6.652437	6.240886	5.876473	5.551737	5.260662	4.998359
45	9.007910	8.282516	7.660864	7.123217	6.654293	6.242143	5.877327	5.552319	5.261061	4.998633
46	9.016135	8.287961	7.664482	7.125629	6.655907	6.243227	5.878058	5.552813	5.261396	4.998861
47	9.023545	8.292822	7.667683	7.127744	6.657310	6.244161	5.878682	5.553231	5.261677	4.999051
48	9.030221	8.297163	7.670516	7.129600	6.658531	6.244966	5.879215	5.553586	5.261913	4.999209
49	9.036235	8.301038	7.673023	7.131228	6.659592	6.245661	5.879671	5.553886	5.262112	4.999341
50	9.041653	8.304498	7.675242	7.132656	6.660515	6.246259	5.880061	5.554141	5.262279	4.999451
51	9.046534	8.307588	7.677205	7.133909	6.661317	6.246775	5.880394	5.554357	5.262419	4.999542
52	9.050932	8.310346	7.678942	7.135008	6.662015	6.247220	5.880678	5.554541	5.262537	4.999618
53	9.054894	8.312809	7.680480	7.135972	6.662622	6.247603	5.880922	5.554695	5.262636	4.999682
54	9.058463	8.315008	7.681841	7.136818	6.663149	6.247934	5.881130	5.554826	5.262720	4.999735
55	9.061678	8.316972	7.683045	7.137559	6.663608	6.248219	5.881307	5.554937	5.262790	4.999779
56	9.064575	8.318725	7.684111	7.138210	6.664007	6.248465	5.881459	5.555032	5.262848	4.999816
57	9.067185	8.320290	7.685054	7.138781	6.664354	6.248676	5.881589	5.555111	5.262898	4.999847
58	9.069536	8.321687	7.685888	7.139281	6.664656	6.248859	5.881700	5.555179	5.262939	4.999872
59	9.071654	8.322935	7.686627	7.139720	6.664918	6.249016	5.881795	5.555237	5.262974	4.999894
60	9.073562	8.324049	7.687280	7.140106	6.665146	6.249152	5.881876	5.555285	5.263004	4.999911
61	9.075281	8.325044	7.687859	7.140443	6.665344	6.249269	5.881945	5.555327	5.263028	4.999926
62	9.076830	8.325932	7.688370	7.140740	6.665517	6.249370	5.882005	5.555361	5.263049	4.999938
63	9.078225	8.326725	7.688823	7.141000	6.665667	6.249457	5.882055	5.555391	5.263066	4.999949
64	9.079482	8.327433	7.689224	7.141228	6.665797	6.249532	5.882098	5.555416	5.263081	4.999957
65	9.080614	8.328065	7.689579	7.141428	6.665911	6.249596	5.882135	5.555437	5.263093	4.999964
66	9.081635	8.328630	7.689893	7.141604	6.666009	6.249652	5.882167	5.555455	5.263104	4.999970
67	9.082554	8.329134	7.690171	7.141758	6.666095	6.249700	5.882194	5.555471	5.263112	4.999975
68	9.083382	8.329584	7.690417	7.141893	6.666170	6.249741	5.882217	5.555484	5.263120	4.999979
69	9.084128	8.329985	7.690634	7.142011	6.666234	6.249777	5.882237	5.555495	5.263126	4.999983
70	9.084800	8.330344	7.690827	7.142115	6.666291	6.249808	5.882254	5.555504	5.263131	4.999986
71	9.085405	8.330664	7.690997	7.142206	6.666340	6.249834	5.882268	5.555512	5.263135	4.999988
72	9.085951	8.330950	7.691148	7.142286	6.666382	6.249857	5.882280	5.555518	5.263139	4.999990
73	9.086442	8.331206	7.691281	7.142356	6.666420	6.249877	5.882291	5.555524	5.263142	4.999992
74	9.086885	8.331434	7.691399	7.142418	6.666452	6.249894	5.882300	5.555529	5.263144	4.999993
75	9.087283	8.331637	7.691504	7.142472	6.666480	6.249908	5.882308	5.555533	5.263147	4.999994
76	9.087643	8.331819	7.691596	7.142519	6.666504	6.249921	5.882314	5.555536	5.263148	4.999995
77	9.087966	8.331981	7.691678	7.142561	6.666525	6.249932	5.882320	5.555539	5.263150	4.999996
78	9.088258	8.332126	7.691751	7.142597	6.666544	6.249941	5.882325	5.555542	5.263151	4.999997
79	9.088521	8.332255	7.691815	7.142629	6.666560	6.249949	5.882329	5.555544	5.263152	4.999997
80	9.088757	8.332371	7.691871	7.142657	6.666574	6.249956	5.882332	5.555546	5.263153	4.999998

(Continued)

Table A-4. Ordinary Annuity Present Worth Factor. To find P for a given R received at the end of each period. $P = R \dfrac{1-(1+i)^{-N}}{i}$

i% N	11	12	13	14	15	16	17	18	19	20
81	9.089971	8.332474	7.691922	7.142682	6.666586	6.249962	5.882335	5.555547	5.263154	4.999998
82	9.089163	8.332566	7.691966	7.142703	6.666596	6.249968	5.882338	5.555548	5.263155	4.999998
83	9.089336	8.332648	7.692005	7.142722	6.666606	6.249972	5.882340	5.555550	5.263155	4.999999
84	9.089492	8.332722	7.692040	7.142739	6.666614	6.249976	5.882342	5.555550	5.263156	4.999999
85	9.089632	8.332787	7.692071	7.142753	6.666620	6.249979	5.882344	5.555551	5.263156	4.999999
86	9.089759	8.332846	7.692098	7.142766	6.666626	6.249982	5.882345	5.555552	5.263156	4.999999
87	9.089873	8.332898	7.692122	7.142777	6.666632	6.249985	5.882346	5.555552	5.263156	4.999999
88	9.089975	8.332945	7.692144	7.142787	6.666636	6.249987	5.882347	5.555553	5.263157	4.999999
89	9.090068	8.332986	7.692162	7.142796	6.666640	6.249989	5.882348	5.555553	5.263157	5.000000
90	9.090151	8.333023	7.692179	7.142803	6.666644	6.249990	5.882349	5.555554	5.263157	5.000000
91	9.090226	8.333057	7.692194	7.142810	6.666647	6.249991	5.882349	5.555554	5.263157	5.000000
92	9.090294	8.333086	7.692207	7.142816	6.666649	6.249993	5.882350	5.555554	5.263157	5.000000
93	9.090355	8.333113	7.692219	7.142821	6.666652	6.249994	5.882350	5.555555	5.263157	5.000000
94	9.090410	8.333136	7.692229	7.142825	6.666654	6.249995	5.882351	5.555555	5.263158	5.000000
95	9.090459	8.333157	7.692238	7.142829	6.666655	6.249995	5.882351	5.555555	5.263158	5.000000
96	9.090504	8.333176	7.692246	7.142833	6.666657	6.249996	5.882351	5.555555	5.263158	5.000000
97	9.090544	8.333193	7.692253	7.142836	6.666658	6.249997	5.882352	5.555555	5.263158	5.000000
98	9.090580	8.333208	7.692259	7.142838	6.666659	6.249997	5.882352	5.555555	5.263158	5.000000
99	9.090613	8.333222	7.692265	7.142841	6.666660	6.249997	5.882352	5.555555	5.263158	5.000000
100	9.090642	8.333234	7.692270	7.142843	6.666661	6.249998	5.882352	5.555555	5.263158	5.000000
101	9.090669	8.333244	7.692274	7.142844	6.666662	6.249998	5.882352	5.555555	5.263158	5.000000
102	9.090692	8.333254	7.692278	7.142846	6.666662	6.249998	5.882353	5.555555	5.263158	5.000000
103	9.090714	8.333262	7.692281	7.142847	6.666663	6.249999	5.882353	5.555555	5.263158	5.000000
104	9.090733	8.333270	7.692284	7.142849	6.666663	6.249999	5.882353	5.555555	5.263158	5.000000
105	9.090751	8.333277	7.692287	7.142850	6.666664	6.249999	5.882353	5.555555	5.263158	5.000000
106	9.090766	8.333283	7.692290	7.142851	6.666664	6.249999	5.882353	5.555555	5.263158	5.000000
107	9.090781	8.333288	7.692292	7.142851	6.666665	6.249999	5.882353	5.555555	5.263158	5.000000
108	9.090793	8.333293	7.692293	7.142852	6.666665	6.249999	5.882353	5.555555	5.263158	5.000000
109	9.090805	8.333297	7.692295	7.142853	6.666665	6.249999	5.882353	5.555555	5.263158	5.000000
110	9.090815	8.333301	7.692297	7.142853	6.666665	6.249999	5.882353	5.555555	5.263158	5.000000
111	9.090824	8.333305	7.692298	7.142854	6.666665	6.250000	5.882353	5.555556	5.263158	5.000000
112	9.090833	8.333308	7.692299	7.142854	6.666666	6.250000	5.882353	5.555556	5.263158	5.000000
113	9.090840	8.333310	7.692300	7.142854	6.666666	6.250000	5.882353	5.555556	5.263158	5.000000
114	9.090847	8.333313	7.692301	7.142855	6.666666	6.250000	5.882353	5.555556	5.263158	5.000000
115	9.090853	8.333315	7.692302	7.142855	6.666666	6.250000	5.882353	5.555556	5.263158	5.000000
116	9.090859	8.333317	7.692302	7.142855	6.666666	6.250000	5.882353	5.555556	5.263158	5.000000
117	9.090864	8.333319	7.692303	7.142856	6.666666	6.250000	5.882353	5.555556	5.263158	5.000000
118	9.090868	8.333320	7.692303	7.142856	6.666666	6.250000	5.882353	5.555556	5.263158	5.000000
119	9.090872	8.333322	7.692304	7.142856	6.666666	6.250000	5.882353	5.555556	5.263158	5.000000
120	9.090876	8.333323	7.692304	7.142856	6.666666	6.250000	5.882353	5.555556	5.263158	5.000000

(Continued)

Table A-4. Ordinary Annuity Present Worth Factor. To find P for a given R received at the end of each period. $P = R \dfrac{1 - (1 + i)^{-N}}{i}$

$i\%$ / N	21	22	23	24	25	26	27	28	29	30
1	.826446	.819672	.813008	.806452	.800000	.793651	.787402	.781250	.775194	.769231
2	1.509460	1.491535	1.473990	1.456816	1.440000	1.423532	1.407403	1.391602	1.376119	1.360947
3	2.073934	2.042241	2.011374	1.981303	1.952000	1.923438	1.895593	1.868439	1.841953	1.816113
4	2.540441	2.493641	2.448272	2.404277	2.361600	2.320189	2.279994	2.240968	2.203064	2.166241
5	2.925984	2.863640	2.803473	2.745384	2.689280	2.635071	2.582673	2.532006	2.482996	2.435570
6	3.244615	3.166918	3.092254	3.020471	2.951424	2.884977	2.821002	2.759380	2.699997	2.642746
7	3.507946	3.415506	3.327036	3.242316	3.161139	3.083315	3.008663	2.937015	2.868214	2.802112
8	3.725576	3.619268	3.517916	3.421222	3.328911	3.240726	3.156428	3.075793	2.998616	2.924702
9	3.905434	3.786285	3.673102	3.565502	3.463129	3.365656	3.272778	3.184214	3.099702	3.019001
10	4.054078	3.923184	3.799270	3.681856	3.570503	3.464806	3.364392	3.268917	3.178064	3.091539
11	4.177924	4.035397	3.901846	3.775691	3.656403	3.543497	3.436529	3.335091	3.238809	3.147338
12	4.278450	4.127375	3.985240	3.851363	3.725122	3.605950	3.493330	3.386792	3.285899	3.190260
13	4.362355	4.202766	4.053041	3.912390	3.780098	3.655516	3.538055	3.427180	3.322402	3.223277
14	4.431698	4.264562	4.108163	3.961605	3.824078	3.694854	3.573272	3.458734	3.350699	3.248675
15	4.489007	4.315215	4.152978	4.001294	3.859263	3.726074	3.601001	3.483386	3.372635	3.268211
16	4.536369	4.356734	4.189413	4.033302	3.887410	3.750853	3.622836	3.502645	3.389640	3.283239
17	4.575512	4.390765	4.219035	4.059114	3.909928	3.770518	3.640028	3.517692	3.402821	3.294800
18	4.607861	4.418660	4.243118	4.079931	3.927942	3.786125	3.653565	3.529447	3.413040	3.303692
19	4.634596	4.441525	4.262628	4.096718	3.942355	3.798512	3.664225	3.538630	3.420961	3.310532
20	4.656691	4.460266	4.278616	4.110257	3.953883	3.808343	3.672618	3.545805	3.427102	3.315794
21	4.674951	4.475628	4.291558	4.121175	3.963107	3.816145	3.679227	3.551410	3.431862	3.319842
22	4.690042	4.488220	4.302079	4.129980	3.970485	3.822338	3.684028	3.555789	3.435552	3.322955
23	4.702514	4.498541	4.310634	4.137080	3.976388	3.827252	3.688528	3.559210	3.438412	3.325350
24	4.712822	4.507001	4.317588	4.142807	3.981111	3.831152	3.691754	3.561883	3.440630	3.327192
25	4.721340	4.513935	4.323243	4.147425	3.984888	3.834248	3.694295	3.563971	3.442349	3.328609
26	4.728380	4.519619	4.327839	4.151149	3.987911	3.836705	3.696295	3.565602	3.443681	3.329700
27	4.734199	4.524278	4.331577	4.154152	3.990329	3.838655	3.697870	3.566877	3.444714	3.330538
28	4.739007	4.528096	4.334615	4.156575	3.992263	3.840202	3.699110	3.567873	3.445515	3.331183
29	4.742981	4.531227	4.337086	4.158528	3.993810	3.841430	3.700087	3.568650	3.446135	3.331679
30	4.746265	4.533792	4.339094	4.160103	3.995048	3.842405	3.700856	3.569258	3.446617	3.332061
31	4.748980	4.535895	4.340727	4.161373	3.996039	3.843178	3.701461	3.569733	3.446990	3.332355
32	4.751223	4.537619	4.342054	4.162398	3.996831	3.843792	3.701938	3.570104	3.447279	3.332581
33	4.753077	4.539032	4.343134	4.163224	3.997465	3.844280	3.702313	3.570394	3.447503	3.332754
34	4.754609	4.540190	4.344011	4.163890	3.997972	3.844666	3.702609	3.570620	3.447677	3.332888
35	4.755875	4.541140	4.344724	4.164428	3.998377	3.844973	3.702842	3.570797	3.447811	3.332991
36	4.756922	4.541918	4.345304	4.164861	3.998702	3.845217	3.703025	3.570935	3.447916	3.333070
37	4.757786	4.542555	4.345776	4.165211	3.998962	3.845410	3.703169	3.571043	3.447997	3.333131
38	4.758501	4.543078	4.346159	4.165492	3.999169	3.845564	3.703283	3.571127	3.448059	3.333177
39	4.759092	4.543507	4.346471	4.165720	3.999335	3.845685	3.703372	3.571193	3.448108	3.333213
40	4.759580	4.543858	4.346724	4.165903	3.999468	3.845782	3.703443	3.571245	3.448146	3.333241

(Continued)

Table A-4. Ordinary Annuity Present Worth Factor. To find P for a given R received at the end of each period. $P = R \dfrac{1 - (1 + i)^{-N}}{i}$

i% N	31	32	33	34	35	36	37	38	39	40
1	.763359	.757576	.751880	.746269	.740741	.735294	.729927	.724638	.719424	.714286
2	1.346075	1.331497	1.317203	1.303186	1.289438	1.275952	1.262720	1.249737	1.236996	1.224490
3	1.790897	1.766285	1.742258	1.718795	1.695880	1.673494	1.651621	1.630245	1.609350	1.588921
4	2.130456	2.095671	2.061848	2.028952	1.996948	1.965804	1.935490	1.905974	1.877230	1.849229
5	2.389661	2.345205	2.301411	2.260412	2.219961	2.180738	2.142693	2.105778	2.069950	2.035164
6	2.587527	2.534246	2.482813	2.433143	2.385157	2.338778	2.293937	2.250564	2.208597	2.167974
7	2.738571	2.677459	2.618656	2.562074	2.507523	2.454984	2.404333	2.355481	2.308343	2.262839
8	2.853871	2.785954	2.720794	2.658244	2.598165	2.540429	2.484915	2.431508	2.380103	2.330599
9	2.941886	2.868147	2.797590	2.730033	2.665308	2.603257	2.543733	2.486600	2.431729	2.378999
10	3.009073	2.930414	2.855331	2.783607	2.715043	2.649454	2.586667	2.526522	2.468870	2.413571
11	3.060361	2.977587	2.898745	2.823587	2.751884	2.683422	2.618005	2.555451	2.495590	2.438265
12	3.099512	3.013323	2.931387	2.853423	2.779173	2.708398	2.640880	2.576413	2.514813	2.455904
13	3.129399	3.040396	2.955930	2.875689	2.799387	2.726764	2.657576	2.591604	2.528642	2.468503
14	3.152213	3.060906	2.974384	2.892305	2.814363	2.740267	2.669764	2.602612	2.538592	2.477502
15	3.169628	3.076444	2.988258	2.904705	2.825453	2.750197	2.678660	2.610588	2.545749	2.483930
16	3.182922	3.088215	2.998690	2.913959	2.833669	2.757497	2.685153	2.616368	2.550899	2.488521
17	3.193070	3.097133	3.006634	2.920865	2.839755	2.762866	2.689893	2.620557	2.555603	2.491801
18	3.200817	3.103888	3.012432	2.926019	2.844263	2.766813	2.693352	2.623592	2.557269	2.494144
19	3.206731	3.109006	3.016866	2.929865	2.847602	2.769715	2.695878	2.625791	2.559186	2.495817
20	3.211245	3.112884	3.020200	2.932735	2.850076	2.771850	2.697721	2.627385	2.560566	2.497012
21	3.214691	3.115821	3.022707	2.934877	2.851908	2.773419	2.699066	2.628540	2.561558	2.497866
22	3.217321	3.118046	3.024592	2.936475	2.853265	2.774573	2.700048	2.629377	2.562272	2.498476
23	3.219329	3.119732	3.026009	2.937668	2.854270	2.775421	2.700765	2.629983	2.562786	2.498911
24	3.220862	3.121009	3.027074	2.938558	2.855015	2.776045	2.701289	2.630423	2.563155	2.499222
25	3.222032	3.121977	3.027875	2.939223	2.855567	2.776504	2.701670	2.630741	2.563421	2.499444
26	3.222925	3.122710	3.028478	2.939718	2.855975	2.776841	2.701949	2.630972	2.563612	2.499603
27	3.223607	3.123265	3.028931	2.940088	2.856278	2.777089	2.702153	2.631139	2.563750	2.499717
28	3.224127	3.123685	3.029271	2.940364	2.856502	2.777271	2.702301	2.631260	2.563849	2.499798
29	3.224525	3.124004	3.029527	2.940570	2.856668	2.777405	2.702410	2.631348	2.563920	2.499855
30	3.224828	3.124246	3.029720	2.940724	2.856791	2.777504	2.702489	2.631412	2.563971	2.499897
31	3.225060	3.124428	3.029864	2.940839	2.856882	2.777576	2.702547	2.631458	2.564008	2.499926
32	3.225236	3.124567	3.029973	2.940925	2.856950	2.777630	2.702589	2.631491	2.564035	2.499947
33	3.225371	3.124672	3.030055	2.940989	2.857000	2.777669	2.702619	2.631515	2.564054	2.499962
34	3.225474	3.124751	3.030117	2.941036	2.857037	2.777698	2.702642	2.631533	2.564067	2.499973
35	3.225553	3.124812	3.030163	2.941072	2.857064	2.777719	2.702658	2.631545	2.564077	2.499981
36	3.225613	3.124857	3.030198	2.941098	2.857085	2.777734	2.702670	2.631555	2.564084	2.499986
37	3.225659	3.124892	3.030224	2.941118	2.857100	2.777746	2.702679	2.631561	2.564089	2.499990
38	3.225694	3.124918	3.030243	2.941133	2.857111	2.777754	2.702685	2.631566	2.564093	2.499993
39	3.225720	3.124938	3.030258	2.941144	2.857119	2.777761	2.702690	2.631570	2.564096	2.499995
40	3.225741	3.124953	3.030269	2.941152	2.857125	2.777765	2.702694	2.631572	2.564098	2.499996

(Continued)

Table A-4. Ordinary Annuity Present Worth Factor. To find P for a given R received at the end of each period. $P = R\dfrac{1-(1+i)^{-N}}{i}$

$i\%$ / N	41	42	43	44	45	46	47	48	49	50
1	.709220	.704225	.699301	.694444	.689655	.684932	.680272	.675676	.671141	.666667
2	1.212213	1.200159	1.188322	1.176698	1.165279	1.154063	1.143042	1.132213	1.121571	1.111111
3	1.568945	1.549408	1.530295	1.511596	1.493296	1.475385	1.457852	1.440685	1.423873	1.407407
4	1.821947	1.795357	1.769937	1.744164	1.719515	1.695469	1.672008	1.649111	1.626761	1.604938
5	2.001381	1.968562	1.936669	1.905669	1.875527	1.846212	1.817693	1.789940	1.762927	1.736626
6	2.128639	2.090536	2.053615	2.017826	1.983122	1.949460	1.916798	1.885095	1.854313	1.824417
7	2.218893	2.176434	2.135395	2.095712	2.057326	2.020178	1.984216	1.949388	1.915646	1.882945
8	2.282903	2.236925	2.192584	2.149800	2.108500	2.068615	2.030079	1.992830	1.956810	1.921963
9	2.328300	2.279525	2.232576	2.187361	2.143793	2.101791	2.061278	2.022182	1.984436	1.947975
10	2.360496	2.309525	2.260543	2.213445	2.168133	2.124515	2.082502	2.042015	2.002977	1.965317
11	2.383331	2.330651	2.281100	2.231559	2.184920	2.140078	2.096940	2.055416	2.015421	1.976878
12	2.399525	2.345523	2.293776	2.244138	2.196496	2.150739	2.106762	2.064470	2.023877	1.984585
13	2.411011	2.356006	2.303340	2.252874	2.204480	2.158040	2.113444	2.070588	2.029377	1.989724
14	2.419157	2.363385	2.310028	2.259940	2.209986	2.163041	2.117989	2.074722	2.033139	1.993149
15	2.424934	2.368581	2.314705	2.263153	2.213784	2.166467	2.121081	2.077515	2.035664	1.995433
16	2.429031	2.372240	2.317975	2.266078	2.216403	2.168813	2.123184	2.079402	2.037358	1.996955
17	2.431937	2.374817	2.320263	2.268110	2.218209	2.170420	2.124615	2.080677	2.038496	1.997970
18	2.433998	2.376632	2.321862	2.269521	2.219454	2.171520	2.125589	2.081538	2.039259	1.998647
19	2.435459	2.377910	2.322980	2.270501	2.220313	2.172274	2.126251	2.082121	2.039771	1.999098
20	2.436496	2.378810	2.323762	2.271181	2.220906	2.172791	2.126701	2.082514	2.040115	1.999399
21	2.437231	2.379443	2.324309	2.271653	2.221314	2.173144	2.127008	2.082780	2.040345	1.999599
22	2.437753	2.379890	2.324692	2.271982	2.221596	2.173386	2.127216	2.082959	2.040500	1.999733
23	2.438122	2.380204	2.324959	2.272209	2.221790	2.173552	2.127358	2.083081	2.040604	1.999822
24	2.438385	2.380425	2.325146	2.272368	2.221924	2.173666	2.127454	2.083163	2.040674	1.999881
25	2.438571	2.380581	2.325277	2.272478	2.222017	2.173744	2.127520	2.083218	2.040721	1.999921
26	2.438703	2.380691	2.325369	2.272554	2.222081	2.173797	2.127565	2.083255	2.040752	1.999947
27	2.438796	2.380768	2.325433	2.272607	2.222125	2.173834	2.127595	2.083281	2.040773	1.999965
28	2.438863	2.380823	2.325477	2.272644	2.222156	2.173859	2.127616	2.083298	2.040787	1.999977
29	2.438910	2.380861	2.325509	2.272669	2.222176	2.173876	2.127630	2.083309	2.040797	1.999984
30	2.438943	2.380888	2.325531	2.272687	2.222190	2.173888	2.127639	2.083317	2.040803	1.999990
31	2.438967	2.380907	2.325546	2.272699	2.222200	2.173896	2.127646	2.083322	2.040808	1.999993
32	2.438983	2.380920	2.325557	2.272708	2.222207	2.173901	2.127650	2.083326	2.040810	1.999995
33	2.438995	2.380930	2.325564	2.272714	2.222212	2.173905	2.127653	2.083328	2.040812	1.999997
34	2.439004	2.380937	2.325569	2.272718	2.222215	2.173907	2.127655	2.083330	2.040814	1.999998
35	2.439010	2.380941	2.325573	2.272721	2.222217	2.173909	2.127657	2.083331	2.040815	1.999999
36	2.439014	2.380945	2.325575	2.272723	2.222219	2.173910	2.127658	2.083332	2.040815	1.999999
37	2.439017	2.380947	2.325577	2.272724	2.222220	2.173911	2.127658	2.083332	2.040816	1.999999
38	2.439019	2.380948	2.325578	2.272725	2.222221	2.173912	2.127659	2.083333	2.040816	2.000000
39	2.439021	2.380950	2.325579	2.272726	2.222221	2.173912	2.127659	2.083333	2.040816	2.000000
40	2.439022	2.380950	2.325580	2.272726	2.222221	2.173912	2.127659	2.083333	2.040816	2.000000

(Continued)

Table A–4. Ordinary Annuity Present Worth Factor. To find P for a given R received at the end of each period. $P = R \dfrac{1 - (1 + i)^{-N}}{i}$

$i\%$ / N	51	52	53	54	55	56	57	58	59	60
1	.662252	.657895	.653595	.649351	.645161	.641026	.636943	.632911	.628931	.625000
2	1.100829	1.090720	1.080781	1.071007	1.061394	1.051940	1.042639	1.033488	1.024485	1.015625
3	1.391277	1.375474	1.359988	1.344810	1.329932	1.315346	1.301044	1.287018	1.273261	1.259766
4	1.583627	1.562812	1.542475	1.522604	1.503182	1.484196	1.465633	1.447480	1.429724	1.412354
5	1.711012	1.686060	1.661749	1.638054	1.614956	1.592433	1.570467	1.549038	1.528128	1.507721
6	1.795372	1.767145	1.739705	1.713022	1.687068	1.661816	1.637240	1.613315	1.590018	1.567326
7	1.851240	1.820490	1.790657	1.761703	1.733593	1.706292	1.679771	1.653997	1.628942	1.604578
8	1.888238	1.855586	1.823959	1.793314	1.763608	1.734803	1.706860	1.679745	1.653423	1.627862
9	1.912741	1.878675	1.845725	1.813840	1.782973	1.753079	1.724115	1.696041	1.668819	1.642413
10	1.928967	1.893865	1.859951	1.827169	1.795466	1.764794	1.735105	1.706355	1.678503	1.651508
11	1.939713	1.903859	1.869249	1.835824	1.803527	1.772304	1.742105	1.712883	1.684593	1.657193
12	1.946830	1.910433	1.875326	1.841444	1.808727	1.777118	1.746564	1.717015	1.688423	1.660745
13	1.951543	1.914759	1.879298	1.845092	1.812082	1.780204	1.749404	1.719629	1.690832	1.662966
14	1.954664	1.917604	1.881894	1.847463	1.814246	1.782182	1.751213	1.721284	1.692347	1.664314
15	1.956731	1.919477	1.883591	1.849002	1.815643	1.783450	1.752365	1.722332	1.693300	1.665221
16	1.958100	1.920708	1.884700	1.850001	1.816544	1.784263	1.753099	1.722995	1.693899	1.665763
17	1.959007	1.921519	1.885425	1.850650	1.817125	1.784784	1.753566	1.723414	1.694276	1.666102
18	1.959607	1.922052	1.885899	1.851072	1.817500	1.785118	1.753864	1.723680	1.694513	1.666314
19	1.960005	1.922402	1.886208	1.851345	1.817742	1.785332	1.754053	1.723848	1.694663	1.666446
20	1.960268	1.922633	1.886411	1.851523	1.817898	1.785469	1.754174	1.723955	1.694756	1.666529
21	1.960442	1.922785	1.886543	1.851638	1.817999	1.785557	1.754251	1.724022	1.694815	1.666581
22	1.960558	1.922885	1.886629	1.851713	1.818064	1.785614	1.754300	1.724064	1.694852	1.666613
23	1.960634	1.922951	1.886686	1.851762	1.818106	1.785650	1.754331	1.724091	1.694876	1.666633
24	1.960685	1.922994	1.886723	1.851793	1.818133	1.785673	1.754351	1.724109	1.694890	1.666646
25	1.960719	1.923022	1.886747	1.851814	1.818150	1.785688	1.754364	1.724119	1.694900	1.666654
26	1.960741	1.923041	1.886763	1.851827	1.818161	1.785697	1.754372	1.724126	1.694905	1.666658
27	1.960755	1.923053	1.886773	1.851836	1.818169	1.785703	1.754377	1.724130	1.694909	1.666662
28	1.960765	1.923061	1.886780	1.851841	1.818173	1.785707	1.754380	1.724133	1.694911	1.666663
29	1.960772	1.923067	1.886784	1.851845	1.818176	1.785710	1.754382	1.724135	1.694913	1.666665
30	1.960776	1.923070	1.886787	1.851847	1.818178	1.785711	1.754384	1.724136	1.694914	1.666665
31	1.960779	1.923072	1.886789	1.851849	1.818180	1.785712	1.754384	1.724137	1.694914	1.666666
32	1.960781	1.923074	1.886790	1.851850	1.818180	1.785713	1.754385	1.724137	1.694915	1.666666
33	1.960782	1.923075	1.886791	1.851851	1.818181	1.785714	1.754385	1.724138	1.694915	1.666666
34	1.960783	1.923076	1.886791	1.851851	1.818181	1.785714	1.754386	1.724138	1.694915	1.666666
35	1.960783	1.923076	1.886792	1.851851	1.818181	1.785714	1.754386	1.724138	1.694915	1.666667
36	1.960784	1.923076	1.886792	1.851852	1.818182	1.785714	1.754386	1.724138	1.694915	1.666667
37	1.960784	1.923077	1.886792	1.851852	1.818182	1.785714	1.754386	1.724138	1.694915	1.666667
38	1.960784	1.923077	1.886792	1.851852	1.818182	1.785714	1.754386	1.724138	1.694915	1.666667
39	1.960784	1.923077	1.886792	1.851852	1.818182	1.785714	1.754386	1.724138	1.694915	1.666667
40	1.960784	1.923077	1.886792	1.851852	1.818182	1.785714	1.754386	1.724138	1.694915	1.666667

Index

Index

Abandonment, 150n, 201–213, 281
Accounting costs, 21
Accounting method, 21, 58–61
Accounting profits, 26, 58
Accounting revenues, 16
Adjunct investment measures, 197
Adverse minimum, 109–113, 192, 211
Alchian, Armen A., 92
Alexander, Jason, 322
Algorithm, 55
"Algorithm for Finding Exact Rates of Return, An" (Fisher), 72
Amling, Frederich, 53, 58
Arithmetic mean, 187–188
Asset depreciation range (ADR) system, 30, 33–35
Average cost, 106–108
Average discounted rate of return, 188–192
Average return on average investment (ARAI), 58–61

"Backward searching" algorithm, 210, 210n

Bacon, Peter, 190, 190n, 192
Balas, Egon, 218, 218n
BASIC, 71–72
Basic valuation model, 14–16, 44
　vs. NPV equation, 78–79
Baum, Sanford, 278, 278n, 279, 280, 281
Beginning-of-period principal balance, 90
Behavioral theories of management decision-making, 13
Bell, Earl J., 217n
Bell, M. D., 218, 218n, 278
Bellman, R. E., 211, 211n
Beta, 41–42, 42n, 308–314, 326, 326n
Bierman, Harold, Jr., 150, 176, 178
Binary vector, 218
Black, Fisher, 303
Bonds, 42n, 43, 44, 72–74
　government, 41n
　mortgage, 134
Borrowing rate, 148–149, 155
Boulding, Kenneth E., 192–194, 192n
Bower, Richard S., 162–163

392 INDEX

Breakeven lease payment, 166–167, 168n
Brennen, Edward P., 139n
Business Investment Policy, 103

Calculators, 65n, 67, 67n, 79n
Campanella, Joseph A., 174, 175, 184
Canadian depreciation, 33–34
Capacity disparities, 112–113
Capital, defined, 3n
Capital asset pricing model (CAPM), 41–42, 268, 279, 288, 303–314
   and inflation, 326
Capital budgeting
   CAPM and, 311, 313–314
   defined, 7–8
   objective of, 12–17
"Capital consumption or cost allowance," 33–34
Capital cost, 106–107. *See also* Cost of capital
Capital gains, 305–306
Capital-intensive production, 6–7
Capital investment, 3–7
   in 1980s, 321–344
Capital/labor ratio, 325
Capital market line (CML), 306, 307, 308
Capital rationing, 7, 15, 215
Capital recovery factor (CRF), 68, 84–85, 84n, 106–107, 157
Carlson, Robert C., 278, 278n, 280
Cash flow(s). *See also* Cash inflows; Cash outflows
   and CAPM, 314
   "compressed," 137, 137n
   and computer simulation, 293–295
   depreciation and, 29–30
   discounted, 9, 15, 113, 292–293
   earliest positive, 141
   estimates, 8
   for individual projects, 16
   and investment tax credits, 35
   mixed or nonuniform, 65–66, 67, 68, 92, 116–159, 175
   negative, 81, 136, 136n
   positive, 139, 139n, 141
   and project cost estimates, 18–19, 23, 26–29
   and public sector, 16
   quarterly, IRR and, 74
   reinvested, 89–90
Cash inflows, 26, 27–28, 113
   given or fixed, 105
Cash outflows, 26–29
Certainty equivalents, 256–259, 260, 288, 310
Challenger, 105–106, 108–110
Chicago, University of, 6
Childs, C. Rogers, Jr., 150, 179–183

Childs and Gridley leveraged lease example, 179–183
Christy, G. A., 53, 149
Chrysler Corporation, 342
Classical economic theory of management decision-making, 12–13
Coefficient of risk aversion, 277, 278, 278n, 280
Coefficient of variation, 247, 273–274
Committee for Economic Development, 323–324
Commodity markets, 313
Common stock, 40–42, 43, 44
Component projects, 22, 103, 105
   cash flow estimates for, 26–27
   defined, 18–19
Computer, 220, 279, 280
   program methods for IRR solution, 67, 69–72, 71n
Computer simulation
   and multiple project selection, 289–298
   and risk, 261–268
Constraint specification, 220–224
Contingency planning, 20, 211, 341–343
Contingent projects, 217, 271n
Converse, A. O., 19, 211, 211n
Convertible debentures, 39
Convertible preferred stock, 40
Copeland, Thomas E., 307n, 309n, 310n
Corporations, 13, 39
Correlation coefficient, 273–274
Cost-benefit analysis, 7, 338–339
Costless information, 305–306, 306n
Cost minimization, 19, 105, 113
Cost of capital, 8–9, 15, 38–46, 85
   average, 42, 43, 311, 312
   vs. capital cost, 106
   and CAPM, 310–311
   and inflation, 326
   interaction between cash flow, risk and, 15
   marginal, 79
   in two-stage method, 149, 150, 150n
Cost of capital components, 39–42
Cost of debt, 39, 45
   and CAPM, 311
Cost of equity, 40–41
Cost of new shares, 41n
Cost of preferred stock, 40, 42, 42n
Cost per unit, 112, 113
Cost reduction, 16. *See also* Cost minimization
Coupon rate, 73, 74
Covariance, 272, 279, 281
   -variance matrix, 277, 278, 279, 283
Cutting-plane approach, 217
Cyert, Richard M., 13, 13n

Daellenbach, Hans G., 217n
Davis-Bacon legislation, 335
Dean, Joel, 114
Debt, 39, 39n, 43, 45-46
    and equity mix, 43-44
    vs. leasing, 161, 164, 168-169
Debt capacity, 167-168, 169
Decision-making, 12-13
Decision trees, 285-289
Declining-balance depreciation, 33
Defender, 105-106, 110
Depreciable lifetime, 31n
Depreciation, 14, 29-35, 325, 327
    and inflation, 36
    tax shields, and leases, 161, 166-168
    unrecovered tax reductions for, 21
Descartes' rule of signs, 65, 69, 69n, 117-118
Deviational variables, 226
Diagonal model. See Sharpe model
Discounted cash flow (DCF) method, 15, 113, 292-293
Discounting, 29
Discount rate, 9, 93
    in NPV calculation, 79, 79n
    in present value simulations, 266
    risk-adjusted, 259-261
    as variable, 261
Distribution of returns, 259n
Diversification, 312
Divestiture, 278
Dividend capitalization model, 41, 41n, 42
Dividends, 40
Doctrine of rational expectations, 323
Dominant point, 278, 278n
Donosky, Lea, 331n
Double-declining-balance (DDB) depreciation, 31-33, 34, 35
Dreyfus, S. E., 211, 211n
Dual problem, 103-105
Durand, David, 58n, 149, 194, 194n, 197
Duration, 194-195, 197
Dyl, Edward, 12, 201, 201n
Dynamic Equipment Policy (Terborgh), 103, 203, 211

Dynamic programming approach, 210-211, 210n
DYNAMO, 261

Economic capital, 3n
Economic life. See Useful economic life
Effective interest rate, 72-74
Efficient frontier, 280n, 307, 307n
Efficient portfolio, 275-278, 280, 304-305, 306, 310

Elasticity of capital, 194
Employment, 4-5
Environmental Protection Agency, 333
Equal market valuation curve, 257n
Equated time, 192
Equilibrium, 307
Equity, 39, 40-42, 45-46
    change in value of, 190
    and debt mix, 43-44
    return on, 135
Ex ante inflation, 327
Excess present value, 94
Existing enterprise, 278
Expected return
    and CAPM, 310, 314
    and inflation, 326
Expected value, 247, 259, 266
Ex post inflation, 327

Factors of production, 4-7, 330
Fair bet, 238
Fama, Eugene F., 309, 309n, 314
Farrar, Donald E., 276
Federal Power Commission, 334
Federal Trade Commission, 334
Federal Water Pollution Control Act Amendments (1972), 335
Feller, William, 250n
Financial capital, 3n
Financial leases, 160
Financial management theory, 14, 15
Financing. See also Cost of capital
    interaction of investment and, 46
    -investment relationship, 72-74
First standard assumption, 109
Fisher, Irving, 92, 197
Fisher, Lawrence, 72
Fisher's intersection and rate, 92-96, 97
Flow chart, 296-297
Food and Drug Act, 334
Forecasts, 27-28
"Forgotten Consumer, The" (Weidenbaum), 333-340
FORTRAN, 71, 72, 218, 261
Frequency distribution, 263-264
Fringe benefits, and cash flow estimates, 29
Future challengers, 108-109
Future riskless rate, 314
Future value formulation
    conversion of IRR and NPV to, 89
    for TRM, 119

Gaines, Tilford, 323n

Galbraith, John K., 13, 13*n*
Game theory, 12
General guidelines (GG) depreciation system, 30, 32–33, 34, 35
Geometric mean, 187–188
Geometric mean rate of return, 187–188, 189, 192
Goal programming, 224–227
Gomory, R. E., 217, 217*n*
Government, 12, 323. *See also* Public sector
  bonds, 41*n*
  capital investment, 4
  and productivity, 330–331
  regulations, 324, 332–341
GPSS, 261
Gridley, William G., Jr., 150, 179–183
Gross national product (GNP), 4–5
Gross present value, 79, 83
Gross private domestic investment, 4*n*

Haessler, Robert, 190, 190*n*, 192
Haley, Charles W., 306*n*
Harlow, Charles V., 240, 245, 250
Harper, Chris, 331*n*
Hasan, Sayeed, 290*n*
"Has MAPI a Place in a Comprehensive System of Capital Controls?" (Dean and Smith), 114
Hempel, G. H., 197
Henkoff, Ronald, 331*n*
Herbst, Anthony-F., 74*n*, 164*n*, 169, 290*n*
Hichens, Antony, 185
Hicks, John R., 194
Hillier, Frederick S., 259
Hirschleifer, J., 126
Holthausen, Duncan M., 313
Horner's method of polynomial evaluation, 67
Horvath, P. A., 218
Hughes, John S., 313
Human capital, 7

Ideographic model, 13
Immunization, 194–195
Income Tax Act of Canada (1949), 33
Indifference curves, 280, 304, 306
Indivisibility, 227, 274–275, 277, 278, 280
Inefficient asset portfolio, 307
Inflation, 36, 323–330, 333
  and CAPM, 305
  and depreciation, 30
Inflation premium, 326
Initial cost, 19, 20–23
Initial investment, 107
Initial investment method (IIM), 136–146

and leveraged leases, 177, 179–184
Initial investment rate, 136
Installation costs, 22
Insurance cost, 22
Integer linear programming algorithm, 217, 224, 227
Interest expenses
  and cash flow estimates, 29
  and tax deductions, 39, 39*n*, 44
Interest rate, 72–74
Interest tax shield, 166, 168
Internal rate of return (IRR), 64–72, 85, 107, 149
  and computer simulation of risk, 266
  conflicting rankings with NPV, 92–96
  and mixed cash flows, 116–129
  and NPV, 81–82, 88–89, 96–97
  with quarterly cash flows, 74
  reinvestment rate assumptions for, 88–92
  and time spread, 193
  unique, real, as incorrect measure of return on investment, 126–128
Interpolation, 67, 70
Interstate Commerce Commission, 334
Interval bisection method, 67, 69–70
Introduction to Business Investment Analysis, An, 103
Investment curve, 245–246, 257
Investment policy, financing and, 46, 72–74
Investment return, financial measures of, 292–293
Investment tax credit, 35
  and leveraged leases, 174
"Is Average Maturity a Proxy for Risk?" (Yawitz, Hempel, and Marshall), 197
Iso-utility curve, 257
Istvan, Donald E., 53

Jean, W. H., 126
Journal of Business, 72
Jucker, James V., 278, 278*n*, 280

KAPSIM, 261
Kellner, Irwin L., 322*n*
Kessler, Felix, 342*n*
Keynesian theory, 134, 134*n*
Klammer, T. P., 149
Koopmans, Tjalling C., 194–195
Kuo, Shan S., 72

Labor, 4–7
Labor-intensive production, 7
Lawler, E. L., 218, 218*n*, 278
Lawler and Bell algorithm, 218–220, 219*n*

Leases
  leveraged, 133n, 148, 150, 174–185
  ordinary financial, 160–172
Lease valuation equation, 164, 171–172
Lessee, 162
  debt capacity of, 164, 167–168, 169
Lessor, 162, 164–168
  valuation model of, 165–166
Level annuities, 84–85
Leverage, 45–46
Leveraged leases, 133n, 148, 174–185
Levy, Robert E., 313–314, 314n
Lewellen, Wilbur G., 149, 265, 267, 267n
Lewellen-Long criticism, 265–268
License or royalty cost, 22
Linearly weighted average, 309–310
Linear programming, 215–217, 224, 227
Lintner, John, 303
"Loan" rate, 149, 150, 150n, 151–153
Loans, and IRR, 72–73
Long, Hugh W., 201, 201n
Long, Michael S., 265, 267, 267n
Long-run profits, 13, 14
Lorie, J. H., 130
Lorie and Savage "pump" project, 130

Macaulay, Frederick R., 194, 194n
MacBeth, James D., 309
Magee, John F., 286
Major projects, 18–19, 22, 26, 105
Management
  decision-making, 12–13
  satisficing, 15
Management of Corporate Capital, The
  (Solomon), 114
"Manager's Journal" (Kessler), 342
Mao, James C. T., 41n, 53, 92, 96–97, 118, 126,
  149, 247, 248n, 249, 251, 260n, 265, 276–
  277, 278, 279, 281n
MAPI (Machinery and Allied Products Institute)
  method, 19, 103–113, 203
  and abandonment, 203–207, 211
March, James G., 13, 13n
Marginal analysis, 12
Marginal cost of capital, 42, 43
Marginal efficiency of capital (MEC), 134, 134n
Marginal utility, 238
Market portfolio, 306–307, 308
Markov chains, 286, 286n
Markowitz, Harry M., 275–276, 278–280, 281,
  289, 312, 314
Marshall, W. J., 197
Masseé, Pierre, 286
Mathematical programming, 103–105

Maximization of value, 14–16, 105. *See also*
  Basic valuation model
Maximization problems, relation of, to
  minimization problems, 103–105
Maximum value increase, 15
Miller, M. H., 44, 44n
Miller, Merton, 309
Minimization problems, 103–105
Minimum profitability rate, 8–9
Minimum wage, 6, 335
Mixed cash flows, 116–159
  and leveraged leases, 175
Mixed investment theorem, 128–129
Mixed project, 119
Modified sinking fund method (MSFM), 139n
Modigliani, F., 44, 44n
Money supply, 324, 327
Montalbano, M., 132
Monte Carlo experimentation. *See* Computer
  simulation
Mortgage bond amortization flows, 134
Mossin, Jan, 303
Multiple investment sinking fund method
  (MISFM), 136, 136n, 143–146
Multiple project selection, 214–232
  when portfolio approach not applicable,
    285–298
  under risk, 271–281
Multiplicative combinations of stochastic
  variables, 266
Mutual exclusivity, 215, 216, 256, 256n
Myers, Stewart C., 268, 313
Myers, Dill, and Bautista (MDB) model, 164–
  165, 166, 169

Naive rate of return (NROR), 55
  and IRR, 68
National Association of Accountants, 58n
National Environmental Policy Act (1969), 335
National Federation of Independent Business,
  332
National policy goals, 4–6, 8n
Negative capital accumulation, 6
Negative cash flows, 81
  in sinking funds methods, 136, 136n
Negative correlation, 273–274
"Negative investment or loan" phase, 149
Negative root rule, 67–68
Nelson, Charles R., 325, 325n
Net cash flows, 8, 19, 26
Net future value, 79
Net present value (NPV) method, 64, 69, 72,
  78–85, 146
  computer simulation of risk, 266

Net Present Value (NPV) method (continued)
    conflicting rankings of, with IRR, 92–96
    estimating, and computer simulation, 295
    and initial investment, 107
    and IRR, 81–82, 88–89, 96–97
    and leveraged leases, 176–178, 184
    in multiple project budgeting, 214–215
    ranking, 325
    reinvestment assumptions for, 88–92
    under risk, 259, 260
    and two-stage method, 149, 153, 154–156
Net working capital increases, 23
Newton-Raphson method, 67, 69, 70–71
Nominal interest rates, 72–74
Nomothetic model, 13
Noncash costs, 21, 23
Nonprofit institutions, 12
Nonsymmetrical cash flow distributions, and computer simulations, 266
Nonuniform cash flows, 65–66, 67, 68, 92
Nonuniversal model, 13
Normative model, 13–14
Numerical Methods and Computers (Kuo), 72

Occupational safety and health, 337–338
OPEC, 327–330
Operating inferiority, 23, 25, 107–108
Operating leases, 160
Operational adaption, 15–16
Operator training costs, 22–23
Opportunity costs, 89, 90, 106, 148, 149, 209
Optimal capital structure, 44–46
Owner trustee, 175
"Own" risk, 267

Pappas, James L., 211, 211n
Parkinson, C. Northcote, 4n
Partnerships, 39, 245
Payback method, 53–57, 293, 293n
    and IRR, 68
    as risk-coping method, 255–256
    traditional, 196, 196n, 215n
    vs. two-stage method, 149–150, 156
Payout, 160, 160n
Percentage rate, 156
Perg, Wayne F., 164n, 169
Perpetuity, 40, 40n
Personal utility, 240–245
Pettway, Richard H., 218, 218n
Physical deterioration, 23, 24–25, 107–108
Point estimates, vs. computer simulation, 265–268
Portfolio approach, 15, 46n, 267, 275–280, 289, 314

    vs. CAPM, 312
Portfolio risk, 10, 310
Positive cash flows, 139, 139n
Positive correlation, 273–274
Preferred stock, 40, 42n, 45
Present worth of annuity factors, 79, 79n
Price controls, 324
"Price of risk," 307, 310, 314
Prices, and money supply, 327–329
Primal problem, 103–105
Principal repayment, 91–92
Priority level coefficients, 225
Private sector, 7
Probabilities, 9–10
Production theory, 330
Productivity, 6, 330–332
Profitability index (PI), 83, 84, 96
Profit maximization, 12, 13, 15
Profits, 13–14, 331–332
Project characteristics, estimating, 18–36
    indivisibility, 227, 274–275, 277, 278
    life, 83–85, 261, 266
    NPV of unequal, 82–85
    types, 18–19
Project balance equations, 119
Project financing rate (PFR), 120
Project investment rate (PIR), 120
"Propitious maximum" NPV, 203, 204
Proprietorships, 39
Public sector, 7, 8, 16, 268
Pure financing project, 119
Pure investment project, 119, 120

Qualitative parameters of investment, 19–20
Quantitative parameters of investment, 19

Railroad trust certificate leases, 175
Random number generator, 261
Rationality, 12
Redington, F. M., 195, 195n
Regression equation, 247
Reinvestment rate assumptions, 88–92
Rendleman, Richard J., Jr., 313, 313n
Replacement policy, 325
Required additional working capital investment, 22
Required equity investment, 134
Retained earnings, 40
Return on invested capital (RIC), 92, 97
    and MISFM, 146
    -NPV conflict for leveraged leases, 178
    TRM measure of, 118, 120
Return on investment, 6
    IRR as incorrect measure of, 126

INDEX

Return to equity, 175
Revenue Act (1971), 30
Risk, 9–10, 39n, 42, 96, 153n, 165n, 211
  -adjusted discount rate, 259–261
  attitudes toward, 238–240
  CAPM and, 303–314
  and cost of capital, 15, 46, 46n
  measures of, 246–248
  and multiple project selection, 271–281, 285–298
  single project analysis under, 255–268
  vs. uncertainty, 157, 344
  and utility, 238–251
Risk aversion, 238, 257, 277, 278, 278n, 280
Risk-free asset, 304–307, 308
Risk-free rate, 258, 258n, 266, 326
Risk lover, 239–240
Risk neutral individual, 239
Risk of ruin, 250–251, 250n, 276n, 314
Risk-return trade off, 257, 275–280, 281
Robichek, Alexander A., 118, 201, 201n
Robichek-Van Horne (R-VH) analysis, 201–203, 208–210
Robinson, E. A. G., 8
Roll, Richard, 309
Roots, multiple, 64–65, 67–68, 69, 69n, 71n, 117n
Roy, A. D., 276

Salvage value, 19, 22, 29, 31, 32, 33, 203, 203n, 204, 209
Satisficing, 12, 13, 15
Savage, L. J., 130
Schall, Lawrence D., 306n
Scholes, Myron, 309
Scientific subroutine package (SSP), 71
Second standard assumption, 109
Securities, 42, 42n
  long maturity, 40, 40n
Security market line (SML), 308–310, 311, 312
Semivariance, 248, 248n, 249
Sensitivity analysis, 143
Sequential, event-contingent decisions, 285–286
Shadow prices, 104
Shamblin, James E., 286
Sharpe, William F., 279–280, 281, 289, 303
Sharpe model, 279–280
Short-run profits, 13–14
Short-term financing, 38
Simon, Herbert A., 12, 12n
Simple project, 119, 156
Simplex method, 217, 217n
SIMSCRIPT, 261
Single project analysis under risk, 255–268
Sinking fund earnings rate, 136

Sinking fund method. *See* Traditional sinking fund method
Sinking fund rate, 136, 146
Sinking fund methods, 136–146
  alternative to, 148–157
Smith, Sidney O., 341
Smith, Winfield, 114
Social institutions, 3–4
Soldofsky, Robert M., 8, 53, 149
Solomon, Ezra, 114
"Some Comments on the Dean-Smith Article on the MAPI Formula" (Terborgh), 114
Standard deviation, 247
Standard error of the estimate, 247
Standard of living, 4, 7–8
Stevens, G. T., Jr., 286
Stochastic dependence, 271, 271n
Stone, Herbert L., 240, 245, 250
Straight-line depreciation, 30–33, 34, 35
Sturm's theorem, 71n
Summation of a geometric progression formula, 65n
Sum-of-the-year's digits (SYD) depreciation, 31–33, 34, 35
Sunk cost, 21–22
Survival of the enterprise, 276–277
Systematic risk, 308, 312

Targeted value, 248, 248n
Taxes
  vs. corporate profits, 332
  and debt, 39, 39n
  and depreciation, 29–35
  inflation and, 326–327, 331
Tax shields, and leases, 166–168
Technological obsolescence, 23, 25–26, 108
Teichroew, Daniel, 118, 136, 210n
Teichroew, Robichek, and Montalbano (TRM) method, 118–129, 136, 148
  and leveraged leases, 177, 179–183, 184
  vs. sinking fund methods, 137
Terborgh, George, 19, 23, 23n, 25, 56–57, 103, 107n, 109, 110, 114, 203, 211
Teweles, Richard J., 240, 245, 250
Time, 341
Time-adjusted average present value, 83–84, 84n
Time-related measures, 192–195
Time spread (TS), 192–194
Time value of money, 58, 64–74, 78–85, 149
Tobin, James, 238, 239
Total risk, 308
Trade-off functions, 226, 227

Traditional sinking fund method (TSFM), 136, 137–143, 146
  and leveraged leases, 177, 178, 179–183, 184
Transportation costs, 22
Treynor, Jack, 303
Trippi, Robert R., 189, 189n, 190, 190n, 192, 192n
True lease, 175
Trusts, 174–175
Turnbull, Stuart W., 313
Two-stage method (TSM), 148–157
  and leveraged leases, 177, 179–183, 184

Uncertainty, 10, 156–157, 281
  in 1980s, 323, 324, 344
Underemployment of capital, 6
Unemployment, 6–7
Uniform annual equivalents, 84–85
U.S. Energy Resources Council, 335
Unrecovered investment, 58, 149, 195–196
Unsystematic risk, 308
Useful economic life, 19, 23–26
  vs. depreciable lifetime, 31n
  and multiple project selection, 289–298
Utility, 237–238, 240–245, 256, 257, 259n, 276, 276n, 280
Utility functions, 276, 276n, 280

Value maximization, 19. *See also* Basic valuation model
Value of the enterprise, 15, 16
Van Horne, James C., 201, 201n
Variance, 246–247, 308
  -covariance matrix, 277, 278, 279, 281
  of linear combinations of variables, 273n
  of NPV, and certainty equivalent, 258–259
Vector partial ordering, 218

Wage and price controls, 326
Wages, and cash flow estimates, 29
Weidenbaum, Murray L., 333–340
Weighted average cost of capital, 42, 43, 311, 312
Weil, Roman L., 194, 194n
Weston, J. Fred, 307n, 309n, 310n
White, Andrew Dickson, 321
Wiar, Robert, 133
Wiar method (WM), 133–135
  for leveraged leases, 179–183, 184
Williams, Richard, 190, 190n, 192
"Worst case" forecast, 27

Yawitz, J. B., 197

Zero-one (0–1) integer programming, 216, 217–224, 227–228, 278, 279